African Diasporas
in the New and Old Worlds

Consciousness and Imagination

Cross Cultures

Readings in the Post/Colonial
Literatures in English

69

Series Editors

Gordon Collier	Hena Maes–Jelinek	Geoffrey Davis
(Giessen)	(Liège)	(Aachen)

African Diasporas
in the New and Old Worlds

Consciousness and Imagination

Edited by

Geneviève Fabre and Klaus Benesch

Amsterdam - New York, NY 2004

The paper on which this book is printed meets the requirements of "ISO 9706:1994, Information and documentation - Paper for documents - Requirements for permanence".

Second edition 2006
ISBN: 90-420-0870-9
©Editions Rodopi B.V., Amsterdam - New York, NY 2004
Transferred to digital printing 2006
Printed in The Netherlands

We dedicate this book to the memory of Tom Feelings (1933–2003),
whose inspired creative artwork illuminated the narrative
of the ordeal and endurance of African Americans
on their passage to the New World

Contents

VISUAL ART AND PERFORMANCE

POSTSCRIPT

APPENDIX

Illustrations

Acknowledgements

W E WISH TO THANK both the institutions that helped to organize the Paris conference that was the starting-point for the present essays and those that contributed to the preparation of the collection: the Conseil scientifique of the University of Paris 7 (Denis Diderot), the CIRNA (Centre interdisciplinaire de recherche scientifique sur l'Amérique du Nord), the CEAA (Cercle d'études africaines américaines), the rectorate of the Universities of Paris, and the Cultural Services of the American Embassy in Paris. Most of all we want to express our gratitude to the Florence Gould Foundation for the sustained support that it has extended to the Research Center for the Study of the African Diasporas.

We are also indebted to friends and colleagues who have accompanied us through the various stages of this project, among them Bénédicte Alliot, who gave it much of its initial impetus, helped collect the essays, and was attentive to many editorial queries. Special credit should also be given to Arlette Frund and Viviane Lelièvre. Members of the research group "Africans in the Americas" at the University of Bayreuth (Germany) have read early versions of the essays and provided valuable suggestions. We are also thankful to the editors of Rodopi and, especially, to Gordon Collier for his interest in this project and the useful hints he has given us. We appreciate the patience and care with which the contributors to this volume have worked with us. Finally we would like to thank all those who were present at the conference and could not be included in this collection: scholars who shared aspects of their research, writers who gave readings, and artists who presented shows or gave performances. All have in significant ways helped us reach a deeper understanding of the field and concept we were exploring.

❖

Introduction
The Concept of African Diaspora(s):
A Critical Reassessment

> I think that our migrations are an archetype of those
> of the dispossessed and I want somehow to tell the
> story of how the dispossessed become possessed of
> their own history without losing sight, without for-
> getting the meaning or the nature of their journey.[1]

T HE CONCEPT OF DIASPORA, though indelibly inscribed in
the consciousness and imagination of the twentieth century, has
long been disregarded as an adequate heuristic tool for capturing
the experience of slavery and forced migration shared by millions of Africans. Today, after a long subterranean life, the term 'diaspora' has finally
emerged as a promising, powerful new idea. In the humanities, the social
sciences, and cultural studies, among other fields, it is now challenging
modes of thinking and assumptions not only about the unfolding of contemporary cross-cultural or multicultural societies and communities, but also
about the past, about power relations, frontiers and boundaries, about cultural transmission, communication and translation, about revolt or revolution. It invites reconsiderations of current theoretical assumptions and, most
importantly, it opens up new ways of approaching familiar issues: migratory
flux, identity formation, structures of society as well as structures of mentality and emotion; it also encourages reflection on the meaning of nationalism, colonialism or neocolonialism, pan-Africanism, on established notions

---

[1] Sherley Anne Williams, preliminary note on "Meditations on History," in *Black-
Eyed Susans/Midnight Birds: Stories of Contemporary Black Women Writers*, ed.
Mary Helen Washington (Garden City NY: Doubleday, 1980): 197.

such as people and nation, race and gender, modernity and progress. What is more, it affects our conception of the relation between time and space, history and geography. The past and present of both Africans and Europeans are now being reconsidered, organized along new lines and according to new priorities; perspectives are shifting, stakes are being reshuffled, continuities broken.

In its broadest sense, the linking of 'African' and 'diaspora' compels acknowledgement of the fact that people of African descent living 'out of Africa' have formed a shared tradition of values and cultural behavior in the Old World as well as in the New. The application to other ethnic groups of the term 'diaspora', traditionally associated with the fate of Jewish people, was often questioned, despite the common experience of a dramatic uprooting accompanied by geographical dispersion. The existence of an African diaspora, though compelling as a point of reference, was neither taken for granted nor, once claimed, easily accepted. Etymologically, the Greek term referred to forced or voluntary dispersion (primarily with regard to Hellenistic Jews or early Jewish Christians) that resulted in exile and separation from the homeland. In Hebrew, the term *galuth*, signifying 'exile', already designated a more or less permanent condition. In the seventeenth century, its meaning was extended to groups or peoples displaced for religious or political reasons, such as Huguenots, Armenians or Palestinians. Defined in general terms, the notion of diaspora thus provides a frame within which to assess the experience of exile and cultural alienation. It also spells out a number of assumptions and characteristics shared by most peoples living in diaspora: first, the existence of a homeland, real or mythic, that is rarely forgotten and with which one seeks to establish a new relation (this mythic homeland is often associated with the memory of the event that initially caused the separation and loss); second, the new life in a foreign environment and the concomitant estrangement, humiliations and ordeals not only necessitate a continuous struggle for recognition, equality, and justice but call for the identification of social and cultural forces as yet unknown; and, finally, the creation of (or connecting to) a composite diasporic community with its distinctive set of ethnic, national, and linguistic identities, unified by collective memory, by shared sensibilities and affinities, by kinship and solidarity. This is achieved through a complex blending of dream (or utopia) and determination, as well as through an attempt to negate separation, restore ties, and retrieve lost identity. In this sense, then, diaspora is less a condition or a state than a search for identity that is constantly contested, re-imagined, and re-invented.

If the appropriation of the term 'diaspora' for people of African descent is recent, the experience or reality to which it refers is not. Just consider the

slave trade and its aftermath, an historical juggernaut that plundered a continent and sent millions of Africans as slaves either to Europe or to the
plantations of the New World, and the diasporic implications of the Black
Odyssey become immediately apparent. To the exiled population, Africa
was irretrievably lost. What is more, the traumatic experience of the Middle
Passage marked a violent and brutal uprooting. Real or imagined, Africa is
the matrix of the African diaspora, the lost homeland and center. For people
of African descent who had been abducted from or driven out of Africa, the
'dark' continent is the place of origin, the guarantor of identity and filiation;
it is a mythic site, a source of inspiration and consolation, to which one
longs to return. The massive exodus of Africans and their dispersal throughout the Western World remains the most compelling image of black discourse. Even today, as the memoir of artist Tom Feelings toward the end of
this collection attests, images of slave ships, of capture and enslavement, of
flight, revolt and resistance, still endure and keep haunting the imagination
of black artists and writers.

For the African diaspora, the return to Africa has proved to be a dream
deferred but never abandoned. It has taken many forms, teleological (as a
'natural' design and purpose), ideological, and political. The myth of origin,
of "homeland and return," as Safran put it in the first issue of the journal
Diaspora in 1991, had always been an essential component of African
diasporic consciousness.[2] It may take the form of romance and longing, of
moral obligation and loyalty, or of political commitments that mobilize the
'black world' and inspire intellectual or artistic projects. Whatever its
guises, the notion of return serves as a unifying theme that raises fundamental questions about the relation to Africa, a fragile relation that is constantly
explored and rethought. To be sure, there were many actual returns: the
efforts of the colonization movement to transplant African Americans back
to Africa in the nineteenth century or, on a smaller scale, individual captives
or refugees who were temporarily brought back to Africa. Yet myth and history merge, while new definitions of the relations between Africa and the
diaspora evolve. As historians and anthropologists have pointed out, Africa
is a complex continent made up of many nations and a plethora of ethnic
and linguistic groups. The assumption of unity, already questioned by historians of the slave trade, has been increasingly challenged and is now confronted with evidence of an amazing cultural diversity marked, more often

---

[2] William Safran, "Diasporas in Modern Societies: Myths of Homeland and
Return," *Diaspora: A Journal of Transnational Studies* 1 (Spring 1991): 83–99.

than not, by ethnic fervor and division.[3] Though still a land of origin, Africa has shifted conceptually: it has finally become an ambiguous place, a conflict-ridden continent. This may also explain why the diaspora has gradually turned into an agent of the social, political, and economic processes of modernity.

With decolonization and the independence movements of the 1950s, there occurred a decisive shift in the apprehension of Africa by its diaspora. Africa was no longer a thing of the past; its future and its implication in the future of the diaspora (artistic as well as political) suddenly became an issue of utmost and widespread concern. Among the many concepts associated with these new orientations towards Africa in the twentieth century, the following are of particular importance and should therefore not go unnoted here: Ethiopianism, Pan-Africanism, and Negritude. A secessionist movement that swept through South Africa when Reverend Magena Mokone founded the Ethiopian Church in 1892, Ethiopianism also garnered a considerable number of followers among African Americans. When Bishop Henry McNeal Turner of the African Methodist Episcopal Church visited South Africa in 1896, he created upon his return a vital network between African-American and South African churches. The Ethiopianist tradition in America, Iris Schmeisser argues in her contribution to this volume, had its origins in late-eighteenth-century black thought in the New World. Prophesying a return to an earlier efflorescence, it took such later forms as Garveyism and other back-to-Africa movements, and its potent vision of cultural renewal invested the Harlem Renaissance with the mission of reconstructing an "Ethiopian Golden Age."

Pan-Africanism, mainly through the work of W.E.B. Du Bois, developed as a cultural network of interaction between Africa, North America, the Caribbean and Europe. Significantly if somewhat paradoxically, however, the international orientation of this movement also created a new awareness of the differences among the various African diasporas: it changed their respective relation to the homeland and marked, for example, the emergence of a Caribbean consciousness that was more radical and more directly involved in decolonization than its African-American counterpart. As Winston James points out in his essay on pan-Africanist projects and the Caribbean diaspora, the latter dates back as far as the early nineteenth century and later included people who left the islands to live in close contact with the former colonizers in France or England, a fact that made their cultural,

---

[3] See, for example, Philip D. Curtin, *The Atlantic Slave Trade: A Census* (Madison: U of Wisconsin P, 1970) and *Cross Cultural Trade in World History* (Cambridge & New York: Cambridge UP, 1984).

linguistic, and political situation even more complex and led to further differences with other diasporic groups. The idea of an African diaspora was thus gradually replaced by that of multiple diasporas, unified solely through their lost center and mythic homeland, Africa.

Whereas African-Americans intellectuals such as W.E.B. Du Bois took the lead in developing an idea of Africa that was connected to cultural splendor and ancient images, the Negritude movement, which originated within the francophone diaspora, focussed more on common cultural traditions and ethical values of contemporary Africans living in exile.[4] The idea took shape in Paris and was launched by two writers, Léopold Sédar Senghor of Senegal and Aimé Césaire from Martinique, who both played a significant political role in their respective countries. According to Senghor, *négritude* is the whole complex of civilized values that characterizes the Negro African world.[5] Negritude symbolized an unprecedented convergence of two French colonies, one from Africa, the other from the New World, a fact that is further reflected in the vital contribution of writers such as Léon Damas from French Guiana and the Martinican psychiatrist Frantz Fanon. If Césaire voiced his own poetic and political version of "le retour au pays natal," Fanon's work introduced a strong political overtone and striking metaphors: that of dark skins, white masks, and of a false consciousness crippling the lives of the "wretched of the earth."

The idea of an "African presence" also developed in Paris; originally promulgated by the *Revue du monde noir* in 1931, it was especially propagated by Niam N'goura Diop's *Présence Africaine*, founded in 1947, and the journal *African Forum*, both of which lent it a more official existence. The idea soon spread to North America. An intensive network of communication was established; African congresses in Paris (1956) and Rome (1959) brought together black artists and intellectuals from both sides of the Atlantic; arts festivals, such as the one held in Dakar in 1966, and societies, such as the "Société africaine de culture" or the "American Society of African Culture," were created to spur interest in African cultures. All of these efforts led to a revaluation of the African diaspora and, eventually, ushered in a new brand of pan-Africanism that, in the words of St. Clair Drake, became increasingly continental.[6] Triggered by as well as reinforc-

---

[4] See the essays by Kirschke and Edwards in this collection.

[5] See Léopold Senghor, "Problématique de la Négritude," *Présence Africaine* 78 (1971): 3–26.

[6] St. Clair Drake, "Diaspora Studies and Pan Africanism," in *Global Dimensions of the African Diaspora*, ed. Joseph Harris (Washington DC: Howard UP, 1982): 359–66.

ing new ways of 'seeing and imaging' Africa, these developments also need to be studied as part of a shifting politics of representation.

While the various political and cultural manifestations of the African diaspora – and their conceptualization in postcolonial and diaspora studies – guide most of the essays in the theoretical, introductory section "Thinking Diasporas," the changing artistic representations of Africa are at the center of the section on "Visual Art and Performance." As Amy Kirschke's and Iris Schmeisser's analyses of graphic representations of Africa between the Wars reveal, African and African-American artists both in Europe and the Americas were instrumental in establishing a visual vocabulary that helped to create a new sense of identity with the lost African homeland.

In view of these developments, we can see how the term 'African diaspora' cannot be comprehended exclusively in terms of its relation to Africa. With the rise of new, postcolonial African nations and, concomitantly, an increase of migratory flux and the appearance of multiple, temporary homelands, the cultural, historical, and geographical differences within the black diaspora itself are being increasingly recognized. Today scholars are more interested in how these various forms of diaspora are connected to each other rather than in links between the dispersed former Africans and a mythic homeland or spiritual center. As James Clifford has recently argued, "transnational connections linking diasporas need not be articulated primarily through a real or symbolic homeland."[7] What is more, with globalization in full swing, attention is shifting to the global dimensions of diaspora, to traveling circuits, border crossings and constant geographical dispersal and redistribution. If immigration is now seen as a major factor in the formation of diasporic communities, the contemporary understanding of diaspora seems to be blurring the distinction between immigrant, exile, refugee, and expatriate (but at the same time emphasizing their interaction). The international perspective embraced at the beginning of the twentieth century by black intellectuals such as W.E.B. Du Bois has shifted, at the turn of the new millennium, to the *trans*-national aspects of an astonishingly hybrid, globalized market economy. Accordingly, in the first issue of the journal *Diaspora,* Khachig Tölölyan speaks of the new diasporas as "exemplary communities of the transnational moment."[8] If 'roots' have been the metaphoric focus of the twentieth century, it seems that scholarly

---

[7] James Clifford, "Diasporas," in *Routes: Travel and Translation in the Late Twentieth Century* (Cambridge MA: Harvard UP, 1997): 249.

[8] Khachig Tölölyan, "Introduction" to *Diaspora: A Journal of Transnational Studies* 1.1 (1991): 4.

attention today is drawn to 'routes', to the mapping of the complex, rhizomatic, cross-cultural itineraries of African diasporas.

This volume is a selection of papers and keynote lectures presented at an international conference at the Université Denis Diderot in Paris on "African Diasporas in the Old and the New Worlds: Consciousness and Imagination" (October 2000). The conference brought together a large number of scholars, critics, historians, writers and artists who were asked to discuss the following question: To what extent can the concept of diaspora be considered as a useful tool or help develop new perspectives for theoretical reflection and literary or artistic creation? Though many participants focussed on African diasporas in the Americas, historical and contemporary developments in Britain, France and Italy were also addressed, often from a comparative perspective. The conference was in part organized so as to add to the ongoing scholarly debate about Paul Gilroy's recent publication *Against Race* (2000) and to link up with a twin conference on diaspora at New York University and the Schomburg Library in September 2000. The Paris conference thus provided yet another welcome opportunity for renewed dialogue and exchange. Paris has long been a major crossroads in the travel-routes of African diasporas and has continued to offer possibilities for new passages, circuits, and audiences. The particular setting thus allowed for a unique viewpoint from which to examine the history and theory of African diasporas and the diasporic experience in general.

This collection of essays is bears upon the following key issues: the concept of African diaspora, its possible origin, its historical development and the many, often divergent interpretations it has received (some inducing heated debates or controversy); the political uses of diaspora; implications for special fields (history, art history, intellectual history, anthropology, etc.); and, more generally speaking, its validity in defining new approaches, providing new definitions and perspectives, new fields of inquiry. Since 'diaspora' is not just a historical phenomenon but also an idea or ideology and an object of representation, theorizing diaspora(s) carries important implications for scholars in cultural studies, African-American studies, ethnic studies, and African studies.

Some of the essays in this volume examine the concept of diaspora itself and the meanings it has received in the last decades (Edwards, Palumbo–Liu, Feith). The term 'diaspora' is often associated with the following notions:

1. exile, homeland and expatriation;
2. an impossible or deferred return, dispersal and 'reunification', multiple displacement;
3. borders, contacts and intersections; and 4. interpretations, knowledge, and translation.

All of these aspects evoke, literally or metaphorically, movement, place and space. Yet they also refer to specific historical moments fraught with projects and desires, painful or exalting experiences and emotions, memories and silences.

The complex and often contradictory dimensions of the African diasporas (collective, international, multi-ethnic, multi-cultural or multi-lingual) are analysed in relation to significant sites and figures (Frey, Dhanvantari, James), as well as through the various theoretical models such as the "black Atlantic" (Palumbo–Liu) that have been proposed. The essays consider these movements as they have occurred across societies, languages and cultures, between the New (Latin America or Anglo-America) and the Old Worlds (Europe and Africa), or between islands (such as the Caribbean) and the American continent. Many also address the crucial issue of how to think, express or write the diaspora, with what words and what images (Peterson, Benesch, Birat, Moglen). Further, some authors examine the resources (collections and archives) and iconographies that are available today and the new technologies through which they are made accessible (Kirschke, Schmeisser, Bettelheim, Bischof). The question is raised of how these far-reaching changes and innovations in publishing and/or exhibition policies have affected – or have been affected by – the attention given to the diasporic phenomenon. Most importantly, while some studies are concerned with the modes and modalities of creative expression from the perspective of both artists/writers and their audiences, others highlight the ways in which literature and the arts interact, especially photography, film, and the graphic arts (Benesch, Moglen, Feelings).

This collection does not claim to be exhaustive, nor does it claim to reflect the wealth of papers presented at the conference in Paris, the discussions that took place, or the tremendous impact created by visual and musical performances, or the public readings by African and African-American writers. Yet we hope that this interdisciplinary volume will provide invigorating and original insights into the consciousness and imagination of African diasporas, past and present.

GENEVIÈVE FABRE AND KLAUS BENESCH

WORKS CITED

Clifford, James. "Diasporas," in Clifford, *Routes: Travel and Translation in the Late Twentieth Century* (Cambridge MA: Harvard UP, 1997): 244–78.

Curtin, Philip D. *The Atlantic Slave TraA Census* (Madison: U of Wisconsin P, 1970).

——. *Cross Cultural Trade in World History* (Cambridge & New York: Cambridge UP, 1984).

Drake, St. Clair. "Diaspora Studies and Pan Africanism," in *Global Dimensions of the African Diaspora*, ed. Joseph Harris (Washington DC: Howard UP, 1982): 359–66.

Safran, William. "Diasporas in Modern Societies: Myths of Homeland and Return," *Diaspora: A Journal of Transnational Studies* 1 (1991): 83–99.

Senghor, Léopold Sédar. "Problématique de la Négritude," *Présence Africaine* 78 (1971): 3–26.

Tölölyan, Khachig. "Introduction" to *Diaspora: A Journal of Transnational Studies* 1.1 (1991): 3–7.

Williams, Sherley Anne. "Meditations on History," in *Black-Eyed Susans/Midnight Birds: Stories of Contemporary Black Women Writers*, ed. Mary Helen Washington (1975–79; Garden City NY: Doubleday, 1980): 197–79.

❖ THINKING DIASPORAS

The Uses of 'Diaspora'

BRENT HAYES EDWARDS

O NE OF THE MORE VEXING PROBLEMS of recent histo-
rical work on black culture and politics in an international sphere
is that the term 'diaspora', so attractive to many of our analyses,
does not appear in the literature under consideration until surprisingly late
after the Second World War. Of course, black artists and intellectuals, from
Edward Wilmot Blyden, Martin Delany, and Pauline Hopkins in the nineteenth century to W.E.B. Du Bois, Marcus Garvey, and Tiemoko Garan
Kouyaté in the early twentieth, have long been engaged with themes of
internationalism; but 'diaspora' has only in the past forty years been a term
of choice to express the links and commonalities among groups of African
descent throughout the world. Here I will engage this problem by taking up
Khachig Tölölyan's signal call to "return to diaspora": the confusing multiplicity of terms floating through recent work ('exile', 'expatriation', 'post-
coloniality', 'migrancy', 'globality', and 'transnationality', among others),
he argues, makes it

> necessary to 'return to diaspora,' which is in danger of becoming a promiscu-
> ously capacious category that is taken to include all the adjacent phenomena
> to which it is linked but from which it actually differs in ways that are con-
> stitutive, that in fact make a viable definition of diaspora possible.[1]

---

[1] Khachig Tölölyan, "Rethinking *Diaspora*(s): Stateless Power in the Transnational Moment," *Diaspora: A Journal of Transnational Studies* 5.1 (Spring 1996): 8.

Both Tölölyan and James Clifford have recently written valuable comparative overviews of the use of the term.[2] I will limit consideration here, however, to the politics of 'diaspora' in black historical work and cultural
criticism, as the term marks a quite specific intervention in that arena, one
that may not be subsumable under some overarching frame of inquiry.[3] I
will be particularly concerned with excavating the function performed by
the term in the work of Paul Gilroy, as he is the one theorist cited in almost
all recent considerations of these issues. The reception of his brilliant 1993
study, *The Black Atlantic*, threatens continually (despite Gilroy's own qualifications) to conflate 'diaspora', and its particular history of usage in black
cultural politics, with Gilroy's proposition of that field he calls the "black
Atlantic" – a phrase rapidly being canonized and institutionalized in the US
academy.

I am not suggesting that one must limit the term's object of study to more
contemporary phenomena. On the contrary, I want to excavate a historicized
and politicized sense of diaspora for my own work, which focusses on black
cultural politics in the interwar period, particularly in transnational circuits
of exchange between the so-called Harlem Renaissance and pre-Negritude
francophone activity in France and West Africa.[4] I am rethinking the uses

---

[2] James Clifford, "Diasporas," in *Routes: Travel and Translation in the Late
Twentieth Century* (Cambridge MA: Harvard UP, 1997): 244–78.

[3] Tölölyan comments that African Americans make up a community that "remains
exceptional, not least in its formation as a diaspora, and it is both an intellectual and
political disservice to cloud that exceptionality by the piety of a solidarity that
conjoins all peoples of color in some ethnodiasporan or multiculturalist discourse"
("Rethinking *Diaspora*(s)," 23). Although I follow Tölölyan here in arguing that the
intellectual history of an "African diaspora" discourse is singular, it should be noted
that my approach breaks with the emphasis on what might be termed "comparative
diasporas" exemplified by the editorial policy of *Diaspora*, the journal he edits, as
well as with other recent work (some of it quite useful) that reads the African diaspora as only one example in a typology. Other examples are *Diaspora and
Immigration*, a special issue of the *South Atlantic Quarterly* 98.1–2 (Winter–Spring
1999), ed. Valentine Y. Mudimbe & Sabine Engel; Kim Butler, "Defining Diaspora,
Refining a Discourse," *Diaspora: A Journal of Transnational Studies* 10.2 (Fall
2002): 189–219; Robin Cohen, *Global Diasporas: An Introduction* (Seattle: U of
Washington P, 1997); and William Safran, "Diaspora in Modern Societies: Myths of
Homeland and Return," *Diaspora: A Journal of Transnational Studies* 1.1 (Spring
1991): 83–99.

[4] Brent Hayes Edwards, "Three Ways to Translate the Harlem Renaissance," in
"Temples for Tomorrow": Looking Back at the Harlem Renaissance, ed. Geneviève
Fabre & Michel Feith (Bloomington: Indiana UP, 2001): 359–96; and Edwards, *The*

of diaspora more precisely to compel a discussion of the politics of nomi-
nalization, in a moment of prolixity and careless rhetoric when such a question is often the first casualty. An intellectual history of the term is needed,
in other words, because diaspora is taken up at a particular conjuncture in
black scholarly discourse to do a particular kind of epistemological work.[5]

The use of 'diaspora' emerges directly out of the growing scholarly interest in the pan-African movement in particular, and in black internationalism
in general, that began to develop in the 1950s. It is important to recall that
pan-Africanism, referring both to Henry Sylvester Williams's Pan-African
Conference in 1900 and to the Congresses organized by W.E.B. Du Bois
and others in 1919, 1921, 1923, 1927, 1945, and 1974, arises as a discourse of
internationalism aimed generally at the cultural and political *coordination*
of the interests of peoples of African descent around the world. As Du Bois
declared in 1933, in a celebrated piece published in *Crisis*, "Pan-Africa
means intellectual understanding and co-operation among all groups of
Negro descent in order to bring about at the earliest possible time the industrial and spiritual emancipation of the Negro peoples."[6]

This emphasis on vanguardist collaboration toward a unified articulation
of the interests of "African peoples" at the level of international policy is
generally considered to have been influenced by a number of popular currents; the most important of these included the diverse ideologies of
"return" that were so often a component of the African experience in the
New World. Indeed, Du Bois would go so far as to claim that the motiva-
tions of pan-Africanism are paradigmatically African *American*. If black
New World populations have their origin in the fragmentation, racialized
oppression, and systematic dispossession of the slave trade, then the pan-
African impulse stems from the necessity to confront or heal that legacy
through racial organization itself – through ideologies of a real or symbolic
return to Africa. Even toward the end of his life, when he became more

---

*Practice of Diaspora: Literature, Translation, and the Rise of Black International-
ism* (Cambridge MA: Harvard UP, 2003).

[5] In taking up a politics of the usage of 'diaspora', I am foregrounding the analytical function of the term, because (athough some recent historical work confuses
the issue) 'diaspora' has not been a dominant term of political *organization*. When
black activists have assembled transnational movements, they have turned to a wide
range of terms (including Ethiopianism, pan-Africanism, anti-fascism, communism,
civil rights, Black Power, afrocentrism, anti-racism, anti-apartheid), but seldom and
only very recently to 'diaspora' as rallying cry or group appellation.

[6] W.E.B. Du Bois, "Pan-Africa and the New Racial Philosophy," *Crisis* 40 (November 1933): 247.

directly involved – particularly in Ghana – in what has been termed "continental Pan-Africanism," Du Bois clung to this New World orientation,
writing, for example:

> The idea of one Africa to unite the thought and ideals of all native peoples of
> the dark continent belongs to the twentieth century and stems naturally from
> the West Indies and the United States. Here various groups of Africans, quite
> separate in origin, became so united in experience and so exposed to the
> impact of new cultures that they began to think of Africa as one idea and one
> land.[7]

By the 1950s, scholars were beginning to consider this paradigmatically
New World impulse, which St. Clair Drake memorably encapsulated in the
phrase "Africa interest," as a broad force in African-American identity
formation.[8] At times the "Africa interest" was inflected toward a *return* to
the African continent itself, as in the nineteenth-century colonization and
missionary movements, for instance. But in a larger sense, scholarship on
the history of the "Africa interest" was a way of coming to terms with the
consistent necessity of an ideological 'return' to the question of Africa, as a
figure for the question of origins – a return to what Édouard Glissant calls
the "point of entanglement [*intrication*]." The problematic of 'return' in this
sense consistently animated black ideologies as diverse as Garveyism, Negritude, and the numerous black New World discourses of "Ethiopianism"; it
also animated a great deal of the ground-breaking African-American history
and sociology in the first decades of the century (by Du Bois, Carter G.
Woodson, and Arturo Schomburg, among others).[9] In the interwar period,

---

[7] Du Bois, *The World and Africa: An Inquiry into the Part Which Africa Has
Played in World History* (1946; expanded edition, New York: International Pub-
lishers, 1965): 7. For another version of this argument, see J.A. Langley, "New-
World Origins of Pan-Negro Sentiment," in *Pan-Africanism and Nationalism in
West Africa, 1900–1945: A Study in Ideology and Social Classes* (Oxford: Oxford
UP, 1973): 17–40.

[8] Drake, "Negro Americans and the Africa Interest," in *The American Negro
Reference Book*, ed. John P. Davis (Englewood Cliffs NJ: Prentice–Hall, 1966): 662–
705.

[9] Glissant, *Caribbean Discourse*, tr. J. Michael Dash (Charlottesville VA: UP of
Virginia/CARAF, 1989): 26. The original is *Le Discours antillais* (Paris: Seuil,
1981): 36. Arguments from this period that a problematic of 'return' shapes both
Negritude and Ethiopianism include St. Clair Drake, "Hide My Face? – On Pan-
Africanism and Negritude," in *Soon, One Morning: New Writing by American
Negroes, 1940–1962*, ed. Herbert Hill (New York: Alfred A. Knopf, 1966): 77–105;

these roots were extended in the emerging discipline of anthropology, especially through the influential work of scholars such as Jean Price–Mars and Melville Herskovits on "African survivals" in New World black cultures.[10] These issues of cultural retention were equally dominant in the historical and archival work that developed after the 1945 Manchester Pan-African Congress, work by scholars including St. Clair Drake, George Shepperson, Rayford Logan, Harold Isaacs, James Ivy, Dorothy Porter, Adelaide Cromwell Hill, and E.U. Essien–Udom.[11]

I will return below to francophone articulations of 'diaspora', but I want to mention here the specific role of the journal *Présence Africaine*, often cited as a fertile ground for diasporic work. On the one hand, it should be recalled that at its outset, *Présence Africaine* was not primarily conceived as a diasporic project, focussing on issues of connection and collaboration among peoples of African descent. It was more expressly conceived as an

---

and George Shepperson, "Ethiopianism and African Nationalism," *Phylon* 14 (First Quarter 1953): 9–18. Drake comments more generally on "'The Return' as a Pan-African Theme" in his "Diaspora Studies and Pan-Africanism," in *Global Dimensions of the African Diaspora*, ed. Joseph Harris (Washington DC: Howard UP, 1982): 359–66.

[10] An excellent introduction is David Scott, "That Event, This Memory: Notes on the Anthropology of African Diasporas in the New World," *Diaspora: A Journal of Transnational Studies* 1.3 (Winter 1991): 261–84.

[11] Here is a small sampling of the wealth of "Africa interest" work in this period, which focussed in particular on black New World projects of return and on African American ideological influences on Africa: Harold R. Isaacs, "The American Negro and Africa: Some Notes," *Phylon* 20 (Fall 1959): 219–33; George Shepperson, "Notes on Negro American Influences on the Emergence of African Nationalism," *Journal of African History* 1.2 (1960): 299–312, and "The Afro-American Contribution to African Studies," *Journal of American Studies* 8.3 (December 1974): 281–301; E.U. Essien–Udom, "The Relationship of Afro-Americans to African Nationalism," *Freedomways* 2 (Fall 1962): 391–407, and "Black Identity in the International Context," in *Key Issues in the Afro-American Experience*, vol. 2: *Since 1865*, ed. Nathan Huggins, Martin Kilson & Daniel Fox (New York: Harcourt Brace Jovanovich, 1971): 233–58; Richard B. Moore, "Africa Conscious Harlem," *Freedomways* 3 (Summer 1963): 315–34; *Apropos of Africa: Sentiments of Negro American Leaders on Africa from the 1800s to the 1950s*, ed. Adelaide Cromwell Hill & Martin Kilson (London: Frank Cass, 1969). See also Sterling Stuckey, "Black Americans and African Consciousness: Du Bois, Woodson, and the Spell of Africa," in *Going through the Storm: The Influence of African American Art in History* (New York: Oxford UP, 1994): 120–37.

African incursion into modernity. In the mission statement of the first issue,
Alioune Diop writes:

> Reaching beyond the confines of French colonization, [*Présence Africaine*]
> intends to raise and study the general problem of Europe's relations with the
> rest of the world, taking Africa as an example, especially since her black
> mankind finds itself to be the most disinherited. [...] The black man [*Le noir*],
> conspicuous by his absence in the building up of the modern city, will be able
> to signify his presence little by little by contributing to the recreating of a
> humanism reflecting the true measure of man. [...] As to us Africans, we are
> expecting concrete results from these cultural activities. To enable us to merge
> with modern society and to identify ourselves clearly in that society,
> PRESENCE AFRICAINE, while revealing us to the world, will, more than
> anything else, persuade us to have faith in ideas.[12]

It should not be surprising that the journal was conceived in the European
metropolis by a group of "overseas students" (*étudiants d'outre-mer* – more
precisely, students from the overseas French colonies, or *France d'outre-
mer*), who felt, after the ravages of the war, that they constituted "a new
race, mentally mixed [*mentalement métissée*]," and who began to reconsider
their position in European discourses of "universal" humanism.[13] *Présence
Africaine*, as the title announces, inscribes an African presence in modernity
and inaugurates the "re-creation" of the humanist project through that intervention.[14] The aims of such a project are notably different than those
announced by interwar francophone journals in Paris, like *La Dépêche Africaine*, which explicitly strove to foster "correspondence" among blacks
throughout the world, or *La Revue du Monde Noir*, which intended "to
create among Negroes [*les Noirs*] of the entire world, regardless of nationality, an intellectual, and moral tie, which will permit them to better know
each other[,] to love one another, to defend more effectively their collective

---

[12] Diop, "Niam N'Goura, or *Présence Africaine*'s *raison d'être*," tr. Richard
Wright & Thomas Diop, *Présence Africaine* 1 (October–November 1947): 190–91.
The French original appears in the same issue, 7–14.

[13] Diop, "Niam N'Goura, or *Présence Africaine*'s *raison d'être*," 186.

[14] Bernard Mouralis, "*Présence Africaine*: The Geography of an 'Ideology'," in
*The Surreptitious Speech: "Présence Africaine" and the Politics of Otherness,
1947–1987*, ed. Valentine Y. Mudimbe (Chicago: U of Chicago P, 1992): 6. See also
the account by Jacques Howlett, the French philosopher who worked closely with
Diop on the journal: "*Présence Africaine, 1947–1958*," tr. Mercer Cook, *Journal of
Negro History* 43 (April 1958): 140–50.

interests and to glorify their race."[15] On the other hand, even given the express aims of *Présence Africaine*, one should not forget that the translation of Diop's "Niam N'Goura" quoted above is by Thomas Diop and Richard Wright, the African-American writer, then living in Paris. Even if *Présence Africaine* did not initially aim to theorize black internationalism, it represents black internationalism *in practice*, particularly through its translations[16] and through the International Congresses of black artists and intellectuals it hosted in Paris in 1956 and Rome in 1959. Moreover, especially in its "new series" after 1955, *Présence Africaine* explicitly espoused an anticolonialist stance and argued that "our common national aspirations" provided the foundation for the "solidarity of colonized peoples."[17] In the context of independence struggles in Africa, the journal would prove receptive to work on 'diaspora' as it emerged in the 1960s.[18]

Toward a Genealogy of the African Diaspora Concept

The turn to 'diaspora' in the early 1960s marks in no small degree a break with the "Africa interest" orientation, which, as Penny von Eschen has poin-

[15] *La Dépêche Africaine*, under the direction of the Guadeloupean Maurice Satineau, began publication in February 1928. The paper's masthead presented it as a "grand organe républicain indépendant de correspondence entre les Noirs et d'Études des Questions Politiques et Économiques Coloniales." The quotation comes from an editorial by Paulette Nardal and Léo Sajous, "Our Aim" ["Ce que nous voulons faire"], tr. Nardal & Clara W. Shepard, *La Revue du Monde Noir / Review of the Black World* 1 (1931).

[16] The first issue included Wright's "Bright and Morning Star," translated by Boris Vian, and Gwendolyn Brooks' poem "The Ballad of Pearl May Lee." Wright, working with the journal's editorial board until 1950, was also responsible for *Présence Africaine*'s publishing Frank Marshall Davis, Samuel Allen, Horace Cayton, and C.L.R. James. Like *La Revue du Monde Noir* in the early 1930s, *Présence Africaine* also printed an English edition.

[17] "Foreword," *Présence Africaine*, New Series 1–2 (April–July 1955): 8.

[18] In a sense, the international congresses mark a convergence between the intellectual formations around the "Africa interest" in the USA and the "African presence" in France, culminating in publications such as *Africa Seen by American Negro Scholars*, the volume published in 1958 as a joint venture between Diop's Société Africaine de Culture and its US cousin, the American Society of African Culture, headed by John A. Davis. See also the American Society of African Culture, *Pan-Africanism Reconsidered* (Berkeley: U of California P, 1962).

ted out, was greatly molded by the exigencies of the Cold War. Even when
in collaboration with francophone scholarship, much of the work emanating
from the USA during that period was conditioned by an unrelenting American exceptionalism.[19] Of course, the figurative elements of the turn were by
no means new: syncretic African-American slave cultures had found resonance in the Old Testament tales of Exodus, and references to the "scattering" of Africans into the New World were common at least since the work
of Blyden in the nineteenth century. But the crystallization of these figurative allusions into a theoretical discourse of diaspora, explicitly in dialogue
with the long-standing Jewish traditions behind the term, responds to a set
of historiographic needs particular to the late 1950s and early 1960s, especially in the work of the historians George Shepperson and Joseph Harris.

Although it is often overlooked, the necessity of this conceptual turn is
first developed in a work in the growing field of African history, specifically around the issue of African resistance to colonialism. The 1958 book
Independent African, by George Shepperson and Thomas Price, is a celebrated study of the revolts that took place in British Central Africa in 1915,
often considered to be the first in a long series of African resistance movements in the modern period that led via discontinuous eruptions to the
independence struggles of the 1950s and 1960s. Shepperson and Price,
attempting to explain the development of John Chilembwe, the African
minister who led the uprising out of his mission in the Shire Highlands in
what was then called Nyasaland, spend a significant amount of time considering his trip to the USA in 1897, where Chilembwe became associated
with the National Negro Baptist Convention, studied at the Virginia Theological Seminary, and entered the ministry.[20] The authors are at pains to
come to terms with the influence of that New World context, given the great
flux of black cultural and intellectual work that emerges at the turn of the

---

[19] Von Eschen argues, more particularly, that the "Africa interest" was not always
articulated with the exigencies of decolonization and independence. There were loud
silences around the wealth of radical work that was specifically seeking such an
internationalization in the period (most prominently, the work of George Padmore,
Kwame Nkrumah, Paul Robeson, Alphaeus Hunton, and the Council on African
Affairs). Penny von Eschen, *Race against Empire: Black Americans and Anticolonialism, 1937–1957* (Ithaca NY: Cornell UP, 1997): 176.

[20] George Shepperson & Thomas Price, *Independent African: John Chilembwe
and the Origins, Setting and Significance of the Nyasaland Native Rising of 1915*
(Edinburgh: Edinburgh UP, 1958): 112 (further page references are in the main text).
For commentary on *Independent African*, see particularly Cedric Robinson, "Notes
on a 'Native' Theory of History," *Review* 4 (Summer 1980): 45–78.

century in the USA in particular: the struggle against US imperialism in the Caribbean and the Philippines, which in part was expressed in the Niagara movement of 1905 (103); the cultural histories of the "African background" that would emerge in the work of Du Bois and Woodson; the histories of black insurrection in the USA and the Caribbean (106–107); and the prevalence of diverse nineteenth-century "return" ideologies and "Back to Africa" projects such as the American Colonization Society. For Shepperson and Price, the explanation of Chilembwe's intellectual development in this milieu requires an understanding of transnational black influences that would have to diverge sharply from de-politicized, vanguardist considerations of an "Africa interest."

In an oft-cited essay published in *Phylon* in 1962, Shepperson extended this work theoretically by reconsidering the uses and limitations of the term 'pan-African'. Attempting to clear a field that had become increasingly crippled by indiscriminate references to "pan-Africanism" in terms of any consideration of racial organization or black internationalism, Shepperson broke the term down into its "proper" and "common" senses: "Pan-Africanism" (capital P) indicates the history of the transnational movement itself, the limited parameters of the Pan-African Congress from 1900 on. But another derivation of the term was required: "On the other hand, 'pan-Africanism' with a small letter is not a clearly recognizable movement, with a single nucleus such as the nonagenarian Du Bois. [...] It is rather a group of movements, many very ephemeral."[21] For Shepperson, the "cultural element often predominates" in this diverse grouping of "pan-African" movements, but these formations are not at all limited to this focus (this is not a split between 'political' and 'cultural' versions of pan-Africanism, as it sometimes has been misread). Shepperson considers the small-'p' term to cover both aesthetic evocations and political institutions, such as church organizations, academic conferences and associations, lobbying groups, and various radical pressure groups. Finally, the ideological diversity that falls under the broad rubric including both Pan-Africanism and pan-Africanism, Shepperson argues, demonstrates that Africa itself emerges as a concept only historically, mainly through *external* evocations of "continental unity," and calls for return (349).

I will highlight two components of this revision or splitting of pan-Africanism. On the one hand, Shepperson re-reads the term precisely to

---

[21] George Shepperson, "Pan-Africanism and 'pan-Africanism': Some Historical Notes," *Phylon* 23.4 (Winter 1962): 346 (further page references are in the main text).

make room for ideological difference and disjuncture in considering black cultural politics in an international sphere. He specifically invokes the need to consider the ways in which black internationalisms have been refracted through the Caribbean, for example, especially through the disproportionate contributions of Caribbean migrants to US ideologies of liberation in the early years of the century.[22] In Shepperson's view, it is crucial to be able to account for the transformative "sea changes" that Pan-African thought undergoes in a transnational circuit. One instance involves the work of Marcus Garvey, who was often described as a "pan-Negroist" after the first World War even as Du Bois's Pan-African Congress initiatives were articulated directly in opposition to Garvey's populist and racialist version of "Back to Africa." Later, though, as Shepperson points out, Garvey is factored into the pan-African tradition, especially through the African intellectuals who dominated the movement after the 1945 Manchester Pan-African Congress, such as Kwame Nkrumah, who expressly cited Garvey's *Philosophy and Opinions* as one of the main influences in the development of continental African race consciousness and independence ideologies (347–48). At the same time, Shepperson claims that many of these discontinuities in pan-Africanism and Pan-Africanism are rooted not just in ideological disjunctures but also in the linguistic difference that necessarily has crucial consequences for any consideration of black internationalism. He notes the role of the Liga Africana, the federation of Portuguese African associations, in the 1923 Pan-African Congress in Lisbon (355), but considers the most important arena of linguistic difference to arise in French, particularly through French participation in the first and second Pan-African Congresses, and through the influence of Negritude after World War Two:

> Above all, the story of French-speaking African participation in Pan-Africanism and pan-Africanism has yet to be told. Blaise Diagne, Deputy from Senegal, and Gratien Candace, deputy from Guadeloupe, played important roles in the 1919 and 1921 Pan-African Conferences. But their ultimate split with the Du Bois forces was to be seen in their references to themselves as 'we Frenchmen,' whereas the English-speaking delegation called themselves 'we Negroes.' By 1921, the difference between the two groups was revealed when Du Bois felt that he had to stand out against the flood of anti-Garvey statements from Diagne and Candace and took the unusual step of saying in public that he agreed with the Jamaican's main principles. (355–56)

---

[22] Shepperson, "Pan-Africanism and 'pan-Africanism'," 356. We now have a definitive history of this dynamic, Winston James's impressive *Holding Aloft the Banner of Ethiopia: Caribbean Radicalism in Early Twentieth-Century America* (London: Verso, 1998).

The point is that Shepperson is attempting to push here toward a revised or expanded notion of black international work that would be able to account for such an unavoidable dynamic of difference, rather than either assuming a universally applicable definition of 'pan-African' or presupposing an exceptionalist version of New World 'pan-African' activity. He goes so far as to suggest "all-African" as a "collective term" (346) for this wider, more various context of black internationalism. Shepperson closes his essay with a call to consider all-Africanism "in its international context: If it is necessary to study Pan-Africanism and pan-Africanism in a wider African context than the specifically West African, it is of equal importance to look at it in its full international perspective, in time as well [as] in space" (358).

In October 1965, Shepperson formalized this intervention in his paper "The African Abroad, or the African Diaspora," originally delivered on a panel arranged by Joseph Harris at the International Congress of African Historians at University College, Dar es Salaam.[23] It is this paper that is usually credited with introducing the notion of "diaspora" into the study of black cultural politics and history. Shepperson starts by explicitly invoking the "Jewish Dispersal or Diaspora" with a quotation from Chapter 28 of Deuteronomy ("Thou shall be removed into all the kingdoms of the earth"); then he extends the analogy:

> Although it cannot be said that the dark-skinned peoples of Africa, the so-called Negroes, have been dispersed into all kingdoms and countries of the world, they have certainly migrated to a very large number of them. And the forces which have driven them abroad, slavery and imperialism, have been similar to those which scattered the Jews. It is, therefore, not difficult to understand why the expression 'the African Diaspora' has gained currency as a description of the great movement which, according to one estimate made in

---

[23] Shepperson, "The African Abroad, or the African Diaspora," in *Emerging Themes of African History*, ed. T.O. Ranger (Nairobi: East African Publishing House, 1968): 152–76. It is crucial to note that this essay was first published in *Africa Forum*, the journal of the American Society of African Culture; in that arena, it marks an explicit intervention into the assumptions of the "Africa interest." The citation (note the inversion of the title: the essay is identical, but this title emphasizes the 'diaspora' concept rather than African history) is Shepperson, "The African Abroad, or the African Diaspora," *Africa Forum: A Quarterly Journal of African Affairs* 1.2 (Summer 1966): 76–93. For Joseph Harris's comments on the Dar es Salaam conference, and on the introduction of the diaspora concept, see Joseph E. Harris, "Introduction to the African Diaspora," in *Emerging Themes* 146–51; and Harris, "The International Congress on African History, 1965," *Africa Forum* 1.3 (Winter 1966): 80–84.

1946, has been responsible for creating over 41 million people of African descent in the Western hemisphere.[24]

The essay is a rather schematic elaboration of the uses of 'diaspora' in a re-visioning of African historiography; it moves by list-making, by enumerating the objects of study that might fall under the rubric of "the African abroad." Again, Shepperson uses the term precisely to push beyond the ways in which 'pan-African' limits the scope of analysis: 'diaspora' studies would involve not only attention to the "idea and practice of African unity" (ie, Pan-Africanism and pan-Africanisms) (168–69) but also an understanding of slavery influenced in particular by the historical work of W.E.B. Du Bois and C.L.R. James, which considers the slave trade as central to any understanding of Western modernity or "universal history" (161); an investigation into the effects of slave trade and subsequent imperialism on Africa itself, and patterns of dispersal internal to the continent (162, 170); an analysis of "African survivals" in the black cultures of the New World (162–66); and a consideration of the influence of African Americans on the emergence of African nationalism (166).

In Shepperson's usage, in other words, the term is quite flexible: he suggests that the concept of diaspora "can be considerably extended, both in time and space," and part of the use of the concept is precisely in its extensions (152). The "African diaspora" here adheres to many of the elements considered common to the three 'classic' diasporas (the Jewish, the Greek, and the Armenian): in particular, an origin in the scattering and uprooting of communities, a history of "traumatic and forced departure," and also the sense of a real or imagined relationship to a "homeland," mediated through the dynamic of collective memory and the politics of "return."[25] As a frame for knowledge production, the "African diaspora" likewise inaugurates an ambitious and radically decentered analysis of transnational circuits of culture and politics that are resistant to or deviant from the frames of nations and continents.

The turn to diaspora arises not in terms of black cultures in the New World but in the context of revising what Shepperson calls "isolationist" and restrictive trends in African historiography – hence the apposition enunciated by the essay's title ("The African Diaspora, or the African Abroad," 173). In addition, the "African diaspora" is formulated expressly through an attempt to come to terms with diverse and cross-fertilized black traditions of

---

[24] Shepperson, "The African Abroad," 152 (further page references are in the main text).

[25] See Tölölyan, "Rethinking *Diaspora*(s)," 12–15.

resistance and anticolonialism. On a theoretical level, this intervention focusses especially on relations of difference and disjuncture in the varied interactions of black internationalist discourses, both in ideological terms and in terms of language difference itself.[26]

This is not to suggest that Shepperson is definitively the first intellectual to use the phrase 'African diaspora'. Shepperson has insisted that the use of the expression was "certainly established" in scholarly vocabulary before the 1965 Dar es Salaam conference.[27] In his 1982 essay "African Diaspora: Concept and Context," he sketches the development of the term:

> At some time between the mid-1950s and the mid-1960s, the period in which many African states were breaking away from European empires and achieving independence, the expression *African diaspora* began increasingly to be used by writers and thinkers who were concerned with the status and prospects of persons of African descent around the world as well as at home. Who first used this expression, I do not know; and I wish very much that someone would attempt the difficult task of tracing the employment of the Greek word for dispersal – which, until it began to have the adjective *African* or *black* attached to it, was used largely for the scattering abroad of the Jews.[28]

I am less concerned here with unearthing the 'originator' or first use of what Shepperson calls "the African diaspora concept." Etymologies are seductive in part because of the ruse of origin – the implication that one can discover the roots of language use and transformation. They are most instructive, though, in the ways in which they provide a sedimentation of the social construction of linguistic meaning over time: as something not unlike Raymond

---

[26] In the 'diaspora' articles, both Shepperson and Harris call again for attention to be paid to the French influence on discourses of pan-Africanism and black internationalism. See Shepperson, "The African Abroad," 167; Harris, "Introduction," 149–50. The first studies to follow up on this call included Imanuel Geiss's 1968 *The Pan-African Movement: A History of Pan-Africanism in America, Europe and Africa*, tr. Ann Keep (New York: African Publishing & London: Methuen, 1974), especially the chapter on "Nationalist Groups in France: The Roots of Négritude" 305–21, and J.A. Langley, "The Movement and Thought of Francophone Pan-Negroism: 1924–1936," which originally appeared in a shorter version in the *Journal of Modern African Studies* in 1969, and was later published as chapter 7 of Langley's *Pan-Africanism and Nationalism in West Africa, 1900–1945*, 286–325.

[27] Shepperson, "Introduction" to *The African Diaspora: Interpretive Essays*, ed. Martin L. Kilson & Robert I. Rotberg (Cambridge MA: Harvard UP, 1976): 2. I have not yet found an earlier example in print, however.

[28] Shepperson, "African Diaspora: Concept and Context," in Harris, *Global Dimensions of the African Diaspora*, 46.

Williams's notion of the "keyword," which Michael McKeon has felicitously described as an "antithetical structure expressing a historical contradiction."[29] Rather than originary usage, the question is why it becomes necessary at a certain historical conjuncture to employ the term 'diaspora' in black intellectual work. Shepperson himself begins to point toward an answer, as he conjectures why the nineteenth-century black intellectual Edward Wilmot Blyden never used the term:

> Considering Blyden's knowledge of Hebrew, his interest in Jewish history, and his sympathy with Zionist aspirations, it is surprising that he did not employ the expression 'the African diaspora.' If, however, Blyden had popularized the expression 'African diaspora' in the nineteenth century and it had gained support amongst early African nationalist intellectuals, it could have acquired political overtones which would have rendered it useless for scholars today who find it convenient to employ in their studies of the too long neglected subject of the African abroad. Without political overtones, it serves as a satisfactory although sometimes fluctuating focus for the various aspects of the African outside of Africa.[30]

The point is not that 'diaspora' is apolitical but that it has none of the 'overtones' that make a term like 'pan-Africanism' already contested terrain. In this sense, the turn to 'diaspora' as a term of analysis allows for an account of black transnational formations that attends to their constitutive differences, the political stakes of the organization of the "African abroad." The accepted risk is that the term's analytic focus 'fluctuates'. Like 'pan-African', it is open to ideological appropriation in a wide variety of political projects, from anticolonial activism to what has long been called "Black Zionism" – articulations of 'diaspora' that collapse the term into versions of nationalism or racial essentialism.

Unfortunately, some of the most celebrated work on 'diaspora' in the past thirty years has served to undo this complex history of emergence. It is impossible to take on the "African diaspora concept" without a great debt to the work of the historian St. Clair Drake, who may be the single intellectual with the most impressive long-term commitment to its elaboration. Still, it is difficult to endorse Drake's conclusions in "Diaspora Studies and Pan-Africanism," a 1982 essay that offers a historically rich but theoretically

---

[29] Michael McKeon, review of *Keywords*, *Studies in Romanticism* 16 (Winter 1977): 133.

[30] Shepperson, "Introduction," 3.

misleading overview of the development of "diaspora studies."[31] Without fully coming to terms with Shepperson's argument about the great diversity of Pan-Africanist and pan-Africanist movements, Drake simply periodizes a split between what he terms "traditional Pan-African activity" (which encapsulates both of Shepperson's senses of the term)[32] and a subsequent "continental Pan-Africanism" that develops as a discourse of political unity in Africa itself in independence struggles after the second World War.[33] He then discards the precise sense of diaspora as an intervention in Shepperson's work, by cataloging "diaspora studies as an aspect of traditional Pan-African activity." This ends up needlessly conflating the two terms:

> A concept of the black world is necessary in defining Pan-African activity. It would include all of those areas where the population is actually black in a phenotypic sense, that is, Negroid, or where the people think of themselves as black despite considerable miscegenation, or where they are so defined by others. For almost a century a conscious and deliberate movement has been developing within various parts of the black world to increase cultural contacts between its diverse segments and to unite them in the pursuit of common interests. I refer to this as traditional Pan-African activity. *For diaspora studies to be considered an aspect of this activity, an aspect operating in the cultural sector of it, they must contribute toward maintaining and reinforcing black consciousness and must be oriented toward the goal of fostering understanding, solidarity, and cooperation throughout the black world.*[34]

Without even engaging Drake's unfortunate reliance on a genetic ("phenotypic") understanding of black identity, it should be clear that this argument for the "parameters of African Diaspora Studies" departs from Shepperson's

---

[31] St. Clair Drake, "Diaspora Studies and Pan-Africanism," in Harris, *Global Dimensions of the African Diaspora*, 358, 373. But see also Drake's "The Black Diaspora in Pan-African Perspective," *Black Scholar* 7.1 (September 1975), which is more tentative in its claims: "the diaspora analogy," he writes, "like the internal colony analogy, needs constant critical analysis if it is to be a useful guide to research as well as a striking metaphor" (2). Other work has equally moved away from the sense of 'diaspora' as a particular kind of intervention: some have framed the term around questions of foreign policy, while others have continued to worry the question of the historical and cultural "unity" of the diaspora, in a vein that might be more properly termed pan-Africanist – eg, Ruth Simms Hamilton, "Conceptualizing the African Diaspora," in *African Presence in the Americas*, ed. Carlos Moore et al. (Trenton NJ: Africa World Press, 1995): 393–410.

[32] Drake, "Diaspora Studies and Pan-Africanism," 353.

[33] "Diaspora Studies and Pan-Africanism," 358–59.

[34] "Diaspora Studies and Pan-Africanism," 343 (emphasis in the original).

intervention in significant ways. Here 'diaspora' marks a simple continuity
with 'pan-Africanism' – indeed, a reduction to its "cultural sector," rather
than precisely a means to theorize both culture and politics at the transnational level. Whereas Shepperson uses 'diaspora' to break with a depoli-
ticizing emphasis on "unity" and unidirectional return in mid-century black
internationalist scholarship, Drake here reintroduces the pan-African concern with vaguely defined "cultural contacts," with projects of "fostering
understanding, solidarity, and cooperation throughout the black world."
This results in an elision with severe consequences for the politics of 'diaspora' as a term of analysis: in particular, it abandons the insight that 'diaspora' becomes necessary partly because of the increased contestation over
the political scope of 'pan-Africanism' in the independence movement.[35]

Joseph Harris and Locksley Edmondson have provided a more convincing historiographical account of the term. They suggest that we period-
ize the African diaspora to distinguish between an initial history of migration and "involuntary diaspora" (both inside Africa and through the Arab
and European slave trades) and the subsequent transnational formation of a
"mobilized diaspora," a phenomenon particular to the twentieth century.
Harris defines the latter term by noting that, in the early 1900s,

> the major cities of the Western powers [...] became loci for the gathering of
> diverse ethnic and political groups of African origin, facilitating the devel-
> opment of an international network linking Africa to its diaspora; this network
> may be called a mobilized diaspora. [...] Until the 1960s most Africans in
> Africa retained a primary ethnic allegiance, while their descendants abroad
> constituted a 'stateless' diaspora without a common country of origin, lan-

---

[35] In other words, part of the reason for the turn to a discourse of diaspora in the
1960s and 1970s is precisely the growing split in the independence period between
'continental' and 'traditional' visions of pan-Africanism (to use Drake's terms). Although certain explicitly 'cultural' projects continued to flourish (eg, the 1966 First
Festival of Negro Arts in Dakar, Senegal), the pan-African movement reached an
impasse at the Sixth Congress in Dar es Salaam in 1974, when delegates from the
Americas and delegates from the African continent itself argued whether the movement should focus on the concerns of the continent as a unit or on the international
connections between peoples of African descent. Drake notes these difficulties (357–
59), without reconsidering his conflation of 'diaspora' and 'pan-Africanism', how-
ever. See also the essays around the 1974 Congress edited by Horace Campbell, *Pan-
Africanism: Struggle against Neo-Colonialism and Imperialism* (Toronto: Afro-
Carib Publications, 1975); and Joseph Harris & Slimane Zeghidour, "Africa and its
Diaspora since 1935," in *General History of Africa*, vol. 8: *Africa Since 1935*, ed. Ali
A. Mazrui (Berkeley CA: UNESCO/Heinemann, 1993): 716–17.

guage, religion, or culture. The strength of the connection between Africans and the African diaspora remained essentially their common origins in Africa as a whole and a common social condition (social, economic, and political marginalization) throughout the world. It was this combination that paved the way for the development of an effective international network by the mobilized African diaspora, namely, descendant Africans with a consciousness of the identity of their roots, occupational and communications skills, social and economic status, and access to decision-making bodies in their host country.[36]

My point in resuscitating the history of the term itself, however, is that a discourse of diaspora becomes necessary in the same period that the "mobilized diaspora" is taking shape – indeed, the turn to 'diaspora' is precisely part of what allows that mobilization to occur.

At the same time, one might add that Drake's "Diaspora Studies and Pan-Africanism" appears in a collection edited by Joseph Harris, *Global Dimensions of the African Diaspora*, arising out of the 1979 conference of the First African Diaspora Studies Institute at Howard University. Despite the problems of Drake's take on 'diaspora', the collection overall might be considered the culmination of the interventionist use of 'diaspora': it includes essays by a wide range of internationally based intellectuals, among them Harris, Elliott Skinner, George Shepperson, and Lawrence Levine, and is organized precisely to signal both a politicized sense of the stakes of these definitional issues and room for divergence and disagreement, even around the use of the term 'diaspora' as a frame for the conference in general. Moreover, *Global Dimensions* highlights again not just ideological disjuncture but also linguistic divergence as a central issue in any approach to the question: four chapters were originally written in French (by Oruno D. Lara, Daniel Racine, Guerin C. Montilus, and Ibrahima B. Kaké), and

---

[36] Joseph E. Harris, "The Dynamics of the Global African Diaspora," in *The African Diaspora*, ed. Alusine Jalloh (College Station: U of Texas at Arlington, 1996): 14. Although Harris does not cite a source for the phrase, the original application of "mobilized diaspora" to the African diaspora appears to be Locksley Edmondson, "Black America as a Mobilizing Diaspora: Some International Implications," in *Modern Diasporas in International Politics*, ed. Gabriel Sheffer (London: Croom Helm, 1986): 164–211. Other foreign-policy-oriented work in this vein includes Robert Chrisman, "History of Black Involvement in International Politics," in *The Non-Aligned Movement in World Politics*, ed. A.W. Singham (Westport CT: Lawrence Hill, 1977); John A. Davis, "Black Americans and United States Policy Toward Black Africa," *Journal of International Affairs* 23.2 (1969): 236–49; and Yossi Shain, "Ethnic Diasporas and US Foreign Policy," *Political Science Quarterly* 109.5 (Winter 1994–95): 811–41.

there is copious coverage of the divergence of francophone pan-Africanism
and Negritude cultural politics within the wider frame of the "African
diaspora concept."

Cultural Studies and Diaspora

A more complete genealogy of the uses of 'diaspora' in black critical work
after the Second World War would have to turn to the institutionalization of
black studies in the US academy in the 1960s and 1970s.[37] That intervention in the Western academy is an epistemological challenge,[38] explicitly staked out through a politics of diaspora that rejects Western assumptions about a link between knowledge production and the nation. Invocations of diaspora were central and strategic in almost all of the mission
statements of Black Studies and African American Studies departments
founded in the late 1960s and early 1970s – though not necessarily in a
manner consonant with the earlier work of Harris and Shepperson. For
instance, Maulana Karenga's *Introduction to Black Studies*, like much of
the programmatic literature, offers a split conception of diaspora that separates an African past from a US present: it is based on a "Diasporan focus
treating first African Americans and then all other Africans spread across
the world."[39] Karenga explains this privileged division in pragmatic terms:

> just as a point of departure and sound procedure, does not logic demand a
> thrust which is not over-ambitious, but begins where it is, in the US, among
> African Americans, and then as it grows stronger, expands outward? In other
> words, is not the study of African Americans the core of Black Studies in the

---

[37] This is also the period when a discourse of diaspora begins to emerge in black
popular culture. There is no room here, however, to trace the uses of the term on that
level.

[38] On black studies as epistemological intervention, see in particular Russell L.
Adams, "Intellectual Questions and Imperatives in the Development of Afro-Ameri-
can Studies," *Journal of Negro Education* 53.3 (Summer 1984): 204. The essays of
Sylvia Wynter offer the most impressive elaboration of this argument. See, for
example, Wynter, "Columbus, the Ocean Blue, and Fables That Stir the Mind: To
Reinvent the Study of Letters," in *Poetics of the Americas: Race, Founding, and
Textuality*, ed. Bainard Cowan & Jefferson Humphries (Baton Rouge: Louisiana
State UP, 1997): 148–49.

[39] Maulana Karenga, *Introduction to Black Studies* (Los Angeles: U of Sankore P,
1993): 13.

US, the study of an African people neglected more than any other, certainly more than the study of Continentals or Caribbeans?[40]

This begs the question: what are the implications of such a "core" for a Black Studies project? Wouldn't such a "thrust" tend to cement an American exceptionalism already prevalent in the US academy, rather than using diaspora precisely to break up that orientation? Or, as C.L.R. James put it in a 1970 interview,

> The black students believe that black studies concerns them and black people alone. But that is a mistake. Black studies mean the intervention of a neglected area of studies that are essential to the understanding of ancient and modern society. [...] Black studies require a complete reorganization of the intellectual life and historical outlook of the United States, and world civilization as a whole.[41]

The discourse of diaspora, in other words, is both enabling to Black Studies, in the service of such an "intervention," and inherently a risk, in that it can fall back into either racial essentialism or American vanguardism.

More recently, this complex history of institutional intervention has been elided by the 'internationalization' of the discourse of diaspora developed in British cultural studies. Scholars including Mae Henderson, Wahneema Lubiano and Sylvia Wynter have recently expressed fears that the recent 'importing' of cultural studies into the US academy often serves to marginalize or even erase the hard-won gains of Black Studies and African-American Studies programs.[42] The stakes are not solely institutional but also epistemological, since cultural studies methodology is often portrayed in the

---

[40] Karenga, *Introduction to Black Studies*, 492.

[41] James, "The *Black Scholar* Interviews C.L.R. James," *Black Scholar* 2.1 (September 1970): 43. St. Clair Drake has often pointed out the role of 'diaspora' in the institutionalization of Black Studies: see his "Diaspora Studies and Pan-Africanism," 380–84, and his more recent "Black Studies and Global Perspectives: An Essay," *Journal of Negro Education* 53.3 (Summer 1984): 226–42.

[42] See Mae G. Henderson, "'Where, By the Way, is This Train Going?' A Case for Black (Cultural) Studies," *Callaloo* 19.1 (Winter 1996): 60–67; Wahneema Lubiano, "Mapping the Interstices Between Afro-American Cultural Discourse and Cultural Studies: A Prolegomenon," *Callaloo* 19.1 (Winter 1996): 68–77; Manthia Diawara, "Black Studies/Cultural Studies," in *Borders, Boundaries and Frames: Cultural Criticism and Cultural Studies*, ed. Mae G. Henderson (New York: Routledge, 1995): 202–12; Wynter, "Columbus, the Ocean Blue, and Fables That Stir the Mind," 193–94, n. 34.

USA as offering a 'new' focus on issues of diaspora. Certainly, what is often called the "turn to race" in the trajectory of work associated with the Centre for Contemporary Cultural Studies at Birmingham University demands to be read equally as a *turn to diaspora.* The scholarship that began to critique the presupposition of an "English" national frame (particularly in Raymond Williams's development of a cultural studies paradigm) moves to a diasporic register as a counterbalance to the constitutive links between racism and nationalism.[43] This strategic move arises, however, as a discourse discontinuous with the invocations of diaspora in African-American and African historiographic and cultural work.[44] The question of the possible conjunction of these different turns to 'diaspora', then, is central to the issue of the uses of 'diaspora' for contemporary critical scholarship with a transnational focus.

As in Shepperson's work, a transnational imperative emerges in cultural studies before it is crystallized with an explicit discourse of the "African diaspora" in the mid-1980s. For example, the superb 1978 study *Policing the Crisis*, written collaboratively by Stuart Hall and others, points towards a nascent diasporic register. The book is usually celebrated for its prescient claims about the emergence of "authoritarian populism" in British politics – which predict the ascent of 1980s Thatcherism in many of its most vicious details – and for its theoretical insight that race should be understood as the "modality in which class is lived."[45] But in the last chapter, "The Politics of 'Mugging'," the authors turn from their patient and polemical investigation of the social significance of the aura of "moral panic" surrounding race, crime, and youth at a particular moment of ideological crisis in British society at the end of the 1970s and offer a ground-breaking analysis of the overall situation of black "settler" communities in England in the postwar

---

[43] The most obvious sources of this critique are *The Empire Strikes Back: Race and Racism in '70s Britain* (London: Hutchinson/Centre for Contemporary Cultural Studies, University of Birmingham, 1982); chapter 2 of Paul Gilroy's *'There Ain't No Black in the Union Jack': The Cultural Politics of Race and Nation* (Chicago: U of Chicago P, 1987); and Stuart Hall's essay "Culture, Community, Nation," *Cultural Studies* 7 (October 1993): 349–63.

[44] In his discussion of Blyden in the final chapter of *The Black Atlantic*, Gilroy does cite Shepperson's essay "African Diaspora: Concept and Context," but without taking up the introduction of the term itself. Gilroy, *The Black Atlantic: Modernity and Double Consciousness* (Cambridge MA: Harvard UP, 1993): 211.

[45] Stuart Hall, Chas Critcher, Tony Jefferson, John Clarke & Brian Roberts, *Policing the Crisis: Mugging, the State, and Law and Order* (New York: Holmes & Meier, 1978): 394 (further page references are in the main text).

period. In a context of underemployment and racialization, certain cultural features of the "settler colony," particularly the range of activities that fall under the popular term 'hustling', are reconceived as "modes of survival" and even as the potential ground of black consciousness and community resistance, rather than as bearing the taint of black pathology and backward behavior (352–53). "The dynamic factor," the authors write,

> is the change in the way this objective process is collectively understood and resisted. Thus, the social content and political meaning of 'worklessness' is being thoroughly transformed from inside. Those who cannot work are discovering that they do not want to work under those conditions. [...] this black sector of the class 'in itself' has begun to undergo that process of becoming a political force 'for itself' [...] This qualitative shift has not happened spontaneously. It has a history. It began with the discovery of black identity, more specifically the *re*discovery, inside the experience of emigration, of the African roots of 'colony' life. (381)

Policing the Crisis describes this turn to "African roots" as inherently transnational. The emergence of British black consciousness is never a purely national phenomenon: it is influenced in particular by postwar African independence movements and by the black rebellions of the 1960s in the USA. Indeed, like Shepperson, *Policing the Crisis* expressly raises the question of how black internationalist and liberationist ideologies are *translated* from one 'national' context to another. They specifically invoke the "adoption and adaptation of Fanonism within the *black* movement in the USA" (especially through the Black Power movement and the Black Panthers), and they note that this "movement" of black ideological work had a formative "impact on the developing consciousness of black people everywhere, including those in Britain [...] because it suggested that a political analysis, initiated in terms of colonial society and struggle, *was* adaptable or transferable to the conditions of black minorities in developed urban capitalist conditions" (386).

Stuart Hall has extended this work, most notably in his well-known 1980 essay "Race, Articulation, and Societies Structured in Dominance," which, like the last chapter of *Policing the Crisis*, attempts to theorize the function of difference in a global capitalist mode of production. Here Hall returns more directly to Marx, to excavate a notion of 'articulation' that is crucial to any consideration of the politics of diaspora. To understand capitalist production on a "global scale," Hall writes (drawing on the work of Louis Althusser and Ernesto Laclau), Marx began to theorize an articulation [*Gliederung*] between two modes of production, the one 'capitalist' in the true sense, the other only 'formally' so: the two combined through an articulating principle, mechanism, or set of relations, because, as Marx observed, 'its beneficiaries participate in a world market in which the dominant productive sectors are already capitalist.' That is, the object of inquiry must be treated as a complex articulated structure which is, itself, 'structured in dominance.'[46]

Articulation here functions as a concept-metaphor that allows us to think of relations of "difference within unity," non-naturalizable relations of linkage between disparate societal elements. The functional "unity" of specific and strategically conjoined structures, then, is emphatically

> not that of an identity, where one structure perfectly recapitulates or repro-
> duces or even 'expresses' another; or where each is reducible to the other. [...]
> The unity formed by this combination or articulation is always, necessarily, a
> 'complex structure,' a structure in which things are related, as much through
> their differences as through their similarities. This requires that the mecha-
> nisms which connect dissimilar features must be shown – since no 'necessary
> correspondence' or expressive homology can be assumed as given. It also
> means – since the combination is a structure (an articulated combination) and
> not a random association – that there will be structured relations between its
> parts, i.e., relations of dominance and subordination.[47]

The notion of articulation is crucial not just because it combines the structural and the discursive but also because it has a flip sisuch "societies
structured in dominance" are also the ground of cultural resistance. Hall,
following Gramsci, contends that ideology must be considered the key site
of *struggle* over competing articulations.[48] In a transnational circuit, then,

---

[46] Stuart Hall, "Race, Articulation, and Societies Structured in Dominance," in *Sociological Theories: Race and Colonialism* (UNESCO, 1980), reprinted in *Black British Cultural Studies: A Reader*, ed. Houston A. Baker, Manthia Diawara & Ruth H. Lindeborg (Chicago: U of Chicago P, 1996): 33.

[47] Hall, "Race, Articulation," 38.

[48] Other work touching upon the importance of the term in Birmingham cultural studies includes Jennifer Daryl Stack, "The Theory and Method of Articulation in Cultural Studies," in *Stuart Hall: Critical Dialogues in Cultural Studies*, ed. David Morley & Kuan–Hsing Chen (New York: Routledge, 1996): 112–30; and the inter-view with Hall, "On Postmodernism and Articulation," 131–50, in the same volume. Fredric Jameson offers a more idiosyncratic genealogy of the term (in his review essay "On 'Cultural Studies'," *Social Text* 34 [1993]: 30–33), but elegantly notes the

articulation offers the means to account for the diversity of black 'takes' on 'diaspora', which Hall himself explicitly begins to theorize in the late 1980s as a frame of cultural identity determined not through "return" but through difference: "not by essence or purity, but by the recognition of a necessary heterogeneity and diversity; by a conception of 'identity' which lives with and through, not despite, difference."[49]

The turn to an explicit discourse of 'diaspora' in cultural studies comes in 1987 in Paul Gilroy's *'There Ain't No Black in the Union Jack'*, although Gilroy's fifth chapter, "Diaspora, Utopia and the Critique of Capitalism," departs in significant ways from Hall's more strictly Marxist vocabulary of articulation. It is crucial to recognize that 'diaspora' functions in this work, written at the height of Thatcherite domination in Britain, very differently from the way it does in Shepperson's African historiography. Whereas for Shepperson 'diaspora' is a way of coming to terms with transnational circuits of intellectual influence in the development of black internationalism and resistance to colonialism, in Gilroy's work it is invoked to account for the peculiar position of black communities in Britain during a period when nationalism was being perniciously expressed through recourse to populist racism. Gilroy writes:

> Black Britain defines itself crucially as part of a diaspora. Its unique cultures draw inspiration from those developed by black populations elsewhere. In particular, the culture and politics of black America and the Caribbean have become raw materials for creative processes which redefine what it means to be black, adapting it to distinctively British experience and meanings. Black culture is actively made and re-made.[50]

Reading this passage, one wonders what is lost in positioning black US and Caribbean cultures as "raw materials" for "black British" expressive culture

---

ways in which the term implies a "poetic" between the structural and the discursive (32).

[49] Stuart Hall, "Cultural Identity and Diaspora," in *Identity: Community, Culture, Difference*, ed. Jonathan Rutherford (London: Lawrence & Wishart, 1990): 235. This approach has been extended by theorists, including Kobena Mercer and Hazel Carby, who have considered the ways in which diaspora as an articulated structure of difference is constituted not only by race and colonization but also by representation, sexuality, gender, and cultural production.

[50] Gilroy, *'There Ain't No Black in the Union Jack'*, 154. On the next page he writes that "this chapter introduces the study of black cultures within the framework of a diaspora as an alternative to the different varieties of absolutism which would confine culture in 'racial', ethnic or national essences."

– such a trajectory would seem to efface the equally syncretic 'made-ness' (and the equally transnational sources) of black culture in those supposedly "raw" New World contexts. (Moreover, is "adaptation," in Gilroy's terminology, the same process as active 'making and re-making'?) But Gilroy's inattention to the 'raw material' metaphor is not surprising when we consider the degree to which his project is shaped by the needs of theorizing black British culture as beyond the orbit of the nation-state. 'Diaspora' is only one of the terms Gilroy uses in attempting to define what he sees as a "new structure of cultural exchange" that in the twentieth century has been "built up across the imperial networks which once played host to the triangular trade of sugar, slaves and capital" (157). He also writes of black culture as "exported" (157, 184), "transferred" (157), "translated" (194), as "syncretic" (155), as "articulated" in something approaching Hall's sense (160, 187), even rhapsodizing on the "living bridge" between performance and improvisation in black British popular music and "African traditions of music-making which dissolve the distinctions between art and life" (164). Such slippage among terms, I would suggest, is mainly due to Gilroy's salutary efforts to identify that "new structure of cultural exchange," especially in terms of popular musical forms like hip hop, dub, and soul – forms which at that time were just beginning to be investigated in more detail by cultural critics including Gilroy and Dick Hebdige. Still, the chapter is ultimately less interested in theorizing 'diaspora' itself than in evading the limiting confines of the British nation. Gilroy turns to "the framework of a diaspora" not in order to specify that space but "as an alternative to the different varieties of absolutism which would confine culture in 'racial,' ethnic or national essences" (155). He contends that "national units are not the most appropriate basis for studying this history for the African diaspora's consciousness of itself has been defined in and against constricting national boundaries" (158). The result of this insistence on the evasion of the national (even while, in the quote above, "diaspora" is confusingly defined at least partially *in* national boundaries) is that Gilroy's use of the term fluctuates, to use Shepperson's word. One is left uncertain about what "the African diaspora's consciousness of itself" might refer to – where that self-awareness might be located. "Diaspora" here ultimately functions more as one of the figures for Gilroy's obstinate anti-absolutism and anti-essentialism than as an elaboration of that "new structure of cultural exchange."

This discourse of diaspora undergoes a shift in Gilroy's 1993 *The Black Atlantic*, the work that is often made to stand for this entire complex and discontinuous tradition of intervention – or, indeed, that is sometimes viewed as itself the 'origin' of such a transnational focus in black cultural criticism. The issue, of course, is the stakes of 'black Atlantic' as a term that (particularly in the adoption of Gilroy's work in the US academy) often usurps the space that might otherwise be reserved for 'diaspora'. The success of *The Black Atlantic* has cleared space for a wide range of intellectual work in the academy; still, this development makes it all the more crucial to ask about the risks of 'black Atlantic' as a term of analysis that is not necessarily consonant with the sense of 'diaspora' as intervention that I have described above.[51]

It is sometimes overlooked that Gilroy himself is careful to propose 'black Atlantic' as a provisional or heuristic term of analysis, more in order to open up a certain theoretical space that would radically dislodge any inquiry grounded in singular frames – whether 'race', 'ethnicity', or 'nation' – than in order to formalize that space. For instance, in a telling passage at the beginning of the book, he writes of "the stereophonic, bilingual, or bifocal cultural forms originated by, but no longer the exclusive property of, blacks dispersed within the structures of feeling, producing, communicating, and remembering that I have heuristically called the black Atlantic world."[52] (I read the characteristic tumble and stammer of Gilroy's adjectives describing the "black Atlantic" as the performance of the category's heuristic nature.) At the same time, Gilroy often pushes toward something like a typology of cultural politics in the "black Atlantic," especially in terms of the local and global circuits of production and reception of black music. To this end, he enjoins cultural historians to think "the Atlantic as one single, complex unit of analysis in their discussion of the modern world and use it to produce an explicitly transnational and intercultural perspective" (15). Or, as he writes soon thereafter,

> The history of the black Atlantic since [Columbus], continually crisscrossed by the movements of black people – not only as commodities but engaged in

---

[51] Indeed, one measure of the book's influence is the number of formidable scholars who have felt the need to contest Gilroy's more provocative propositions in print. Some of the more significant analysts of *The Black Atlantic* are Neil Lazarus, "Is a Counterculture of Modernity a Theory of Modernity?" *Diaspora* 4.3 (Winter 1995): 323–39; Ronald A.T. Judy, "Paul Gilroy's *Black Atlantic* and the Place(s) of English in the Global," *Critical Quarterly* 39.1 (Spring 1997): 22–29; Laura Chrisman, "Journeying to death: Gilroy's *Black Atlantic*," *Race and Class* 39.2 (October–December 1997): 51–64; the reviews by Brackette F. Williams and George Lipsitz, *Social Identities* 1.1 (1995): 175–92 and 192–220, respectively; and the essays collected in *Research in African Literatures* 27.4 (Winter 1996), particularly Joan Dayan, "Paul Gilroy's Slaves, Ships, and Routes: The Middle Passage as Metaphor," 7–14.

[52] Gilroy, *The Black Atlantic*, 3 (further page references are in the main text).

various struggles towards emancipation, autonomy, and citizenship – provides a means to reexamine the problems of nationality, location, identity, and historical memory. They all emerge from it with special clarity if we contrast the national, nationalistic, and ethnically absolute paradigms of cultural criticism to be found in England and America with those hidden expressions, both residual and emergent, that attempt to be global or outer-national in nature. These traditions have supported countercultures of modernity that touched the workers' movement but are not reducible to it. (16)

Gilroy simultaneously signals the importance of the term 'diaspora' itself, as an equally "heuristic means to focus on the relationship of identity and non-identity in black political culture" (81), and the final chapter of the book is a sensitive consideration of the resonances of diaspora both in Jewish and in black New World thought, elaborated through readings of Toni Morrison's *Beloved* and the work of the nineteenth-century intellectual Edward Wilmot Blyden. This continuing discourse of diaspora begs the question of the introduction of the notion of the "black Atlantic," which would seem to impose an assumption of geographical specificity (what we might term a 'hemispheric' limit) and a 'racial' context on a field that might be much more broad and more various.

Gilroy adapts the conceptual unit of the Atlantic most notably from the remarkable recent work of Peter Linebaugh (12–13). But Linebaugh's scholarship, and his recent collaborations with Marcus Rediker, are explicitly focussed on the rise of a working class in complex cultural histories of sailors and vagabonds in ports around the Atlantic basin, who, from the beginnings of the slave trade onward, so often resisted being pressed into serving the expansion of capitalist modes of production on a transnational scale.[53] This antinomian "proletarian internationalism" is linked to the development of black consciousness and the antislavery movement, for Linebaugh, but at the same time, he does not suggest that we can extract a singular or autonomous 'black' transnational circuit of cultural and political exchanges.[54] Gilroy in any case is more concerned with individual stories

---

[53] See Peter Linebaugh, "All the Atlantic Mountains Shook," *Labour/Le Travailleur* 10 (Autumn 1982): 87–121; Peter Linebaugh & Marcus Rediker, "The Many-Headed Hydra: Sailors, Slaves, and the Atlantic Working Class in the Eighteenth Century," *Journal of Historical Sociology* 3 (September 1990): 225–52; Linebaugh & Rediker, *The Many-Headed Hydra: Sailors, Slaves, Commoners, and the Hidden History of the Revolutionary Atlantic* (Boston MA: Beacon, 2000).

[54] For cautions in this vein concerning the "black Atlantic," see Colin Palmer's review in *Perspectives* 36.6 (September 1998): 24–25; and Alasdair Pettinger, "Enduring Fortresses: A Review of *The Black Atlantic*," *Research in African Literatures*

of travel (Du Bois' sojourns in Germany, Richard Wright living in France, the Fisk Jubilee Singers touring Europe in the late nineteenth century) and abstract notions of transnational circuits of culture than with specific ground-level histories of culture in port cities and on ships around the world. The risk here is that 'black Atlantic' loses the broad range of the term 'diaspora', without even replacing it with a contextualized history of transnational cultures in the Western hemisphere. Although these questions are not worked through in *The Black Atlantic* itself, Gilroy has explained this strategy in a 1994 interview:

> First we have to fight over the concept diaspora and to move it away from the obsession with origins, purity and invariant sameness. Very often the concept of diaspora has been used to say, 'Hooray! we can rewind the tape of history, we can get back to the original moment of our dispersal!' I'm saying something quite different. That's why I didn't call the book diaspora anything. I called it *Black Atlantic* because I wanted to say, 'If this is a diaspora, then it's a very particular kind of diaspora. It's a diaspora that can't be reversed.'[55]

I share Gilroy's concern but find that, ironically, the terminology in *The Black Atlantic* operates in a nearly inverse fashion: in the work itself, it is the fascination with the Atlantic frame, and its focus on the triangular slave trade in particular, that continually draws Gilroy back into the quagmire of origins, by imposing (as he himself admits) "a tension that gets set up around modernity as a chronological and temporal category – when did modernity begin?"[56] At the same time, we have started to see a reductive kind of 'serial logic' at work in studies of black transnational circuits of

---

29.4 (Winter 1998): 142–47. Philip D. Curtin, among others, has argued that the Mediterranean must be considered coextensive with the Atlantic in terms of the development of the slave trade. He goes so far as to argue for the "Mediterranean origins of the South Atlantic system"; see Curtin, "The Slave Trade and the Atlantic Basin: Intercontinental Perspectives," in *Key Issues in the Afro-American Experience*, vol. 1, ed. Nathan Huggins, Martin Kilson & Daniel Fox (New York: Harcourt Brace Jovanovich, 1971): 75–77.

[55] Tommy Lott, "Black Cultural Politics: An Interview with Paul Gilroy," *Found Object* 4 (Fall 1994): 56–57.

[56] Lott, "Black Cultural Politics," 75. Gilroy comments, "If I were going to write the book again, I would not use modernity as the framework for it." He notes that in the book he is interested in a "particular history of modernity," the one "generated through and from the systemic and hemispheric trade in African slaves." That "hemispheric" focus – the Atlantic, in other words – implicitly leads to the work's concern with modernity and the question of origins.

culture, in which the 'black Atlantic' would have to be set beside a parallel oceanic frame of the 'black Mediterranean' or the 'black Pacific'. I remain unconvinced that such oceanic frames can be thought of as separate in any consistent manner, and I would argue that it is precisely the term 'diaspora', in the interventionist sense I have sketched here, that would allow us to think beyond such limiting geographic frames, and without reliance on an obsession with origins.[57]

Another way to make this point is to note that a discourse of diaspora functions simultaneously as abstraction and as anti-abstraction. We have generally come to have recourse unquestioningly to its level of abstraction, grounding identity claims and transnational initiatives in a history of 'scattering of Africans' that putatively offers a principle of unity – in Gilroy's phrase, "purity and invariant sameness" – to those dispersed populations. I am arguing here neither to disclaim this history of dispersal nor to substitute another abstraction (an alternative principle of continuity, like the oceanic frame offered by 'Atlantic'), but instead to emphasize the anti-abstractionist uses of 'diaspora'. As I have pointed out, a return to the intellectual history of the term itself is necessary because it reminds us that 'diaspora' is introduced in large part to account for difference among African-derived populations, in a way that a term like 'pan-Africanism' could not. Moreover, 'diaspora' points to difference not only internally (the ways transnational black groupings are fractured by nation, class, gender, sexuality, and language) but also externally: in appropriating a term so closely associated with Jewish thought, we are forced to think not in terms of some closed or autonomous system of African dispersal but explicitly in terms of a complex past of forced migrations and racialization – what Earl Lewis has called a history of "overlapping diasporas."[58] (For a specific example, in a history of black internationalism in France between the World Wars, 'diaspora' points not just to the encounter in Marseilles between the Senegalese radical Lamine Senghor and the Jamaican novelist Claude McKay, but also to the

---

[57] Indeed, there is a prior model for precisely this kind of work through the 'diasporic' lens I have been espousing: see Joseph Harris's "A Comparative Approach to the Study of the African Diaspora," in Harris, *Global Dimensions of the African Diaspora*, 112–24, which attempts to consider both the African-American presence in Sierra Leone and Liberia, and the histories of African communities in India, Turkey, the Middle East, and Asia. The main source for the latter part of the African diaspora is, of course, Harris' unprecedented *The African Presence in Asia: Consequences of the East African Slave Trade* (Evanston IL: Northwestern UP, 1971).

[58] Earl Lewis, "To Turn as on a Pivot: Writing African Americans into a History of Overlapping Diasporas," *American Historical Review* 100 (June 1995): 765–87.

collaboration in the French Communist Party between Senghor and the Vietnamese radical Nguyen Ai Quoc, later better known as Ho Chi Minh.) The use of the term 'diaspora', I am suggesting, is not that it offers the comfort of abstraction, an easy recourse to origins, but that it forces us to consider discourses of cultural and political linkage only through and across difference.

Reading *Décalage*

I return in closing to Stuart Hall's notion of diaspora as 'articulated', as a structured combination of elements "related as much through their differences as through their similarities." If a discourse of diaspora articulates difference, then one must consider the status of that difference – not just linguistic difference but, more broadly, the trace or the residue, perhaps, of what resists translation or what sometimes cannot help refusing translation across the boundaries of language, class, gender, sexuality, religion, the nation-state. Whenever the African diaspora is articulated (just as when black transnational projects are deferred, aborted, or declined) these social forces leave subtle but indelible effects. Such an unevenness or differentiation marks a constitutive *décalage* in the very weave of the culture, one that cannot be either dismissed or pulled out. Léopold Senghor, in an important short essay called "Négro-Américains et Négro-Africains," writes suggestively about the differences and influences between US blacks and African blacks as spun out across such a gap:

> Le différend entre Négro-Américains et Négro-Africains est plus léger malgré les apparences. Il s'agit, en réalité, d'un simple décalage – dans le temps et dans l'espace. [Despite appearances, the difference between Negro-Americans and Negro-Africans is more slight. In reality it involves a simple *décalage* – in time and in space.][59]

Décalage is one of the many French words that resists translation into English; to signal that resistance and, moreover, to endorse the way that this term marks a resistance to crossing over, I will keep the term in French here.[60] It can be translated as 'gap', 'discrepancy', 'time-lag', or 'interval';

---

[59] Senghor, "Problématique de la Négritude" (1971), in *Liberté III: Négritude et civilisation de l'universel* (Paris: Seuil, 1977): 274. My translation.

[60] The historian Ranajit Guha is one of the few scholars writing in English who regularly makes recourse to the term *décalage*, using it to indicate a structural

it is also the term that French speakers sometimes use to translate 'jet lag'. In other words, a *décalage* is a difference or gap *either* in time (advancing or delaying a schedule) *or* in space (shifting or displacing an object). I would suggest, reading somewhat against the grain of Senghor's text, that there is a possibility here in the phrase "in time *and* space" of a 'light' (*léger*) and subtly innovative model with which to read the structure of such unevenness in the African diaspora.

The verb *caler* means 'to prop up or wedge something' (as when one leg on a table is uneven). So *décalage* in its etymological sense refers to the removal of such an added prop or wedge. *Décalage* indicates the re-estab-lishment of a prior unevenness or diversity; it alludes to the taking away of something that was added in the first place, something artificial, a stone or piece of wood that served to fill some gap or to rectify some imbalance. This black diasporic *décalage* among African Americans and Africans, then, is not simply geographical distance, nor is it simply difference in evolution or consciousness; instead, it is a different kind of interface that might not be susceptible to expression in the oppositional terminology of the 'vanguard' and the 'backward'. In other words, *décalage* is the kernel of precisely that which cannot be transferred or exchanged, the received biases that refuse to pass over when one crosses the water. It is a changing core of difference, it is the work of "differences within unity,"[61] an unidentifiable point that is incessantly touched and fingered and pressed.

Is it possible to rethink the workings of 'race' in black cultural politics through a model of *décalage*? Any articulation of diaspora in such a model would be inherently *décalé* or disjointed by a host of factors. Like a table with legs of different lengths, or a tilted bookcase, diaspora can be discur-sively propped up (*calé*) into an artificially 'even' or 'balanced' state of 'racial' belonging. But such props, of rhetoric, strategy, or organization, are always articulations of unity or globalism, ones that can be 'mobilized' for a variety of purposes but can never be definitive: they are always prosthetic. In this sense, *décalage* is proper to the structure of a diasporic 'racial' formation, and its return in the form of 'disarticulation' – the points of mis-understanding, bad faith, unhappy translation – must be considered a neces-

---

overlap or discrepancy, a period of "social transformation" when one class, state bureaucracy, or social formation "challenges the authority of another that is older and moribund but still dominant"; Guha, *Dominance without Hegemony: History and Power in Colonial India* (Cambridge MA: Harvard UP, 1997): 13, 157. See also Guha, *Elementary Aspects of Peasant Insurgency in Colonial India* (Durham NC: Duke UP, 1999): 173, 330.

[61] Senghor, "Problématique de la Négritude," 278.

sary haunting. This reads against the grain of Senghor, if one can consider his Negritude one influential variety of this diasporic propping-up. Instead of reading for the *efficacy* of the prosthesis, this orientation would look for the *effects* of such an operation, for the traces of such haunting, reading them as constitutive of the structure of any articulation of diaspora.[62]

Recall that Hall points out that the word 'articulation' has two meanings: "both 'joining up' (as in the limbs of the body, or an anatomical structure) and 'giving expression to'."[63] He suggests that the term is most useful in the study of the workings of race in social formations when it is pushed away from the latter implication, of an "expressive link" (which would imply a predetermined hierarchy, a situation where one factor makes another 'speak'), and toward its etymology as a metaphor of the body. Then the relationship between factors is not predetermined; it offers a more ambivalent, more elusive model. What does it mean to say, for example, that one 'articulates a joint'? The connection speaks. Such 'speaking' is functional, of course: the arm bends at the elbow to reach down to the table, the leg swivels at the hip to take the next step. But the joint is a curious place, as it is both the point of separation (the forearm from the upper arm, for example) and the point of linkage. Rather than a model of ultimate debilitation or of predetermined retardation, then, *décalage*, in providing a model for what escapes or resists translation through the African diaspora, alludes to this strange two-ness of the joint. It directs our attention to what I described earlier as the "antithetical structure" of the term 'diaspora', its risky intervention. My contention, finally, is that articulations of diaspora demand to be approached this way, through their *décalage*. For, paradoxically, it is exactly such a haunting gap or discrepancy that allows the African diaspora to 'step' and 'move' in various articulations. Articulation is always a strange and ambivalent gesture, because, finally, in the body it is *only* difference – the separation between bones or members – that allows movement.[64]

---

[62] My emphasis on diaspora as a discursive tradition echoes David Scott's suggestion that the African diaspora be read less as a culturally unified continuity than as "embodied disputes" among black populations throughout the globe about the very meaning of 'Africa', slavery, or black identity. Scott, *Refashioning Futures: Criticism After Postcolonialism* (Princeton NJ: Princeton UP, 1999): 123–24.

[63] Hall, "Race, Articulation, and Societies Structured in Dominance," 41.

[64] I would like to thank the graduate students in my seminar "Black Cultural Studies: Issues and Approaches" at Rutgers University in the fall of 1998, where much of the framework of this piece was conceived. Shorter versions of this essay were presented at the City University of New York Americanist Group colloquium

WORKS CITED

Adams, Russell L. "Intellectual Questions and Imperatives in the Development of Afro-American Studies," *Journal of Negro Education* 53.3 (Summer 1984): 201–25.

American Society of African Culture. *Pan-Africanism Reconsidered* (Berkeley: U of California P, 1962).

Butler, Kim. "Defining Diaspora, Refining a Discourse," "Defining Diaspora, Refining a Discourse," *Diaspora: A Journal of Transnational Studies* 10.2 (Fall 2002): 189–219.

Campbell, Horace, ed. *Pan-Africanism: Struggle against Neo-Colonialism and Imperialism* (Toronto: Afro-Carib Publications, 1975).

Chrisman, Laura. "Journeying to Death: Gilroy's *Black Atlantic*," *Race and Class* 39.2 (October–December 1997): 51–64.

Chrisman, Robert. "History of Black Involvement in International Politics," in *The Non-Aligned Movement in World Politics*, ed. A.W. Singham (Westport CT: Lawrence Hill, 1977): 197–202.

Clifford, James. "Diasporas," in *Routes: Travel and Translation in the Late Twentieth Century* (Cambridge MA: Harvard UP, 1997): 244–78.

Cohen, Robin. *Global Diasporas: An Introduction* (Seattle: U of Washington P, 1997).

Curtin, Philip D. "The Slave Trade and the Atlantic Basin: Intercontinental Perspectives," in *Key Issues in the Afro-American Experience*, vol. 1, ed. Nathan Huggins, Martin Kilson & Daniel Fox (New York: Harcourt Brace Jovanovich, 1971): 75–77.

Davis, John A. "Black Americans and United States Policy Toward Black Africa," *Journal of International Affairs* 23.2 (1969): 236–49.

Dayan, Joan. "Paul Gilroy's Slaves, Ships, and Routes: The Middle Passage as Metaphor," *Research in African Literatures* 27.4 (Winter 1996): 7–14.

Diawara, Manthia. "Black Studies/Cultural Studies," in *Borders, Boundaries and Frames: Cultural Criticism and Cultural Studies*, ed. Mae G. Henderson (London & New York: Routledge, 1995): 202–12.

Diop, Alioune. "Niam N'Goura, or *Présence Africaine*'s *raison d'être*," tr. Richard Wright & Thomas Diop, *Présence Africaine* 1 (October–November 1947): 190–91. The French original appears in the same issue, 7–14.

Drake, St. Clair. "The Black Diaspora in Pan-African Perspective," *Black Scholar* 7.1 (September 1975): 2–13.

and at the American Studies Association conference in Seattle in October 1998, and I am grateful to my co-panelists from both occasions: Alys Weinbaum, David Kazanjian, Miranda Joseph, Melissa Wright, and Michael Denning. In addition, Phillip Brian Harper, Daphne Lamothe, Randy Martin, Chandan Reddy, and Bruce Robbins made invaluable suggestions for revision.

——. "Black Studies and Global Perspectives: An Essay," *Journal of Negro Education* 53.3 (Summer 1984): 226–42.

——. "Diaspora Studies and Pan-Africanism," in *Global Dimensions of the African Diaspora*, ed. Joseph Harris (Washington DC: Howard UP, 1982): 359–66.

——. "Hide My Face? On Pan-Africanism and Negritude," in *Soon, One Morning: New Writing by American Negroes, 1940–1962*, ed. Herbert Hill (New York: Alfred A. Knopf, 1966): 77–105.

——. "Negro Americans and the Africa Interest," in *The American Negro Reference Book*, ed. John P. Davis (Englewood Cliffs NJ: Prentice–Hall, 1966): 662–705.

Du Bois, W.E.B. "Pan-Africa and the New Racial Philosophy," *Crisis* 40 (November 1933): 247.

——. *The World and Africa: An Inquiry into the Part Which Africa Has Played in World History* (1946; expanded ed., New York: International Publishers, 1965).

Edmondson, Locksley. "Black America as a Mobilizing Diaspora: Some International Implications," in *Modern Diasporas in International Politics*, ed. Gabriel Sheffer (London: Croom Helm, 1986): 164–211.

Edwards, Brent Hayes. *The Practice of Diaspora: Literature, Translation, and the Rise of Black Internationalism* (Cambridge MA: Harvard UP, 2003).

——. "Three Ways to Translate the Harlem Renaissance," in *"Temples for Tomorrow": Looking Back at the Harlem Renaissance*, ed. Geneviève Fabre & Michel Feith (Bloomington: Indiana UP, 2001): 359–96.

Eschen, Penny von. *Race against Empire: Black Americans and Anticolonialism, 1937–1957* (Ithaca NY: Cornell UP, 1997).

Essien–Udom, E.U. "Black Identity in the International Context," in *Key Issues in the Afro-American Experience*, vol. 2: *Since 1865*, ed. Nathan Huggins, Martin Kilson & Daniel Fox (New York: Harcourt Brace Jovanovich, 1971): 233–58.

——. "The Relationship of Afro-Americans to African Nationalism," *Freedomways* 2 (Fall 1962): 391–407.

Geiss, Imanuel. *The Pan-African Movement: A History of Pan-Africanism in America, Europe and Africa*, tr. Ann Keep (New York: Africana & London: Methuen, 1974).

Gilroy, Paul. *The Black Atlantic: Modernity and Double Consciousness* (Cambridge MA: Harvard UP, 1993).

——. *'There Ain't No Black in the Union Jack': The Cultural Politics of Race and Nation* (Chicago: U of Chicago P, 1987).

Glissant, Edouard. *Le Discours antillais* (Paris: Seuil, 1981). *Caribbean Discourse*, sel., tr. & intro. J. Michael Dash (Charlottesville: CARAF/UP of Virginia, 1989).

Guha, Ranajit. *Dominance without Hegemony: History and Power in Colonial India* (Cambridge MA: Harvard UP, 1997).

——. *Elementary Aspects of Peasant Insurgency in Colonial India* (Durham NC: Duke UP, 1999).

Hall, Stuart. "Cultural Identity and Diaspora," in *Identity: Community, Culture, Difference*, ed. Jonathan Rutherford (London: Lawrence & Wishart, 1990): 222–37.

——. "Culture, Community, Nation," *Cultural Studies* 7 (October 1993): 349–63.

——. "On Postmodernism and Articulation," interview, in *Stuart Hall: Critical Dialogues in Cultural Studies*, ed. David Morley & Kuan–Hsing Chen (London & New York: Routledge, 1996): 131–50.

——. "Race, Articulation, and Societies Structured in Dominance," in *Sociological Theories: Race and Colonialism* (UNESCO, 1980), repr. in *Black British Cultural Studies: A Reader*, ed. Houston A. Baker, Manthia Diawara & Ruth H. Lindeborg (Chicago: U of Chicago P, 1996): 16–60.

——, Chas Critcher, Tony Jefferson, John Clarke & Brian Roberts. *Policing the Crisis: Mugging, the State, and Law and Order* (New York: Holmes & Meier, 1978).

Hamilton, Ruth Simms. "Conceptualizing the African Diaspora," in *The African Presence in the Americas*, ed. Carlos Moore et al. (Trenton NJ: Africa World Press, 1995): 393–410.

Harris, Joseph E. *The African Presence in Asia: Consequences of the East African Slave Trade* (Evanston IL: Northwestern UP, 1971).

——. "The Dynamics of the Global African Diaspora," *The African Diaspora*, ed. Alusine Jalloh (College Station: U of Texas at Arlington, 1996): 7–21.

——. "The International Congress on African History, 1965," *Africa Forum* 1.3 (Winter 1966): 80–84.

——. "Introduction to the African Diaspora," in *Emerging Themes of African History*, ed. T.O. Ranger (Nairobi: East African Publishing House, 1968): 146–51.

——, with Slimane Zeghidour. "Africa and its Diaspora Since 1935," in *General History of Africa*, vol. 8: *Africa Since 1935*, ed. Ali A. Mazrui (Paris: UNESCO; Berkeley: U of California P & Oxford: Heinemann, 1993): 705–23.

Henderson, Mae G. "'Where, By the Way, is This Train Going?' A Case for Black (Cultural) Studies," *Callaloo* 19.1 (Winter 1996): 60–67.

Hill, Adelaide Cromwell, & Martin Kilson, ed. *Apropos of Africa: Sentiments of Negro American Leaders on Africa from the 1800s to the 1950s* (London: Frank Cass, 1969).

Howlett, Jacques. "*Présence Africaine*, 1947–1958," tr. Mercer Cook, *Journal of Negro History* 43 (April 1958): 140–50.

Isaacs, Harold R. "The American Negro and Africa: Some Notes," *Phylon* 20 (Fall 1959): 219–33.

James, Winston. "The *Black Scholar* Interviews C.L.R. James," *Black Scholar* 2.1 (September 1970): 35–43.

——. *Holding Aloft the Banner of Ethiopia: Caribbean Radicalism in Early Twentieth-Century America* (London: Verso, 1998).

Jameson, Fredric. "On 'Cultural Studies'," *Social Text* 34 (1993): 30–33.

Judy, Ronald A.T. "Paul Gilroy's *Black Atlantic* and the Place(s) of English in the Global," *Critical Quarterly* 39.1 (Spring 1997): 22–29.

Karenga, Maulana. *Introduction to Black Studies* (Los Angeles: U of Sankore P, 1993).

Langley, J. Ayodele. "The Movement and Thought of Francophone Pan-Negroism: 1924–1936," *Journal of Modern African Studies* (1969), repr. (expanded) in Langley, *Pan-Africanism and Nationalism in West Africa, 1900–1945: A Study in Ideology and Social Classes* (Oxford: Clarendon, 1973): 86–325.

——. "New-World Origins of Pan-Negro Sentiment," in Langley, *Pan-Africanism and Nationalism in West Africa, 1900–1945*, 17–40.

Lazarus, Neil. "Is a Counterculture of Modernity a Theory of Modernity?" *Diaspora* 4.3 (Winter 1995): 323–39.

Lewis, Earl. "To Turn as on a Pivot: Writing African Americans into a History of Overlapping Diasporas," *American Historical Review* 100 (June 1995): 765–87.

Linebaugh, Peter. "All the Atlantic Mountains Shook," *Labour/Le Travailleur* 10 (Autumn 1982): 87–121.

——, & Marcus Rediker. "The Many-Headed Hydra: Sailors, Slaves, and the Atlantic Working Class in the Eighteenth Century," *Journal of Historical Sociology* 3 (September 1990): 225–52.

——, & Marcus Rediker. *The Many-Headed Hydra: Sailors, Slaves, Commoners, and the Hidden History of the Revolutionary Atlantic* (Boston MA: Beacon, 2000).

Lipsitz, George. Review of Paul Gilroy's *Black Atlantic*, *Social Identities* 1.1 (1995): 192–220.

Lott, Tommy. "Black Cultural Politics: An Interview with Paul Gilroy," *Found Object* 4 (Fall 1994): 56–57.

Lubiano, Wahneema. "Mapping the Interstices Between Afro-American Cultural Discourse and Cultural Studies; A Prolegomenon," *Callaloo* 19.1 (Winter 1996): 68–77.

McKeon, Michael. Review of *Keywords*, *Studies in Romanticism* 16 (Winter 1977): 133.

Moore, Richard B. "Africa Conscious Harlem," *Freedomways* 3 (Summer 1963): 315–34.

Mouralis, Bernard. "*Présence Africaine*: The Geography of an 'Ideology'," in *The Surreptitious Speech: "Présence Africaine" and the Politics of Otherness, 1947–1987*, ed. Valentine Y. Mudimbe (Chicago: U of Chicago P, 1992): 3–13.

Mudimbe Valentine Y., & Sabine Engel, ed. *Diaspora and Immigration*, a special issue of the *South Atlantic Quarterly* 98 (Winter–Spring 1999).

Nardal, Paulette, & Léo Sajous. "Our Aim" ['Ce que nous voulons faire'], tr. Nardal & Clara W. Shepard, *Revue du Monde Noir/Review of the Black World* 1 (1931).

Palmer, Colin. Review of Paul Gilroy's *Black Atlantic*, *Perspectives* 36.6 (September 1998): 24–25.

Pettinger, Alasdair. "Enduring Fortresses: A Review of *The Black Atlantic*," *Research in African Literatures* 29.4 (Winter 1998): 142–47.

Safran, William. "Diaspora in Modern Societies: Myths of Homeland and Return," *Diaspora: A Journal of Transnational Studies* 1.1 (Spring 1991): 83–99.

Scott, David. *Refashioning Futures: Criticism After Postcolonialism* (Princeton NJ: Princeton UP, 1999)

——. "That Event, This Memory: Notes on the Anthropology of African Diasporas in the New World," *Diaspora: A Journal of Transnational Studies* 1.3 (Winter 1991): 261–84.

Senghor, Léopold Sédar. "Problématique de la Négritude" (1971), in *Liberté III: Négritude et civilisation de l'universel* (Paris: Seuil, 1977): 268–89.

Shain, Yossi. "Ethnic Diasporas and US Foreign Policy," *Political Science Quarterly* 109.5 (Winter 1994–95): 811–41.

Shepperson, George. "The African Abroad, or the African Diaspora," *Africa Forum: A Quarterly Journal of African Affairs* 1.2 (Summer 1966): 76–93. Repr. in *Emerging Themes of African History*, ed. T.O. Ranger (Nairobi: East African Publishing House, 1968): 152–76.

——. "African Diaspora: Concept and Context," in Harris, *Global Dimensions of the African Diaspora*, 46–53.

——. "The Afro-American Contribution to African Studies," *Journal of American Studies* 8.3 (December 1974): 281–301.

——. "Ethiopianism and African Nationalism," *Phylon* 14.1 (1953): 9–18.

——. "Introduction" to *The African Diaspora: Interpretive Essays*, ed. Martin L. Kilson & Robert I. Rotberg (Cambridge MA: Harvard UP, 1976): 1–17.

——. "Notes on Negro American Influences on the Emergence of African Nationalism," *Journal of African History* 1.2 (1960): 299–312.

——. "Pan-Africanism and 'pan-Africanism': Some Historical Notes," *Phylon* 23.4 (Winter 1962): 346–58.

Stack, Jennifer Daryl. "The Theory and Method of Articulation in Cultural Studies," in *Stuart Hall: Critical Dialogues in Cultural Studies*, ed. David Morley & Kuan–Hsing Chen (London & New York: Routledge, 1996): 112–30.

Stuckey, Sterling. "Black Americans and African Consciousness: Du Bois, Woodson, and the Spell of Africa," in *Going through the Storm: The Influence of African American Art in History* (New York: Oxford UP, 1994): 120–37.

The Empire Strikes Back: Race and Racism in '70s Britain (London: Hutchinson/ Centre for Contemporary Cultural Studies, U of Birmingham, 1982).

Tölölyan, Khachig. "Rethinking Diaspora(s): Stateless Power in the Transnational Moment," *Diaspora: A Journal of Transnational Studies* 5.1 (Spring 1996): 3–36.

Williams, Brackette F. Review of Paul Gilroy's *Black Atlantic*, *Social Identities* 1.1 (1995): 175–92.

Wynter, Sylvia. "Columbus, the Ocean Blue, and Fables That Stir the Mind: To Reinvent the Study of Letters," in *Poetics of the Americas: Race, Founding, and Textuality*, ed. Bainard Cowan & Jefferson Humphries (Baton Rouge: Louisiana State UP, 1997).

Against Race: Yes, But At What Cost?

DAVID PALUMBO–LIU

P AUL GILROY'S LATEST BOOK, *Against Race* (2000), is the
third and final component of a series of monographs that began
with *'There Ain't No Black in the Union Jack'* (1987) and continued
with *The Black Atlantic* (1993). Through these books, and a number of
influential articles and essays, Paul Gilroy has proved to be one of our most
exciting and provocative thinkers on race, ethnicity, and cultural studies. In
particular, he has reinvented the notion of 'diaspora' and linked it to a
notion of culture that is both proof against and remedy for what he considers to be one of the most debilitating and destructive aspects of modern
cultural and political thinking – that of 'ethnic absolutism'. In this mode of
thinking, people are indelibly marked by a single and unchanging identity;
culture is the mere reiteration of the same and unchanging. In this final part
of the triology, Gilroy ties together and extends the key themes of his prior
work; *Against Race* may be seen as the logical culmination of a longstand-
ing trajectory of interests.

Here I will first focus on a few of these themes, then show how they both
form a constellation of issues which have an immediate impact on the theoretical formulation of 'race' and at the same time compel us to confront a
series of profound questions that have deep implications not only for African studies, but also for diasporic studies and our study of race and culture
in general. To get a sense of why and how these questions are of central
importance to this work, I first sketch out the main themes of his previous
work and show how he has elaborated them in *Against Race*. Next, I outline
the main components of his thesis, again showing its relation to his *corpus*.
Given the primacy Gilroy awards his notion of 'diaspora' and diasporic cultures, the two basic questions for this essay will be, first, what 'contains'

'diaspora' as a concept and a reality (how to define 'diaspora' if not by taking recourse to the very terms that Gilroy wishes to problematize: ie, geography and race)? Can we conceive of diaspora without race? Second, how can we think *historically* in the terms Gilroy asks us to in order to go "against race"?

We might isolate five key components of Gilroy's triology: first, he defined diaspora as a historical concept – taking his lead from the historical event of the Jewish exile, the first recognized manifestation of what will become called "diaspora," he previously argued that the transatlantic movements of African peoples under slavery constituted another historical instance of diaspora. Earlier expressions of this argument focussed on the phenomenon of forced dispersal and the designation of the transatlantic ship as a particular "chronotope" which temporally and spatially constituted the common reality and symbol of the "Black Atlantic." In this later work, Gilroy elaborates the connection between Jewish and African diasporas by focussing on another common bond – the shared legacy of racism aimed against them. But Gilroy does not simply mention racism as an act perpetrated against Jews and blacks, but attaches racism to fascism and argues that both blacks and Jews also have historically engaged in fascist practices themselves. This is most evident in manifestations of intense nationalistic fervor, whether it be Zionistic or in terms of certain formations of black liberation. Therefore, the very mechanisms that set diaspora in motion – racial thinking which reduces humans to ethnic or racial objects – are not the sole deficit of non-Jews and non-blacks, but the shared deficit of all human beings who follow racial thinking. And such racial thinking is most evident in the discourses that assume an absolute ethnic, racial, or national identity. This critique is the logical culmination of Gilroy's critique of "ethnic absolutism," found throughout his work.

Second, Gilroy considered diaspora as a structure of feeling, an intuitive relation to the homeland. The fact of movement out of Africa is a remembered experience; the symbol of the slave ship persists as a touchstone in which is figured a common historical experience referencing a common origin. What is crucial here is not the detailed remembrance of an originary event so much as it is a registering of the effects of displacement not only in sentimental terms, but also in recognizing its material historical effects – how has the fact of displacement and enslavement taken various forms historically, how has racism in particular been manifested in this act and re-articulated historically? In *Against Race*, "Home," that form of memory of origin, is reconfigured such that it is neither nativist nor fascistic. The very structure of feeling that undergirds diaspora is to be opened up to newer forms of identification that necessarily avoid the reductiveness of racial thinking and fascist violence, most evident in extreme nationalistic thinking that insists on situating certain peoples in certain places.

Third, diaspora previously had been considered as cultural practice – as a practiced reiteration/reformulation of 'culture', with culture understood as the expression of the emotional and material forms of life just described. Emphasis is placed on its hybrid, dynamic, unsettled and open-ended aspects, as opposed to a static, place- and race-bound narrative of 'tradition'. In *Against Race,* this connects critically with the specific cultural forms which embody and articulate diaspora. Here Gilroy's own preference for music becomes renewed and strengthened. We remember that, in his earlier works, Gilroy counterposed music to textuality. The idea of textuality was seen as a key element in modernity, with its obsession with referentiality, representation, and objectification. Such issues of referentiality and representation had everything to do with not only the production of knowledge but also its commodification. Against the linearity and referentiality of texts, Gilroys posed black music culture as intuitive, multidirectional, resistant to stratification and objectification, and, importantly, as a collective and communal enterprise. Instead of a private, individualistic mode of consumption, for Gilroy music calls for and enables a particularly contestational notion of 'consumption'. Music was thus for Gilroy not only the preferred form of cultural expression, but the only possible form adequate to the task of conveying the multifaceted, constantly diversifying nature of diasporic cultures.

In *Against Race*, this valuation of music as diasporic cultural form *par excellence* is located differently in two respects. First, it is not now set against textuality, but is opposed urgently to visual media. Second, music as the preferred form of diasporic consciousness is now regarded, regretfully, as a historically past (or at least absent) phenomenon. The two work together. Gilroy argues that blackness today is predominantly conveyed by visual media that fixate on, project, and reproduce in myriad forms a reified image of blackness that is at once masculinist, heterosexual, intensely individualistic and privatized (in a private space that is seen as repressive and sexist), and, last but not least, absolutely commercialized. Crucially, these visual 'bites' are in no way dialogic, shared, communal, collective, but instead, according to Gilroy, celebrate the individual black figure in a strictly delimited (ie, absolutist) manner.

If this were not depressing enough, Gilroy sees this movement in music as well – the same privatized, masculinist, misogynistic, self-centered aspect of visual representations of blackness are dominant in today's music. Hence he laments the near-disappearance of the transglobal, humanistic, cosmic progressive politics of Bob Marley and notes its displacement by the music of self-gratification. Music's transatlantic, liberatory capacity has been set aside, its anti-capitalist, anti-textual, anti-modernist potential negated. Instead, we find a potential for racism and fascism, the twin evils that Gilroy has set out to address and neutralize in this book.

Fourth, diaspora is seen as produced in and by *modern* culture – that is, its non-arbitrary historical nature. The logic that underlay and drove slavery is part and parcel of a tradition of Enlightenment philosophy whose primary component is a dialectic that at once argued for the resolution of antimonies and estrangement, yet maintained the fundamental antinomy of race. It was the preservation of this antimony that allowed for 'development', for Western 'progress' on the backs of racialized peoples.

Whereas before Gilroy's diasporic critique is held up as anti-modern in the sense that it resists national form, embracing instead a postmodern notion of diaspora that refuses to be confined to one national model of authenticity and belonging over another, and sees instead constantly shifting hybrid formations, in this latest work such an anti-modern formation of diaspora is jeapordized by exactly the disappearance of collective liberatory models and their replacement by absolutist values that shift away from diaspora as a cultural value and form and toward a static, race-centered culture that is allied with nationalistic, and fascistic, thinking.

Finally, we have the notion of diasporic culture as *postmodern* culture – again, we find the hybrid articulation of diaspora. Resisting the categories offered to this experience by modernity, Gilroy has characterized diasporic culture as heterogeneous and mixed, hybrid, in accordance with the historical process that has both a common origin and wildly discrepant points of recombination. Understanding diasporic culture as hybrid has not only the positive value of tracing within it the various elemental strands of diverse national and local cultures which make up diasporic culture, but also the negative value of guarding against a modernist reduction of diasporic culture as ultimately belonging to one or another national culture. This critique of the nation-state as the proper 'container' for diasporic culture harks back, of course, to the postmodern critique of modern forms of social and philosophical organization.

As Gilroy previously balanced his enthusiasm for an anti-modern model with a caution against an uncritical and ahistorical postmodernism that would subscribe to the notion of an unanchored, free-floating model of diaspora, so in this book he sees the current formation of blackness stripped of any real historical sense. Instead, he laments its retreat into absolutist myths and nationalistic nostalgia. The primary goal of the current work is to dissolve the absolutism of 'race': Gilroy proposes that we emulate the advances of nanoscience, which have shown a universal human being in genetic codes which do not change from race to race. This *in*visible truth of human commonality is set against the ascent of the visual iconicity of 'blackness', which silently references a set of behaviors (deemed by Gilroy to be eminently heterosexual, misogynistic, hedonistic) that imprisons black culture and isolates it. But he also urges us to develop a very different sense of historical time. In the next two sections, I first detail Gilroy's particular lines of reasoning in these three books, then conclude by addressing my questions regarding race, history, and diaspora.

I

Gilroy's argument is concise and clear: he demands "liberation not from white supremacy alone [...] but from all racializing and raciological thought, from racialized seeing, racialized thinking, and racialized thinking about thinking."[1] But despite the originality and force of the particular components of his argument, Gilroy rightly suspects that, when all is said and done, his basic argument – that the human race needs to think beyond 'race' as an absolute marker of identity – will be seen as nothing new: "There is a danger that this argument will be read as nothing more than a rather old-fashioned plea for disabusing ourselves of the destructive delusions of racism" (30). To pre-empt this accusation, he articulates his points of distinction:

> All earlier arguments conform to the same basic architecture. They posit the particular, singular, and specific against the general, universal, and transcendent that they value more highly. In contrast, the approach I favor attempts to break up these unhappy couples. It has less to say about the unanswerable force of claims to singularity and particularity that have fuelled ethnic absolutism. Instead, it directs attention toward the other side of these simultaneous equations. We should, it suggests, become concerned once again with the notion of the human into which reluctant specificity has been repeatedly invited to dissolve itself. (30)

As if to make good on this claim at the onset, and as a gesture that confirms Gilroy's attention to visual signifiers, this third book conspicuously deletes

---

[1] Gilroy, *Against Race: Imagining Political Culture Beyond the Color Line* (Cambridge MA: Harvard UP, 2000): 40 (further consecutive page references are in the main text).

the term 'black' from its title.[2] And yet, at the end of this essay, I will return to ask whether Gilroy has actually fulfilled this promise, or whether this assertion does not, rather, outline the difficulty of negotiating that point of tension. What is his notion of the human, where is it to be found, or at least searched for, and what relation does it bear to the 'human' as we have previously understood it? This question is especially important because Gilroy declares that his solution is "the only ethical response" (41). And that presents us with a quandary – for to object to any aspect of the entirety of his anti-racist program (and it does come as a piece) is to risk being accused of being unethical. Gilroy has raised the stakes considerably; we must, then, carefully discern what, exactly, the costs might be of accepting this moral imperative, especially with regard to the social institutions of justice.

It is precisely an unmistakable sense of urgency and of the moment that informs Gilroy's book. What he sees as the general condition of thinking on race, and in particular as manifested in black culture, is the resurgence of fascistic thinking:

> The persistence of fascism and the widespread mimicry of its styles constitute only the most alarming sign that modernity's best culture is assailed from all sides by political movements and technological forces that are working toward the erasure of ethical considerations and the deadening of aesthetic sensibilities. (93)

This finds particular expression in the notion of identity:

> The reduction of identity to the uncomplicated, militarized, fraternal versions of pure sameness pioneered by fascism and Nazism in the 1930s is now routine, particularly where the forces of nationalism, 'tribalism', and ethnic division are at work. (103)

In this light, identity ceases to be something dynamic, changing, and, most important, self-fashioned. Instead, "it becomes [...] a thing to be possessed and displayed. It is a silent sign that closes down the possibility of communication across the gulf between one heavily defended island of particularity and its equally well fortified neighbors, between one national encampment and others" (103).

Throughout Gilroy's work, there has always been the possibility (and reality) of such thinking. He has always been attentive to the fact that racism is founded upon racial thinking, and that racial thinking can not only

---

[2] The title of the book for publication outside the USA is, *Between Camps*. We will address this issue of "camps" later in the essay.

aid and abet racists, but also, ironically, anti-racist forces. For if one side argues the supremacy of one race over the other, the other side can, in defending the degraded *group*, make the mistake of accepting offhand the very categorization of peoples that particularized them as such: "By defining 'race' and ethnicity as cultural absolutes, blacks themselves and parts of the anti-racist movement risk endorsing the explanatory frameworks and political definitions of the new right."[3] In his latest book, Gilroy advocates the wholesale rejection of the very discourse of race as irremediably contaminated: "Revitalizing ethical sensibilities [...] requires moving away from antiracism's tarnished vocabulary while retaining many of the hopes to which it was tied."[4] He urges us to think against race, but in terms freed from the absolutist assumptions of the past. The present historical moment offers him a token: if we have historically been rooted in epidermal, phenotypical determinations of racial identity, if the visible sign of difference has dominated our view of human beings and blinded us to any common ground, then nanoscience and the new vision it offers provides us with a sense of commonality: "[The] biotechnological revolution demands a change in our understanding of 'race,' species, embodiment, and human specificity" (20). If we have unlocked the human genome, isn't it worth considering how this foundation of human life trumps the epidermis? If genes can be switched, organs manufactured that "fit all," isn't this a better and more practical way of viewing human beings? His critique of visual culture thus has two related targets: the ubiquitous, commodifed image of "blackness," and the fixation on the body's surface as a sign of its eternal psychic, mental, and moral content.

Counterposed to any liberatory movement away from the visual and racial determinism, we have what he calls a "camp" mentality. Whereas before the chronotope that informed his theory of diaspora was the transatlantic sailing vessel,[5] in *Against Race* he calls attention to "camps," emphasizing the "territorial, hierarchical, and militaristic qualities"[6] of the fascistic thinking that has come to deeply inform racial thinking. Both have been fostered by the media, which have allowed (and even promoted) these forms of thinking: "The ubiquity of the camp in our mediascape conveys the routinization of the exceptional and our habituation to it" (93).

---

[3] Gilroy, *'There Ain't No Black in the Union Jack': The Cultural Politics of Race and Nation* (Chicago: U of Chicago P, 1987): 13.

[4] Gilroy, *Against Race*, 6.

[5] Gilroy, *The Black Atlantic: Modernity and Double Consciousness* (Cambridge MA: Harvard UP, 1993): 4.

[6] Gilroy, *Against Race*, 68.

In his notion of the "camp," Gilroy draws together the 'territorial' aspects of nationalism and racial thinking that similarly insists on the purity and locatedness of identities. If the former is rooted most conspicuously in the soil, the latter finds its foundation in racial biology. From his earliest book, Gilroy has insisted on the association between British racism and British nationalism[7] and has critiqued the "limits of a political strategy based on appeals to a homogeneous and cohesive nation" (28) and a "variety of black nationalism that relies on mystical and essentialist ideas of a transcendental blackness" (65). The danger of such equations of race and cultural nation is that "this crypto-nationalism means that they are often disinclined to consider the cross catalytic or transverse dynamics of racial politics as significant."[8] It is in cultural production and a revised notion of consumption that Gilroy finds the most promise for a life practice which would resist and counter the mentality of the territorial and absolutist "camp."

Against the "overintegrated conceptions of culture which present immutable, ethnic differences as an absolute break in the histories and experiences of 'black' and 'white' people" (2), and the "especially crude and reductive notions of culture that form the substance of racial politics today [that] are clearly associated with an older discourse of racial and ethnic difference which is everywhere entangled in the history of the idea of culture in the modern West" (7), Gilroy posits the cultural "not as an intrinsic property of ethnic particularity but as a mediating space between agents and structures."[9] It has long been his intention, and a benchmark of his originality, to introduce "a more sophisticated theory of culture into the political analysis of 'race' and racism in Britain by claiming the term back from ethnicity. The active, dynamic aspects of cultural life have been emphasized" (17). Nowhere is this dynamic, rootless vision of culture found better than in Gilroy's discussions of diaspora.

It is in diaspora that Gilroy discovers "an intricate web of cultural and political connections binds blacks here to blacks elsewhere" (156). These connections are manifested not the least in the form of "cultural commodities – books and records – [which] have carried inside them oppositional ideas, ideologies, theologies and philosophies [...] have been consumed in circumstances far removed from those in which they were originally created, new definitions of 'race' have been born" (157). Finally, and most

---

[7] Gilroy, *'There Ain't No Black in the Union Jack'*, 26.

[8] Gilroy, *The Black Atlantic*, 4.

[9] Gilroy, *'There Ain't No Black in the Union Jack'*, 16.

explicitly, "Diaspora is a useful means to reassess the idea of essential and absolute identity precisely because it is incompatible with [...] nationalist and raciological thinking."[10]

If a dynamic, revisional, unpredictable identity that steps outside the boundaries of the nation and what it implies is what is made possible in diaspora, then sound-system culture follows suit in the cultural realm. In this critical sphere, Gilroy finds both a model for and a testament to an inventive, hybrid form of both production and consumption, both of which step outside the circuits of exchange laid out by capitalism:

> Sound system culture redefines the meaning of the term performance by separating the input of the artists who originally made the recording from the equally important work of those who adapt and rework it so that it directly expresses the moment in which it is being consumed."[11]

Importantly, this dynamic indicates an entirely new social identity and public sphere:

> A relationship of identity is enacted in the way that the performer dissolves into the crowd. Together, they collaborate in a creative process governed by formal and informal, democratic rules. [...] Both story-telling and music-making contributed to an alternative public sphere.

> Consumption is turned outwards; no longer a private, passive or individual process it becomes a procedure of collective affirmation and protest in which a new authentic public sphere is brought into being.[12]

---

[10] Gilroy, *Against Race*, 125.

[11] Gilroy, *'There Ain't No Black in the Union Jack'*, 165.

[12] *The Black Atlantic*, 200;*'There Ain't No Black in the Union Jack'*, 210. Passages like these are legion, and reflect the centrality and urgency of this cultural and social dynamic. For instance:

A more profound and complex struggle against the political, ideological and economic structures of capitalism. [...] constitutes the hub of a makeshift answer, part intuitive, part calculated, to the problems which the commodification of art has set for radical, committed artists and their audiences. (*'There Ain't No Black in the Union Jack'*, 212)

The playful, utopian celebration of change and entropic city life coupled with the deconstructive, radical forms of signification (dubbing, scratching, break-dancing and the 'visual pollution' of graffiti) which have been developed, out of necessity. [...] The cultural and political practices with which [I] have been concerned indicate a more substantive 'postmodern' vision where they have

It is crucial that Gilroy registers the political importance of this active, rather than passive, consumption. We should retain this image, for one of the key historical transitions he will note in *Against Race* regards the super-session of this practice of consumption. The stakes are clear:

> The term 'consumption' has associations that are particularly problematic, and needs to be carefully unpacked. It accentuates the passivity of its agents and plays down the value of their creativity as well as the micro-political signi-ficance of their actions.[13]

In *Against Race*, Gilroy traces a sea-change in black culture – away from music culture (which already marked a salutary distance from a textual cul-ture Gilroy found too complicitous with the weaknesses and limitations of of modern thought) and to a particular kind of visual culture that places black culture squarely within the circuits of capitalism consumption.[14] This change is intimated in the transformation of music. Gilroy argues that black music formerly "expressed and confirmed unfreedom."[15] In contrast, "to-day the memory of slavery has itself been repressed or set aside, and the tradition of dynamic remembrance it founded is being assaulted from all sides" (195). Once this defining element is taken away, black music be-comes "nothing more than a distracting accompaniment for the postmodern self-discipline of working out" (201).

The historical transformation that takes black culture out of the positive dynamic of consumption and into the circuits of commodification is no better seen than in the juxtaposition of these two passages:

---

stepped outside the confines of modernity's most impressive achievement – the nation state. (*'There Ain't No Black in the Union Jack'*, 219)

[The anti-modernity of these forms] seeks not simply to change the relation-ship of these cultural forms to newly autonomous philosophy and science but to refuse the categories on which the relative evaluation of these separate domains is based and thereby to transform the relationship between the production and the use of art, the everyday world, and the project of racial emancipation. (*The Black Atlantic*, 74).

[13] *The Black Atlantic*, 103.

[14] For example, Gilroy argues, "The vitality and complexity of this musical cul-ture offers a means to get beyond the related oppositions between essentialists and pseudo-pluralists on the one hand and between totalizing conceptions of tradition, modernity, and postmodernity on the other. It also provides a model of performance which can supplement and partially displace concern with textuality"; *The Black Atlantic*, 36.

[15] *Against Race*, 200.

[Black cultural forms] have struggled to escape their status as commodities and the position within the cultural industries it specifies [...] Their special power derives from a doubleness, their unsteady location simultaneously inside and outside the conventions.

Black culture is not just commodified but lends its special exotic allure to the marketing of an extraordinary range of commodities and services that have no connection whatever to these cultural forms or to the people who have developed them.[16]

Instead of "unfreedom" and a sense of struggling for liberation and joy, now black culture expresses "homophobia, misogyny, anti-semitism, and fundamentalist nationalisms."[17]

To account for this, and at once to stand as evidence of this change, Gilroy notes the suppression of both music and text in favor of the visual. He had already sensed this happening in *The Black Atlantic*: "the power of music and sound are receding not just relative to the power of the text and the performer but also as the relentless power of visual culture expands."[18] In *Against Race*, this tendency has developed fully and visual culture has achieved hegemony. This visual culture stands in opposition to all the positive aspects of music culture – stagnant, privatized consumption replaces dynamic, interactive consumption; flexible, hybrid identities are replaced by objectified, essentialized ones; a broad range of possibilities are whittled down to a narrow set of ideal types; and blackness, thus reduced, becomes legible only as an accoutrement to an equally essentialized whiteness for the sake of marketing and advertising:

The stimulating pattern of this hyper-visibility supplies the signature of a corporate multiculturalism in which some degree of visible difference from an implicit white norm may be highly prized as a sign of timeliness, vitality, inclusivity, and global reach. A whole crop of black models, stylists, photographers, and now, thanks to the good offices of Spike Lee, a black advertising agency, have contributed to this change of climate in the meaning of racialized signs, symbols, and bodies.[19]

The mix of essentialism and visual culture, according to Gilroy, is by no means accidental. The modern flourishing of visual culture arrives with the

---

[16] Gilroy, *The Black Atlantic*, 73; *Against Race*, 214.

[17] *Against Race*, 198.

[18] *The Black Atlantic*, 203.

[19] *Against Race*, 21–22.

Nazi propaganda films of Leni Riefenstahl. Modern visuality cuts off dialogue and simply declares a static and inflexible image/identity:

> The distinctive qualities of fascist political style [...] have long been associated with the enhanced power of visuality. [...] The application of image-building and image-maintaining techniques has created a condition in which icons severely qualify and often dominate the vivid authority of the spoken word in ways that recall the operations of fascist propaganda. (149–51)

The visual thus becomes a "sources of solidarity, identification, and belonging" precisely because it obviates anything other than a passive and binary form of identification: either one accepts or denies what it offers.[20]

Along with deadening the potential utopian power of music culture, the very site of black corporeality is transformed by this imaging and confined differently in the service of capital. Whereas in *'There Ain't No Black in the Union Jack'* Gilroy notes that "a sense of the body's place in the natural world can provide [...] a social ecology and an alternative rationality that articulate a cultural and moral challenge to [...] exploitation and domination,"[21] in *Against Race* he gloomily writes: "The body, in motion on the ball court, striving against machinery in the gym, at the wheel of the sports utility vehicle, between the sheets, and finally decked out in branded finery on the mortuary slab, is now all there is."[22] Rebuffing those who might come up with some heroic script for this image, he declares:

> It is best to be absolutely clear that the ubiquity and prominence currently accorded to the exceptionally beautiful and glamorous but nonetheless racialized bodies do nothing to change the everyday forms of racial hierarchy. The

---

[20] Gilroy, *Against Race*, 155. Gilroy terms this "logosolidarity" (*Against Race*, 160). It is beyond the bounds of this review to tackle Gilroy's claims regarding visual culture. My sense of it is that it is partial and suffers significantly by lacking any phenomenological basis – how do we know the effects of this visual culture are what Gilroy claims them to be? Further questions might relate to the solidity and absolute nature he attributes to visual culture, and to whether his very delineation of it does not ignore other possibilities. Much work has been done in this area – useful titles include Martin Jay, *Downcast Eyes*; *Vision and Visuality*, ed. Hal Foster (Boston MA: Beacon, 1988); *Vision in Context*, ed. Teresa Brennan & Martin Jay (New York: Routledge, 1996); Raymond Boudon, *The Crisis in Sociological Epistemology* (London: Macmillan, 1980), esp. ch. 5; Raymond Boudon & Paul Lazarsfeld, *L'analyse empirique de la causalité* (Paris: Mouton, 2nd ed. 1969).

[21] Gilroy, *'There Ain't No Black in the Union Jack'*, 227.

[22] Gilroy, *Against Race*, 198.

historic associations of blackness with infrahumanity, brutality, crime, idleness, excessive threatening fertility, and so on remain undisturbed. (22)

After such a debilitating description of the present day, the question thus becomes, what now? A simple return to the past would seem impossible in terms of Gilroy's historical narrative. Furthermore, such a linear logic seems out of place given the basic principles of rhizomatic dynamism at the core of Gilroy's work. These problems point to a series of issues which show the real knottiness of his argument, which cannot be taken piecemeal but, rather, as an ensemble of mutually dependent elements.

The fact that history, or at least a particular vision of history, should take center-stage is only natural, given the way *Against Race* itself is organized temporally. Thus, the question, "what now?" becomes "what should be?," the present projected against the backdrop of a future: "Corrective or compensatory inclusion in modernity should no longer supply the dominant theme." Instead, he proposes a difficult "temporal adjustment that warrants this sharp turn away from African antiquity toward our planet's future" (335). To make the transition from present time to future time, from the depressing and seemingly all-pervasive iconicity of fascist visual race essentialism and, what is more, the cultural and political life it unremittingly inculcates, is no easy task. To attempt this, Gilroy carries forward two important strains of thought from his previous works. First, his well-established line of thinking on utopia, which has a precise anti-racist, anti-essentialist core. Second, his specification of what sort of politics might be engaged to help us manifest, in however partial a manner, such a world.

He articulates two 'politics': the "normative" "politics of fulfillment," which is predicated on "the notion that a future society will be able to realise the social and political promise that present society has left unaccomplished";[23] and a utopian "politics of transfiguration," which "emphasizes the emergence of qualitatively new desires, social relations, and modes of association with the racial community of interpretation and resistance and between that group and its erstwhile oppressors" (37). Nevertheless, it is this second, utopian model of politics that would seem to be eliminated under the historical conditions outlined in *Against Racism*, for this quotation continues: "It [the politics of transfiguration] points specifically to the formation of a community of needs and solidarity which is magically made audible in the music itself and palpable in the social relations of its cultural utility and reproduction" (37). If music culture has now been subordinated to the form and the logic of the visual, then it would

---

[23] Gilroy, *The Black Atlantic*, 37.

seem to obviate the positive practice of antiphony, "which symbolises and anticipates (but does not guarantee) new, non-dominating social relationships" (79). As it stands now, there is no resonance, no harmony or dissonance, no give-and-take, no recombinatory aspect of visual culture. Every possible meaningful articulation of black culture apparently has been collapsed beneath the glossy surface of the Image, whose singularity attests to not only the condensation of diverse forms of being, but the reduction of political effect to a single, deadening message.

To get out of this impasse, in *Against Race* Gilroy adjusts his time frame, away from race altogether. He suggests that we make more precise the content of utopian society, the aspirations to be fulfilled, and the transformations in our own thinking of ourselves necessary to get beyond race. Gilroy urges us to bracket 'race', because its very discursive assumptions, which contain a specifically delimited reality, can lead us only further into trouble, or at the very least keep us mired in the same old raciology that we have inherited:

> I urge a fundamental change of mood upon what used to be called 'anti-racism.' It has been asked in an explicitly utopian spirit to terminate its ambivalent relationship to the idea of 'race' in the interest of a heterocultural, post-anthropological, and cosmopolitan yet-to-come.[24]

Again, Gilroy suggests that

> it may be better to welcome a change of scale and work toward a more complex picture in a longer time frame, perhaps also within a conceptual scheme that reorients our thinking away from the glamour of ethnos and redirects it toward what used to be called 'the problem of species being.' This could be presented as an exercise in 'strategic universalism.' (96)

To revive Marx's notion of "species being" in this case means to revive a notion of human collectivity and social being that is neither private nor, in Gilroy's usage, absolutely partisan. He sets his eyes on "a world in which racial solidarities no longer enjoy an automatic allegiance or uncontested priority over the competing collectivities based on age, religion, language, region, health, gender, or sexual preference" (210).

However, here his temporal scheme becomes more complex, and this new turn marks both the originality and problematic nature of *Against Race*. Ingeniously, Gilroy brings the future back to the present:

---

[24] Gilroy, *Against Race*, 334.

> our challenge should now be to bring even more powerful visions of planetary humanity from the future into the present and to reconnect them with democratic and cosmopolitan traditions that have been all but expunged from today's black political imaginary. (356)

That is, while he advocates a "sharp turn away from African antiquity" (335), he draws on whatever residual elements of past modern black culture may be found precisely because they were able, *in their particular historical situation*, to envision a future in ways that today's black culture cannot. This powerful and emphatic turn to the future via the past is thus at once pragmatic (to bring back from a vision of the future the tools to revise the present) and also utopian (this reworking of the present is aimed at a better world to come). This ingenuity only points out more forcefully the need to come to terms with history. In conclusion, I turn to two areas where this new temporal dynamic raises important issues. First, Gilroy must decide how much of the past is to be retained, and how and why. Second, he must decide at what point race actually can be relinquished. And this second point has everything to do with the cohesion and futurality of his key term, "diaspora."

II

The first issue – how much history to retain, and why – is made necessary by Gilroy's long-tanding complaint against conceiving black culture purely as a negative term articulated against the backdrop of whiteness: "anti-racist policies must not have the effect of appearing to reduce the complexity of black life to an effect of racism."[25] To do this requires "bringing blacks into history outside the categories of problem and victim, and establishing the historical character of racism" (27). This double movement found at the beginning of his 1987 book is essentially the program of the book he published thirteen years later. He seeks here both to make more complex our understanding of black life, outside the categories imposed from the perspectives of whites, and to show that racism is neither natural nor static – its historical manifestations are to be linked to larger social, political, and cultural phenomena. Nevertheless, while all three books share the same purpose, in this third book Gilroy's critique of victim as identity is much more biting and accusatory: "The identity of the victim, sealed off and presented as an essential, unchanging state, has become, in the years since [Dr King's]

---

[25] Gilroy, *'There Ain't No Black in the Union Jack'*, 150.

murder, a prized acquisition not least where financial calculations have sought to transform historic wrongs into compensatory monies."[26]

This raises an important question: what is *wrong* with seeking "compensatory monies"? Or, better yet, *any* kind of compensation? It is clear that Gilroy believes that victimage is not a satisfactory political platform. Such claims come not from the status of victim *per se* but from the collective voice of a group victimized because of race. Here is where things get very tricky. If one is forced to see victimization occurring because of racial thinking, to undo this dynamic one has to think "against race," to reject the categories of race that led to the violence in the first place. But that leaves us with the unrelenting, indelible historical fact – these people were aggrieved because of racial thinking on *another's* part, not (necessarily) their own.

But Gilroy's concerns exceed that of simply naming victims and perpetrators – he seeks to move beyond of us/them binaries and englobe all "camps" under the common sign of humanity:

> The intellectual challenge defined here is that histories of suffering should not be allowed exclusively to their victims. [...] This proposed change of perspective about the value of suffering is not then exclusively of interest to its victims and any kin who remember them. Because it is a matter of justice, it is not just an issue for the wronged "minorities" whose own lost or fading identities may be restored or rescued by the practice of commemoration. It is also of concern to those who may have benefitted directly and indirectly from the rational application of irrationality and barbarity. Perhaps above all, this attempt to reconceptualize modernity so that it encompasses these possibilities is relevant to the majority who are unlikely to count themselves as filiated with either of the principal groups: victims and perpetrators. This difficult stance challenges that unnamed group to witness sufferings that pass beyond the reach of words and, in so doing, to see how an understanding of one's own particularity or identity might be transformed as a result of a principled exposure to the claims of otherness. (115)

This seems to re-state the common (though by no means illegitimate) notion that racism not only does deep damage to its most explicit victims (explicit because it is their bodies that bear witness to the wrongs done to them), but also dehumanizes those who perpetrate racism. But this argument always runs the risk of flattening out questions of agency and involvement in ways that turn an issue of social justice into a more purely philosophical point. What weight do words like "witness," "understanding," "transformation," "principled exposures," and "claims" actually have? Although Gilroy can-

---

[26] Gilroy, *Against Race*, 113.

not be expected to predict how any of these terms might apply in specific historical cases, the level of abstraction both enhances his argument and makes it more difficult to picture:

> And yet, unsettled claims deriving from past injustices are still alive, as, for example, where the remnants of the Herero people seek economic redress for the genocide wrought upon them by General Von Tritha and his associates, or the surviving descendants of the Nazis' slave laborers launch courtroom battles for reparation against the multinational companies that they were compelled to serve on pain of death. Making raciology appear anachronistic – placing it squarely in the past – now requires careful judgement as to what histories of our heterocultural present and our cosmopolitan future should entail. (335)

My point here is that what we clearly gain in terms of a speculative, philosophical point, with some potential political effect, we almost equally lose in terms of a practical political and legal voice. It places enormous weight on those who would be given the right to make those "careful judgments." We are presented with the exciting challenge to think differently, but the wheels of the courts keep moving on. This is surely one of the most controversial parts of his book, yet it is especially difficult to take an oppositional stance, because to do so would run the risk of being accused of being "unethical," if not simply politically correct.

Finally, let us turn to the issues of race and diaspora. First, it is somewhat eerie that, while Gilroy opens his book to a universal species being, his conclusion is founded on a particular conception of 'blackness' that re-specifies race, rather than moves beyond it. He sets up a historical narrative that privileges a particular origin:

> Before I enlist the raceless future in the service of my own willfully dislocated argument, I am bound to acknowledge the history of black appeals to the future and must now look toward the vernacular formations where these themes constantly cross one another." (337)

Although he claims a "willful dislocatedness" to his argument, on the one hand, on the other he feels the obligation to acknowledge a tradition of sorts within black cultures. Thus we are drawn to the *telos* of a particular history – black culture occupies a specific and valorized historical precedent in his line of reasoning: "extraterrestriality, futurology, and fictions of techno-science have been articulated in the everyday rhythms of forms of what might be termed 'the mainstream' of black vernacular expression" (337). Gilroy is right to be reluctant to downplay the specific cultural history of blacks, and their contributions to the kinds of futurology he endorses. Yet this attention ignores the possibility that other peoples of other races may not also have had cultural forms that housed such intimations of the future. Gilroy, if presented with such evidence, would probably not disavow it but, rather, welcome it. But it is striking that his effort to map a raceless utopia where "species being" would reign is so emplotted along one particular racial narrative. If only for symbolic purposes, one might have expected him to entertain the possibilities of other traditions of post-racial utopianism.

But even if we keep to a discussion of only black cultural forms, we are not left without deep questions about its coherence. Indeed, the very values that Gilroy holds to, of hybridity and post-racial thinking, raise crucial issues as to the identity of diasporic cultures. As in the case of justice and victimization, Gilroy senses the real problem behind his broad recommendations:

> The main problem that we face [...] is the lack of a means of adequately describing, let alone theorizing, intermixture, fusion, and syncretism without suggesting the existence of anterior 'uncontaminated' purities. (250)

He will lay claim to the production of 'black' culture, yet urges us to think of race and culture as more complex and hybrid, pointing to

> the stereophonic, bilingual, or bifocal cultural forms originated by, *but no longer the exclusive property of*, blacks dispersed within the structures of feeling, producing, communicating and remembering that I have heuristically called the black Atlantic world.[27]

In these two passages we find the paradox of diaspora – how can we at once imagine recombinatory, freely-inventing cultural production and name it as the product of *anything or anyone in particular*? Crucially, this is not simply a matter of proper attribution; rather, it points to a deep cultural issue: "It becomes important to consider how the vital symbolic and cultural links between Africa and its modern diaspora might be protected."[28] I would simply add, "without resorting to race." What Gilroy does not (and perhaps cannot) specify is not only at what point on the horizon of a constantly hybridizing notion of culture race drops off the edge of our vision, but also what would happen to our sense of origin at that point: ie, where does blackness end? When is culture no longer the 'property' of a single group?

---

[27] Gilroy, *The Black Atlantic*, 3 (my emphasis).
[28] Gilroy, *Against Race*, 211.

This point is driven home forcefully when we encounter phrases that speak of "black culture" as if it were easily identifiable. Given Gilroy's argument for a sense of diaspora over and against 'race' – for an open and evolving notion of *culture* against a static and biologically anchored racial *identity* – we would expect that race itself would be erased from his notion of diaspora. Geography might still operate as some distant point of reference (ie, Africa), but that origin would be a remote and idealistic one. But even if we retain geography, how and why should we retain 'race', given both the inescapable fact that races are impure, hybrid, shifting in 'racial' content, and more particularly the specific argument of Gilroy's book. In short, what is particular about it? Why does he continue, unselfconsciously, to speak of culture "made by black hands"? Are 'culture' and diaspora still anchored for Gilroy in 'race'?

III

It is at the interstices of these problems of history, culture, and race that we find the core not only of the problems that have informed Gilroy's work, but also of a problematic which is not to be dismissed simply for its contradictions but, rather, confronted with even more energy. We are ultimately brought back to another motif that runs throug Gilroy's work: the notion of the sublime; for the centerpiece of his politics is transfiguration, which, precisely, "strives in pursuit of the sublime, struggling to repeat the unrepeatable, to present the unpresentable."[29] *Against Race* is a brave and extremely useful attempt to do exactly that; more than just about anyone else, Gilroy has mapped out the most obstinate, entrenched paradoxes of race in the modern age. But in the end we need to return the point Gilroy poses near the beginning of his book, where he defines the particularity of an argument that has been in the making for over a decade:

> All earlier arguments conform to the same basic architecture. They posit the particular, singular, and specific against the general, universal, and transcendent that they value more highly. In contrast, the approach I favor attempts to break up these unhappy couples. It has less to say about the unanswerable force of claims to singularity and particularity that have fueled ethnic absolutism. Instead, it directs attention toward the other side of these simultaneous equations. We should, it suggests, become concerned once again with the

---

[29] Gilroy, *The Black Atlantic*, 38.

notion of the human into which reluctant specificity has been repeatedly invited to dissolve itself.[30]

As my discussion of history and victimage, race and diaspora has tried to indicate, it is precisely at this point of tension, this moment of dissolution, that Gilroy's work may be situated. The real question becomes how much will be left behind, and to what effect, once we cross over.

WORKS CITED

Boudon, Raymond. *The Crisis in Sociological Epistemology* (London: Macmillan, 1980).

——, & Paul Lazarsfeld. *L'Analyse empirique de la causalité* (Paris: Mouton, 2nd ed. 1969).

Brennan, Teresa, & Martin Jay, ed. *Vision in Context: Historical and Contemporary Perspectives on Sight* (London & New York: Routledge, 1996).

Durand, Gilbert. *Figures mythiques et visages de l'œuvre: De la mythocritique à la mythanalyse* (Paris: Berg International, 1979).

Foster, Hal, ed. *Vision and Visuality* (Dia Art Foundation Discussions in Contemporary Culture 2; Seattle WA: Bay Press, 1988).

Gilroy, Paul. *Against Race: Imagining Political Culture Beyond the Color Line* (Cambridge MA: Harvard UP, 2000).

——. *The Black Atlantic: Modernity and Double Consciousness* (Cambridge MA: Harvard UP, 1993).

——. *'There Ain't No Black in the Union Jack': The Cultural Politics of Race and Nation* (Chicago: U of Chicago P, 1987).

Jay, Martin. *Downcast Eyes: The Denigration of Vision in Twentieth-Century French Thought* (Berkeley & London: U of California P, 1993).

Pelton, Robert. *The Trickster in West Africa: A Study of Mythic Irony and Sacred Delight* (Berkeley: U of California P, 1980).

Sartre, Jean–Paul. *Qu'est-ce que la littérature?* (Paris: Seuil, 1949).

---

[30] Gilroy, *Against Race*, 30.

Henry Louis Gates, Jr.'s
Signifying Monkey
A Diasporic Critical Myth

MICHEL FEITH

G ATES'S *THE SIGNIFYING MONKEY: A Theory of African-American Literary Criticism* (1986) is, as its subtitle indicates, an attempt to constitute a literary and critical tradition around the vernacular trope of "Signifyin(g)," defined as "repetition with a difference."

> Signifyin(g) is black double-voicedness; because it always entails formal re-vision and an intertextual relation, and because of Esu's double-voiced representation in art, I find it an ideal metaphor for black literary criticism, for the formal manner in which texts seem concerned to address their antecedents. Repetition, with a signal difference, is fundamental to the nature of Signifyin(g).[1]

This innovative, fertile approach immediately gained the book the status of a classic, and has provided guidelines for much pertinent criticism. After almost a decade and a half, a reassessment may be in order: one is naturally led to interrogate the prominence given in Gates's analyses to the trickster figures of the Monkey and his African antetype Esu–Elegbara. The vision of diaspora stemming from this mythic genealogy may be confronted with more recent analyses, such as Paul Gilroy's *Black Atlantic* (1993). Trick-sters, who can be found in most traditional cultures of the world, are parti-

---

[1] Henry Louis Gates, Jr., *The Signifying Monkey: A Theory of African-American Literary Criticism* (New York: Oxford UP, 1988): 51. Where clear, further page references are in the main text.

cularly ambiguous characters, as Paul Radin reminds us in his classic study
of the Winnebago stories:

> In what must be regarded as its earliest and most archaic form, as found
> among the North American Indians, Trickster is at one and the same time
> creator and destroyer, giver and negator, he who dupes others and who is
> always duped himself. He wills nothing consciously. [...] He knows neither
> good nor evil yet he is responsible for both. He possesses no values, moral or
> social, is at the mercy of his passions and appetites, yet through his actions
> values come into being.[2]

Radin's reading is more psychological than structural: his vision of the
trickster as a purely unconscious agency should be taken with a pinch of
salt. Yet, being at one and the same time culture-hero and universally subversive agent, linguistic equivocator and benevolent translator, embodiment
of a tribe's ethos and transgressor of the very values he helped promote, this
character stands at the boundaries of civilization and savagery, nature and
culture, instincts and their sublimation. The institution of such an a-normal
figure as the tutelary deity of criticism and tradition may seem paradoxical,
given the rather normative nature of literary interpretation and patterns of
influence. How essential, then, is it to Gates's demonstration to give the
trope a local habitation, a body and a name? What does the myth add to the
rhetoric? This first question is intimately linked to that of the Monkey's
diasporic dimension, his reconstructed genealogy from Africa through the
Caribbean to the USA. Should it be construed as mere background information, or does it unveil a crucial component of the story?

The title of the first chapter – "A Myth of Origins: Esu–Elegbara and the
Signifying Monkey" (3) – is in itself programmatic. Emphasis has to be laid
on both terms: myth and origins. First, the filiation between the African
trickster and the American folk figure, especially the prominence given to a
minor character of the original legend, is "extremely difficult to reconstruct" (15). Then, the derivation of contemporary literary and critical practices from a myth, be it an analogue to the European Hermetic narrative,
seems to invert a received relationship. Literature having strong connections
with myth, considered either as sacred narrative[3] or as ideological imposi-

---

[2] Paul Radin, *The Trickster: A Study in American Indian Mythology* (New York:
Bell, 1956): x.

[3] Mircea Eliade, *Myth and Reality*, tr. Willard Trask (New York: Harper & Row,
1963).

tion,[4] the task of criticism is usually construed as an exposure of the hidden mythologies present in cultural texts, so as to deepen understanding, or in an enterprise of demystification. Yet the different schools of interpretation themselves are not exempt from ideological or mythological premises, as perceptively analysed in Tzvetan Todorov's *Critique de la critique* (1986). Gates's project is more complex, in the sense that he intends to reveal a critical myth. The stories of Esu and the Monkey seem to be more than propaedeutic allegories, and will be envisaged as true myths, in spite of their secularized context and the intellectual distance at work in their theoretical re-writing. In the course of what Gilbert Durand calls a "myth-analyse,"[5] the Signifyin(g) Monkey will be considered first as a paradigm of identity, then as a mediating figure, and finally as a tool for the (re-)invention of a tradition; at all these levels the central question will be that of the symbolic efficacy of this vernacular figure in the management of the contradictions facing the black writer and, more pointedly, the contemporary African-American critic.

A Paradigm of (Diasporic) Identity

In his *Blues, Ideology and Afro-American Literature* (1984), Houston Baker, Jr. outlined a crisis in African American literary criticism, which his book and Gates's *Signifying Monkey* were attempts at solving. According to this description, there had been by the mid-1980s three main schools of black criticism in the USA, all of which presented serious drawbacks. The first movement was an already-faded "integrationist poetics" whose idealistic belief in the progress of democracy was a correlative of its defense of a single standard of literary criticism. The second trend, the Black Arts movement, advocated closeness to vernacular expression, an insistence on the 'blackness' of the work. "It propose[d] a separate symbolism, mythology, critique and iconography" connected with the "inner life" of the folk,

---

[4] Roland Barthes, *Mythologies*, tr. Annette Lavers (New York: Hill & Wang, 1972).

[5] Gilbert Durand, *Figures mythiques et visages de l'œuvre: De la mythocritique à la mythanalyse* (Paris: Berg International, 1979): 313. "Mytho-critique," according to Gilbert Durand, aims at identifying the leading myths and their variations, in the works of an author, a time or a society; whereas "myth-analysis," a word he coined in reference to psychoanalysis, purports to analyse these myths in order to discover their psychological and sociological meanings.

and fully accessible only to insiders.[6] Such notions belong to what Baker calls a "Romantic Marxism," reminiscent of Herderian cultural nationalism in its rather essentialist assumption of an irreducible folk spirit, or *Volksgeist*. The third critical streak was that of the "reconstructionists," who accepted Afro-American literature as an "autonomous cultural domain," yet analysed it according to the critical tools of Western theory, "alien to the implicitly vernacular approach of the Black Aesthetics."[7] The "reconstructionist" option seemed the most sophisticated, yet was plagued by contradiction. It was an 'impure' middle ground, caught between two extremes, and was often denounced as a new integrationism that didn't spell its name.

Baker's and Gates's books aimed at unraveling this skein of contradictions, by bridging the gap between the vernacular culture and the sophistication of European and Euro-American theory. Hence the 'rooting' function of their key concepts: the "blues matrix" reconfigured along Foucaldian lines in the former, and the trope of "Signifying" in the latter. The symbolic gesture of this confrontation between the two epistemologies is particularly charged. In a first stage, it amounts to an anti-eurocentric move: the vernacular is as sophisticated as poststructuralist thought. Signifyin(g), the slave's trope, is characterized by such postmodern traits as parody, word play and the destabilization of meaning.[8] The very name chosen by African Americans for their specific language 'shadows' standard meaning in such a way as to express their status as linguistic Others, and their opposition to the order of things enforced by the dominant ordering of signs.

> For Signifiyin(g) constitutes all of the language games, the figurative substitutions, the free associations held in abeyance by Lacan's and Saussure's paradigmatic axis, which disturbs the seemingly coherent linearity of the syntagmatic chain of signifiers, in a way analogous to Freud's notion of how the unconscious relates to the conscious. The black vernacular trope of Signifyin(g) exists on this vertical axis, wherein the materiality of the signifier (the use of words as things, in Freud's terms of the discourse of the unconscious) not only ceases to be disguised but comes to bear prominently as the dominant mode of discourse. (58)

Black discourse is, then, the opposite of Western linear thought, and of the sets of binaries that govern language. The parallel Gates establishes between the linguistic, psychological and political domains makes it clear that

---

[6] Houston A. Baker, Jr.. *Blues, Ideology and Afro-American Literature: A Vernacular Theory* (Chicago: U of Chicago P, 1984): 74.

[7] Baker, *Blues, Ideology and Afro-American Literature*, 89.

[8] Gates, *The Signifying Monkey*, 45.

among those oppositions that define the culture is that between black and white, complete with the assumed superiority of one over the other. Repression works in similar ways in the three fields: Signifyin(g) simultaneously implies an awareness of this situation, and a distancing from it.

The black vernacular is therefore imbued with the insights of a post-modern critique of logocentrism and domination, but at the cost of a re-phrasing in the idiom of classical Western rhetoric, Lacanian psycho-analysis and Derridean grammatology. Such a rephrasing is a renaming: ie, a translation and a distortion. Gates's vernacular is not the jazzman's verna-cular – so little so, that some critics have deemed it a paradoxical tribute, "for it seems that the more the black theorist writes in the interest of black-ness, the greater his Eurocentrism reveals itself to be."[9] Sandra Adell seems here to ignore the dearth of historical alternatives to Gates's position. Assimilationism goes most of the way toward Euro-American positions; whereas black nationalism is perhaps even more influenced by the thought it claims to repudiate – the German romantic discourse on nations and the essential "inner life" of peoples that finds expression in a specific language. The concept of Signifyin(g), at least, is centered on the "double-voicedness" of the black text, and incorporates this duality into black criticism. Inciden-tally, Jacques Derrida's and Michel Foucault's philosophies are attempts to explore the consequences of decolonization and to de-center European thought away from the former justifications of imperialism. Born of a West-ern locus and European preoccupations, they hardly qualify as eurocentric.

By defining the Afro-American community by its formal idiom, Gates founds "the Signifyin(g) black difference" neither on a purely socio-econo-mic *situation*, nor on some ineffable romantic 'essence'. On the contrary: identity resides in the manipulation of signs that bear the imprint of history and, in turn, subvert that history. Such a position is very close to Fredrik Barth's definition of ethnicity as the building and maintenance of symbolic boundaries.[10] The relation of exclusion and difference that obtains in the linguistic realm is equivalent to the discrimination existing in the political and economic sphere of the nation-state. At this juncture, the necessity of the mythic figure becomes more obvious. Even though the prerequisite (and hidden agenda) of Gates's endeavour to unveil the "blackness of the sign" is to define that blackness, and blackness in turn is to be found as a sign or

---

[9] Sandra Adell, *Double Consciousness / Double Bind: Theoretical Issues in Twen-tieth-Century Black Literature* (Urbana: U of Illinois P, 1994): 132.

[10] Fredrik Barth, "Introduction" to *Ethnic Groups and Boundaries: The Social Organization of Culture Difference* (London: Allen & Unwin, 1969): 9–38.

tropological performance, the trope is not enough as a support for identity. Or it must be personified. "The Monkey, in short, is not only a master of technique [...] he *is* technique, or style, or the literariness of literary language; he is the great Signifier."[11] The Monkey not only represents a *corpus* of black vernacular texts and a rhetoric of figuration and revision; it is also a character that serves as a support for individual and communal identification. It is a "Figure in Black,"[12] a literary construction, a trope of black identity: identity through difference, identity as text. The trickster embodies this paradox: an anti-essentialist model of identity. It stands at the crossroads between different discursive universes, as a synthetic or syncretic figure which does not erase difference into a Hegelian third term. Opposing the openness of discourse to the closure of identity, it must be distinguished from the hero, or the John Henry type, who also transgresses boundaries, only to affirm, in the epic-serious mode, a strong communal ethos. The playful Monkey, rather, proposes an image of the black subject as Kristeva's "*sujet en procès*," a subject who is at the same time a never-ending process, and always (self-) subversive.[13]

This paradigm of linguistic and social identity has, up to now, been strictly contained within the system of African-American experience; its diasporic dimension seems to be only so much background information, without being of the essence. Yet recourse to the genealogy – or gene-analogy – of the Monkey, back to the Yoruba deity Esu–Elegbara, has a definite role to play in the North American myth of criticism. The "double-voicedness" of the vernacular and the literature is homothetic to the "double consciousness" of the black subject, as defined by W.E.B. Du Bois. The Afro-American idiom, then, opens a space of radical Otherness. Yet this Otherness is a play of difference *within* the English language: its originality may be lost when confronted with other instances of appropriation and diversion of a dominant language by minority groups. Irish and Jewish humour may serve as examples of such troping on the oppressor's tongue. After all, Gates himself declares that "Signifyin(g), of course, is a principle of language use and is not in any way the exclusive province of black people, although blacks named the term and invented its rituals."[14] This

---

[11] Gates, *The Signifying Monkey*, 54.

[12] Gates, *Figures in Black: Words, Signs, and the "Racial" Self* (New York: Oxford UP, 1987).

[13] Julia Kristeva, "Le sujet en procès: le langage poétique," in *L'Identité*, ed. Claude Lévi–Strauss (Paris: Presses Universitaires de France, 1977): 224.

[14] Gates, *The Signifying Monkey*, 90.

way of speaking, like the figure of the trickster itself, could well be found in most cultures of the world. In that case, the Afro-American instance is only a local variant of a more universal rhetorical category; its specificity can then only be apprehended through the genealogical principle: ie, through recontextualization within the framework of the African diaspora.

A Figure of (Anti)Mediation

This reinscription within the diasporic dimension gives a new twist to any analysis of the title of the first chapter: "A Myth of Origins." The Esu narratives appear as the source of the Signifying Monkey poems, but what is at stake is, rather, a reconstruction of origins, since the filiation is somewhat hypothetical, and functions more as a figure of analogy. When it becomes a founding myth for the African-American literary tradition, this compound story, like most myths, is multi-layered, for it bears the memory of the historical process by which new versions accrete within a basic, invariant structure. The history of the African diaspora is that of the triangular trade between Europe, Africa, and the Americas. This is transposed in the Signifying Monkey text, as recomposed by Gates, into a triangular 'commerce' of meaning between three poles: African myth (Esu); mainstream America, a part of the European diaspora (the semantic axis); and "Aframerica" (the Monkey, Signifyin(g), the rhetorical axis). These symbolic transactions take place by way of passages – the crossing of oceans as well as the crossing of linguistic and ethnic boundaries. Depending as they do on multiple mediations, they open a strategic slot for this arch-mediator, the trickster. Lewis Hyde, recalling that tricksters, like Hermes or Esu, are at the origin of such activities as sacrifice, market exchange, divination or translation, insists on the peculiar nature of these mediations.

This idea that lively articulation requires a kind of built-in ambivalent force that can "join by separating" suggests a new way to describe the trickster's inventions and activities. To take the invention of sacrifice as a first example, one striking thing – at least in the Greek tradition – is that the ritual simultaneously separates and connects. Then, in West African stories where a trickster translates for the gods and divines for human beings, both these arts – translation and divination – connect without connecting. Each builds a bridge, but in so doing reveals a distance. Neither one involves *union*, the pure overcoming of separation.[15]

---

[15] Lewis Hyde, *Trickster Makes This World: Mischief, Myth, and Art* (New York: Farrar, Straus & Giroux, 1998): 263.

As a transgressor of borders, the trickster carries out a syncretic operation whose ultimate synthesis is continually deferred. Gates rephrases it as
follows: "Indeed, the Monkey is a term of (anti) mediation, as are all trickster figures, between two forces he seeks to oppose for his own contentious
purposes, and then to reconcile."[16] In the book, these ambiguous (anti-)
mediations concern primarily three essential sets of opposites: center and
periphery; black and white; orality and literacy.

Center and periphery

Chapters One and Two retrace the Middle Passage of the deported slaves
from Africa to the Caribbean (Esu) and to the USA (Monkey). In order to
elucidate the function of the myth of origins, this history has to be read
backwards. First of all, it roots Signifyin(g) in an African-derived epistemology. It therefore contradicts the thesis of the complete eradication of the
slaves' culture during the Middle Passage, and the notion that black American culture, having fallen under the spell of the Western center, is merely
mimetic of white ways. The Monkey verse bear witness to the transplantation, not of assorted traits, but of a whole cultural *Weltanshauung*: seeing
the New World through African eyes, and transmitting this way of seeing.
Against another prejudice according to which American blacks were purely
reactive, they are here presented as taking the symbolic initiative.

> Nevertheless, this topos functions as a sign of the disrupted wholeness of an
> African system of meaning and belief that black slaves recreated from
> memory, preserved by oral narration, improvised upon in ritual – especially in
> the rituals of the repeated oral narrative – and willed to their own subsequent
> generations, as hermetically sealed and encoded charts of cultural descent. (5)

The pun on "hermetically" in the last clause draws our attention to the
double dimension of this act of transmission and re-creation. Hermes is the
trickster equivalent of Esu in Greek mythology and, like Esu, the tutelary
figure of criticism and interpretation, or 'hermeneutics'. Since Gates draws
the connection himself, there is a possibility that his theory is inspired in
part by the academic corpus on the classical God. Hermetic knowledge is
reserved to initiates, because of its sacred nature. The treasury of African
survivals at the core of black identity in the USA was such a precious,
numinous substance, its preservation ensured by the in-group linguistic rites
that Gates elsewhere defines as "masks."[17] The masking operation aims at

---

[16] Gates, *The Signifying Monkey*, 56.
[17] Gates, *Figures in Black*, 171–72.

investing the common language (English) with additional, private meanings that are peculiar to the minority group and ensure an 'intimacy' from which the mainstream is excluded, "hermetically sealed." It turns language inside out, so to speak, by inverting the relation of domination and exclusion imposed by the oppressor. Changing language into a sort of Moebius strip – a paradoxical topological object, in which the inside is simultaneously the outside, and vice versa – it amounts to the trickster operation of subverting the binary logic of exclusion encoded in the semantics of the culture.

The story bears the mark of history, yet it is also able to heal the split brought about by that history. The violent dis-location at the root of the diaspora, the Middle Passage, is partly relieved by the unveiling or estab-lishment of continuities and filiations. True to Esu's other connection, with medicine and healing,[18] the myth of origins is endowed with the curative powers of "symbolic efficacy" born of narrative mediation.[19] First of all, Signifyin(g) ensures the kind of mental liberation that comes from subvert-ing the master's *doxa*, and finding a space of freedom within language. Moreover, Gates's reconstruction imbues the folkloric figure of the Monkey with the force and depth of African mythology. This tentative restoration of a lost wholeness, through the acknowledgment of the stratified nature of the myth, allows the composition of an empowering pan-African narrative of identity. What makes a diaspora more than a dispersion or exodus is the

---

[18] "Divination, then, seeks to open these [clogged] passages of life by trans-forming them into *limina*, ways out of rigidity, thresholds of larger meaning [...] In mending the breaks or in widening the scope of that network [of relationships], the divinatory process is a true sociotherapy, concerned with revealing the meanings of the outer as well as the inner environment of the client"; Robert Pelton, *The Trick-ster in West Africa: A Study of Mythic Irony and Sacred Delight* (Berkeley: U of California P, 1980): 143. Esu is the founder of, and godly intermediary in, Yoruba divination; and individual and communal healing go hand in hand in African con-ceptions of the world.

[19] Describing the shamanic cure of a woman about to give birth in difficult con-ditions, Claude Lévi–Strauss comments: "It is unimportant that the mythology of the shaman should not correspond to an objective reality: the patient believes in it, and she belongs to a society which believes in it [...] What she does not accept are those incoherent, arbitrary pains, which constitute an element alien to her system, but which, through a recourse to myth, the shaman is going to replace in a whole where everything fits [...] The shaman provides his patient with a *language*, in which unspoken, and otherwise unspeakable states can find immediate expression"; Lévi–Strauss, *Structural Anthropology*, tr. Claire Jacobson & Brooke G. Schoepfe (*An-thropologie structurale*, Paris: Plon, 1958; tr. New York: Basic Books, 1963): 226.

dogged persistence of memory, a memory that is also a perpetual re-creation.

Esu and the Monkey (rather, the composite figure born of their filiation narrative) become the symbol of diasporic identity. Esu is a mediator between spaces, among which the most striking are the world of gods and the world of men, problematically linked in the act of divination. He also represents the unity of past, present and future:

> The most fundamental absolute of the Yoruba is that there exist, simulta-neously, three stages of existence: the past, the present and the unborn. Esu represents these stages, and makes their simultaneous existence possible, "without any contradiction," precisely because he is the principle of discourse both as messenger and as the god of communication. Discourse among three parallel phases of existence renders the notion of contradiction null.[20]

The power of uniting heterogeneous times and spaces transforms Esu into Gates's figure of the diaspora, bridging the gap of the Middle Passage and the various stages of estrangement between Mother Africa and the African-derived cultures in the Americas. He personifies the diaspora as unity in diversity, and his mediating influence renders him apt to create a common sense of belonging, a pan-African vision that leaves room for local differ-ences. "Inadvertently, African slavery in the New World satisfied the pre-conditions for the emergence of a new African culture, a truly Pan-African culture fashioned as a colorful weave of linguistic, institutional, metaphysi-cal, and formal threads" (4). Thus a culture caught between two centers, Africa and Euro-America, produced a powerful new image and became the new center from which to interpret origins.

Yet this story of emergence is itself problematic. Re-reading Esu with the eyes of the Monkey may bring new insights, but might also lead to mis-conceptions about the original African trickster. Isolated from the cultural system of which it partakes, its meaning might be impoverished, reduced to a mere prop of the African-American tradition. Despite Gates's many qualifications, one has the impression that, in his mythic vision of diaspora, continuity in time and space is overemphasized over disjunction. Even though he refers mainly to the Yoruba belief system, he often takes his ex-amples from the Fon of Dahomey, thus eliding the differences between these cultures. This is fully understandable only from a Western-Hemi-sphere viewpoint, given the fusion of African influences that occurred there. Yet this American bias not only has the effect of a radical homogenizing of spaces and cultures, it also depends on a homogenization of time. The

---

[20] Gates, *The Signifying Monkey*, 37.

trajectory from Esu to the Monkey is described as a linear, or concentric, evolution away from Africa, rather than as a reciprocal network of influences. Gates's interests lie, after all, in the constitution of a black literary tradition in the USA; his 'usable diaspora' is not really a comparative one, but the validation of one center via its derivation from a previous one. Like all myths, Gates's critical myth fulfils contradictory aspirations: its transnational frame apparently belies parochialism, yet the nostalgia for centering and wholeness that it betrays stops short of recent visions of diaspora concerned, like Paul Gilroy's, "with the flows, exchanges, and in-between elements that call the very desire to be centered into question."[21]

Between black and white: a mongrel Monkey

Diasporas, like nations, can be pictured as "imagined communities,"[22] drawing their cohesion from memory-links to the point of origin. Yet an exclusive focus on cultural survivals can obscure the diversity of local situations born of contact with other civilizations. The Americas particularly have been a locus of multiple *métissages*, as illustrated, in *The Signifying Monkey*, by the traditional story of Esu's hat (32–34). Esu came riding on the path between two friends' fields, wearing a cap that was black on one side and white on the other. The friends later disagreed on the color of his hat and, without Esu's intervention, would have done violence to one another.

'Hermeneutically' speaking, this tale raises awareness about the ambiguities of the word and the duality of the world. It corresponds to the Janus-faced, two-mouthed representations of Esu in sculpture. The trickster in motley apparel appears once more as a liminal figure, moving on the border of two (cognitive) fields. Even though Gates does not connect it explicitly with the problem of race relations – it is, after all, an African episode outside the context of racist America – I guess most readers would draw the link.[23] Depending on the versions of the story, the cap can be of different colors;[24] in Cuba, the dispute bears on a black man and a white man.[25] In

---

[21] Paul Gilroy, *The Black Atlantic: Modernity and Double Consciousness* (Cambridge MA: Harvard UP, 1993): 190.

[22] Benedict Anderson, *Imagined Communities: Reflections on the Origins and Spread of Nationalism* (London: Verso, 1991).

[23] As Lewis Hyde does in "The Color Line," in *Trickster Makes This World*, 227–51.

[24] Pelton, *The Trickster in West Africa*, 141.

[25] Hyde, *Trickster Makes This World*, 240.

the next chapter of *Monkey*, a similar topology is reiterated, this time in relation to criticism:

> The critic of comparative black literature also dwells at a sort of crossroads, a discursive crossroads at which two languages meet, be these languages Yoruba and English, or Spanish and French, or even (perhaps more importantly) the black vernacular and standard English. (65)

Esu of the black-and-white hat can thus be a valid mythic representation of African-American literature and culture, as a mediating principle between two discursive universes. Such a vision of the double determination of American cultural artefacts, at the crossroads between two diasporas (to which should be added, in South America, the third term of Native American cultures) corresponds to Gates's discussion of the black text in his introduction to *Black Literature and Literary Theory*, as the "double-voiced" meeting-point between black and white, and between formal literature and the vernacular.[26]

Yet the potentiality of the Esu–Monkey figure to represent a 'mongrel' culture on the borderline between black and white is not fully exploited in Gates's theory. Not that it is absent from it; quite the contrary, it is the very prerequisite of all the other developments in the book. "Black literature shares much with, far more than it differs from, the Western literary tradition [...] One can readily agree with Susan Willis that black texts are 'mulattoes' (or 'mulatas'), with a two-toned heritage."[27] But Gates seems to play down this dimension, in favor of a definition of Signifyin(g) as a communal practice establishing a tradition, and as a vernacular theory of interpretation and figuration. All these terms stress the in-group, "hermetically sealed" nature of the concept. There is one border that the trickster had difficulties in subverting: the color line. After all, "whereas black writers most certainly revise texts in the Western tradition, they often seek to do so 'authentically,' with a black difference, a compelling sense of difference based on the black vernacular."[28] What is described here corresponds, more than to a *métissage*, to one of the variants of what George Devereux calls "antagonistic acculturation," by which a community integrates practical and ideological tools coming from the outside, but diverts them to serve its

---

[26] Gates, "Criticism in the Jungle," in *Black Literature and Literary Theory*, ed. Gates (New York: Methuen, 1984): 12.

[27] Gates, *The Signifying Monkey*, xxii–xxiii.

[28] *The Signifying Monkey*, xxii.

specific ends, including the maintaining of its existence.[29] The type of radical subversion of the color line implicit in the story of Esu's hat is several times hinted at in *The Signifying Monkey*, as in the following passage, where Gates explains the importance of the third term in the Monkey tales:

> The third term both critiques the idea of the binary opposition and demonstrates that Signifyin(g) itself encompasses a larger domain than merely the political. It is a game of language, independent of reaction to white racism or even to collective black wish-fulfillment vis-à-vis white racism. I cannot stress too much the import of the presence of this third term, or in Hermese E. Roberts's extraordinarily suggestive phrase, "The Third Ear," an intraracial ear through which encoded vernacular language is deciphered. (70)

Even though most uses of the Signifying Monkey tales and rhetoric have been in-group and have served to strengthen the African-American sense of purpose and identity, it is somewhat surprising that the "third ear" is only defined as "intraracial." In a mixed country like the USA, the two-toned hat of Esu might signify *métissage*, the possibility of an 'interracial' ear subverting the color line by showing its epistemological and ontological absurdity, as well as its historically fallacious nature, and proposing the utopian project of its demise. This project is actually encoded in black art, on the reception sithe dual nature of the black artist's intended public – white liberals as well as African Americans, pending a universal reach – can already serve as an image of such a bridge.[30] Could we, then, state that, despite all the symbolic subversion of the color line in *The Signifying Monkey*, Gates does not wholly transcend what George Hutchinson calls "American racial discourse," the illusory belief in the separation of the 'races' and the denial of New World mixing of bloods and cultures?[31] Gates's awareness of the mixed nature of African-American culture and of the dependence of Signifyin(g) practices on the dominant language it subverts is unquestionable; yet he does not present us with a mongrel Monkey. Once again, we are led to the figure of the Esu–Monkey as a 'pure–impure'

---

[29] George Devereux, "L'Acculturation antagoniste," in Devereux, *Ethnopsychanalyse complémentariste*, tr. Tina Jolas & Henri Gobard (*Ethnopsychoanalysis: Psychoanalysis and Anthropology as Complementary Frames of Reference*, Berkeley: U of California P, 1978; tr. Paris: Flammarion, 1985): 267.

[30] Gates reproduces Sartre's discussion of the double public of Richard Wright's novels; see *Qu'est-ce que la littérature?* (Paris: Seuil, 1949) and "Criticism in the Jungle."

[31] George Hutchinson, *The Harlem Renaissance in Black and White* (Cambridge MA: Belknap P/Harvard UP, 1995): 231.

support for communal identification: the aim is a reinforcement of the black
ethos, through the isolation of the "Signifyin(g) black difference," in common linguistic practice as well as in literature. This persisting divide can be
seen partly as a consequence of the racial situation in the USA. "Where the
community at large can maintain the fiction of its color line, a man forgets
the color of his skin at his own peril."[32] The particular position of Henry
Louis Gates. Jr. as a prominent critic of African-American literature may
also bear on the case: after all, the fight for the recognition of this discipline
is not yet over in the American academy. The rule of the game is that disci-
plines must be self-contained, or autonomous, to a certain degree: too much
emphasis on impurity might weaken the cause.

Orality and literacy

According to the traditional apportionment, the black vernacular is an oral
culture, whereas literacy characterizes the Western frame of mind. This
dichotomy, and its mediation, is essential in establishing two of the major
tropes of the black tradition: the "trope of the Talking Book," and that of the
"speakerly text." The former concept illustrates how, in "the literature of the
slave" published between 1760 and 1865, learning to read and writing an
autobiography represented a self-fashioning, the passage from object- to
subject-position. At the same time, it Signifies upon Western discourse and
prejudice, showing the arbitrariness of this intellectual color line by crossing the reputedly impassable 'natural' boundary of literacy. The "speakerly
text," initiated by Zora Neale Hurston, is a reverse transgression, from the
written to the spoken. It uses the resources of formal literature to pay
homage to the richness of the black vernacular, thereby subverting the
former's claim to superiority.

> Its obvious oral base, nevertheless, suggests that Hurston conceived of it as a
> third language, as a mediating third term that aspires to resolve the tension
> between standard English and black vernacular, just as the narrative device of
> free indirect discourse aspires to define the traditional opposition between
> mimesis and diegesis as a false opposition.[33]

In trickster language, the creation of crossover paradoxes and a "Third Ear"
position displaces the boundaries between black and white, and between
orality and literacy, by questioning traditional assumptions about literature
(the opposition between mimesis and diegesis giving way to performance),

---

[32] Hyde, *Trickster Makes This World*, 247.
[33] Gates, *The Signifying Monkey*, 215.

and by creating a non-white type of writing through infusion of black speech acts. Once again we meet the mediating function of the trickster, and the creation of hybrid forms in the Americas, resulting from the meeting of two, black and white, diasporas.

An acute awareness of the valorization of literacy over orality in the encounter between Western and traditional cultures pervades *The Signifying Monkey*. It is, significantly, by referring to Derrida's philosophy that Gates defines both Esu and the Monkey as figures of writing in an oral culture, thus allowing him to turn the tables on claims of white superiority. The two tricksters, and their rhetorical strategies, are characterized by *"différance"* of meaning (meaning is deferred and, being polysemic, differs from itself).

In Yoruba divination, the dictates of Ifa, the god of destiny, are considered as a form of speech, imbued with numinous presence. Yet they are known to man, through the mediation of Esu, as configurations of palm-nuts on a divining board. This is called by the practitioners the "writing" of Ifa, a first level of mediation. Then the *babalawo* (diviner) chooses and recites one of several brief sayings corresponding to the diagram. These fixed lines can also be construed as a form of writing, since they are learnt by heart, hence invariable; they constitute a second level of mediation. The third level is the subjective interpretation of these oracles by the "analysand."

> The language of the Ifa oracle is of the textual, or discursive, order, precisely because it is mediated, like writing. The text of Ifa is neither spoken nor written, because the relationship between them is an irresolvable moment, or an aporia [...] Esu is analogy, but also every other figure, for he is the trope of tropes, the figure of the figure. Esu is meta-discourse, the writing of the speech-act of Ifa.[34]

The Monkey's status as the representative of the written in an oral framework also depends on mediation and deferral of meaning; it is even more clearly associated with the figurative. "If we think of rhetoric as the 'writing' of spoken discourse, then the Monkey's role as the source and encoded keeper of Signifyin(g) helps to reveal his functional equivalency with his Pan-African cousin, *Esu–Elegbara*, the figure of writing in Ifa" (75).

Read between the lines, Gates's massive recourse to Derrida's somewhat arbitrary distinction between speech and writing can shed light on his mythic apprehension of diasporic literature. The cultural facts of diaspora can be theorized as *différance*, the becoming-Other of the same, embodied in the gaps and divergences that Brent Edwards calls *décalages*. Following

---

[34] Gates, *The Signifying Monkey*, 39–40, 42.

the etymological track, one is led to the close kinship between diaspora and "dissemination," Derrida's later elaboration of the concept.[35] This analogy is more than a chance one: on the linguistic and literary level, Signifyin(g) has the effect of disseminating meaning by opening up the paradigmatic axis.[36] The African-American vernacular is therefore placed under the sign of writing because of its figurative nature and subversion of mainstream language, but also because it conveys traces of absent African tongues. The Monkey stories, in their stratified structure, bear the imprint of African cosmologies and practices. In so doing, they bear witness to the presence/ absence of their authenticating source. Yet what is looked for in Africa is more than a healing presence; it is another Derridean questioning of it:

> To figure Esu as a trope of indeterminacy is to reinforce the critique of the immediacy and transcendence of presence implicit in the priority of speaking, which the oral forms of Ifa divination might suggest without Esu.[37]

This complicity between African premodernity and contemporary post-modernity may be seen as an attempt to bypass modernity and the trauma of slavery.[38] Paradoxically, Derrida's anti-mythic discourse serves to support nostalgia for a lost wholeness of tradition: a nostalgia that might seem anti-thetical to the notion of dissemination.

The (Re)Invention of Tradition

Paul Gilroy opposes two visions of diaspora: one that is founded on tradition, and another that takes into account the plurality of African-derived cultures. The former is often characterized by an essentialist dimension, whereas the latter is historically more accurate. "The invocation of tradition becomes both more desperate and more politically charged as the sheer irrepressible heterology of black cultures becomes harder to avoid."[39] Does, then, Gates's desire to root his own African-American tradition in African structures of thought stem from a misguided notion of diaspora and cultural transmission? Placing black literary criticism, in the person of "that sly

---

[35] Jacques Derrida, *Dissémination*, tr. Barbara Johnson (Chicago: U of Chicago P, 1981): 1981.

[36] Gates, *The Signifying Monkey*, 46, 58.

[37] *The Signifying Monkey*, 39.

[38] Gilroy, *The Black Atlantic*, 188.

[39] *The Black Atlantic*, 195.

simian himself,"[40] under the tutelage of trickster figures implies, on the contrary, an anti-essentialist perspective based on the principle on indeterminacy. Esu's role in Ifa divination becomes the metaphor for the relation between the text and its reading. "For the literary critic, the concept of 'Two Ogboni, it becomes three' accounts for the curious process by which author, text and criticism interact. The third principle, we see readily, is criticism itself."[41] The Ogboni are a secret society whose revered symbol is a couple of masculine and feminine statues connected by a chain, this third element being the mystery, the shared secret making a synthesis possible (38). Esu is associated with this synthesis, creating a third element out of two. "At the crossroads of differences, there is no direct access, or contact, with truth or meaning [...]. Esu endlessly displaces meaning, deferring it by the play of signification" (41–42). The role of the critic, then, is to multiply the meanings of the text by unveiling its polysemy, by offering readers multiple angles of vision on it. It mirrors processes of diasporic dissemination.

The main purpose of *The Signifying Monkey*, that of establishing the claims of 'a' tradition of African-American literature, based on the systematic use of a single critical concept – be it a figure of indeterminacy – runs counter to such pluralistic conceptions of literary activity. The fact that the 'authenticity' of the concept is grounded in its African origins betrays a vision of diaspora that fails to transcend the ideological frame of the nation. Gates's theory appears as a delicate balancing act between a form of cultural nationalism, sifted through a constructive criticism of the Black Aesthetics of the 1960s, and a postmodern denial of the essentialist assumptions of nationalism. The specificity of *The Signifying Monkey* is that it identifies the core of the tradition, not in some specific essence out of which there 'spontaneously' springs 'authentic' expression, but in a process of criticism and rewriting, a "revelation of mind."[42]

Centering tradition on Signifyin(g), a non-essentialist rhetoric of revision and commentary, makes it a continuous creation: "an everyday plebiscite," to use Renan's definition of a nation.[43] Belonging to the tradition is a function of artistic choice, the choice of entering the dialogue by troping other works belonging to it. It is thus a deeply self-reflexive tradition, shorn of the

---

[40] Adell, *Double Consciousness / Double Bind*, 230.

[41] Gates, *The Signifying Monkey*, 38.

[42] Hyde, *Trickster Makes This World*, 296.

[43] Ernest Renan, "Qu'est-ce qu'une nation?," in Renan, *Œuvres complètes*, vol. 1 (Paris: Calmann–Lévy, 1947): 904.

belief in a reified "so-called Black Experience."[44] This conception actually echoes T.S. Eliot's "Tradition and the Individual Talent,"[45] and seems to betray what Sandra Adell calls a "nostalgia for tradition":

> For to summon a tradition, for example, by reconstructing it, is to search for an authority, that of the tradition itself. Such an attempt, even as it pits two or more traditions against each other, or even as it attempts to fuse traditions, is inherently conservative.[46]

If we do take seriously the privileging of literary "consent" over "descent,"[47] then the notion of 'a' tradition is a contradiction in terms: there must be many traditions of African-American literature, and a single work may belong to several, not all of which are 'black'.

This is what Gates recognizes: "While most, if not all black writers seek to place their works in the 'larger' tradition of their genre, many also revise tropes from substantive antecedent texts in the Afro-American canon."[48] The invention of any tradition is based on principles of inclusion and exclusion. The most notable misfit in the canon-formation at hand is Richard Wright, who, in *Monkey*, is much more Signified-upon than Signifyin(g). Interestingly enough, Houston Baker, Jr. gives Wright a prominent position in his own blues matrix, even deeming him a trickster along Gatesian lines.[49] The agenda in Gates's and Baker's enterprises is to propose a canon of 'great' texts supported by theoretical concepts – Signifyin(g) or the blues matrix – which are elaborated from these very texts. These concepts, being evolved from the vernacular, are seen as more 'authentic' than others; so, implicitly, is the fiction deriving from them. While this represents a defense of African-American literature against those academics who deny its value, it runs the risk of reproducing, within this new field, the practices that mainstream canonists have used to keep black writers out.

Once the Monkey's diasporic genealogy is established, Gates more or less confines the African-American literary dialogue to the USA. He neglects an aspect that Paul Gilroy sets in relief: the writer as traveler, as

---

[44] Gates, *The Signifying Monkey*, 111.

[45] T.S. Eliot, "Tradition and the Individual Talent" (1919), in Eliot, *Selected Essays* (London: Faber & Faber, 1972).

[46] Adell, *Double Consciousness / Double Bind*, 137.

[47] Werner Sollors, *Beyond Ethnicity: Consent and Descent in American Culture* (New York: Oxford UP, 1986).

[48] Gates, *The Signifying Monkey*, 122.

[49] Baker, *Blues, Ideology and Afro-American Literature*, 160–68.

part of a transnational network of communication between Africa, the Caribbean, Europe and America. Thus, Chapters 4 and 5 of *The Black Atlantic* examine the complex dialectic of "roots" and "routes" (190) in the formation of W.E.B. Du Bois' and Richard Wright's global comprehension of modernity. Gates, using Signifyin(g) and the trickster figure of indeterminacy as a prop for his own version of the tradition, is able to make discontinuity the very engine of continuity. The in-built *différance* of black literature – in its relations with the mainstream and with its ethnic ante-cedents – simultaneously opens up avenues for dialogue and provides (per-haps unwittingly) a rationale for a normative canonization of some works and approaches at the expense of others.

In order to become usable in literary theory (and despite the wealth of contextual information provided by Gates), the Monkey and, more speci-fically, Esu are drawn away from the whole cultures to which they belong and limited to their linguistic attributes. But these are the formal aspects that lend similarity to trickster figures all over the world, so as to constitute a kind of 'archetype'. If the potential universality of the modes of figuration and of the trickster himself tend to invalidate any claims to ethnic specifi-city, the 'rooting' function of the Monkey appears once more to be a myth-ology, in the Barthesian sense.

The Signifying Monkey is a myth of African-American literature and criticism, grafted onto a myth of the diaspora. It partakes of an identity-building process, in seeming contradiction to the Western critical tools it uses, such as postmodernism or deconstruction. Similarly, its genealogical approach to diaspora seems to play down the differences between the vari-ous cultural elements of the dispersal. Does Gates's recourse to the trickster therefore amount to what Brent Edwards calls, in this volume, a merely "prosthetic" synthesis?

> But such props, of rhetoric, strategy, or organization, are always articulations of unity or globalism, ones that can be 'mobilized' for a variety of purposes but can never be definitive: they are always prosthetic. In this sense, *décalage* is proper to the structure of a diasporic 'racial' formation, and its return in the form of *disarticulation* – the points of misunderstanding, bad faith, unhappy translation – must be considered a necessary haunting.[50]

Yet these *décalages* are precisely what trickster myths deal with in the first place, whether they occur at the juncture of the divine and human worlds, or between the fooler and the fooled in the sublunar universe. So the trickster

---

[50] Edwards, 35 above.

could be a very apt symbol to represent the diasporic imagination, one that transcends the national limitations of Gates's work through the power of his own 'disseminating' insights.

As it is used in contemporary ethnic American literature and criticism, the figure of the trickster is an essential element in the reappropriation of postmodernism, since he is both a culture-hero and an arch-transgressor, characterized by the existential and linguistic mediation of ambiguity. One might explain his present fortune by the fact that he represents the return of the repressed in European and Euro-American culture – the body and desire – as well as principles of contradiction and ambiguity running contrary to the binary logic of Western rationalism. Given his role as a mediator, he can also function as a support for identification in minority or hybrid cultures, embodying a split yet assertive subject in the face of hardship or oppression. It also corresponds to recent notions of subjective and communal identities as texts. The particular richness of the Signifyin(g) Monkey seems to us to reside in the recognition of the presence of the Other at the very core of identity. In this sense, it is a fit symbol for the contemporary world: it may help define the African diaspora as 'disseminated identity', in the deconstructionist sense of the word. Gilroy's advocacy of a "non-traditional tradition," or a use of the word restricted to "the nameless, evasive, minimal qualities that make these diaspora conversations possible,"[51] sometimes comes quite close to Esu–Monkey's main attributes. "The ethics of antiphony," "the chronotope of the crossroads," and "a stereoscopic sensibility, adequate to build a dialogue with the West: both within and without"[52] – all correspond to Gates's description. Signifying on the national limitations of the myth, one might find in Esu and the Monkey a syncretic figure of the diaspora, one that illustrates both its baffling mixture of unity and diversity, 'roots' and "routes," faithfulness and transgressions. As the anthropologist Claude Lévi–Strauss phrased it, "myth [is] an attempt to solve contradictions – a losing battle if the contradictions are real."[53]

---

[51] Gilroy, *The Black Atlantic*, 198–99.

[52] *The Black Atlantic*, 200, 199, 196 respectively.

[53] Lévi–Strauss, *Structural Anthropology*, 264.

WORKS CITED

Adell, Sandra. *Double Consciousness / Double Bind: Theoretical Issues in Twentieth-Century Black Literature* (Urbana: U of Illinois P, 1994).

Anderson, Benedict. *Imagined Communities: Reflections on the Origins and Spread of Nationalism* (London: Verso, 1991).

Baker, Houston A., Jr. *Blues, Ideology and Afro-American Literature: A Vernacular Theory* (Chicago: U of Chicago P, 1984).

Barth, Fredrik. "Introduction" to *Ethnic Groups and Boundaries: The Social Organization of Culture Difference* (London: Allen & Unwin, 1969): 9–38.

Barthes, Roland. *Mythologies*, tr. Annette Lavers (New York: Hill & Wang, 1972).

Derrida, Jacques. *Dissémination*, tr. Barbara Johnson (Chicago: U of Chicago P, 1981).

Devereux, George. "L'Acculturation antagoniste," in Devereux, *Ethnopsychanalyse complémentariste*, tr. Tina Jolas & Henri Gobard (*Ethnopsychoanalysis: Psychoanalysis and Anthropology as Complementary Frames of Reference*, Berkeley: U of California P, 1978; tr. Paris: Flammarion, 1985): 253–90.

Durand, Gilbert. *Figures mythiques et visage de l'œuvre: De la mythocritique à la mythanalyse* (1979; Paris: Dunod, 1992).

Eliade, Mircea. *Myth and Reality*, tr. Willard Trask (New York: Harper & Row, 1963).

Eliot, T.S. "Tradition and the Individual Talent" (1919), in Eliot, *Selected Essays* (London: Faber & Faber, 1972): 13–22.

Gates, Henry Louis, Jr. "Criticism in the Jungle," in *Black Literature and Literary Theory*, ed. Gates (New York: Methuen, 1984): 1–24.

——. *Figures in Black: Words, Signs, and the "Racial" Self* (New York: Oxford UP, 1987).

——. *The Signifying Monkey: A Theory of African-American Literary Criticism* (New York: Oxford UP, 1988).

Gilroy, Paul. *The Black Atlantic: Modernity and Double Consciousness* (Cambridge MA: Harvard UP, 1993).

Hutchinson, George. *The Harlem Renaissance in Black and White* (Cambridge MA: Belknap P/Harvard UP, 1995).

Hyde, Lewis. *Trickster Makes This World: Mischief, Myth, and Art* (New York: Farrar, Straus & Giroux, 1998).

Kristeva, Julia. "Le sujet en procès: le langage poétique," in *L'Identité*, ed. Claude Lévi–Strauss (Paris: Presses Universitaires de France, 1977): 223–56.

Lévi–Strauss, Claude. *Structural Anthropology*, tr. Claire Jacobson & Brooke G. Schoepfe (*Anthropologie structurale*, Paris: Plon, 1958; tr. New York: Basic Books, 1963).

Pelton, Robert. *The Trickster in West Africa: A Study of Mythic Irony and Sacred Delight* (Berkeley: U of California P, 1980).

Radin, Paul. *The Trickster: A Study in American Indian Mythology* (New York: Bell, 1956).

Renan, Ernest. "Qu'est-ce qu'une nation?," in Renan, *Œuvres complètes*, vol. 1 (Paris: Calmann–Lévy, 1947).

Sollors, Werner. *Beyond Ethnicity: Consent and Descent in American Culture* (New York: Oxford UP, 1986).

Todorov, Tzvetan. *Critique de la critique* (Paris: Seuil, 1986).

❖   DIASPORIC HISTORICAL SITES

Cultural Migrations
A Time-&-Space Outline of Black Atlantic Evangelical Protestantism

SYLVIA FREY

I NTERNATIONAL REVIVALISM, which swept the Atlantic world in the eighteenth and early nineteenth centuries, is one of the turning events in the history of the modern world. The outpouring of literature on American religious history since the 1930s has produced many excellent books about the international evangelical Protestant movement that transformed the religious landscape of the Atlantic world. In recent years, the focus has been on the breadth and diversity of evangelicalism and on the transatlantic character of the First Great Awakening, with special emphasis on the close relationship between the British and American evangelical communities. In all but a few of those works, the story of black evangelicals, when they figure at all, consistently takes second place to that of white evangelicals.

This essay seeks to question the accepted notion that the Atlantic revival was launched by white pioneers and remained their exclusive property, and that African-American revivalists failed to touch the mainstream of evangelical life. Instead, it will argue that while black evangelical Protestantism had British antecedents, owing its earliest beginnings to Wesley and Whitefield, it quickly metamorphized into a uniquely African-American strain of religion that was symbiotically linked to the larger American evangelical culture but radically separate from it; that the theology of the first generation of African-American evangelicals was the theology of the radical First Awakening with its emphasis on universality and the experiential nature of Christianity and revivalistic conversion-centered forms of worship and preaching; and finally, that the story of African-American revivalism left an indelible mark on American religion and had an international significance out of all relation to its numerical size.

In his seminal work on Rebekka Freundlich, the earliest known black missionary in the Americas, Jon Sensbach has suggested that black Protestantism has been transatlantic from the start. Sensbach finds in Rebekka's travels as a missionary to Europe and Africa and to the Dutch island of St. Thomas in the Caribbean in the 1740s the beginnings of an international movement that would have repercussions throughout the Atlantic world.[1] Black evangelical Protestantism was broadly related to English evangelicalism, but it had its own local and independent sources of origin. Within the anglophone world were particular driving centers, areas of special activity that became the heartlands of black revivalism. This was especially true on the North American mainland, where many early evangelical preachers undertook conversion in rural isolation. The spread of revivalism in Georgia is a case in point. Sometime in the 1760s, two men, one black and the other white, traveled together from Virginia to Georgia. Their arrival in Georgia marked the beginning of something important, the transformation of the religious landscape of the American South. The black man, George Liele, was born into slavery in Virginia, and was taken to Georgia by his master, Henry Sharp. After a lengthy conversion experience, Liele became a New Light Baptist and was baptized by Matthew Moore sometime in 1773. Soon afterward, he "began to discover his love to other negroes, on the same plantation with himself, by reading hymns among them, encouraging them to sing, and sometimes by explaining the most striking parts of them."[2] Following an invitation to "exercise his gift" at a Baptist quarterly meeting, Liele was licensed as a probationer, and in 1775 he was ordained. Three months later he constituted the First African Baptist Church of Savannah, composed largely of bond-people from the different plantations around Savannah and up and down the Savannah River.[3]

---

[1] Jon Sensbach, "Rebekka's Revival: Afro-Christian Women and the Origins of the Black Protestant Movement," an unpublished paper presented at the conference "Diasporas africaines dans l'ancien et le nouveau monde: Conscience et imaginaire," Paris, 26–28 October 2000.

[2] "Letters Showing the Rise and Progress of the Early Negro Churches of Georgia and the West Indies," *Journal of Negro History* 1 (1916): 70.

[3] Sylvia R. Frey & Betty Wood, *Come Shouting to Zion: African American Protestantism in the American South and British Caribbean to 1830* (Chapel Hill: University of North Carolina P, 1998): 116.

Liele's itinerant ministry carried broad significance. First, because the revivals he promoted established the Baptist faith in Georgia and among part of the enslaved population of South Carolina. Secondly, because from the ranks of his converts came the future leaders of the Black Atlantic Protestant movement. Thirdly, because the New Light legacy Liele passed on to his disciples had a significant impact on the religious cultures of Jamaica, Canada, and West Africa. Fully intent on inventing a new Christianity, black evangelicals, men and women, unobtrusively claimed membership in an expanding Atlantic religious universe, which in many ways and in many places survives today as a monument to a black vision of Christian society.

Transatlantic evangelicalism can be divided into two clearly defined segments of roughly equal length, separated by a decade of turbulence created by the American Revolution. The arc of George Liele's life neatly encapsulates these developments. Liele's revival marks the beginning of the first phase of the continental black Protestant evangelical movement that lasted until the outbreak of the American Revolution, when revivalism subsided temporarily. Markedly radical, ecumenical, biracial, intercolonial, even international in scope, revivalism everywhere challenged the gendered and racial divisions of society and the traditional world of deference and hierarchy. Although women held no formal leadership roles, they enjoyed unprecedented freedom to speak at religious meetings, and exercised religious authority through their charismatic leadership.

The first generation of black evangelical leaders were converted at the height of the First Awakening, when the democratic spirit of religious tolerance and religious experimentation were at a high-water mark. As a consequence, they absorbed elements of New Light theology, Arminian Methodism, and the New Divinity. As their theology coalesced, they became itinerant throughout the hurting world of the enslaved population, coaxing revivals into existence throughout the American South.[4]

The most dramatic episode in the story of black evangelical Protestantism, an event which had repercussions throughout the Atlantic world, was the American Revolution. The Revolution altered the course of religious history not primarily because it was immensely disruptive for the evangelical movement but because it contributed directly to unprecedented evangelical expansion in the immediate wake of the Revolutionary War. If a graph of religious frontiers could be constructed, the 1780s and 1790s would probably represent a peak of high intensity. It was during this period that

---

[4] For details, see Frey & Wood, *Come Shouting to Zion*, 80–117.

black Protestantism achieved an international presence. What made these decades especially important was the conjunction of two transatlantic currents, both of which molded the context in which African Protestantism developed and shaped the channels through which it mediated its influence around the North Atlantic. For a quarter of a century the movement of peoples and of cultures had been a gradual process. The ending of the American Revolutionary War and the emergence of popular Protestantism in North America, the British Isles, and the Caribbean unleashed an almost frantic movement of people. No single migration, it consisted of two overlapping yet distinctly different processes in motion throughout the Revolutionary era: the spread of popular Protestantism and the postwar folk migrations. Both linked mainland America to Europe, Africa, and the Caribbean in a highly dynamic relationship.[5]

Although the continuous circulation of people throughout the Atlantic world and the relocation of religious groups had been commonplace since the seventeenth century, two things were unique about the outward migration: it involved the first sizeable exodus of African Americans; and it precipitated the spread of black forms of Protestantism to various locations around the North Atlantic. Thousands of African-American loyalists left the continent via the eastern seaboard during the Revolutionary War and in the organized British evacuation at war's end. Religion shaped the leadership, ethos and, to some extent, direction of the black migration. Although data are scarce and faulty, it can be said that black émigrés shared an essential characteristic: they were often part of older, all-black evangelical congregations and were frequently led by black preachers. Members of the founding generation of African-American evangelical Protestantism, they established a century-long tradition linking emigration and evangelization.

Jon Sensbach has reminded us that the Atlantic Ocean can be crossed in either direction. During the Revolutionary era and afterward, evangelicalism traveled in both directions. Generally speaking, however, the more radical forms of the movement crossed the Atlantic in a west-to-east direction. Beginning in the 1760s, with the emigration of Henry Alline's New Light Congregationalists from Rhode Island to Nova Scotia and continuing through the great black folk movement of the post-Revolutionary era, evangelicalism began to expand beyond its local roots, transplanting revival

---

[5] For details of the postwar evacuation, see Sylvia R. Frey, *Water from the Rock. Black Resistance in a Revolutionary Age* (Princeton NJ: Princeton UP, 1981): 172–205.

fervor and the radical and democratic ideals of the First Great Awakening into more open spiritual environments of the Atlantic Basin.[6]

Among those who set out from the new republic in 1782 were the afore-mentioned George Liele, and David George, credited with the formation of the first permanent black Baptist church in the USA, Nova Scotia, and West Africa. Because their conversions and introduction to evangelical religion took place at the height of the Great Awakening, they carried with them a tradition of revivalistic enthusiasm and a highly democratic ethos, transmit-ting it to other parts of the globe. In the new spiritual spaces, their contact with other, different strands of evangelicalism generated distinctive expres-sions of faith. In some places, the presence of black Protestants both trans-formed other brands of evangelical Christianity and determined the larger Christian agenda.

George Liele's departure for Jamaica forms an important link between the radical First Great Awakening and religious movements on the conti-nent and in the Caribbean basin. Evacuated from Savannah as an indentured servant of a British officer, he settled in Kingston and, after working out his contract, acquired a little plot of land and a trading cart. Before Liele began preaching in a small private home to a congregation consisting of "four brethren from America besides myself," there was no religious instruction of slaves. In fact, for the first century of British possession there were only sixteen churches to serve nearly a half million inhabitants.[7] Exploiting his mobility as a waggoner, Liele began itinerating in neighboring parishes. Within two years he had gathered "a good smart congregation," which formed the basis for the first Baptist church in Kingston, Jamaica and the launching of the Native Baptist movement.[8] From that fragile beginning, Liele and a handful of Black Christians from North America laid the foun-dation of the Baptist mission to Jamaica and influenced Afro-Jamaican religious developments for the next half-century.

The Baptism Liele originally carried to Jamaica was American in many respects. As a popular preacher of the continental revivals, Liele resorted to the itinerancy developed by Wesley and Whitefield. In addition to the American freedmen George Lewis and George Gibb, and two free people

---

[6] George A. Rawlyk, *Ravished by the Spirit: Religious Revivals, Baptists, and Henry Alline* (Kingston, Ontario: McGill–Queen's UP, 1984).

[7] Peter Duncan, *Report of the Speeches of the Rev. Peter Duncan, Wesleyan Missionary, and the Rev. W. Knibb, Baptist Missionary, at a Public Meeting in 1832* (London, 1832): 5.

[8] "Letters Showing the Rise and Progress of the Early Negro Churches of Georgia and the West Indies," *Journal of Negro History* 1 (1916): 71.

from New York, Moses Baker, a barber, and his wife, a milliner, Liele raised up trainees like Thomas Swiegle and Richard Peart from among black Jamaicans. Likewise largely itinerant, they radiated out to the north and east from Liele's original Kingston base, through the parishes of St. Mary and St. Thomas-in-the Vale, and into the western parishes of Vere, Manchester, St. James and St. Elizabeth.[9]

Unlike the American version of evangelism, which was already tacitly abandoning the emotionalism and egalitarianism of the First Awakening in favor of a more orderly and harmonious society and relative decorum in religious worship, the ethos of the Jamaican variant remained highly democratic and egalitarian. Liele himself had much more in common with the radical Separate Baptists and the early Moravians than with the second generation of North American evangelists. An "earnest and good man," who "taught the essentials of religion and maintained strict discipline in the church," Liele also held "some peculiar views, such as the washing of feet and anointing the sick." A rite of cleansing and humility, washing of feet was abandoned by mainland radical religious groups because the physical intimacy of touching not only confirmed the spiritual bond between believers but symbolically erased the carefully drawn boundaries between race, class and gender.[10]

But Liele and his disciples were not merely bearers or reproducers of culture but cultural creators and innovators, often fusing indigenous and transatlantic dynamics. The Native Baptist movement is a case in point. Predominantly Jamaican, it was led by several of Liele's converts and maintained close ties with Liele's more orthodox Christians. More radical, more egalitarian, more populist than the Liele-led Baptists, the eclectic new sect practiced a more africanized form of Christianity that embraced healing, visions and dreams as evidence of conversion. A well-organized movement, the Native Baptists were controlled through a ticket and leader system, which led to the establishment of class-houses in almost every African village in Jamaica. Class leaders, known in Jamaica as daddies and mammies, conducted prayer meetings, prepared candidates for baptism, and monitored the moral conduct of members. In spite of the formal leadership

---

[9] See Mary Turner, *Slaves and Missionaries: The Disintegration of Jamaican Slave Society, 1784–1834* (1982; Kingston, Jamaica: UP of the West Indies, 1998).

[10] William J. Gardner, *A History of Jamaica from its Discovery by Christopher Columbus to the Present Time* (London, 1873): 344. The Moravians stopped washing the feet of black brethren in 1809; see Jon Sensbach, *A Separate Canaan: The Making of an Afro-Moravian World in North Carolina, 1763–1840* (Chapel Hill: U of North Carolina P, 1998): 201.

roles of male deacons and ministers, in the Jamaican variant of evangelicalism women like Mammy Faith emerged as powerful religious leaders.
If European reports of Faith's power can be trusted, "this wretched woman
was only one of many scattered over the island" to whom "deluded negroes
like herself, prayed for pardon, and who asserted that she had power to
forgive sin."[11] During the forty years before the British missions gained a
foothold in Jamaica, members of the Native Baptist groups were regularly
reinforced by black emigrants from the southern USA. By the nineteenth
century they would increasingly define their spiritual mission in political
terms.[12]

   One of the most powerful vehicles of black Atlantic Protestantism was
David George. Through his aggressive proselytizing and obsession with
religious ecstasy and dramatic conversion, George, along with the blind
black Methodist preacher Moses Wilkinson and the Huntingdonian John
Marrant, stamped a different version of radical evangelicalism on the religious culture of the Canadian Maritimes and West Africa. Born of African
parents in Essex County, Virginia, David George embarked on his remarkable spiritual trajectory in South Carolina, where he was converted under
the preaching of Liele. In 1773, George and eight others formed the Savannah River Silver Bluff Baptist church, the first black Baptist church in
North America.[13] Under the leadership of other Liele converts, Jesse Peter
or Galphin and Andrew Bryan, the Savannah River churches came to dominate numerically the Savannah River Association.

   In 1782, George and some five hundred Southern New Light Baptists,
Methodists, and Huntingdonians joined the loyalist evacuation to Nova
Scotia, where they encountered several marked variants of radical evangelicalism that were shaping the evangelical ethos of the region: Henry
Alline's New Light congregation, originally part of a large Yankee migration from New England; and the somewhat more orthodox Methodist followers of William Black, a twenty-three-year-old evangelist from a York-
shire immigrant family. Despite theological differences, each of the different groups favored enthusiastic forms of worship, which helped fuel a series
of biracial revivals and brought into existence Maritime Canada's First
Great Awakening.

---

[11] The story of Faith is from Gardner, *History of Jamaica*, 358.

[12] James W. St. G. Walker, *The Black Loyalists: The Search for a Promised Land
in Nova Scotia and Sierra Leone, 1783–1870* (Dalhousie African Studies Series;
London: Longman & Dalhousie UP, 1976): 68–69, 73–74; Ellen Gibson Wilson, *The
Loyal Blacks* (New York: Capricorn, 1976): 124–29, 129–31.

[13] Rawlyk, *Ravished by the Spirit*, 3.

To be sure, the preconditions for the Awakening were present, and it may well have occurred without foreign assistance, but George shared with many of the North American black loyalists a concern for religious and spiritual innovation. Although the Allinites saw no need for baptism, George, who had himself been baptized in a Georgia millstream, adhered to the Southern New Light belief in public baptism by total immersion. The first Baptist preacher to immerse in the St John River in 1784, George introduced this practice into the Yankee regions of Nova Scotia – something that, for that time and place, was radically innovative.[14] The "rage for dipping" and the "dangerous excesses of revivalism" that swept certain parts of New Brunswick and Nova Scotia during the 1790s ignited white hostility, and actual rioting broke out after George baptized a white couple. Baptism of believers remained central to Maritime evangelicalism.[15]

Driven by the burden of unremitting racial oppression, David led over 1,110 black Nova Scotians to Sierra Leone in West Africa. The blending of Alline's "socialistic evangelism" with American Southern New Light popular evangelicalism, the essence of which was a compelling belief in the primacy of religious feelings over religious instruction and of public baptism by immersion over the conversion experience, had profound implications for black Protestantism in both Nova Scotia and West Africa.[16] It was this unique blend of American Southern and Nova Scotian New Light evangelism that George, Marrant, Wilkinson and their followers brought to Sierra Leone in 1792, as part of the largest migration of free blacks in history.

It would be a mistake to suppose that African-American influence was limited to a few well-known figures. For every George Liele, Moses Wilkinson or David George, there were scores of men and women whose voices complemented those of the better-known leaders of black evange-

---

[14] George Rawlyk, *The Canada Fire: Radical Evangelicalism in British North America 1775–1812* (Montreal: McGill–Queen's UP, 1994): 163–80; *Fire on the Water: An Anthology of Black Nova Scotian Writings*, ed. George Elliott Clarke (Porters Lake, Nova Scotia: Pottersfield Press, 1991): 36.

[15] See especially Rawlyk, *The Canada Fire* 171; Clarke, ed. *Fire on the Water*, 140–56.

[16] Clarke, ed. *Fire on the Water*, 14; *Black Itinerants of the Gospel: The Narratives of John Lea and George White*, ed. Graham R. Hodges (Madison: U of Wisconsin P, 1993): 4; Mark A. Noll, "Revolution and the Rise of Evangelistic Social Influences in North Atlantic Societies," in *Evangelicalism: Comparative Studies of Popular Protestantism in North America, the British Isles and Beyond, 1700–1990*, ed. Mark A. Noll, David W. Bebbington & George A. Rawlyk (New York: Oxford UP, 1994): 119.

licalism. Joseph Paul, one of Whitefield's converts, was the first Methodist in the Bahamas. Paul arrived in Abaco with American loyalists in 1783 and moved to Nassau sometime between 1786 and 1794. He started preaching in a small wooden shed and soon thereafter built the first Methodist church in the Bahama Islands and established the earliest private school for blacks in Nassau. Brother Amos, probably a member of Liele's African Baptist church in Savannah, was the first black Baptist revivalist in the Bahamas. Amos built the first Baptist church in Providence, which by 1791 had a membership of three hundred.[17] A runaway Baptist preacher, Sambo Scriven, became pastor of the Society of Anabaptists in Nassau after gaining his freedom in 1790. In 1801, Scriven's congregation purchased the land on which the present Bethel Baptist church stands. Today the Baptist Church is the largest denomination in the Bahamas.[18] According to Thomas Coke, Methodism was implanted on the Dutch island of St. Eustatius by two former American slaves, Harry and "a black woman" brought from the continent "to prepare our way," as Coke put it. Before Coke left St Eustatius he formed six classes, three of whom he gave to the care of Harry, one "to our North-American Sister," and one to Samuel.[19] Successive waves of black émigrés not only directly from the USA but also via the Bahamas, Santo Domingo, and, from 1802 onward, from the new black republic of Haiti, increased the black Protestant network and contributed to the cross-fertilization of African-American Protestantism.

How shall we evaluate the significance of African-American Christians in the transatlantic evangelical movement? Obviously the movement was not based in or dependent on African-American participation. Just as obviously, African Americans played a key role in the transformation of the religious landscape of the Atlantic world. Internationalists at heart, the founding generation of black Christians left as their legacy the re-creation of black forms of Protestantism and a black Christian value structure in Jamaica, Nova Scotia, Sierra Leone, Liberia and a score and more West Indian islands. Although many African-American converts had embraced much of white religion and culture, they carried with them a distinctive brand of Protestantism. Although they retained certain assumptions and religious conventions borrowed from white evangelical Protestantism, their

---

[17] "Letters Showing the Rise & Progress of the Early Negro Churches," 73.

[18] Gail Saunders, *Bahamian Loyalists and Their Slaves* (London & Kingston, Jamaica: Macmillan Caribbean, 1983): 63.

[19] Thomas Coke, *A Farther Account of the Late Missionaries to the West Indies in a Letter from the Reverend Dr. Coke to the Reverend John Wesley* (London, 1789): 202–203.

theology was the radical variety of the First Great Awakening with its emphasis on universality and the experiential nature of Christianity, and on revivalistic conversion-centered forms of worship and preaching.[20]

Themselves the products of popular revival culture, black evangelicals held on to the chief components of the eighteenth-century international awakening: a passionate revival preaching style, which they in large measure had helped shape; itinerancy; and extraordinary conversions. Infusing evangelical linguistic forms with inherited African speech and performance patterns that emphasized musicality, spontaneity and emotion, black evangelicals cultivated new forms of oratory.[21] Unpremeditated and unrehearsed, their blending of prose sermon and music thrilled audiences. When Harry preached on St. Eustatius, his "hearers fell down as if they were dead."[22] In contrast to the "whining" and "barking" style still used by some Methodist itinerants, black preaching styles were often described as "sonorous" or "charming." Little if any attention has been paid to the influence of black rhetorical styles on white preaching, although it is clear that the success that such black preachers as the illiterate Harry Hosier had in attracting crowds and winning converts was viewed with much admiration and not a little envy by white evangelicals.[23]

Something less than a true missionary movement, the founding generation were the precursors of the nineteenth-century movement, anticipating by almost a decade the earliest of the new European missionary societies. Organized missionary societies to enslaved peoples evolved almost directly from their example. The great English itinerant Thomas Coke's life work began "only after he had actually seen on a chance visit to Antigua" the flourishing Methodist society of slaves founded by Mary Alley and Sophia Campbell.[24] Moses Wilkinson had already gathered a congregation of two hundred black Methodists in Birchtown by the time the first Wesleyan missionary arrived in 1784. The first British Baptists did not arrive in Jamaica until 1814, when at Liele's request the Baptist Missionary Society

---

[20] Turner, *Slaves and Missionaries*, 68.

[21] Sandra M. Gustafson, *Eloquence Is Power. Oratory & Performance in Early America* (Chapel Hill: U of North Carolina P, 2000): 101, 110, 159.

[22] Thomas Coke, *A Continuation of Dr. Thomas Coke's Journal in Two Letters to the Reverend John Wesley* (London, 1787): 11.

[23] For more on the black preaching style, see Sylvia R. Frey, "'The Year of Jubilee Is Come': Black Christianity in the Plantation South in Post-Revolutionary America," in *Religion in a Revolutionary Age*, ed. Ronald Hoffman & Peter J. Albert (Charlottesville: UP of Virginia, 1994): 115.

[24] Turner, *Slaves and Missionaries*, 7.

dispatched missionaries to Jamaica to assist him.[25] The leader system developed by Liele's Native Baptists was adopted by the British missionaries because it was the only way to spread the Christian message. Eventually, their example inspired the creation of the mission to Liberia. Liele's contact with Dr John Ryland made the Bristol Baptist Academy a regular recruiting ground for missionaries to Jamaica, and no fewer than eight missionaries to Jamaica trained there.[26] Although in the nineteenth century white Protestants dominated missionary work in East and North Africa, in many parts of Africa it was African Americans who were the first American missionaries.[27] With the development of a coherent philosophy of mission in the nineteenth century, black missionary activity was no longer a local or even a regional event but a constituent element of an international and pan-Protestant phenomenon.[28] As a direct result of Liele's efforts, over forty Jamaican Baptist missionaries were dispatched to Africa in 1842.[29]

Although the founding evangelicals existed on the periphery of the print revolution that swept the Atlantic in the late eighteenth century, they thought and acted within an Atlantic world. Extant correspondence reveals that this remarkable collection of black evangelists knew of each other's labors and believed themselves to be part of a worldwide evangelical movement. George Liele regularly communicated with Andrew Bryan in Savannah, David George in Nova Scotia, Amos in Providence in Nassau, thereby contributing to the shaping of a New World African culture. As early as 1806 Baker, Liele, and Swiegle appear to have begun a correspondence with John Rippon, editor of the *Baptist Annual Register*, and John Ryland, principal of the Bristol Baptist Academy.[30] Through the medium of auto-biography and memoirs, literate black evangelists like John Marrant, David George, and Boston King managed to penetrate the circulating web of literature that defined the Great Awakening of the eighteenth century as a truly international event. John Marrant's *Narrative of the Lord's wonderful dealings with John Marrant* was published in 1785; David George's dictated

---

[25] Turner, *Slaves and Missionaries*, 17, 69.

[26] Turner, *Slaves and Missionaries*, 68.

[27] Jacobs, Sylvia M., ed. *Black Americans and the Missionary Movement in Africa* (Westport CT: Greenwood, 1982): 17.

[28] John Walsh, "Methodism and the Origins of English-Speaking Evangelicalism"; Susan O'Brien, "Eighteenth-Century Publication Networks in the First Years of Transatlantic Evangelicalism," in Noll et al. ed. *Evangelicalism*, 20, 41.

[29] Wallace Brown, "The American Loyalists in Jamaica," *Journal of Caribbean History* 26.2 (1992): 139.

[30] Turner, *Slaves and Missionaries*, 69; Gardner, *History of Jamaica*, 351.

memoirs, "An Account of the Life of Mr. David George, from Sierra Leone in Africa," appeared in 1795; and the Rev. Boston King's autobiography, *Memoirs of the Life of Boston King* was published in 1798.[31]

In the process, Afro-Christians forged a new black Christian identity, separate from the root that had brought it into being. Largely independent of any white hierarchy, the separate forms their churches took intentionally or otherwise created an expanding sense of corporate identity and a "genuine sense of separateness," based not on 'nation' or estate but on race. John Thornton has pointed out that through most of the eighteenth century Africans in the Americas lived "at the intersection of the two groups to which they belonged – the estate community, where they lived and worked, and the nation, where they might find cultural and linguistic familiarity." The network of linguistic unity that was the basis of the nation expressed itself in a variety of forms including runaways paired by language, plots, and revolts such as the Stono Rebellion of 1739 in South Carolina (Kongo-lese), or the Jamaica Revolt of 1760 (Coromantee).[32]

Gradually, over the course of the eighteenth century, the biological family and the evangelical church emerged as alternatives to the nation, especially in North America, where the church community was more promi-nent than elsewhere.[33] The paucity of black church records makes it virtual-ly impossible to determine precisely when early separate churches began to take racially specific names, but the tendency to differentiate themselves racially is clearly there: in the exodus of entire congregations from Nova Scotia to West Africa; in the tendency of black evangelicals to categorize white churchmen by a subjective assessment of their physical appearance at the same time as they increasingly defined themselves by their place of birth as "Ethiopian Baptists," and later to designate their separate churches as "African," designations that connote both a claim to independent social personality and a sense of themselves as a select group of Christians. The emergence of a race-centered focus for community ultimately affected pat-terns of black resistance.[34]

---

[31] "Letters Showing the Rise & Progress of the Early Negro Churches," 73, 83, 86, 88; Clarke, ed. *Fire on the Water*, 12.

[32] John K. Thornton, *Africa and Africans in the Making of the Atlantic World 1400–1800* (1992; Cambridge & New York: Cambridge UP, 1998): 324, 326–27.

[33] Thornton, *Africa and Africans in the Making of the Atlantic World*, 330.

[34] Frey, "The Year of Jubilee Is Come" 93–95; James Sidbury, *Ploughshares into Swords. Race, Rebellion, and Identity in Gabriel's Virginia, 1730–1810* (Cambridge: Cambridge UP, 1997): 37, 65; "Letters Showing the Rise & Progress of the Early Negro Churches" 78, 84, 89, 90, 92; Walker, *Black Loyalists*, 76, 78–79.

Black evangelicalism, transported abroad from North America, carried radical social and political implications that transcended strictly religious renewal. The internationalization of black Protestantism as a distinctive entity and the remarkable circulation of revival news and preaching personalities throughout the Caribbean basin and the black Atlantic world combined to create a combustible theology that was simultaneously spiritual and political. For most early Afro-Atlantic Christians, the primary medium of expression for religious values was conversion, not revolution. Nevertheless, the part played by the churches in the political education of African Americans should not be underestimated. Churches were the starting point of serious friendships, centers where men and women from different plantations and locales could converse on matters of general interest, ethical as well as religious.

Apprenticeship in politics operated through a series of psychological steps. The initial impetus derived from the notion of spiritual equality, which enabled enslaved people to cross the threshold of liberty psychologically if not actually. Spiritual affinity and social fellowship quickly translated into the principal of solidarity. Concern for the spiritual freedom of Christian brethren was of a piece with zeal for mental emancipation. Black churches throughout the Atlantic world steadily expanded both their social and evangelistic work, which led them into varied social programs such as the establishment of schools and mutual aid societies. Mobilized by the power of a word – liberty – black Christians advanced their struggle for liberation by refusing to accept discriminatory seating in biracial churches. The development of separate black churches in North America in the 1780s was a declaration of spiritual freedom and cultural independence.[35]

Even a crude survey of major North Atlantic regions reveals the consistent connection between rebellion and the presence of separate black churches. Not coincidentally, the growth of radical black evangelism in Nova Scotia and West Africa, the spread of the Native Baptist movement in Jamaica, and the emergence of a deliberately separatist black church in the USA coincided with great Atlantic revolutions and the development of British antislavery. In the nineteenth century it was translated into actuality by black radical evangelists, in Gabriel's Rebellion in Virginia, in the Denmark Vesey rebellion and the Nat Turner Revolt in South Carolina, in the Baptist War in Jamaica.

---

[35] Frey, *Water from the Rock* 284–88; Mechal Sobel, *The World They Made Together: Black and White Values in Eighteenth-Century* (Princeton NJ: Princeton UP, 1987): 3; see also Sobel's *Trabelin' On: The Slave Journey to an Afro-Baptist Faith* (Westport CT: Greenwood, 1979).

African Americans like Gabriel Prosser of Virginia were increasingly enmeshed in the trade-driven communication and ideological webs of the Atlantic world and through the spread of revolutionary doctrines and inter-national evangelicalism. All of these elements, secular and religious, are present in Gabriel's attempt to overthrow slavery in Virginia in 1800, as James Sidbury's study of the development of black identities in Virginia clearly shows. But Sidbury assigns to Christianity "a central and active role in the insurrectionaries' view of the world, in their conception of resistance, and in the conspiracy," which occurred in the heavily black-Baptist James River region, where separate churches had first emerged. Frequent use of biblical references to depict slaves as God's chosen people and to foment rebellion, the use of swords as a symbolic assertion of the right to power, recruitment at religious meetings – all point to the conspirators' religious commitment.[36]

A similar case has been made for the importance of religion in the Vesey Rebellion. A minister class leader for biblical instruction in the A.M.E. church in the Charleston suburb of Hampstead, the free black carpenter Denmark Vesey, used the structure of the African church to organize and recruit soldiers for the rebellion. Sixteen of those hanged for their part in the 1822 revolt and four of Vesey's lieutenants were former members of the African church.[37] Douglas Egerton's important new study of the revolt argues that Vesey's "profound religious faith and the troubled history of the A.M.E. church laid the basis for his conspiracy." Indeed, Egerton observes, had the "African church not existed, neither, most likely, would his dream of a modern-day exodus." Like other black Atlantic leaders of nine-teenth-century revolts, Vesey drew his moral imperative for radical social change from the Bible. But whereas most black insurgents, including Gabriel and Toussaint L'Ouverture, fought for equality within political society, Vesey's struggle was to lead his followers out of the USA. His revolutionary theology was drawn from the Book of Exodus and the Jewish Bible's edicts on slavery.[38]

The connection between black revolutionary theology and resistance is also apparent in the Baptist War in Jamaica. Mary Turner's seminal study of

---

[36] Sidbury, *Ploughshares into Swords*, especially 36, 38–39, 77, 146. See also Douglas R. Egerton, *Gabriel's Rebellion: The Virginia Slave Conspiracies of 1800 and 1802* (Chapel Hill: U of North Carolina P, 1993), which emphasizes the influ-ence of republican ideology.

[37] David Robertson, *Denmark Vesey* (New York: Alfred A. Knopf, 1999): 47.

[38] Egerton, *He Shall Go Free: The Lives of Denmark Vesey* (Madison: U of Wisconsin P, 1999): 236; for Vesey's revolutionary theology, see ch. 3, 101–25.

mission work in Jamaica points out that the spread of mission churches marked a significant step in the political development of Jamaica. Christianity emerged as a political force first in the form of corporate action to protect customary rights to provision grounds and special food allotments. The growth of the missions led to the expansion of plantation organization beyond the boundaries of the estate and thereby contributed to the development of a network of religious connections. During the late 1820s, corporate action escalated to political action in response to the acute suffering caused by an increasingly exploitative labor regimen.

Significantly, the movement began in the western parishes, where Baptists and independent sects were most numerous. It was signalled by a work stoppage over just wages: "They said they would leave off work; and their argument was, that they had worked long enough to pay their masters for bringing them from Africa, and that they would not work any more unless they were paid."[39] By the time news of the emancipation campaign in Britain reached Jamaica, Christian converts had already "transposed the claim to religious freedom [...] to a claim to free status." Christian converts like General Ruler Sam Sharp, a Native Baptist, had discovered in the Bible a positive justification for rebellion, and used it to launch a revolution.[40]

None of these things brought down slavery, but all had an impact. A great deal has been written about the influence of white evangelical Christianity on African-American spiritual life. Much less is known about African-American influences on Europeans. Historians should look for the convergence between the actions of slaves and their relationship to social and political reforms. Continuing contact with the small body of earnest black Christians from various Protestant denominations influenced the conscience of white evangelical leaders, who in turn were the main inspiration both for abolition of the transatlantic slave trade (1807) and for emancipation (1833–34). John Wesley was gradually awakened to the plight of slaves and the horrors of slavery by his first-hand look at slavery in Georgia and his conversations with enslaved people. His *Thoughts Upon Slavery* (1774) and *Serious Address to the People of England with Regard to the State of the Nation* (1777) are important turning events in the history of antislavery. A similar case can be made for Whitefield and other early abolitionists. By initiating and directing a spiritual movement latent with moral imperatives, black Christians opened the springs of human conscience and

---

[39] Duncan, *Report of the Speeches of the Rev. Peter Duncan*, 5–6, 10.
[40] Turner, *Slaves and Missionaries*, 148–73.

understanding, which in turn inspired and nourished a change in attitudes and finally in structures.

WORKS CITED

Brown, Wallace. "The American Loyalists in Jamaica," *Journal of Caribbean History* 26.2 (1992): 121–46.

Clarke, George Elliott, ed. *Fire on the Water: An Anthology of Black Nova Scotian Writings* (Porters Lake, Nova Scotia: Pottersfield Press, 1991).

Coke, Thomas. *A Continuation of Dr. Thomas Coke's Journal in Two Letters to the Reverend John Wesley* (London, 1787).

——. *A Farther Account of the Late Missionaries to the West Indies in a Letter from the Reverend Dr. Coke to the Reverend John Wesley* (London, 1789).

Duncan, Peter. *Report of the Speeches of the Rev. Peter Duncan, Wesleyan Missionary, and the Rev. W. Knibb, Baptist Missionary, at a Public Meeting in 1832* (London, 1832).

Egerton, Douglas R. *Gabriel's Rebellion: The Virginia Slave Conspiracies of 1800 and 1802* (Chapel Hill: U of North Carolina P, 1993).

——. *He Shall Go Free: The Lives of Denmark Vesey* (Madison: U of Wisconsin P, 1999).

Frey, Sylvia R. *Water from the Rock: Black Resistance in a Revolutionary Age* (Princeton NJ: Princeton UP, 1981): 172–205.

——. "'The Year of Jubilee Is Come': Black Christianity in the Plantation South in Post-Revolutionary America," in *Religion in a Revolutionary Age*, ed. Ronald Hoffman & Peter J. Albert (Charlottesville: UP of Virginia, 1994): 87–124.

——, & Betty Wood. *Come Shouting to Zion: African American Protestantism in the American South and British Caribbean to 1830* (Chapel Hill & London: U of North Carolina P, 1998).

Gardner, William J. *A History of Jamaica from its Discovery by Christopher Columbus to the Present Time* (London, 1873).

Gustafson, Sandra M. *Eloquence Is Power: Oratory & Performance in Early America* (Chapel Hill: U of North Carolina P, 2000).

Hodges, Graham R., ed. *Black Itinerants of the Gospel: The Narratives of John Lea and George White* (Madison: U of Wisconsin P, 1993).

Hoffman, Ronald, & Peter J. Albert, ed. *Religion in a Revolutionary Age* (Charlottesville: UP of Virginia, 1994).

Jacobs, Sylvia M., ed. *Black Americans and the Missionary Movement in Africa* (Westport CT: Greenwood, 1982).

"Letters Showing the Rise and Progress of the Early Negro Churches of Georgia and the West Indies," *Journal of Negro History* 1 (1916): 69–92.

Noll, Mark A. "Revolution and the Rise of Evangelistic Social Influences in North Atlantic Societies," in *Evangelicalism: Comparative Studies of Popular Protestantism in North America, the British Isles and Beyond, 1700–1990*, ed. Mark A.

Noll, David W. Bebbington & George A. Rawlyk (New York: Oxford UP, 1994): 113–36.

O'Brien, Susan. "Eighteenth-Century Publication Networks in the First Years of Transatlantic Evangelicalism," in Noll et al., ed. *Evangelicalism*, 38–57.

Rawlyk, George A. *The Canada Fire: Radical Evangelicalism in British North America 1775–1812* (Montreal: McGill–Queen's UP, 1994).

——. *Ravished by the Spirit: Religious Revivals, Baptists, and Henry Alline* (Kingston, Ontario: McGill–Queen's UP, 1984).

Robertson, David. *Denmark Vesey* (New York: Alfred A. Knopf, 1999).

Saunders, Gail. *Bahamian Loyalists and Their Slaves* (London & Kingston, Jamaica: Macmillan Caribbean, 1983).

Sensbach, Jon. "Rebekka's Revival: Afro-Christian Women and the Origins of the Black Protestant Movement" (unpublished conference paper presented at "Diasporas africaines dans l'ancien et le nouveau monconscience et imaginaire," Paris, 26–28 October 2000).

——. *A Separate Canaan: The Making of an Afro-Moravian World in North Carolina, 1763–1840* (Chapel Hill: U of North Carolina P, 1998).

Sidbury, James. *Ploughshares into Swords: Race, Rebellion, and Identity in Gabriel's Virginia, 1730–1810* (Cambridge: Cambridge UP, 1997).

Sobel, Mechal. *Trabelin' On: The Slave Journey to an Afro-Baptist Faith* (Contributions in Afro-American and African Studies 36; Westport CT: Greenwood, 1979).

——. *The World They Made Together: Black and White Values in Eighteenth-Century Virginia* (Princeton NJ: Princeton UP, 1987).

Thornton, John K. *Africa and Africans in the Making of the Atlantic World 1400–1800* (1992; Cambridge: Cambridge UP, 1998).

Turner, Mary. *Slaves and Missionaries: The Disintegration of Jamaican Slave Society, 1784–1834* (1982; Kingston, Jamaica: The Press, U of the West Indies, 1998).

Walker, James W. St. G. *The Black Loyalists: The Search for a Promised Land in Nova Scotia and Sierra Leone 1783–1870* (Dalhousie African Studies Series; London: Longman & Dalhousie UP, 1976).

Walsh, John. "Methodism and the Origins of English-Speaking Evangelicalism," in Noll et al., ed. *Evangelicalism*, 19–37.

Wilson, Ellen Gibson. *The Loyal Blacks* (New York: Capricorn, 1976).

❖

French Revolutionary Song in the Haitian Revolution 1789–1804

SUJAYA DHANVANTARI

Comment empêcher qu'il ne circule, qu'il ne mobilize ce "message" qui se veut emblée universel, les droits de l'homme et les droits des peuples à disposer d'eux-mêmes?[1]

NATIONS TRADITIONALLY CLASSIFY their histories according to their geographical boundaries. However, the rules and limits of this representation cannot account for the circular movement of ideas and images in a transnational and transcultural system of communication. As a result, some recent debates in diaspora studies attempt to break down the borders among separatist, static national images so as to more adequately interpret fluid historical narratives. The classification of colonial events in historiography is even more complex, since the former colonial and colonized territories are viewed apart from one another in order to create the illusion of mono-ethnic identities. For this reason, postcolonial scholars limit their description and interpretation of events to national borders.

A great challenge to this categorical approach to world history comes from Paul Gilroy's *The Black Atlantic*. In this study of the black diaspora,

---

[1] Anne Pérotin–Dumon, *Être patriote sous les tropiques: La Guadeloupe, la colonisation, et la révolution (1789–1794)* (Basse-Terre: Société d'histoire de la Guadeloupe, 1985): 10 (How does one stop this "message" that wants to be universal from the beginning, the rights of man and the rights of people to act for themselves, from mobilizing and circulating?).

Gilroy identifies the ship as the symbol of cultural dispersion that predates the technological development of modern communications systems. The ship functions as the 'chronotope' of discourse, following Bakhtin's definition: "an optic for reading texts as x-rays of the forces at work in the culture system from which they spring" (426). In disseminating European cultural histories, ideas, political projects and instruments of technology in the Americas, these ships served as mechanisms for the dispersal of objects and ideas, creating the incentive for an initial form of communication that encouraged intercultural exchange. Postcolonial studies of the eighteenth century need to consider the process of cultural dissemination depicted in historical narratives in order to show how black and white histories viewed separately cannot help us to comprehend how European cultural ideas mixed with African and indigenous practices. If we continue to isolate these fields of study from one another, we will not be able to get past the mono-ethnic rhetoric of national histories.

Responding to the critical climate of national and racial approaches to history, Gilroy constructs diaspora studies as an intercontinental field of research into the black Atlantic, calling for the periodization of black colonial histories relative to the dissemination of European ideas. He criticizes both contemporary British and American cultural studies, as well as black studies, since every field identifies its object of inquiry as racially homogeneous. These types of field studies, Gilroy passionately argues, ignore the vital role of transcultural production represented by the history of the black Atlantic.

In order to extend this argument, I will focus on black/white discursive relations in the colonial narrative, keeping in mind, however, that historical reproduction has been controlled by those who have had access to print technology. Consequently, the scholar is left largely with the master-discourse, which silences the voice of the colonized subject. Yet examining the details of the printed text draws our attention to many often overlooked images of the 'Other' which undermine notions of the colonized as the silent figure of discourse. My interpretation thus reconstructs the colonial space in which the European, the African and the Indian interacted. I reflect on the particular case of the Haitian Revolution in Saint Domingue not merely to provide an example but to demonstrate the broader implications of this particular diasporic community, since it was the first colony in the Caribbean world to gain its independence, in 1804. Known as the first black republic ever since its victory, Haiti has been seen as the site of continual black and white/mulatto antagonism. The racially separatist history that arises from this disjunction, I will argue, is not convincing when one looks more closely at the details in colonial histories. Therein, marginal statements and images reveal the interaction that occurred between these races and cultures.

To demonstrate the mixing of cultural identities and discourses, I will analyse an apparently insignificant detail from Général Pamphile de Lacroix's *Mémoires pour servir à l'histoire de la Révolution*, a journal kept during the Haitian revolution. A general in the French army, Lacroix provides the contemporary reader with a written account of colonial conditions. The editor, Pierre Pluchon, underscores the unique perspective offered by Lacroix by stating that he is the only witness to interpret the colonial war as a socially mediated event. In effect, Lacroix's critical commentary on the war gives the diaspora scholar the opportunity to scrutinize the text for images of the colonized subject.

During the famous battle at La-Crête-à-Pierrot, Lacroix records the moral indignation experienced by the French army listening to the rebellious slaves singing the patriotic songs of France, as though these songs belonged to them. These songs have been identified as *La Marseillaise* and *Ça ira*, and other such revolutionary tunes in historical accounts, such as C.L.R James's *The Black Jacobins*. My analysis will explore the double meaning of *La Marseillaise* as both the French and anti-French anthem employed in the Haitian Revolution. In his memoirs, Lacroix proposes an analysis of the French soldiers' reaction to the black adaptation of the revolutionary songs:

> Pendant que nous opérions l'investissement du fort, la musique des ennemis faisait entendre les airs patriotiques adaptés à la gloire de la France. Malgré l'indignation qu'excitaient les atrocités des Noirs, ces airs produisaient généralement un sentiment pénible. Les regards de nos soldats interrogeaient les nôtres: ils avaient l'air de nous dire: "Nos barbares ennemis auraient-ils raison? Ne serions-nous plus les soldats de la République ? Et serions-nous devenus les instruments serviles de la politique?"[2]

In order to describe the displacement of the French soldier, Lacroix verbalizes a fictional face-to-face encounter between general and soldier. This

---

[2] Lacroix, *La Révolution de Haïti: Texte intégral de l'édition originale; Mémoires pour servir à l'histoire de la Révolution de Saint-Domingue, par le Lieutenant-Général Pamphile de Lacroix*, ed. Pierre Pluchon (1819; Paris: Karthala, 1995): 332–33 (While we were taking over the fort, the enemies' music was emitting the patriotic tunes adapted to the glory of France. Despite the indignation that was stirring after the atrocities of the Blacks, these tunes produced a sense of pain. In the eyes of our soldiers, there were these questions: they seemed to say, "Could our barbarous enemies be right? Might we no longer be the soldiers of the Republic? And might we have become the servile instruments of political power?").

illustration reveals the exploitation of the colonial army in the revolutionary war. As General Leclerc's letters show, the condition of the troops was particularly dire during the siege at La-Crête-à-Pierrot, where four thousand men died in less than two months from fatigue, the fires, or murder.[3] For these reasons, it is important to see the French soldier as a multidimensional figure, exploiter and exploited, in this wartime situation, since he is both inferior to his white generals and superior to the black slaves. Occupying both sides of the spectrum, the soldier is ambivalently positioned. As a national martyr, he submits to the demands of his generals; however, as an exploited subject, he identifies with the rank of the slave. In the latter relation, the space of national martyrdom is emptied of meaning, since the Republic for which the soldiers sacrifice themselves is exposed as an instrument of power. In the text, these soldiers become conscious of this vacant symbol when they hear the slaves mimicking the French patriotic songs. Their awareness provokes a deep sense of pain and anxiety over the contradictory repetition of their national anthem.

Many scholars have acknowledged that, in the representation of black or non-European peoples in general, Europe required the reproduction of the 'Other' as beyond jurisdiction. This resulted in the Other's being silenced in European narratives. The postcolonial critic Gayatri Spivak convincingly argues that the "non-European" appears in the margins of Enlightenment discourse as a silent figure, representing the "non-human" in relation to the humanism of the European.[4] Just as Pluchon implies this line of reasoning in his analysis of how Rousseau and Voltaire write the "negro" into discourse as non-human,[5] so does Spivak when she critically assesses Hegel's and Kant's erasure of the non-European.[6] The colonized thus exists in the margins of the written text as the measure by which the colonist confirms European superiority.

As a result, the double meaning of *La Marseillaise* creates confusion in colonial representation, since the singing of the rebellious slaves – the supposedly mute figures of discourse – questions the silence of the colonized subject in European history. For the disillusioned listeners, the singing exposes the difficulties of moral judgement, and, as Lacroix alludes, the

---

[3] Henri Mézière, *Le Général Leclerc (1772–1802) et l'expédition de Saint-Domingue*, preface by Jean–Marcel Champion (Bibliothèque napoléonienne; Paris: Éditions Tallandier, 1990): 200.

[4] Spivak, *A Critique of Postcolonial Reason: Toward a History of the Vanishing Present* (Cambridge MA & London: Harvard UP, 1999).

[5] Pluchon, ed. *Haïti au XVIIIe siècle*, 5–9.

[6] Spivak, *A Critique of Postcolonial Reason*.

French had forfeited their ability to judge by betraying the republican values of liberty and equality. The soldiers' response indirectly indicates the limits of French idealism to Lacroix, who turns the notion of their despair into a synecdoche for this failure. The songs thus demonstrate that the enemy cannot be wholly different, since he repeats the same patriotic narrative. Moreover, the mimicry is ironic, in that it reveals the failure of French identity in the colonial text.

One of the major difficulties of reading the historical narrative for its marginal images is that the written source materials often provide unreliable accounts that portray the slaves as indifferent to their exploitation. In the final chapter of *L'Insurrection des esclaves de Saint Domingue*, Doudou Diène voices this concern about the documentary sources used in studies of the transatlantic slave trade. In expressing the limits of reflection about the slave experience, given the predominance of colonial testimonials and the correlative absence of those of the slaves, Diène describes the trap of contemporary analysis that opens when historians rely on the most accessible written sources of the colonists. This means that the oral narrative of the slave remains outside the limits of history. It is necessary, Diène argues, that both written and oral histories be studied together for a more balanced perspective of the black Atlantic. In considering this problem for historiography, however, Diène implies that the lack of 'factual' oral testimonies is the reason why contemporary scholars continue to base their research on colonial texts.

On the other hand, colonial memory includes the sounds and images of the colonized 'hidden' in the written narrative. Edouard Glissant also refers to this difficulty in debates about the traditions of literature, since Western writing unconsciously conveys a divine presence that draws oral culture into its shadow. Consequently, judgements about historical authenticity tend to honor the written language. In order to undo the power of this regard for writing, I argue, its conceptual limits need to be found in the master-text itself.

Moreover, as I suggested earlier, it is important to recognize the privilege of writing as an outcome of print culture in the global economic context. By controlling the international scope of print culture, the colonial powers were able successfully to spread their message through writing. European literacy allowed Western narratives to establish the rules and limits of access to the representation of colonial histories. Consequently, Glissant raises an important question when he asks whether there is a place to which the histories of the nameless have been relegated, since their stories cannot be found in the existing narrative:

> Est-il un lieu au monde où sont consignées ces déperditions que le monde n'a pas le temps de vérifier? Non pas les grandes calamités qui sont comme les monuments obligés de l'histoire planétaire, mais les accumulations obscures du malheur, l'usure méconnue des peuples coincés, les disparitions insensibles, la lente perte d'identité, la souffrance sans échos?[7]

Glissant refers to the stories of the silent that have never entered the grand narrative of world history. They can still be found, however, in the margins of the existing world. In this sense, there is no 'outside' to the world; rather, the 'outside' of language "without echo" is contained within the world that rejects it. A critical reconstruction of colonial history thus needs to search for signs of these unknown stories.

In historical writing, 'reality' is recorded in a past constructed via the description and interpretation of events that follow the classic structural organization sketched in Aristotle's *Poetics*, which prescribes that the plot have a clear beginning, middle and end in order to complete the sense of narrative truth. According to Glissant, however, the historical text is coiled and fragmented. His concept of history as the poetics of Relation responds to fixed univocal meaning in historical writing by suggesting that a poetics of fragmentation replace Western disciplinary control over historical narrative form.

Such a fragmentation would therefore displace the obsession with narrative historiography, as well as open up an area of ambiguity in which the textual experience of the colonized could be represented. By prescribing a place in the text for loss, Glissant suggests that the space of writing inherits this loss in the written text's shadow-discourse, which also implies that colonial discourse has failed to eliminate the colonized from the text altogether.

In addition to Glissant's notion of loss incorporated into the shadow of colonial discourse, one could refer to Spivak's "native informant," the colonized subject who reflects the master back to himself through the gaze. In distancing himself from the Other, the European becomes the subject who places the native in discourse as a projection of otherness. Spivak draws the term "subaltern" from Antonio Gramsci's analysis of marginalized groups in Italy, employing this term in order to show that the subaltern

---

[7] Glissant, *Le Discours antillais* (Paris: Seuil, 1981): 283–84 (Is there a space to which these losses that the world does not have the time to confirm are consigned? Not the great calamities that are like the unavoidable monuments of world history, but the accumulations of adversity, the wearing down of trapped peoples, the imperceptible disappearances, the slow loss of identity, the suffering without echo?).

does not have access to the print technology that would otherwise allow this voice to be heard. By keeping the native separate from discourse, then, the master manages to maintain a position of superiority. In arguing that the subaltern cannot speak, Spivak claims that no elite can interpret the subaltern, given that this language remains 'foreign' to the written historical narrative.

Spivak, however, stresses that it is the ethical imperative of subaltern studies to analyse the vicissitudes of narrative language in which the subaltern exists as a marginal text. She makes the case that historical agency can be gained for the subaltern by displacing the dominant narrative. In effect, the oppressed subject's mimicry of the master's language dislocates the text, creating differences detectable in the play of language. The scholar, whose ethical imperative is to give the subaltern room for self-recognition, can claim this access by interpreting images that have numerous, sometimes contradictory meanings. In the case of Lacroix's narrative, the French army finds its own reflection contradicted by the slaves' mimicry of song. The repetition derails French identity and its self/Other distinction, since there is a discernible difference in the mimicked lyrics that departs from the meaning of the 'original' version. The ambiguity created by the displacement gives the potential for historical agency to the subaltern, thus freeing this figure from inferior status.

It is difficult to suggest that cultural practices are shared, since such a concept undermines the desire for separate national histories. On the one hand, national identity is rooted in a past guided by the sacredness of the cultural and racial superiority of the European. To suggest that these values do not represent an authentic heritage is to desecrate this notion and replace it with a theory of hybridity. On the other hand, postcolonial historiography has worked hard to write a separate history that is not commanded by the discourse of its former rulers. These two formidable forces in contemporary criticism have led to an isolationist approach in national literary and historical writing. It is thus with prudence that the critic Claude Moïse links the French Revolution to the Haitian Revolution by way of the date 1789:

> Si elle marque le point de départ, en même temps, de la révolution haïtienne et de la Révolution française, c'est que les deux événements sont imbriqués, qu'ils participent d'aventures historiques communes, même si, dans le fond,

ils relèvent de deux sociétés distinctes et qu'à cet égard leur cheminement et
leur orientation respectifs en font deux histoires spécifiques.[8]

Moïse conveys the effect of the French Revolution on the colonies. The
basic demand for secular rights in France created an immediate point of
departure for the liberationist struggle in Saint-Domingue. While it is important to acknowledge the difference between the two revolutionary paths
in order to avoid silencing nascent postcolonial criticism, Moïse's assertion
shows that the events are nevertheless linked.

During the initial period of cultural interaction in the colonies, the exchange of images and ideas among the racial groups resulted in the hybrid-
ization of discourse. In his introduction to *The Potlatch Papers*, a study of
the British colonization of Canada's West Coast, Christopher Bracken
defines the intercultural space by the 'limit', the 'fold' and the 'gift'. The
'limit' in the colonial text is "the line, or set of lines, where Europe attempts
to trace a clean boundary between itself and its exterior."[9] In the text, however, it becomes impossible to keep images isolated from one another. The
result of this failure to separate representations can be seen in Lacroix's
memoirs, wherein the limit of French identity has already been exceeded. In
the colonial space, the patriotic songs signify the slaves' proximity to the
French rather than their difference from them. The mirror effect created by
this closeness is what Homi Bhabha calls "colonial specularity":[10] the
screen of identity splits between the self and its double or hybrid. The slave
thus doubles as *barbare* and *frère*. As such, he is subject to the paternalism
of colonial law, yet he displays a fraternalism in mimicking the French
lyrics. Lacroix discloses the ironic mode of hybridity in asking who the
slave could be Other to, if he already resembles the self. In the hybrid, the
Other is already a part of the self. Both Bracken and Bhabha stress the fact

---

[8] Claude Moïse, "Pour un dictionnaire historique de la revolution haïtienne (1789–
1804)," in *L'Insurrection des esclaves de Saint Domingue (22–23 août 1791)*, ed.
Laënnec Hurbon (Actes de la table ronde internationale de Port-au-Prince, 8 au 10
décembre 1997; Paris: Karthala, 2000): 224 (If the point of departure occurred at the
same time in the Haitian Revolution and the French Revolution, it is because the two
events are imbricated. They participated in common historical ventures, even if,
from the start, they came out of two distinct societies, and, in this regard, their progression and their respective courses created two specific histories).

[9] Christopher Bracken, *The Potlatch Papers: A Colonial Case History* (Chicago:
U of Chicago P, 1997): 5.

[10] Homi K. Bhabha, *Location of Culture* (New York & London: Routledge, 1994).

that the Other is similar to the self to such a degree in the text that the notion of an absolute distinction cannot be justified.

The second occurrence within the space of cultural interaction is the 'fold' or the "bend in the colonial text where Europe brings itself back into an intimate encounter with all that it situates outside of the outer rim."[11] The subaltern, situated outside the limits of the West, cannot have access to the master-narrative. Yet Europe finds itself in close relation to the outside it seeks to reject. By imitating the colonist, the colonized confuses the concept of barbarity; for he cannot be barbaric, since he uses the master's language. The act of mimicry thus destroys the belief that the colonial text convincingly represents self-definition against the Other. In reality, the marginal images reveal that the Other is, ironically, also the same. Lacroix's narrative clearly conveys the uncanny effect of the mimicry on the French soldiers. It is the confusion over the place of the self and the Other that produces the anxiety. The soldiers experience pain upon hearing the lyrics of the patriotic songs in the enemy camp. Due to the collapse of the cultural barrier between the two sides, the soldiers are faced with the notion that the slaves could be morally justified. This questions the self/Other opposition on which the war is based. Contained within the question that the soldiers ask their superiors is the unspoken possibility of a future without difference in which both the self and the Other are rendered alike. The 'fold' predicts this future similarity that already exists in the present act of singing.

The third occurrence in Bracken's theory of the textual border is the 'gift'. The 'gift' is given at the moment when "what Europe identifies as its outside bends back over its interior."[12] Europe gives non-Europe to itself, extending its limits to its outside. The outside is thus inside the living culture of the Europeans. Any attempt to force the cultures apart creates the condition for subordination.

In Bhabha's view, mimicry reveals the political and psychic power relations in which there are continually renegotiated identifications between subordinate and dominant cultures. While Bhabha argues that there is complicity between the colonizer and the colonized, he also suggests that the subordinate figure can gain a certain form of agency by refusing to satisfy the master's demand for recognition and by returning the master's gaze. In *Location of Culture*, mimicry is defined as "the name for the strategic reversal of the process of domination [...] that turns the gaze of the discriminated

---

[11] Bracken, *The Potlatch Papers*, 5.

[12] *The Potlatch Papers*, 6.

back upon the eye of power."[13] Bhabha follows through on Michel Foucault's theory of power relations by characterizing colonial authority as a systematic power that incites challenge, and on Jacques Lacan's theory of psychic relations by showing how the colonized subject imitates the values of the dominant culture. According to Bhabha, the psychic strategy of domination can never succeed, since resistance to colonization is tied to it. Once the dominant culture is repeated in the colonial context, it becomes a "partial presence" of its former "essential" character. This becomes a strategy that threatens the colonist, whose sovereign status depends on the unruptured consolidation of power. In exercising subversion through mimicry at the limits of authority, the colonial subject menaces the ruling party's narcissistic demand for discipline.

The outcome of Bhabha's thinking on mimicry is that Lacroix's journal can be examined for its play of repetition and difference in terms of psychic power relations. In accordance with Bhabha's definition, the singing represents resistance to colonial authority. If we use Spivak's notion of 'catachresis', a concept-metaphor without "any historically adequate referent,"[14] we can see how the colonized peoples seize *La Marseillaise* as their own anthem to symbolize their struggle through the master's language of liberation. This oral expression enables them to orient their experience of slavery to the ideologies of freedom and justice articulated in the anthem. It is particularly significant that the popular song gave the slaves access to the master-narrative, since the acquisition of political power is made legitimate through discourse. *La Marseillaise*, providing narratives of both rule and resistance, thus occupies a contested site for ideas concerning rights and freedoms.

In acknowledging *La Marseillaise* as a symbol of resistance, Madeleine Rebérioux, the former President of the League of the Rights of Man, prefaces the anthology *Marseillaise, Marseillaises* with the statement that European resistance movements have claimed this song as their own over the past one hundred and fifty years. *La Marseillaise*, she argues, has become a quasi-universal weapon.[15] The song exceeded its original context when it became the symbol of revolutionary struggles in all parts of Europe, especially in its use during the storming of the Winter Palace in St Peters-

---

[13] Bhabha, *Location of Culture*, 112.

[14] Spivak, "Constitutions and Cultural Studies," *Yale Journal of Law and the Humanities* 2.1 (1996): 133–48.

[15] Madeleine Rebérioux, "Préface" to *Marseillaise, Marseillaises: Anthologie de différentes adaptations depuis 1792*, ed. Chantal Georgel & Robert Delbart (Paris: Le Cherche Midi, 1992): 1.

burg in 1917. Sung by revolutionaries in Europe, it soon came to convey resistance to authority and the desire for freedom and justice in an independent state.

Even though this historical account of *La Marseillaise* describes its dissemination within and reabsorption into various contexts, Rebérioux stops short of recognizing the important role of the French song in the Haitian Revolution. Rather than referring to the deployment of the anthem as a weapon against the French army in Saint-Domingue, Rebérioux cites the creole *citoyen* Corbin, who proclaimed the abolition of slavery in the Convention on 4 February 1794. Yet Rebérioux fails to mention that the decree was revoked and slavery reinstated by the Napoleonic army, as C.L.R. James notes in *The Black Jacobins* and Pluchon writes in *Histoire de la colonisation française*. By eliminating the historical significance of the Haitian abolitionist revolt, French history consolidates *La Marseillaise* as a perfect discourse of liberation.

In general, French history does not make the link between the two revolutions. Hervé Luxardo, in *Histoire de La Marseillaise*, more directly ignores the extra-European context :

> Hors d'Europe, La Marseillaise ne semble pas avoir eu le même succès. Dans les colonies et protectorats français, on la chantait d'emblée en français. Ailleurs, elle a pu être perçue par les élites comme le chant conquérant des colonisateurs. On connaît toutefois une Marseillaise tamoule du XIXe siècle. Peut-être faut-il y voir l'expression d'un sentiment national indien anti-anglais?[16]

Luxardo seems unaware of the song's anticolonial meaning in Saint-Domingue. Certainly, *La Marseillaise* in the French territories of Guadeloupe, Martinique, French Guiana, Réunion, and French Polynesia, to name the greater number of the French protectorate states, does directly represent French nationalism. However, in Saint-Domingue the song carried with it a counter-cultural expression, analogous to the Tamil version that Luxardo ventures to consider. Although he does comprehend the song's employment as a symbol of domination, Luxardo, like Rebérioux, presents a European object of identification without reflecting on the non-European context. A

---

[16] Hervé Luxardo, *Histoire de la Marseillaise* (Paris: Plon, 1989): 201 (Outside Europe, the Marseillaise appears not have had the same success. In the colonies and the French protectorate states, one sang it immediately in French. Then, it had to have been perceived by the elite as the conquering song of the colonizers. One knows, however, of a Tamil Marseillaise from the nineteenth century. Could it be seen as the expression of a national Indian anti-English sentiment?).

re-reading of *La Marseillaise* could help us to re-think the role of French colonization with respect to the Western values of liberty and equality.

In emphasizing the role of *La Marseillaise*, my intention is to show that nationalist songs are an important part of discourse, providing a contested site for social practices and ideas. As is evident in the singing of *La Marseillaise* by both the colonizer and the colonized, the national anthem can be employed to support any type of communal bond. The critic Iris Zavala asserts that popular songs have been "the figural projections for both the open future and grim imperialism."[17] The text – music and image – can be interpreted to suit the desires of both the ruling and rebellious leaders since both sides seek a popularized political discourse that offers a narrative of communalism:

> Aux armes, citoyens,
> Formez vos bataillons!
> Marchons, marchons,
> Qu'un sang impur,
> Abreuve nos sillons![18]

This chorus reinforces the link between a vision of nationhood and the military defence of territory. The citizens must take up arms and form a communal identity in order to ensure that their territory is not tainted by the blood of the enemy who threatens the integrity of the homeland by infringing on the national borders.

La Marseillaise can thus be viewed as an initial expression of patriotism on an eighteenth-century postcolonial site of contestation. Through the appropriation of this nationalist song, the slaves were able to create an ethnically based communal consciousness that helped them gain their independence. In the lyrics, there are two direct references to the homeland (*la patrie*): "Arise, children of the fatherland" and "Sacred love of the country." These images suggest that a religious character pervades the concept of the nation. Nationalist fervour, akin to spiritual rapture, incites the soldiers to defend the land to which they are devoted as the chosen people. This

---

[17] Iris M. Zavala, "When the Popular Sings the Self: Heterology, Popular Songs, and Caribbean Writing," in *A History of Literature in the Caribbean*, vol. 3, ed. A. James Arnold (Amsterdam & Philadelphia PA: John Benjamins, 1997): 188.

[18] Ginette & Georges Marty. "La Marseillaise," *Dictionnaire des chansons de la Révolution 1787–1799* (Paris: Tallandier, 1988): 9 (To arms, citizens! Form your battalions! / Let us march! Let us march! / That their impure blood may water our fields!).

sacredness of territory is symbolized by the "flags" that wave in opposition to the "blood-stained banner of tyranny." Above all, the divine right of the people counters the "foreign" invader, whose demonic presence taints the purity of god's children.

It is significant that the communal consciousness of the army is male-centered. In order to achieve their "day of glory," the soldiers must enter into a fraternal embrace. The masculine sense of patriotism is evoked in the expression "May victory follow your manly accents." The link between patriotism and fraternity is made clear by the military allusions in *La Marseillaise*. Thierry Bouzard classifies the anthem as a military song. The war song, he writes, galvanizes patriotism, the ardor of combat and the fraternity of the soldiers, who face the hard life of the countryside and require the conjuring of fear before combat and the reinforcement of communal cohesion. In identifying the characteristics of military music, Bouzard clarifies the distinction between a call to arms and a revolutionary song by stating that the latter is more political. In addition to Bouzard's characterization of *La Marseillaise* as a military song, I would include its sense as a revolutionary song, since the discourse is also a site of political contestation.

Finally, the communal bond is romantically expressed through music that conveys the desire for the homeland. The image of father/son love becomes an allegory for the connection between nationalism and territorial defense. In this sense, the music establishes an awareness of political nationhood in the image of familial and spiritual wholeness. Blood relations are envisioned in the perfect reunion of the male family in binary opposition to the enemy's "foul blood." The link between blood and soil is thus made concrete by the right of the community to a defined space. However problematic the mono-ethnicism of the nationalistic lyrics may be, it is undeniable that they expressed the desire for a secular republic.

This reading of *La Marseillaise* raises questions about its employment by the slaves, as one cannot simply conflate their experience with that of the French revolutionaries, since each community is interpolated differently by its particular context. As I suggested earlier, the experience of slavery powerfully oriented the slaves to the discourse of liberation offered by the lyrics of *La Marseillaise*. By singing this "concept-metaphor," they were able to direct the discourse of rights to their struggle for freedom. In a sense, the song as disseminated idea and image formed part of an early global culture, traveling along unpredictable paths.

This mode of cultural reproduction inherent in the early communicative systems of the black Atlantic can account for the particular configurations of power between colonizer and colonized and the nascent development of a

Haitian communal consciousness. By defying the social arrangements that disenfranchised them and by cultivating a sense of cultural bifocality, the slaves placed themselves on a trajectory of empowerment rather than on one of otherness. As a result, I would argue, narratives of colonization that rely on the image of the silent and oppressed 'Other' are inadequate when considering the global system in which 'place' and 'culture' are destabilized by the transcultural and transnational flow of images and ideas.

Furthermore, the dispersion of *La Marseillaise* in the colonies taints the notion of French purity. Viewed as a symbol of national liberation, *La Marseillaise* became a central theme in French literature, repeated in numerous tributes by well-known writers. As François–René de Châteaubriand writes in *Essai sur les Révolutions*, "Cette ode républicaine vivra parce qu'elle fait époque dans notre Révolution. Enfin, elle mena tant de fois les Français à la victoire."[19] "This republican ode will live on because it moved with the times of our Revolution. Finally, it carried the French to victory so many times." In portraying national identity, Chateaubriand stresses the values of the secular republic and their representation in the national anthem. In effect, the literary reproduction of French identity reinforces the sanctity of nationhood associated with the song.

However, the proliferation of the text in diasporic communities such as Saint-Domingue demonstrates the inadequacy of the description and interpretation of *La Marseillaise* prevalent in French literature and history. The transnationalism of the French patriotic songs shows that France's enemies actively engaged in and were formed by *La Marseillaise*, thus revealing the heterogeneous notion of identity and the historical process of hybridity, in which networks, ideas and their ideologies spanned the black Atlantic space in the late eighteenth century.

The critic Jean Price–Mars schematizes the critical similarities between the two histories when he notes that the Haitian desire for liberty was inspired by the French movement of the ideas of social transformation advocated by the French Revolution of 1789.[20] Literary production scattered the information of nationalist rebellion in all directions and crossed all cultural borders, leaving the symbolism open to interpretation. As a result, each rebellion that usurped the lyrics and music oriented them to a specific context. The slaves in Saint-Domingue were thus equally predisposed to a

---

[19] François–René de Chateaubriand, *Essai sur les révolutions*, ed. Frédéric Robert (Paris: Imprimerie Nationale, 1989): 289 (Part I, ch. XXIII: "1797: La Marseillaise").

[20] Jean Price–Mars, *La République d'Haïti et la République dominicaine*, vol. 1 (Port-au-Prince: Fardin, 1953): 18.

discourse that would provide them with a way of striving for social transformation.

A discussion of cultural dissemination cannot ignore the importance of
the communications systems that allowed for the transfer of ideas and
images through discourse. As I discussed earlier, Gilroy's theory of the
ship-in-motion as the conduit for ideas most adequately shows how the
transfer of knowledge back and forth across the Atlantic resulted from the
"modern machine" that transported people and documents. Pluchon also
stresses the role of ships, implying their crucial place in the interpretation of
eighteenth-century transatlantic history. One exemplary moment of the ship
as a communicative system occurred after the 1802 restoration of slavery in
Guadeloupe, when black deportees jumped from the ship *La Cocarde* at
night to inform the former slaves of Saint-Domingue about Napoleon's re-
instatement of slavery.[21] This transfer of information can be viewed as a
socially transformative act that contributed to the development of black
resistance in Saint-Domingue.

On the other hand, the concept of the ship as a social space in which the
transnational movement of ideas created a type of cultural bifocality also
involves the fact that the enforced transfer of Africans to Haiti via the Middle Passage engendered the experience of racial terror. For this reason, one
needs to consider the mutable nature of diasporic space, in which uneven
forms of travel depend on the access to power. But the open-endedness of
travel makes it a useful point of departure to describe the origins of transnational relations between the Old and New Worlds.

It is particularly significant that the ships traveling between France and
Saint-Domingue carried arms, soldiers and slaves, all of which supported
French commercial enterprise. French historians acknowledge Saint-
Domingue's importance as a commercial center of production. Pluchon
summarizes the independence gained by Saint-Domingue in 1804 as a
tragedy that destroyed maritime commercial profits : "Ce désastre [...] se
manifeste [...] par l'effondrement du grand commerce maritime, que le
trafic colonial actionnait, par la ruine de la France atlantique."[22] In this
respect, the transatlantic space can be described as a site of struggle among
the European powers that viewed the exploitation of the colonies as the
necessary condition for the growth of their own economies. Many colonial

---

[21] Pluchon, in Lacroix, *La Révolution d'Haïti*, ed. Pluchon, 368.

[22] Pluchon, in Lacroix, *La Révolution d'Haïti*, ed. Pluchon, 399 (This disaster
manifests itself in the demise of the great maritime commerce that colonial
trafficking put into action and in the ruin of the French maritime provinces).

accounts point to the link between the economic and political goals of colonization, such as that of Villevaleix, a plantation owner, who writes, on 31 July 1790: "L'indépendance politique se doublait d'une indépendance commerciale."[23]

In considering the important role of *La Marseillaise* in the Haitian revolution, I do not seek to prioritize French discourse over other narratives of liberty consciously used by the rebellious slaves. Jack Corzani describes how Jean–François Brièrre's play *Adieu à La Marseillaise* reveals the dangers of Toussaint L'Ouverture's faith in the European doctrine.[24] The narrative is told so as to indicate the drawbacks of devoting oneself completely to colonial fields of power. The ability of the maroons, for example, to establish a non-European form of resistance undermined European authority in the colonies from the seventeenth century onward. As agents of their own liberation, the maroons not only posed a real threat to the consolidation of colonial power in the Caribbean region, but they also created a Caribbean self-awareness that directly contradicted the colonial project.

Both Price–Mars and Glissant emphasize the way in which the figure of the maroon threatened European control by failing to follow the example set by the colonists. Since they did not engage in the process of mimesis, the maroons escaped their expected subordination. According to Price–Mars, the maroon was the most worthy witness to the work of the black for liberty. Glissant also dramatizes maroon resistance as a cultural force at work in the Caribbean world: "Les marrons portaient une odeur de liberté. Nous fabriquions notre République."[25] This statement conveys the crucial role of the maroons in the independence struggle. By putting in place a model of liberation, the maroon offered a seemingly inimitable voice that communicated an initial form of anticolonialism outside of the European colonial context. Yet even this desire for emancipation took the form of European nationhood. This context draws our attention to the cultural integration already in place at the beginning of the colonial project. In this

---

[23] Gabriel Debien, *Études antillaises XVIIIe siècle* (Paris: Association Marc Bloch, 1956): 152 (Political independence doubled as commercial independence).

[24] Jack Corzani, "De l'aliénation révolutionnaire: Toussaint Louverture et la Marseillaise (A propos de *L'Adieu à la Marseillaise* de J. Brièrre)," in *Mourir pour les Antilles: Indépendance nègre ou esclavage (1802–1804)*, ed. Michel Louis Martin & Alain Yacou (Pointe-à-Pitre, Guadeloupe: CERC/Centre d'études et de recherches caraïbéennes/Paris: Éditions caribéennes, 1991): 45–56.

[25] Glissant, *Monsieur Toussaint* (Paris: Gallimard, 1961): 42 (The maroons gave off the scent of liberty. We created our Republic).

sense, narratives of diaspora in Saint-Domingue contain layered references and allusions to both French and maroon histories.

I consequently venture to say that the nationalist boundaries set in place by the colonial powers are discursively monitored. But these border regions remain mutable and prone to transgression. The complex role of *La Marseillaise* in Saint-Domingue demonstrates the open-ended and contingent nature of interpretation, since the singing of the slaves negates strategies that seek to appropriate the song as an authentic symbol. Moreover, the mimicking of the French patriotic songs reveals that the latter are mediated, hence contain only a partial presence of their 'original' sense. This means that *La Marseillaise* contains an element of 'foreignness' and cannot be viewed as a perfect model of emancipation if it could be harnessed against French authority as it was during the Haitian Revolution.

I have reflected on the particular case of *La Marseilllaise* in order to draw upon some of the wider implications of this specific study of an eighteenth-century diaspora community in the black Atlantic. Above all, the particularity of this early-modern revolution provides new insights into the complexities of global culture. The ability of the slaves to appropriate the song undermines static and mono-ethnic notions of community and draws attention to the contingency of discourse. As Gilroy points out, the boundaries of diaspora experience do not coincide with those of nation-states. In this sense, the slaves represent a diaspora that acquired access to the symbolic field of French power.

This access to a field of power also suggests that oppression need not be read as complete disempowerment. Rather, analysis of the slave experience goes beyond consideration of a discourse of silence, however horrific the circumstances of colonization are, in order to convey the way in which the slaves defied the social and political circumstances that disenfranchised them and to describe the borders at which they cultivated cultural bifocality. For these reasons, the complex nature of diaspora narratives cannot rely on the slave being a mute figure of discourse.

Moreover, the layered nature of diasporic movements (eg, goods, arms, slaves) draws attention to the disjunctiveness of global culture. In this sense, one needs to account for the overlaps and resemblances between cultural forms at the same time as one considers the fragmented mode of cultural reproduction and mimesis as a form of power. The particular experience of the eighteenth-century diaspora in Saint-Domingue shows that the dispersion of European discourse created multiple meanings in a specific struggle for independence. As a result, only a historical approach that is attentive to the particular interpretation of discourse can account for the complexities of the diaspora.

Finally, the case of *La Marseillaise* in Saint-Domingue is useful for diaspora studies in providing us with ways to analyse the complexities of resistance in the minutiae of colonial writing. This process enables the analysis of the colonized, whose texts are inscribed in the margins of European narratives.

My point is not to prioritize the symbolic, but to suggest that a transnational approach to the textual study of diaspora identify the relation between the power of cultural ideas and their appropriation in the colonial context. Such an investigation will not only strongly qualify any notion that discourse might be socially inadequate, but will also help us guard against reducing uneven and complex relations to binary models of colonial relations.

Works Cited

Aristotle. *Poetics*, tr. Leon Golden (Tallahassee: Florida State UP, 1981).

Bakhtin, M.M. *The Dialogic Imagination*, ed. & tr. Michael Holquist (Austin: U of Texas P, 1981).

Bhabha, Homi K. *Location of Culture* (New York & London: Routledge, 1994).

Bouzard, Thierry. *Anthologie du chant militaire français* (Paris: Grancher, 2000).

Bracken, Christopher. *The Potlatch Papers: A Colonial Case History* (Chicago: U of Chicago P, 1997).

Corzani, Jack. "De l'aliénation révolutionnaire: Toussaint Louverture et la Marseillaise (A propos de *L'Adieu à la Marseillaise* de J. Brièrre)," in *Mourir pour les Antilles: Indépendance nègre ou esclavage (1802–1804)*, ed. Michel Louis Martin & Alain Yacou (Pointe-à-Pitre, Guadeloupe: CERC/Centre d'études et de recherches caribéennes/Paris: Éditions caribéennes, 1991): 45–56.

Chateaubriand, François–René de. *Essai sur les révolutions*, ed. Frédéric Robert (Paris: Imprimerie Nationale, 1989).

Debien, Gabriel. *Études antillaises XVIIIe siècle* (Paris: Association March Bloch, 1956).

Diène, Doudou, Jean–Michel Deveau, Claude Moïse et al. "Résumé des débats," in *L'insurrection des esclaves de Saint-Domingue (22–23 août 1791)*, ed. Laënnec Hurbon (Actes de la table ronde internationale de Port-au-Prince, 8 au 10 décembre 1997; Paris: Karthala, 2000): 237–44.

Gilroy, Paul. *The Black Atlantic: Modernity and Double Consciousness* (London: Verso & Cambridge MA: Harvard UP, 1993).

Glissant, Édouard. *Le Discours antillais* (Paris: Seuil, 1981).

——. *Introduction à une poétique du divers* (Paris: Gallimard, 1996).

——. *Monsieur Toussaint* (Paris: Gallimard, 1961).

James, C.L.R. *The Black Jacobins: Toussaint L'Ouverture and the San Domingo Revolution* (1938; New York: Vintage, 1963).

Luxardo, Hervé. *Histoire de la Marseillaise* (Paris: Plon, 1989).

Marty, Ginette, & Georges Marty. "La Marseillaise," *Dictionnaire des chansons de la Révolution 1787–1799* (Paris: Tallandier, 1988): 9–10.

Mézière, Henri. *Le Général Leclerc (1772–1802) et l'expédition de Saint-Domingue*, preface by Jean–Marcel Champion (Bibliothèque napoléonienne; Éditions Tallandier, 1990).

Moïse, Claude. "Pour un dictionnaire historique de la révolution haïtienne (1789–1804)," in *L'Insurrection des esclaves de Saint Domingue*, ed. Laënnec Hurbon, 215–36.

Pérotin–Dumon, Anne. *Etre patriote sous les tropiques: La Guadeloupe, la colonisation, et la révolution (1789–1794)* (Basse-Terre: Société d'histoire de la Guadeloupe, 1985).

Pluchon, Pierre. *Histoire de la colonisation française* (Paris: Karthala, 1991).

——, ed. *Haïti au XVIIIe siècle: Richesse et esclavage dans une colonie française, édition du Voyage à Saint-Domingue pendant les années 1788, 1789, 1790 par le baron Alexandre–Stanislas de Wimpffen* (1797; Paris: Karthala, 1993).

——, ed. *La Révolution de Haïti: Texte intégral de l'édition originale; Mémoires pour servir à l'histoire de la Révolution de Saint-Domingue, par le Lieutenant-Général Pamphile de Lacroix* (1819; Paris: Karthala, 1995).

Price–Mars, Jean. *La République d'Haïti et la République dominicaine: Les aspects divers d'un problème d'histoire, de géographie et d'ethnologie*, vol. 1 (Port-au-Prince: Fardin, 1953).

Rebérioux, Madeleine. "Préface" to *Marseillaise, Marseillaises: Anthologie de différentes adaptations depuis 1792*, ed. Chantal Georgel & Robert Delbart (Paris: Le Cherche Midi, 1992): 5–7.

Spivak, Gayatri Chakravorty. "Can the Subaltern Speak?" (1988), in *Colonial Discourse and Postcolonial Theory: A Reader*, ed. Patrick Williams & Laura Chrisman (Hempstead: Harvester Wheatsheaf, 1993): 66–111.

——. "Constitutions and Cultural Studies," *Yale Journal of Law and the Humanities* 2.1 (1996): 133–48.

——. *A Critique of Postcolonial Reason: Toward a History of the Vanishing Present* (Cambridge MA & London: Harvard UP, 1999).

——. "Subaltern Studies: Deconstructing Historiography," in *Selected Subaltern Studies*, vol. 4: *Writings on South Asian History and Society*, ed. Ranajit Guha (New York: Oxford UP, 1985): 330–63.

Zavala, Iris M. "When the Popular Sings the Self: Heterology, Popular Songs, and Caribbean Writing," in *A History of Literature in the Caribbean*, vol. 3, ed. A. James Arnold (Amsterdam & Philadelphia PA: John Benjamins, 1997): 187–202.

❖

The Wings of Ethiopia
The Caribbean Diaspora and Pan-African Projects from John Brown Russwurm to George Padmore[1]

WINSTON JAMES

T HE PHENOMENON OF PAN-AFRICANISM cannot be properly understood without appreciating the responses of different segments of the African diaspora to its appeal and dissemination. Scholars generally speak of the African diaspora in the singular, but for *analytical* purposes I have become more and more convinced that we ought to speak of diasporas. It might even be preferable to avoid the term, singular and plural, altogether. For, despite our common provenance and experience of slavery in the Americas, the variation in the rhythm of transformation and the evolution of our people are so profound that it is sensible to be cautious about generalizations. Unfortunately, there are too many glib and ignorant generalizations on the subject. The experience of one particular national or regional group of the African diaspora, usually that of the USA (which is the most atypical), is often extrapolated to the rest.

It is not insignificant that the Africans in the Americas came from widely differing parts of the continent; that the slave trade ended in 1808 in some parts and the 1860s in others; that slavery ended in 1838 in one part, and

[1] The final version of this essay was written while the author held the Josephus Daniels Fellowship at the National Humanities Center, North Carolina. He also wishes to thank the editors for their comments on an earlier and much longer draft and their suggestions for its abbreviation. The title is borrowed from Wilson Jeremiah Moses' remarkable volume *The Wings of Ethiopia: Studies in African-American Life and Letters* (Ames: Iowa State UP, 1990).

1888 in another; that some slaves had greater autonomy in the labor process than others; ranching in Cuba, diamond mining in Brazil, and work on sugar plantations in Barbados were very different forms of activity with different implications for the evolution of those societies, their cultures and the groups involved. Additionally, the character of the post-emancipation settlement varied, and the economic and political transformation that issued from them in the post-emancipation period cannot be ignored. It is with a consciousness of such broad variations that it should be registered that the Caribbean, the anglophone Caribbean in particular, generated a dispropor- tionately large, second African diaspora, a diaspora of a diaspora, so to speak, a remarkable Caribbean diaspora. While the pan-Africanist contribu- tion of individuals from the anglophone Caribbean has long been recog- nized by scholars, no one has documented, analysed or explained the pattern of this contribution to pan-Africanist projects over time and space.[2]

This Caribbean diaspora began as early as the seventeenth century, when British slave holders in Barbados took their slaves with them as they populated and colonized more and more islands and British North America, most notably Virginia and South Carolina. Within the British archipelago itself, Trinidad and Guyana, by virtue of their more robust post-emancipa- tion economies, served as magnets for over-exploited workers as well as some members of the black intelligentsia of the eastern Caribbean, espe- cially Barbados. It was also in the aftermath of slavery that this intra-Carib- bean diaspora became even more far-flung and, in fact, a decidedly extra- Caribbean one. Central America, Cuba, the Dominican Republic, Puerto Rico, Haiti, Brazil, West, Central and Southern Africa, and North America were some of the key points of circulation and settlement. Some, mainly

---

[2] George Shepperson noted that the "persistence" of what he dubs "the West Indian factor [...] in all-African movements is remarkable"; Shepperson, "Pan-Africanism and 'Pan-Africanism': Some Historical Notes," *Phylon* 23.4 (1962): 356. Imanuel Geiss also points to the importance of the Caribbean and the Caribbean contribution: "The West Indies were, so to speak, the hub of the slave-trade system. They saw the first Negro slaves, they saw also the first successful slave revolts. Later on West Indians were in surprisingly intimate contact with West Africa, Britain and Negroes in the USA. The West Indies were the breeding ground of such men as E[dward] W[ilmot] Blyden, Sylvester Williams, Marcus Garvey, George Padmore, all of whom played a prominent role in the history of Pan-Africanism; Du Bois' father came from the West Indies." "Notes on the Development of Pan-Africanism," *Journal of the Historical Society of Nigeria* 3.4 (1967): 722. This theme is also brought out in Geiss's monumental study, *The Pan-African Movement*, tr. Ann Keep (London: Methuen, 1974): 8–11.

students and seamen, made their way to Europe; others went as far as Australia during the gold rush, as did others to California.[3] And at least one, James Patterson, a Vincentian, went as far as Tahiti to serve as a Seventh Day Adventist missionary after having lived for many years in northern California. He then lived in Panama City before returning to St Vincent to die.[4] Others worked in British India and Ceylon (Sri Lanka), some even ended up in China. Ras Makonnen, a keen observer of the Caribbean diaspora, reported that after the Second World War a number of Barbadians, former seamen, were found living with their Japanese wives in Japan. "Wherever you go in the world," declared Makonnen, "you will find a Bimsha – a Barbadian."[5] There is even island lore, probably apocryphal but no less instructive, of a Bajan, as the Barbadian is commonly called, found running a restaurant in Jerusalem.[6] No other national grouping of Africans in the Americas – not that in the USA, not that in the Spanish Caribbean, not that in Brazil, and not even that in the French territories – has produced such a large and widely scattered diaspora as the British Caribbean, especially over so many centuries. It continues to this very day, with even greater intensity and no sign of abating. Moreover, although this diaspora included important segments of the Afro-Caribbean intelligentsia, it was overwhelmingly proletarian.

---

[3] See Winston James, *Holding Aloft the Banner of Ethiopia: Caribbean Radicalism in Early Twentieth-Century America* (London & New York: Verso, 1998): 9–49 and references therein. The literature on the subject is vast and growing. See, in particular: Bonham Richardson, "Caribbean Migrations, 1838–1985," in *The Modern Caribbean*, ed. Franklin Knight & Colin Palmer (Chapel Hill: U of North Carolina P, 1989): 203–28; Peter Fryer, *Staying Power: The History of Black People in Britain* (London: Pluto, 1984); Peter Fraser, "British West Indians in Haiti in the Late Nineteenth and Early Twentieth Centuries," *Immigrants and Minorities* 7.1 (1988): 79–94; Paul Rich, "The Black Diaspora in Britain: Afro-Caribbean Students and the Struggle for a Political Identity, 1900–1950," *Immigrants and Minorities* 6.2 (1987): 151–73; Jeffrey Green, *Black Edwardians: Black People in Britain, 1901–1914* (London: Frank Cass, 1998); Rudolph Lapp, *Blacks in Gold Rush California* (New Haven CT: Yale UP, 1977): esp. 266–68; Barry Higman, "Jamaicans in the Australian Gold Rushes," *Jamaica Journal* 10.2–4 (December 1976): 38-45.

[4] William Patterson, *The Man Who Cried Genocide: An Autobiography* (New York: International Publishers, 1971): 18–20, 22–23, 46–47.

[5] Ras Makonnen, *Pan-Africanism From Within* as recorded and edited by Kenneth King (Nairobi: Oxford UP, 1973): 57–58.

[6] I have analysed elsewhere the forces behind the creation of this massive Barbadian diaspora. See James, *Holding Aloft the Banner of Ethiopia*, 30–49.

Its relative size, class composition and wide range of destinations are easily explained. From its small beginnings in the seventeenth century, and even after the loss of its North American colonies and before Latin American independence, Britain had emerged as the largest and most powerful imperial force. Britannia *did* rule the waves. Contested by Germany and the USA, especially in the early twentieth century, Britain did not lose its formal world hegemony until the hurricane of postwar anticolonialism blew the Union Jack to shreds. It was their peculiar membership in this far-flung imperial system – one on which the sun never set – that enabled Afro-Caribbeans such easy access and mobility around the globe.

In the Western Hemisphere, especially in the late nineteenth and early twentieth centuries, American capital and its preference for an English-speaking, plentiful, and low-waged proletariat habituated to the rigors of plantation labor induced the anglophone black diaspora in Cuba, the Dominican Republic and Puerto Rico, over which it ruled, *de facto* if not *de jure*. Similarly, American capital through the agency of the Isthmian Canal Commission in Panama, and the United Fruit Company throughout the rest of the isthmus, stimulated the migration of Barbadian and Jamaican workers especially, to toil on the Canal and the banana plantations. But even in this emergent US sphere of influence inspired by the Monroe Doctrine, John Bull still had the capacity in the late nineteenth and early twentieth centuries to pull along the Caribbean proletariat with him on his capitalist adventures to Putamayo and north-eastern Brazil.[7]

Having established, largely inadvertently, these vectors for communicating both people and ideas, the anglophone Caribbean diaspora, not surprisingly, was positioned to play – and did play – a disproportionate role in the spread of pan-Africanist ideas. The fact that they enjoyed a higher rate of literacy compared to their counterparts in the USA, Brazil and the Spanish-speaking Caribbean facilitated their role in the dissemination of these ideas. Largely unaccustomed in the islands to the naked racism they encountered in Oriente province in Cuba, the Jim Crow crackerdom of the Canal Zone in Panama (most of their supervisors on the Canal were un-reconstructed white, Southern, American racists), the apartheid in Cape Town before Apartheid, the naked brutality of colonial rule in West and Central Africa, these Caribbean men and women played a major role in transforming pan-Africanism from a largely inchoate and unarticulated

---

[7] Sidney Greenfield, "Barbadians in the Brazilian Amazon," *Luso-Brazilian Review* 20 (1983): 44–64a; Howard Johnson, "Barbadian Migrants in the Putamayo District of the Amazon, 1909–11," in *Caribbean Migration: Globalised Identities*, ed. Mary Chamberlain (London & New York: Routledge, 1998): 177–87.

political and cultural sensibility to a modern political ideology, movement and social project.

These were the circumstances and forces: *de facto* membership of the largest empire, economic hardship in the islands, extraordinary mobility and willingness to migrate to distant places, the encounter with more brutal forms of racism than that to which they were accustomed at home, high levels of literacy (even among its proletariat); all contributed to the prominence of what George Shepperson calls the "West Indian factor" in the history of pan-Africanism, and the explanation of why pan-Africanism was, as Imanuel Geiss puts it, "largely an English-speaking affair."[8]

What do I mean by pan-Africanism? I mean the basic belief that people of African descent have a common ancestral home, share a history of oppression at the hands of Europeans, constituted a nation (even one without a state), and that it is right to extend solidarity to fellow Africans at home and abroad, thus transcending national and juridical boundaries. Aligned to this belief are practices aimed at their realization: "attempts by African peoples to link up their struggles for their mutual benefit," as Tony Martin puts it.[9] It should be added, however, that such attempts need not take collective organizational form. Pan-African efforts can be highly informal and sometimes even operate at the level of individual endeavor. The term 'pan-Africanism' is of relatively recent vintage. There is no evidence of its usage before Henry Sylvester Williams and his colleagues established the African Association in London in 1897 and soon thereafter began planning the Pan-African Conference of 1900.[10] But if the term is relatively new, the sentiment and practices associated with it go back at least to the beginning of the transatlantic slave trade, and the forced migration of Africans to the New World at the beginning of the sixteenth century.

George Shepperson argued that one should make a distinction between 'Pan-Africanism' with a capital letter and 'pan-Africanism'. The former, he suggested, should be used to describe "a clearly recognizable movement," which he sees as "the five Pan-African Congresses" in which Du Bois played a role – 1919, Paris; 1921, London; 1923, London and Lisbon; 1927, New York; 1945, Manchester. On the other hand, 'pan-Africanism', he

---

[8] Shepperson, "Pan-Africanism and 'Pan-Africanism'," 356; Geiss, "Notes on the Development of Pan-Africanism," 722.

[9] Tony Martin, *The Pan-African Connection: From Slavery to Garvey and Beyond* (Cambridge MA: Schenkman, 1983): vii.

[10] Owen Mathurin, *Henry Sylvester Williams and the Origins of the Pan-African Movement, 1869-1911* (Westport CT: Greenwood, 1976): 52, gives 11 November 1899 as the date for the first documented usage of the term.

argued, is not a clearly recognizable movement, with a "single nucleus" such as the figure of Du Bois. "It is rather a group of movements, many very ephemeral. The cultural element often predominates." He concluded that "pan-Africanism may be used for all those all-African movements and trends which have no organic relationship with the capital 'P' variety."[11] This attempt at establishing a form of conceptual order is admirable; but what Shepperson in the end proposed is unsatisfactory.

There are several problems with the schema. First, it is impossible to separate in so neat a fashion Pan-Africanism and pan-Africanism – the former never operated without organic connections with the latter. Shepperson seemed to be aware of this when he conceded that the dichotomy he proposed is "clearly not absolute and [...] there are obvious interacting elements,"[12] but he pressed on despite his own caveat and apparent misgivings. Second, the schema is highly idiosyncratic. The first Pan-African Conference, organized in London by Williams in 1900, is, surprisingly, dismissed as "pioneering but premature," and is thus precluded from that movement given a capital "P" by Shepperson.[13] Even more peculiar is the explicit preclusion of Garvey's Universal Negro Improvement Association (UNIA). Third, Du Bois' importance in these movements, as recent scholarship reveals, is overstated by Shepperson, and, in any case, there is no good conceptual reason why his relation to these organizations should form a defining principle.[14] Finally, there is an implicit hierarchy of the two types of movements, with 'Pan-Africanism' placed in the position of superordination, which is unwarranted and unsustainable. The fact is that informal pan-African organizations and efforts were frequently far more important in their effects than the five congresses in which Shepperson invested such significance. Garvey and the UNIA, separately and combined, had a far greater and more enduring impact – including upon the 1945 Manchester congress itself – on the mobilization of peoples of African descent and on the decolonization of the African continent and the territories of the Caribbean. It is partly in an attempt to avoid Shepperson's conceptual pitfalls that I have decided to use 'pan-Africanism' as a generic term to cover all the efforts that were made, including those manifested in the two movements

---

[11] Shepperson, "Pan-Africanism and 'Pan-Africanism'," 346.

[12] "Pan-Africanism and 'Pan-Africanism'," 347.

[13] "Pan-Africanism and 'Pan-Africanism'," 353.

[14] Several scholars have pointed out that Du Bois' importance to these congresses has been exaggerated (mainly by Du Bois himself, who was not above self-promotion), but Geiss (in his *The Pan-African Movement*) has made the most persuasive case.

described by Shepperson.[15] In what follows I would therefore like to turn more specifically to the involvement of anglophone Caribbeans in the struggle on the African continent. I will briefly mention their contribution to pan-Africanist projects (broadly defined) and outline its historical and cultural framework.

The Establishment of a Tradition: Some Nineteenth-Century Pioneers

John Brown Russwurm (1799–1851)

As my title suggests, John Brown Russwurm is a good person to start with. Born in Port Antonio, Jamaica, on 1 October 1799, he was the son of a black mother and a white English merchant on the island. After the early death of his mother, Russwurm was sent to school in Montreal by his father. When, a few years later, the elder Russwurm moved to Maine, he brought his son with him. Young John was rather fortunate that after his father married an American widow, Susan Blanchard, who already had three children, he was accepted as a full member of the new family. And after his father died in 1815, Mrs Russwurm remarried, but continued to treat the young Jamaican as her own son. He finished his secondary education in Maine. But he never forgot his Jamaican connections and insisted upon returning to the island. Back in Jamaica, he was unhappy, and returned to the USA. He taught at African schools in Philadelphia, New York and Boston. The former Mrs Russwurm advised him to emigrate to Liberia. Russwurm, however, decided to get a college education first. He entered Bowdoin College, Brunswick, Maine in 1824 and graduated in 1826, one of the first three black people to graduate from an American college.[16]

---

[15] Elsewhere, I have dealt at length with the role of Caribbeans from the various linguistic and colonial regions of the archipelago in radical political projects in the USA. I have also argued that their role and presence in both black nationalist and socialist endeavors were disproportionately large and that the Caribbean involvement in the UNIA and the African Blood Brotherhood – two extraordinarily important black organizations – was profound. See James, *Holding Aloft the Banner of Ethiopia*.

[16] As of today, there is no comprehensive biography of Russwurm. See: William Brewer, "John B. Russwurm," *Journal of Negro History* 13.4 (1928): 413–22; Philip Foner, "John Browne Russwurm: A Document," *Journal of Negro History* 54.4 (1969): 393–95; Floyd Miller, *The Search for a Black Nationality: Black Emigration and Colonization, 1787–1863* (Urbana: U of Illinois P, 1975): 84–85; Clarence

As late as January 1826, Russwurm's ambition was to study medicine
and migrate to Haiti, the heroic, newly created, black republic. It was perhaps because of this fascination with Haiti and his ambition to emigrate
there that Russwurm's commencement address at Bowdoin was on the "The
Condition and Prospects of Haiti" – a remarkable speech that attracted
widespread attention and praise. Russwurm did not "study Medicine in
Boston previous to an emigration to Hayti," as he had promised earlier in
the year. He did, however, attend lectures on anatomy at Bowdoin College
Medical School.[17]

Soon after his graduation, Russwurm moved to New York City and im-
mersed himself in the abolitionist movement. There, largely because of
attacks on black people by some of the New York newspapers, he, Samuel
Cornish and a group of black supporters in the city decided to establish a
newspaper of their own, *Freedom's Journal*, Afro-America's first black
newspaper. Edited by Cornish, a distinguished Afro-American, with Russwurm as the junior partner, *Freedom's Journal* made its intentions clear
from the very first issue, published on 16 March 1827:

> We wish to plead our own cause. Too long have others spoken for us. Too
> long has the publick been deceived by misrepresentations, in things which
> concern us dearly, though in the estimation of some mere trifles; for though
> there are many in society who exercise towards us benevolent feelings; still
> (with sorrow we confess it) there are others who make it their business to
> enlarge upon the least trifle, which tends to the discredit of any person of
> colour; and pronounce anathemas and denounce our whole body by the mis-
> conduct of this guilty one. [...] The civil rights of a people being of the
> greatest value, it shall ever be our duty to vindicate our brethren, when oppres-
> sed, and to lay the cure before the publick.[18]

More a magazine than a newspaper, *Freedom's Journal* reported the news,
but focussed more on history, editorials, essays and poems directly relevant
to the struggle and ambitions of black people. As its "Prospectus" made
clear, the *Journal* was an instrument of uplift through education as well as a
weapon of political combat:

Contee, "John Brown Russwurm," in *Dictionary of American Negro Biography*, ed.
Rayford Logan & Michael Winston (New York: W.W. Norton, 1982): 538–39.

[17] John B. Russwurm, "The Condition and Prospects of Hayti," *Journal of Negro
History* 54.4 (1969): 395–97; Foner, "John Browne Russwurm," 394.

[18] *Freedom's Journal* (16 March 1827). For the hostile ideological context that
issued the birth of the *Journal*, see Bella Gross, "*Freedom's Journal* and *The Rights
of All*," *Journal of Negro History* 17.3 (1932): 241–46.

As education is what renders civilised men superior to the savage: as the dissemination of knowledge is continually progressing among all other classes in the community: we deem it expedient to establish a paper, and bring into operation all the means with which our benevolent C R E A T O R has endowed us, for the moral, religious, civil and literary improvement of our injured race. [...] It shall never be our object to court controversy, though we must at all times consider ourselves as champions of oppressed humanity.[19]

Six months after its first appearance, in September 1827, Russwurm became the sole editor of *Freedom's Journal*.[20] Agents for the *Journal* worked in Canada, England, Haiti, as well as across the U S A. Among them was the militant black abolitionist, David Walker of Boston, whose name appeared in the very first issue as an "Authorised Agent" of the *Journal*. Walker also contributed articles to the paper, and it was in *Freedom's Journal* that his 1828 "Address Delivered Before the General Colored Association," in Boston first appeared in print.[21] A few months later he developed it into his justly famous and militant *Appeal*, published as a pamphlet in 1829.[22]

To advance the fight against the advocates of black colonization in Africa and elsewhere was one of the primary objectives of *Freedom's Journal*. The American Colonization Society, founded in 1817, was one of the primary targets. And Russwurm attacked it as ferociously as Cornish did. As late as July 1827, he criticized the Society for "imposing upon the public, the foolish *idea*, that we are longing to emigrate to their land of *milk and honey*. [...] We are all, to a man, opposed, in every shape, to the Colonization Society."[23]

---

[19] *Freedom's Journal* (16 March 1827).

[20] Cornish, who was a Presbyterian minister, served the paper as one of its directors and its general traveling agent, but his time was largely absorbed by his new post as general agent of the New York African Free School. See Gross, *"Freedom's Journal* and *The Rights of All*," 242, 248.

[21] *Freedom's Journal* (19 December 1828).

[22] The most authoritative edition of the *Appeal* is Peter P. Hinks, ed. & intro. *David Walker's Appeal to the Colored Citizens of the World* (1829; University Park PA: Penn State UP, 2000). In his fine study of Walker, Hinks suggests that the articles carried in *Freedom's Journal*, especially those on African civilizations and culture, had a significant impact on Walker's intellectual formation and the formulation of his *Appeal* – see Hinks, *To Awaken My Afflicted Brethren: David Walker and the Problem of Antebellum Slave Resistance* (University Park PA: Penn State UP, 1997): 179–95.

[23] Quoted in Miller, *Search for a Black Nationality*, 84.

But doubt and disillusionment about Afro-America's prospects in the
USA soon set in. Now under his sole editorship, Russwurm's *Journal*,
against the objections of subscribers, began to provide space for coloniza-
tionists. By February 1829, Russwurm publicly declared his *volte face*: "We
have carefully examined the different plans now in operation for our benefit, and none, we believe, can reach half so efficiently the masses as the plan
of colonization on the West coast of Africa."[24] He later explained that "full
citizenship in the USA is utterly impossible in the nature of things, and
those who pant for it must cast their eyes elsewhere."[25] Russwurm decided
upon Africa: In Europe "overpopulation precluded advance," distance
eliminated Asia, "those who had tried their fortunes in the West Indies were
disappointed and unsuccessful."[26] Apart from its fierce climate – its "bleak
winds of winter" – a rising tide of racism in Upper Canada made north of
the border uncongenial. Thus, Russwurm, writing from Liberia in 1831, concluded that it requires "no prophetic eye to foresee" that to Afro-America
and its posterity

> there is no abiding place on the other side of the Atlantic. [...] Before God, we
> know no other home for the man of color, of republican principles, than
> Africa. Has he no ambition? Is he dead to everything noble? Is he contented
> with his condition? Let him remain in America.[27]

What triggered this change is not entirely clear. But no explanation could
satisfy his former anticolonization comrades. They showered him with
abuse, venality of principle being the primary charge.[28] And when he insisted on holding to his new position, he was burned in effigy. As he had planned before making public his subscribing to colonization, he resigned from
Freedom's Journal in March 1829 and, with the support of the ACS, left for
Liberia later that year.[29] Russwurm was appointed to the office of Superintendent of Schools in Liberia. According to one commentator, what he did

---

[24] Brewer, "John B. Russwurm," 417.

[25] C. Abayomi Cassell, *Liberia: History of the First African Republic* (New York:
Fountainhead, 1970): 49.

[26] Brewer, "John B. Russwurm," 421.

[27] Quoted in Carter G. Woodson, ed. *The Mind of the Negro as Reflected in Letters Written During the Crisis, 1800–1860* (Washington DC: Association for the
Study of Negro Life and History, 1926): 161–62.

[28] For a couple of examples, see Woodson, *The Mind of the Negro,* 161–63.

[29] Brewer, "John B. Russwurm," 417–18; Miller, *Search for a Black Nationality,*
86–88.

for the enlightenment of Liberia "is a long chapter in the history of education of that country. He encouraged missions, stimulated private education,
and established public schools."[30] While working as Superintendent of
Schools, Russwurm founded and edited the *Liberia Herald*. Launched in
1830, the *Herald* was West Africa's, and probably the continent's, first
black newspaper.[31] With the motto "Freedom is the Brilliant Gift of
Heaven," Russwurm, in the first issue, just as he had in *Freedom's Journal*,
emphasized the progressive role of education and his commitment to its
dissemination. He seemed to have perceived the paper as an arm of his port-
folio as Superintendent of Schools. But, like black nationalists before and
after, Russwurm advocated self-improvement through education. In words
almost identical to those of Marcus Garvey a century later, Russwurm
declared:

> Of all employments to which a rational being can devote his leisure hours, that
> of *self-improvement*, is the most honorable, profitable and durable. There is no
> station, to which such an one, especially, if a young man, may not qualify
> himself for in the process of time, and in a free government like ours, aspire
> after. It is true, such an effort is the labor of days, months and years, but what
> then? [D]oes the distant prospect of success deter the merchant from shipping
> his goods to foreign countries – does the prospect of rough and stormy
> weather, and gales *ahead*, deter the adventurous mariner from the ocean?

Moreover, without education "no government can long exist in a state of
freedom: it is the link which binds man to his fellowman, & teaches him his
duty to his kindred, his country, and his God." He narrated the role that
education played in the advancement of Europe and America and counseled
emulation. Africa, however, was no newcomer to the advancement of
knowledge: "As low as Africa has descended in the scale of nations, she can
with propriety claim the invention of letters, as the honor rests between the
Egyptians & Ethiopians."[32]

The *Liberia Herald* quickly became a leading newspaper, demanded at
home as well as elsewhere in West Africa and the USA. Russwurm con-

---

[30] Brewer, "John B. Russwurm," 421.

[31] Charles Huberich reported that an earlier newspaper called *Liberia Herald* was
begun in 1826 by the newly arrived emigrant Charles Force, but the paper died soon
after it began with the death of its founder in the same year. No copies of the paper
has apparently survived. *The Political and Legislative History of Liberia* (New
York: Central Book Co., 1947), vol. 1: 344, 392–93.

[32] *Liberia Herald* (6 March 1830); see Garvey's remarks on education in James,
Holding Aloft the Banner of Ethiopia, 79.

tinued to preach the virtues of colonization, sought greater cooperation among the settlements by linking them with Monrovia, and resisted the encroachment of the Europeans.[33] He wrote for American publications, such as the *African Repository*, encouraging Afro-Americans to settle in Liberia. Liberia, he had said before leaving the USA, was a place where "the Man of Colour [...] may walk forth in all the majesty of his creation – a new born creature – a *Free Man!*"[34] But he persuaded relatively few.

Russwurm also served as Colonial Secretary from 1830 to 1834. But in 1836, after the settlement of the new colony of Cape Palmas under the auspices of the Maryland State Colonization Society, he was appointed Governor[35] – the first black person to hold such office in a colony. He served with distinction for almost sixteen years up to his death in June 1851 at Cape Palmas. Russwurm did live long enough to witness the new spurt of Afro-American emigration to Liberia after the passage of the Fugitive Slave Law in 1850.[36] What with the insecurity added by this law to the already fragile liberty of the free people of color, many of those who had previously pilloried Russwurm now turned their eyes to Liberia.[37]

With more than his fair share of detractors while living, in death Russwurm was, at least in certain quarters, highly praised. His burden was heavy – and in more ways than one. Sir Harry Johnston described him as "a most energetic, capable man," but also suggested that Russwurm died of "overwork and worry."[38] The white ruling class in America watched his every move. Like other black men in positions of esteem, he was not afforded the luxury of the individual to stumble as an individual; on his shoulders was the albatross of the prestige of the African, the fate of an entire race. Thus,

---

[33] Cassell, *Liberia* 123, 211; Antonio McDaniel, *Swing Low, Sweet Chariot: The Mortality Cost of Colonizing Liberia in the Nineteenth Century* (Chicago: U of Chicago P, 1995): 56–57.

[34] *Freedom's Journal* (7 March 1829).

[35] Known as Maryland in Liberia, the new colony had a separate identity until it was amalgamated with Liberia proper in 1857. Harry Johnston, *Liberia* (London: Hutchinson, 1906), vol. 1: 222.

[36] Cassell, *Liberia* 169; McDaniel, *Swing Low, Sweet Chariot*, 61.

[37] The best analysis of the Compromise of 1850, of which the Fugitive Slave Law was an important and the most controversial component, is Holman Hamilton, *Prologue to Conflict: The Crisis and Compromise of 1850* (Lexington: U of Kentucky P, 1964). The Law's impact on the development of black nationalism and emigrationism in the USA is discussed at length in Miller, *Search for a Black Nationality*.

[38] Johnston, *Liberia*, 190, 232.

in an "Address to the People of Maryland in Liberia" the Board of Managers of the Maryland Colonization Society commented on Russwurm's
death:

> If white men have ceased to hold office or exercise authority among you, it is
> because he [Russwurm] illustrated the capacity of your race to fill the highest
> political office with an ability that could not be surpassed. [...] But great and
> distinguished as these may be, their possessors may always resort with profit
> to your earliest history to gather from the records of Governor Russwurm's
> life the most admirable examples of prudence, wisdom and integrity.[39]

The *African Repository*, organ of the American Colonization Society, eulogized Russwurm in notably more human terms:

> He combined with great good sense a quiet and unostentatious manner, a
> gentle, modest, and amiable temper, well adapted to allay excitement, to con-
> ciliate confidence and regard, to satisfy all sober expectations, and all honest
> and reasonable demands. Free from ostentation and arrogance, little disposed
> to the highest exhibition of vanity he fulfilled the trust committed to his hands
> with uniform fidelity.[40]

Edward Wilmot Blyden (1832–1912)

Unlike Russwurm, the next major figure to emerge in the line of Caribbean
pan-Africanists is well-known and blessed with a fine biography. Edward
Wilmot Blyden thus requires relatively little discussion here. Born on the
small island of St Thomas, Virgin Islands, in 1832, Blyden from a very
early age exhibited enormous intellectual promise. Before his eighteenth
birthday he was encouraged to seek a religious education in the USA. But
after being rejected by Rutgers' Theological Seminary and two other theological colleges on account of his color, Blyden, encouraged and supported
by members of the American Colonization Society, set his eyes on Liberia
in particular and Africa in general. He was steadfast in his commitment to
developing the continent and "vindicating the Negro race." He continued
his education in Africa, becoming in 1858 an ordained Presbyterian minister
and a high school principal. From a condescending attitude toward continental Africans – he had promised on leaving the USA to help bring "those
barbarous tribes under civilized and enlightened influences" – he would,

---

[39] Quoted in Huberich, *Political and Legislative History of Liberia*, vol. 1, 438–
39.

[40] Quoted in Brewer, "John B. Russwurm," 422.

with time, grow to respect, revere, celebrate and defend their indigenous institutions and cultures against the white supremacists.[41] Although he regularly traveled abroad (he made eight trips to the USA) and served for short periods as a diplomat in London, Africa was his home. And it was there that he died in 1912, aged 79.

Linguist, educator, diplomat, theologian, politician, statesman, explorer, littérateur, Blyden was, as his biographer claims, "easily the most learned and articulate champion of Africa and the Negro race in his own time." To his black contemporaries, Blyden's achievements "were the most convincing refutation of the oft-repeated white charges of Negro inferiority." Moreover, Blyden raised the ideology and practice of pan-Africanism to a new level of clarity and persuasiveness. And his teachings ceaselessly propounded one lesson:

> Negroes had a history and a culture of which they could be proud, and that with the help of New World Negroes a progressive civilization could be built in Africa.

This, wrote his biographer, "gave members of his race a new pride and hope, and inspired succeeding generations of African nationalists and New World Negro leaders."[42]

Blyden's ideas – disseminated in pamphlets, books and articles as well as by the spoken word – were among the most influential in the black world in the late nineteenth century and early twentieth century. He had a legendary reputation years before he died. On his visit to Lagos in 1890, Blyden was welcome at Hope School on the evening of December 23. Among the festive decorations was a lantern of "exquisite workmanship" made by a black Brazilian returnee. Mounted prominently at the entrance of the School, inscribed on it "in luminous letters" were the lines: "Africa's destiny lay hid in night, God said 'let BLYDEN be,' and there was light."[43] Marcus Garvey and George Padmore, most notably, saw their pan-Africanist work as little more than attempts to finish the work Blyden had begun and hoped to achieve. Little wonder, then, that when Padmore left Trinidad for study in the USA in 1924, he instructed his wife, who remained behind and was pregnant with their first and only child, that the baby must be

---

[41] Hollis Lynch, *Edward Wilmot Blyden: Pan-Negro Patriot, 1832–1912* (London: Oxford UP, 1967): 6.

[42] Lynch, *Edward Wilmot Blyden*, vii.

[43] E.A. Ayandele, *The Missionary Impact on Modern Nigeria, 1842–1914* (London: Longmans, 1966): 217; Lynch, *Edward Wilmot Blyden*, 223.

named Blyden, whether boy or girl. His wife, Julia, dutifully named their little girl "Blyden."[44]

Robert Campbell (1829–84)

Less remembered and sung but no less worthy of attention is Robert Campbell.[45] Born in Kingston, Jamaica, in 1829, Campbell was the son of a mulatto mother and a Scottish father. Little is known about his parents and his family, but his maternal grandmother was of 'pure' African descent, both of her parents having made the Middle Passage. Around 1840, Campbell became a printer's apprentice and five years later took a job in a local printing shop. He left after two years to attend the newly established Normal School, where he studied for two years. Campbell then became a schoolmaster in Kingston. The Jamaican economy was in terminal decline and a series of devastating epidemics between 1850 and 1852 seemed to have helped Campbell to decide on emigration. He left the island in early 1852 and lived in Nicaragua and then Panama, but, quickly disappointed by Central America, a year later he once again moved on in search of greener pastures.

New York was his new destination, but it shocked and alarmed him. Although Campbell was, as he put it, only "twenty five percent of negro blood," and few could tell whether he was black or white when he had his hat on, New York punished him for his African ancestry. Because of widespread racism, it was virtually impossible for Campbell to find work as a printer in the city. Relatively privileged in Jamaica on account of his light

---

[44] James R. Hooker, *Black Revolutionary: George Padmore's Path From Communism to Pan-Africanism* (New York: Praeger, 1967): 4–5. For another and less poetic indication of the esteem in which Padmore held Blyden, see his *Pan-Africanism or Communism? The Coming Struggle for Africa* (London: Dennis Dobson, 1956): 54–55. Throughout the book, Padmore respectfully referred to his hero as "Dr. Blyden."

[45] There is no biography of Campbell. Richard Blackett is the only scholar to have provided a biographical portrait. Blackett's is a pioneering and splendid effort, but there is still much work to be done to fully unveil Campbell's remarkable life. See Blackett, "Return to the Motherland: Robert Campbell, A Jamaican in Early Colonial Lagos," *Journal of the Historical Society of Nigeria* 8.1 (1975); Blackett, "Martin R. Delany and Robert Campbell: Black Americans in Search of an African Colony," *Journal of Negro History* 62.1 (1977), and Blackett, "Robert Campbell and the Triangle of the Black Experience," in Blackett's collective biographical portrait, *Beating Against the Barriers: The Lives of Six Nineteenth-Century Afro-Americans* (Ithaca NY: Cornell UP, 1989): 139–82.

complexion and the color hierarchy on the island, Campbell came face to face, for the first time, with the brutal species of American racial proscription. It was, as Blackett puts it, "a racial baptism of fire for the young Jamaican."[46] Eventually, and through the intervention of an enlightened English abolitionist, John Grey, Campbell gained an opening in Grey's small printing shop in Brooklyn. He worked with Grey, all the while with an eye to a better opportunity, for almost two years until in 1855 he saw an advertisement for principal of the Institute for Colored Youth, a black school in Philadelphia.

When the ICY board met in the fall of 1855 to decide upon the applicants, Campbell was not selected for the principalship. But the board was sufficiently impressed with his application to offer him the assistant principal's position. Campbell accepted the offer and taught natural sciences, geography, elementary algebra and Latin; he was also made responsible for teaching evening classes, open to the public, on electricity, astronomy, anatomy and other subjects. By all accounts, Campbell enjoyed the challenge and distinguished himself as a teacher at the ICY. He would, however, once again encounter racial discrimination.

To satisfy his urge for self-improvement, Campbell applied to attend a series of scientific lectures at the Franklin Institute of Philadelphia. But because of his color, the Institute's agent refused to sell him a ticket. Campbell then wrote to the managers to ascertain whether this was indeed the Institute's policy. Attempting to avoid open admission of its racism, the managers offered Campbell a free ticket on the ostensible grounds that he was a teacher at an incorporated institution. Campbell saw through the ruse and stuck to his principles. If the managers of the Franklin Institute, he told a friend,

> deem it wrong for respectable men of different complexions to partake of knowledge in common, then let them as scientific men, let them as the assumed instructors of the public, fearlessly proclaim it. I could then pity the distortion of their judgement, but would respect their honesty. On the other hand, if they do not, why cater to the weakness and prejudice of the vulgar – why on any pretense evade a direct issue in this matter?[47]

But the managers refused to deal more honestly with the issue, and so Campbell, embittered, refused their offer.

---

[46] Blackett, "Robert Campbell," 143.
[47] Quoted in Blackett, "Robert Campbell," 147.

In an attempt to heal Campbell's wounded pride, the managers of the
ICY, in December 1856, purchased a ticket for him to attend a series of
lectures in the Department of Mines, Arts and Manufactures at the University of Pennsylvania. Campbell attended, thus becoming the first black
person to be admitted to the lecture halls of that university. But it did not
mark an end to the color bar there, for, at the end of the century, there were
still complaints, as W.E.B. Du Bois reported, against the institution's
refusal to admit black students or even allow black people to attend public
lectures.[48]

Infuriated at America's racism, Campbell seized the chance at the end of
1858 to join Martin Delany's emigrationist Niger Valley Exploring Party.
He was sufficiently enthusiastic about the project and tired of the enforced
indignities of black life in the USA to resign his relatively secure, esteemed
and well-paid job to throw in his lot with Delany. In November 1858,
Campbell resigned from the ICY even before funds were secured for
Delany's mission. He was determined to leave the USA and could not be
persuaded to stay. Reluctantly reconciled to his decision, the board of the
ICY praised Campbell for his work over the years with them. Fanny
Jackson–Coppin, who would later become principal of the Institute, and
many others praised his gifts as a teacher. For their part, the students at the
ICY, in December 1858, organized a farewell meeting to express their
appreciation and presented him with a gold watch and a copy of Alexander
von Humboldt's five-volume study, *Cosmos: Sketch of a Physical Description of the Universe*.[49]

Impatient with Delany's efforts to raise funds for the mission, Campbell
sailed for Britain – the first leg of his African journey – in April 1859,
leaving Delany behind. Two months later he had reached Africa. By early
July he was in Lagos, more than two months before Delany arrived. With
Delany, he secured an agreement with the *alake* (king) of Abeokuta,
allowing the settlement of Africans in the Americas in the area. Campbell
spent nine months on the continent and declared it his motherland. He was
home.

In the fall of 1860, Campbell returned to the USA. He traveled across the
country preaching the virtues of African emigration. Dressed in splendid
African robes, acquired during his continental sojourn, he lectured to sym-

---

[48] Blackett, "Robert Campbell," 149; and W.E.B. Du Bois, *The Philadelphia
Negro: A Social Study*, intro. Elijah Anderson (1899; Philadelphia: U of Pennsylvania P, 1995): 88.

[49] Blackett, "Robert Campbell," 149–50.

pathetic black audiences in churches and halls. But he won few converts, and after the outbreak of the Civil War in April 1861, there was even less interest and inclination on the part of Afro-Americans to go to Africa. The Nigerian project suffered another setback in the summer of 1861 when, largely through the pressure of British missionaries in Abeokuta, the colonial authorities disallowed the treaty, thus denying the settlement of an Afro-American colony in Nigeria.[50] But Campbell would not be deterred.

In 1861, he published *A Pilgrim to My Motherland: An Account of a Journey Among the Egbas and Yorubas of Central Africa, in 1859–60*, a remarkable account of his experience in Africa. It was half of a diptych, Delany's *Official Report of the Niger Valley Exploring Party* being the other part, which appeared later the same year.[51] In vivid and lively prose, Campbell tells of the vicissitudes of his journey, the flora and the fauna of the region, the fertility of the soil, the economic prospects for the would-be emigrant, and, most of all, of the people and their institutions. It is a refreshingly clear-eyed and unromantic story of Southern Nigeria. Given the fact that the volume was issued primarily as an advertisement for African emigration, Campbell was surprisingly frank about the less pleasing side of the Africa he saw. Thus, he mentions the several bouts of fever he suffered, and does not refrain from expressing his antipathy toward polygamy as a "disgusting system." He also relates the hard bargain driven by the local carriers, which he calls acts of extortion. He condemns their "unconquerable love of gain, and desire to make if possible a fortune out of us." He was particularly hard on those on the coast, the "semi-civilized, neither Christian nor heathen," who, "acquiring all the vices of the white man, know little and practise still less of his virtues" (174, 208, 236–38). But his primary target of attack was the institution of slavery he encountered in the land of the Yorubas. Although he recognizes the differences between this form of slavery and that in the Americas, he found it no less repugnant. He regards all forms of slavery, whether perpetrated by Africans or Europeans, as "evil" (192) As he explains, "although [...] slavery in Africa is not like slavery in America, or even as it is in Cuba, yet it is still a fact which must not be disregarded, that, more or less, it is slavery" (194–95).

So important to him was this anti-slavery commitment that, before his African journey was over, he placed his own safety and liberty, if not his

---

[50] Miller's *Search for a Black Nationality* provides the most detailed analysis of the negotiations over the treaty and the politics of its rescinding.

[51] These two texts have been conveniently brought together in Howard Bell, ed. *Search for a Place: Black Separatism and Africa, 1860* (Ann Arbor: U of Michigan P, 1969). It is to this combined edition that I shall refer.

life, in jeopardy in order to save a woman and her two children from enslavement (230–33). Campbell perhaps felt the need for this disquisition on slavery because of the charge by some black anti-emigrationists, such as Dr James McCune Smith, accusing both Delany and Campbell of condoning slavery by their recognition of the domestic institutions of the Egba people. Campbell had delivered a powerful riposte to this charge at the beginning of 1861:

> I have no notion of law apart from equity and would respect the 'domestic institutions' in Abeokuta no more than James McCune Smith would respect the Fugitive Slave bill by voting under the Constitution of the USA, by virtue of which that God-defying measure is sustained.

But he perhaps felt it necessary to buttress his argument in his travelogue.[52] It is noticeable that Delany, the more fully formed black nationalist, though far from condoning the institution, was more defensive in speaking of its African expression as he found it. He dismissed as "simply preposterous to talk about slavery, as that term is understood, either being legalized or existing in this part of Africa." The system, he writes, is a "patriarchal one, there being no difference, socially, between the slave (called by their protector *son* or *daughter*) and the children of the person with whom they live."[53]

But despite her shortcomings, so forthrightly enumerated, Africa, to Campbell was his home, his motherland.[54] And she had much to commend her: the warmth with which she received and embraced both Delany and himself, despite his light complexion; and the ingenuity of the arts and crafts of her people, about which Campbell was exceedingly curious and highly complimentary. Although he could not disguise his "disgust" at both polygamy and slavery, he did not display the New World arrogance that so many members of the diaspora, before and after, were to display. He told prospective emigrants that they "must ever remember that the existing rulers must be respected, for they only are the *bona fide* rulers of the place." How this was to be reconciled with his antipathy toward polygamy and slavery Campbell does not clarify. Nevertheless, he felt that the "effort

---

[52] For the charge and Campbell's riposte, see Blackett, "Martin R. Delany and Robert Campbell," 22–23.

[53] Bell, *Search for a Place*, 85–86.

[54] It is interesting to note that in marked contrast to Campbell, Delany, in keeping with the more masculinist and conventional vocabulary of black nationalism, always referred to Africa as his "fatherland."

should be to lift them [the Africans] up to the proper standard, and not to supersede or crush them. If such a disposition is manifested, then harmony and peace will prevail; I am afraid not, otherwise" (244). Against the rising tide of pseudo-scientific racism, Campbell put up a spirited defense. In opposing the naysayers, he asserts from his own experience that "there is not a more industrious people on the face of the earth." He especially noted the industry of the women, and the men, he said, are "builders, blacksmiths, iron-smelters, tanners and leather-workers, tailors, carpenters, calabash-carvers, weavers, basket[-], hat[-] and mat-makers, farmers: the women weave, spin, dye, cook, brew, make pots, oils, soap and I know not what else" (184). In the final passage of his book, he declares:

> Those who believe, among other foolish things, that the Negro is accustomed lazily to spend his time basking in the sunshine, like black-snakes or alligators, should go and see the people they malign. There are, doubtless, among them, as among every other race, not excepting the Anglo-American, indolent people, but this says nothing more against the one than the other. (248)

Campbell could not resist a final jibe, in the very last sentence of his book, at those who malign his motherland: "We landed at Liverpool, Dr. Delany and myself, on the 12th of May, 1860, in good health, although we had been to Africa!" (250).

Even before the signing of the treaty with the Alake and the Yoruba authorities, Campbell had determined to return and settle in Africa:

> My home shall be Africa, though I be the only person from America; and I am satisfied that any man knowing the circumstances, who is not a fool, and is solicitous for his own welfare, having too a heart to labor for the good of his race, would come to the same conclusion.[55]

In his preface to *A Pilgrimage to My Motherland*, he reaffirmed his decision:

> If I am still asked what I think of Africa for a colored man to live and do well in, I simply answer, that with as good prospects in America as colored men generally, I have determined, with my wife and children, to go to Africa to live, leaving the inquirer to interpret the reply for himself.

True to his word, Campbell, with his wife and four children, left the USA in August 1861, spent five months in London, then went on to Africa, never to

---

[55] Quoted in Blackett, "Robert Campbell," 170.

leave his motherland for the rest of his life. Arriving in Lagos in March 1862, Campbell had brought with him £250 worth of cotton machinery. He had intended to settle and cultivate cotton in Abeokuta, export it to Britain and, by so doing, not only make a living for himself and his family but also help, as the black emigrationists had dreamed, to undermine the slave-produced cotton that dominated the world market. But his plan went awry. Southern Nigeria was in turmoil internally with itself and externally with Britain, which had annexed Lagos the previous year. He was forced to abandon the Abeokuta plan along with his idea for a gin machine. Campbell chose instead to settle in Lagos.

He tried his hand at photography for a while and then decided to found a newspaper.[56] At the time, Lagos had no newspapers, and in the whole of what became modern Nigeria there was only a fortnightly, *Iwe Irohin*, put out in English and Yoruba by a white missionary in Abeokuta. Campbell brought in a second-hand printing press from England. But before he could even begin, the British Governor in Lagos, H. Stanhope Freeman, conspired to kill Campbell's paper before it was born. In a dispatch to the Secretary of State for the Colonies, Freeman reported that "a West Indian gentleman lately settled here" had plans to start a newspaper. He complained to White-hall of the "unfortunate dispute and ill-feeling" that "the worse than worth-less" periodicals published in Britain's west-coast colonies were causing.[57] He pointed especially to the *New Era*, a newspaper put out by another Caribbean immigrant, William Drape, in Sierra Leone. Freeman sought the Colonial Secretary's authorization to impose a tax on newspapers published in the colony "as would preclude the possibility of their succeeding as a monetary speculation."[58] Such a measure Freeman regarded as a "trifling check" on the liberty of the press, which, he averred, was "a dangerous instrument in the hands of semi-civilized Negroes." Mindful of the trouble that they had with Drape only a few years earlier when they attempted a similar ploy (about which more later), Whitehall, however, refused to accede to Governor Freeman's request.

Described in the 1880s by another Nigerian broadsheet as the first news-paper "ever seen and read" in Lagos, the *Anglo-African* made its debut on 6 June 1863 and was published weekly until its last issue on 30 December

---

[56] Fred Omu, "The *Anglo-African*, 1863–65," *Nigeria Magazine* 90 (1966): 208.

[57] Omu, "The *Anglo-African*," 209; Blackett, "Return to the Motherland," 137.

[58] Blackett, "Return to the Motherland," 137.

1865.[59] But Freeman did not abandon the hope of controlling the *Anglo-African*. This time, however, he hoped to bribe it into submission. As early as September 1863 a representative of the Church Missionary Society was informing the London headquarters that "it is understood" that the *Anglo-African* is "under the influence of the Government who pay the editor a considerable sum annually for their advertisements."[60] But Campbell was beyond purchase.

From the outset, he made the independent position of his paper explicit. When the *Anglo-African* was accused of bias, Campbell stated:

> The *Anglo-African* was established to promote the interest and welfare of Lagos and its people, and not to serve those of any party, but in all questions to advocate the side of right – right, not in the estimation of this man or that, but in the estimation of the editor; and hence we shall never consult any one as to what we shall say or what we shall forbear to say.[61]

There is still no systematic analysis of the coverage and editorial positions of the *Anglo-African* – a serious lack that cannot be made good here. What is known is that the paper carried news and analysis of the developments in Nigeria and West Africa generally. It also serialized stories and, not forsaking Campbell's New World beginnings, paid considerable attention to developments in the Americas, especially the American Civil War. Campbell devoted an entire issue to the Morant Bay uprising in his native Jamaica in 1865.[62]

It is not clear why Campbell decided to discontinue the paper, but it was probably due to financial difficulties. In Campbell's hands, the *Anglo-African* was more than a newspaper. It was also a training ground for Lagos's first generation of printers and compositors, for Campbell imparted his knowledge of the trade to his fellow Africans. Some of them gained employment as government printers, including Richard Beale Blaize, who was head government printer between 1871 and 1874. Blaize would later start his

---

[59] *Eagle and Lagos Critic* (26 January 1884), quoted in Michael Echeruo, *Victorian Lagos: Aspects of Nineteenth Century Lagos Life* (London: Macmillan, 1977): 3.

[60] Quoted in Blackett, "Return to the Motherland," 138.

[61] *Anglo-African* (6 June 1863, 9 September 1863), quoted in Blackett, "Return to the Motherland," 138.

[62] For some idea of the editorial positions taken by and coverage of the *Anglo-African*, see: Omu, "The *Anglo-African*," 209–12; Blackett, "Return to the Motherland," 138–40; Blackett, "Robert Campbell," 173–77; Geiss, *The Pan-African Movement*, 91; and Echeruo, *Victorian Lagos*, passim.

own newspaper, the *Lagos Times and Gold Coast Colony Advertiser*, in 1880 – the first to appear in Nigeria after the demise of the *Anglo-African*. A Sierra Leonean immigrant, Blaize, by the end of the century, was one of Lagos's most prominent citizens and successful merchants, who also played an important part in the nationalist struggle in Nigeria and British West Africa.[63] According to Fred Omu, an expert on the history of the Nigerian press, "in large measure," the *Anglo-African* "not only helped to produce more printers without whom the subsequent proliferation of newspapers would have been impossible but also set the stage for the growth of the printing industry in Nigeria." He regarded as even more significant the fact that Campbell's newspaper "reinforced the growing awareness of the importance of the newspaper as an essential institution in an enlightened society." The *Anglo-African* was thus of "major significance in the growth and consolidation, from 1880, of the Lagos Press which, until the second decade of the [twentieth] century, was synonymous with the Nigerian Press."[64]

But Campbell's contribution in Africa was not confined to the pioneering role of the *Anglo-African*. He retained his keen interest in education and the broadest dissemination of knowledge. It was in keeping with his character, then, that, during his initial exploration, Campbell took time to help reorganize the Abeokuta Lyceum. When it re-opened in January 1860, he also delivered its first lecture (on the Dignity of Labour), which was attended by over a hundred people, including forty women.[65]

Not surprisingly, Campbell used the *Anglo-African* to promote the expansion and development of education in the colony. He advocated an educational system that went beyond the three Rs and de-emphasized religious instruction, which he distinguished from moral education, something which he supported. Schools should endeavor to develop the moral, intellectual and physical faculties of their students. Students must be trained to think and to acquire new skills. Furthermore, education should be available to all: "The diffusion of learning – the cultivation of the habit of correct thinking – the discipline of the mind which is the consequence of study [...] are

---

[63] Jean Herskovits Kopytoff, *A Preface to Modern Nigeria* (Madison: U of Wisconsin P, 1965): 216–20, 283–84; Omu, "The *Anglo-African*," 212.

[64] Omu, "The *Anglo-African*," 212; Omu, *Press and Politics in Nigeria, 1880–1937* (London: Longman, 1978).

[65] Blackett, "Robert Campbell," 160.

together with religious truths," Campbell claims, the most effective means of ensuring the development of a "respectable community."[66]

Campbell expressed his educational interests concretely during his years in Nigeria, attending the annual examinations of missionary schools and making recommendations for curricula change. As early as 1863, he gave four public lectures on human physiology and other topics. In october 1866 he helped to launch the Lagos Academy, which aimed at promoting literature, the arts and sciences. In 1879, he became the first president of the Lagos Mutual Improvement Society. The Society organized the study of local languages, the work of Edward Wilmot Blyden, the discussion of ethnic loyalties and polygamy. Under the Society's auspices, Campbell demonstrated many of the latest scientific discoveries. He improved a form of colza oil, which was widely used in lamps, developed a steam mill for making salt, and he used local material for the manufacture of soap. No surprise, then, that Campbell was elected the first president of the Lagos Scientific Society when it was formed in the late 1870s. Thus, he helped to establish "a tradition of intellectual investigation" in the early years of the British colony and was recognized as one of Lagos's leading intellectuals.[67]

Campbell seemed to have been as enterprising in seeking a living as he was in his intellectual endeavors. In 1863, to supplement his income, he sold merchandise from the offices of the *Anglo-African*. He owned and ran a brickmaking factory in Ebute Metta on the mainland near Lagos from 1863 to 1878. Toward the end of 1866, Campbell was involved in the Lagos Steam Sawing and Ginning Company, which collapsed before it could engage in the cotton-cleaning side of the business. In the early 1880s he established a distillery to produce "Africana Canna or Pure Cane Juice Spirits," which the colonial surgeon described as "a more wholesome stimulant than much of the imported liquors sold in Lagos."[68] Unfortunately, the Canna did not survive for long.

Critics found it difficult to assess Campbell's many commercial ventures, especially given the "volatile period" in which they were undertaken, a time during which "businesses in Lagos rose and disappeared" rapidly.[69] But at

---

[66] Quoted in Blackett, "Robert Campbell," 177; see also Echeruo, *Victorian Lagos*, 50.

[67] Blackett, "Robert Campbell," 178; for good discussions of nineteenth- and early twentieth-century intellectual life in Nigeria and Campbell's place in it, see Echeruo, *Victorian Lagos*, and Philip Zachernuk, *Colonial Subjects: An African Intelligentsia and Atlantic Ideas* (Charlottesville: UP of Virginia, 2000).

[68] Blackett, "Robert Campbell," 179.

[69] "Robert Campbell," 179.

least one local editor was less reticent in his appraisal. Addressing Campbell publicly in the Lagos *Observer*, he asked:

> Are you forgetful of such a thing as determination of purpose? Is your life so well insured as to admit to further experimentalizing? For your own sake I deprecate the versatility of your intellect. I deny your arguments that former experiments did not pay you because I am convinced that you have relinquished many of them on the threshold of success.[70]

As Blackett shows, the *Anglo-African* was abandoned by Campbell on the verge of success. Many of his business failures can be attributed to impatience. Campbell, according to Blackett, was driven by "an almost frenetic desire to establish a reputation and find financial security."[71] Blackett's own evidence, however, also suggests a more complex explanation. Campbell's energies were too widely dispersed and he did seem guilty of the charge of too much "experimentalizing," as the Lagos *Observer* remarked. He seemed to have been easily bored, which contributed to his commercial restlessness. On top of his educational and business activities, Campbell was for decades the factotum of the local government. He held the posts of government auctioneer, stipendiary magistrate, acting colonial surveyor, and acting chief clerk and warehouse keeper, and served on the Commercial Court of Tribunal as acting surveyor four times between 1866 and 1878.[72] Campbell, despite the general agreement of contemporaries that he was "a most clever and industrious man," quite simply took on far too much at the same time.

On 19 January 1884, Campbell died in Lagos, aged fifty-four. A pan-Africanist and emigrationist, through his own New World experience, especially in the USA, he sought a life free of the indignities of white supremacy in his ancestral homeland. He was not a rhetorical black nationalist of the Delany school. Campbell simply sought to contribute to the advancement of Africa while making a living for himself and his family. He thought that all knowledge is the patrimony of all humanity and tried to harness scientific advances in Europe to the conditions of Africa. Unlike most of his emigrationist contemporaries, he was not a missionary of Christianity, though he was, in his own quiet way, a Christian. Basically a propagandist of knowledge, he took a leading role in the establishment and

---

[70] Lagos *Observer* (10 July 1882), quoted in Blackett, "Robert Campbell," 179.

[71] Blackett, "Robert Campbell," 179.

[72] "Robert Campbell," 180. The colonial authorities were willing to exploit his undoubted talents but were reluctant to give him a permanent, civil service, position.

improvement of educational and cultural institutions and practices among
the black population of Nigeria. Small wonder, then, that, in its obituary, the
Lagos *Observer* bemoaned the loss of one of the colony's "representative
brains [...] a man of rare intellect, and versatility of learning."[73] As Blackett
noted, "From the moment in 1858 when he accepted Delany's invitation to
join the Exploring Party until his death in 1884, Campbell displayed an un-
failing commitment to the 'advancement' of Africa."[74] The young Mojola
Agbebi (1860–1917), man of letters and one of Africa's most distinguished
cultural nationalists of the late nineteenth and early twentieth centuries,
spoke for many when he eulogized Campbell as one of Africa's "priceless
sons."[75]

Russwurm, Campbell and Blyden were pioneers, but they were by no
means the only Caribbeans to figure in the annals of pan-African dissent in
nineteenth-century Africa. Other distinguished figures appeared in West,
Central and Southern Africa. A number of historians have highlighted the
extraordinary role that Caribbean immigrants played in the struggle, especially in Sierra Leone. The most thorough and comprehensive assessment of
their pan-Africanist efforts can be found in Nemata Blyden's recent book
West Indians in West Africa, 1808–1880.[76] Thanks to her work, we now
have a fuller account of the role played by immigrants such as William
Ferguson, Alexander Fitzjames, William Drape and William Rainy. It is
impossible to provide here even a précis of the Caribbean experience in
Sierra Leone in the nineteenth century, but it should be registered that
Drape and Rainy in particular made profound contributions to the articula-

---

[73] Quoted in "Robert Campbell," 182.

[74] Blackett, "Robert Campbell," 182.

[75] David B. Vincent [Mojola Agbebi], "A Dirge," *Eagle and Lagos Critic* (28
June 1884), quoted in Rina Okonkwo, *Heroes of West African Nationalism* (Enugu:
Delta Publications): 12.

[76] See, in particular, Christopher Fyfe, "The Sierra Leone Press in the Nineteenth
Century," *Sierra Leone Studies* 8 (1957): 228–36; Fyfe, *A History of Sierra Leone*
(Oxford: Oxford UP, 1962); Fyfe, *Africanus Horton: West African Scientist and
Patriot* (New York: Oxford UP, 1972); Abioseh Nicol, "West Indians in West
Africa," *Sierra Leone Studies* 13 (1960); Hollis Lynch, "The Native Pastorate Con-
troversy and Cultural Ethno-Centrism in Sierra Leone, 1871–1874," *Journal of
African History* 5.3 (1964): 395–411; Fred Omu, "The Dilemma of Press Freedom in
Colonial Africa: The West African Example," *Journal of African History* 9.2 (1968):
279–98; Omu, "The *New Era* and the Abortive Press Law of 1857," *Sierra Leone
Studies* 23 (1968): 2–14; Nemata Blyden, *West Indians in West Africa, 1808–1880:
The African Diaspora in Reverse* (Rochester NY: U of Rochester P, 2000).

tion of pan-African dissent through legal advocacy and the medium of the press. Drape started the first black newspaper, the *New Era*, in Sierra Leone in 1855. Its outspokenness about government policy in the colony attracted the enmity of the Governor, who unsuccessfully sought its suppression.[77] It was Drape's successful struggle against the heavy hand of Governor Hill in Sierra Leone in 1857 that saved Campbell's *Anglo-African* in Nigeria from being strangled at birth in 1863 and helped to launch other dissenting newspapers in British West Africa in subsequent years.[78]

Rainy, born in Dominica and trained as a barrister in London, was by far the most formidable Caribbean opponent of colonial despotism in Sierra Leone in the nineteenth century. In addition, he boldly raised his voice against the rising tide of pseudo-scientific racism in the second half of the century. He was so incensed by Sir Richard Burton's racist diatribe *Wanderings in West Africa* (1863), which targeted the educated African in particular, that he penned his own riposte in the form of a pamphlet.[79] Rainy could not stand silently by and watch and listen to what he called "the wide-spread conspiracy" to "lower the negro in the scale of creation."[80] His eyes were trained not only upon Africa, but, like Campbell's, also upon developments in the Americas, especially the events surrounding the Morant Bay Rebellion in Jamaica and its bloody suppression.[81] More explicitly than others in Sierra Leone at the time, he expressed a pan-African vision aimed at creating "a spirit of nationality in Africa," and sought to induce others to follow his example. "We have the cause of Africa at heart," he declared in 1866, "and shall welcome every labourer in the field who honestly strives to establish it and strengthen it."[82] Described by a Sierra Leonean correspondent to the London-based *African Times* as "our indefatigable and warmhearted advocate and champion," Rainy was also a hero elsewhere in West Africa. In 1871 he fell ill and left for London in July; he never returned to Sierra Leone.[83] His friends at the *African Times* recog-

---

[77] See Omu, "The *New Era*," and Blyden, *West Indians in West Africa*, 96–100.

[78] Omu, "The *New Era*," 13–14; and Omu, "Dilemma of Press Freedom in Colonial Africa."

[79] Richard Burton, *Wanderings in West Africa: From Liverpool to Fernando Po*, 2 vols. (London: Tinsley Brothers, 1863), see especially vol. 1, 193–281; and William Rainy, *The Censor Censured, or the Calumnies of Captain Burton on the Africans of Sierra Leone* (London: Geo. Chalfont, 1865).

[80] Quoted in Blyden, *West Indians in West Africa*, 151.

[81] Blyden, *West Indians in West Africa*, 151–52.

[82] Quoted in Blyden, *West Indians in West Africa*, 142.

[83] Fyfe, *History of Sierra Leone*, 386–87.

nized the loss that his departure from Africa meant for Sierra Leone and West Africa in general and implored Sierra Leoneans to continue the struggle. "It is difficult to obtain the removal of officials however evil their course may be," the *African Times* editorialized,

> but persistent efforts for their removal, such as Mr. Rainy has made, will at least prevent any perpetuation, in the persons of subsequent officials, of these abominations which they may have practised; and we are sure that in the future African Pantheon the name of "Rainy" will be prominently inscribed by a grateful people.[84]

From London, Rainy emigrated to Australia, where he had spent time in the 1850s, and died near Melbourne in 1878.[85]

Lack of space here precludes discussion of the efforts made by persons of West Indian origin in nineteenth-century Gold Coast anti-colonial politics. Their contribution was remarkable – William Finlason, Francis Grant and the Barbadian-born bishop John B. Small made their mark in this part of West Africa.[86] In Nigeria too, after Robert Campbell's death in Lagos, other Caribbeans, particularly Edward Ricketts (Jamaica) and John Amblestone (Dominica), kept up the pan-Africanist project there, stretching across the late nineteenth into the twentieth century.

The Pattern in the Twentieth Century

1897 is a particularly important year in the history of pan-Africanism, for, in that year, Henry Sylvester Williams (1869–1911), a Trinidadian law student, started the African Association in London, the heart of the largest empire. This organization aspired to give formal expression to pan-Africanist sentiment and aspirations. By organizing the historic Pan-African Conference in London in 1900, the first of its kind, Williams opened the new century with a resolute gathering of people of African descent from the diaspora and the continent. The association did not last after 1902, but its legacy was rich and

---

[84] *African Times*, 23 December 1868, and 22 July 1871, quoted in Blyden, *West Indians in West Africa*, 154 and 156.

[85] Fyfe, *History of Sierra Leone*, 263 and 387.

[86] There are good vignettes of these figures in David Kimble's remarkable and unsurpassed study, *A Political History of Ghana: The Rise of Gold Coast Nationalism, 1850–1928* (Oxford: Clarendon, 1963). Small is also discussed in Geiss, *Pan-African Movement*.

enduring. Williams himself continued to agitate on behalf of oppressed black humanity, including a stint in South Africa, where he practiced as its first black barrister, right up to his untimely death in Trinidad at the age of forty-two.[87]

The First World War and its aftermath galvanized new forces in a pan-African effort. In London, another Trinidadian, Felix Hercules, was one of the founders of the Society of Peoples of African Origin, bringing together Africans and others of the diaspora living in Britain. He, in fact, served as the General Secretary of the Society and as associate secretary of a similar organization, the African Progress Union, before the two merged in 1919. Hercules edited the organization's magazine, the *African Telegraph*, and was uncompromising in expressing the cause of African people around the world. To the alarm of the Colonial Office and the governors in the British West Indies, Hercules made a tour of the region and forcefully expressed the pan-Africanist aspirations of the SPAO. He was frequently made a scapegoat for the labor unrest in the Caribbean in 1919. The *African Telegraph* was sued for libel by the colonial authorities and was thus pushed into bankruptcy. Pleased with this victory, the colonialists were further relieved when Hercules migrated to the USA after his Caribbean tour.[88]

Far more enduring was the effort of Marcus Garvey and the UNIA. Although Garvey never set foot on African soil, his organization had a profound impact on the nationalist struggles on the continent, especially in West and Southern Africa. And here, once again, one finds the mobilization of Caribbean immigrants on the continent, this time through the agency of the UNIA.[89] In Lagos, the center of UNIA activity in West Africa, the

---

[87] For more on Williams, see Mathurin, *Henry Sylvester Williams*, and J.R. Hooker, *Henry Sylvester Williams: Imperial Pan-Africanist* (London: Rex Collings, 1975).

[88] W.F. Elkins, "Hercules and the Society of Peoples of African Origin," *Caribbean Studies* 11.4 (1972): 47–59.

[89] Tony Martin, *Race First: The Ideological and Organizational Struggles of Marcus Garvey and the Universal Negro Improvement Association* (1976; Dover MA: Majority Press, 1986); Rina Okonkwo, "The Garvey Movement in British West Africa," *Journal of African History* 21.1 (1980): 105–17; Rupert Lewis, *Marcus Garvey: Anti-Colonial Champion* (London: Karia, 1987); G.O. Olusanya, "Garvey and Nigeria," in *Garvey: Africa, Europe, the Americas*, ed. Rupert Lewis & Maureen Warner–Lewis (Trenton NJ: Africa World Press, 1994); and the pioneering volumes on Africa among the Garvey Papers, *The Marcus Garvey and Universal Negro Improvement Association Papers*, ed. Robert Hill (Berkeley: U of California P, 1995), vols. 9–10.

President of the organization, Wynter Shackleford, was a Jamaican immigrant, and the Treasurer, Amblestone, was from Dominica.[90] In Southern
Africa, Arthur McKinley and J.G. Gumbs, two Afro-Caribbeans, were leading members of Garvey's organization. Gumbs was also Vice-President and
later President of the Industrial and Commercial Workers' Union, the
primary working-class organization in Southern Africa at the time. In South
West Africa (now Namibia), Fitz Herbert Headley and John De Clue, both
immigrants from the Caribbean, founded and led the UNIA in Luderitz, the
main port city in the territory, and later Windhoek. The list is not
exhaustive. One of the remarkable features of this group in Southern Africa,
unlike that in Lagos, for instance, was that they were deeply involved in the
working-class movement and saw no contradiction between their black
nationalism and radical trade unionism.[91]

The crises of the Great Depression and the Italian invasion of Ethiopia in
1935 brought another Trinidadian to the fore. One of the most distinguished
pan-Africanists of the twentieth century, George Padmore, was born Malcolm Nurse in Arouca, the same Trinidadian town in which Henry Sylvester
Williams was born. He studied in the USA at Fisk and Howard Universities, where his already radical inclinations became more pronounced. After
joining the Communist Party he eventually became, in 1929, the head of
"Negro" work in the Communist International (Comintern) in Moscow.
Disillusioned with Stalin's disinclination to support the anticolonial struggle, he left the Comintern in 1935 and settled in London. There he launched
the International African Service Bureau with like-minded Caribbeans and
Africans, most notably C.L.R. James, a fellow Trinidadian, and Ras Makonnen from British Guiana (Guyana). The Bureau agitated against colonial
oppression in Africa and the Caribbean, particularly the devastation of

---

[90] Okonkwo, *Heroes of West Africa*, ch. iv.

[91] Hill, ed. *The Marcus Garvey and Universal Negro Improvement Association
Papers*, vol. 9: 204–205, 211–12, 267–69, 566; Alan Cobley, "'Far From Home': The
Origins and Significance of the Afro-Caribbean Community in South Africa to
1930," *Journal of Southern African Studies* 18.2 (1992): 349–70; Tony Martin,
"Marcus Garvey and Southern Africa," in Martin, *The Pan-African Connection*; and
Robert Hill & Gregory Pirio, "'Africa for the Africans': The Garvey Movement in
South Africa, 1920–1940," in *The Politics of Race, Class and Nationalism in Twen-
tieth-Century South Africa*, ed. Shula Marks & Stanley Trapido (London: Longman,
1987): 209–53. A thorough account of the evolution and practices of both the ICU
and the UNIA in Namibia during the period is given in Tony Emmett, *Popular
Resistance and the Roots of Nationalism in Namibia, 1915–1966* (Basel: P. Schlettwein, 1999): 125–54.

Ethiopia and its people by Mussolini's fascist troops. Padmore also drew attention to the complicity and inaction of the other members of the League of Nations, especially Britain and the USA, in the suffering of the Ethiopian people.

Padmore's office and small flat in central London became the workshop of the African anticolonial struggle. Nkrumah and Jomo Kenyatta were two of the more distinguished African nationalists to pass through their apprenticeship under Padmore's guidance. Padmore later served as Nkrumah's advisor on African affairs in the newly independent Ghana. In 1959 he became ill, traveled to London for treatment and, at the age of 57, died there under mysterious circumstances.[92]

Towards an Explanation

The question of how we account for the disproportionate contribution of Caribbean people to these pan-Africanist projects (given the size of the British West Indian population at the time and the relatively small number who went to Africa) has never been adequately addressed. Maybe this is due to the complex nature of the answer. I think the following may help us toward an understanding of this striking phenomenon.

1. The Caribbean diaspora was among the most far-flung and widely traveled since the end of the slave trade. This was especially true of Jamaicans and Barbadians, whose lives in the post-emancipation period became especially difficult, even by Caribbean standards.

2. Related to this was the limited economic options in the British West Indies because of the generally depressed state of its economies in the late nineteenth and early twentieth centuries.

3. Many sought new openings in Africa and elsewhere because of the racist, color-related blockages that existed in the Caribbean. Black profes-

---

[92] Hooker's (*Black Revolutionary*) is the only biography of Padmore. See also: Penny von Eschen, *Race Against Empire: Black Americans and Anticolonialism, 1937–1957* (Ithaca NY: Cornell UP, 1997); Philippe Dewitte, *Les Mouvements Nègres en France, 1919–1939* (Paris: L'Harmattan, 1985); and the memoirs of some his associates and comrades: Makonnen, *Pan-Africanism from Within*; C.L.R. James, "George Padmore: Black Marxist Revolutionary – A Memoir," in his *At the Rendezvous of Victory: Selected Writings* (London: Allison & Busby 1984); Dudley Thompson, *From Kingston to Kenya: The Making of a Pan-Africanist Lawyer* (Dover MA: Majority Press, 1993); and Peter Abrahams, *The Black Experience in the Twentieth Century: An Autobiography* (Bloomington: Indiana UP, 2000).

sionals endured severe restrictions in relation to the colonial civil service in the Caribbean. But on migration to Panama, Cuba, the Dominican Republic, the USA and even Africa, they also met with racism; perhaps they felt an even greater legitimacy to resist racist and colonial structures in Africa, their ancestral home, and became determined to wrest a homeland, the "motherland," as Campbell called the continent, from the grip of the imperialists. As J. Albert Thorne put it in 1896, "Africa is the only quarter of the world where we will be permanently respected as a race."[93] Thus the desire to create a liberated oasis in a desert of oppression was a compelling force.

4. There was also a greater willingness on the part of Caribbean intellectuals and workers to settle in Africa than among many of their American counterparts. It is interesting to note that Delany decided to stay in the USA while Campbell returned to Nigeria. Blyden made Africa his home; the Afro-American Alexander Crummell, Blyden's close friend and collaborator, decided, after almost twenty years of living in Liberia, to return to the USA. Afro-Americans generally thought that the USA could be a good place to live, if only it could be reformed. Caribbean people had little hope of transforming the Caribbean and even less the USA, so decided to stay in Africa in larger proportions. In addition, Caribbean people generally had a closer affinity with Africa and Africans than did Afro-Americans. Towards the end of the eighteenth century, the Afro-American population became self-reproducing. Thus the transatlantic slave trade was less important for the USA, while in the Caribbean there was always need for a continued infusion of new blood from Africa as the slave population died out. The USA's was the most creolized population in the New World; those of the British Caribbean had a higher proportion of African-born people. This was especially true of Trinidad, Guyana and Jamaica. Moreover, so-called liberated Africans, those taken from Spanish, Portuguese and Brazilian slave ships after 1808 by the British Navy, were re-settled in the thousands in the Caribbean right up to the 1860s.[94] This brought another infusion of the African presence, especially in Jamaica and Trinidad, where many were re-

---

[93] Quoted in George Shepperson, "Notes on Negro American Influences on the Emergence of African Nationalism," *Journal of African History* 1.2 (1960): 300.

[94] The best overview of the slave experience in the USA is Peter Kolchin, *American Slavery, 1619–1877* (New York: Hill & Wang, 1993); for the British Caribbean pattern in the nineteenth century, see B.W. Higman, *Slave Populations of the British Caribbean, 1807–1834* (Baltimore MD: Johns Hopkins UP, 1984); and for an excellent case study of the impact of indentured Africans in the post-emancipation period: Monica Schuler, *"Alas, Alas, Kongo": A Social History of Indentured African Immigration into Jamaica, 1841–1865* (Baltimore MD: Johns Hopkins UP, 1980).

settled, which is something that is frequently overlooked by scholars of African 'retentions' in the New World. The connection with Africa was thus strengthened even after the slave trade had been abolished. The USA did not undergo this kind of re-infusion.

5. George Shepperson made the important point, albeit *en passant*, that the emergence of pan-Africanism has largely been through "English-speaking agencies."[95] And the fact that British Caribbeans belonged to the largest empire, with the largest holdings on the continent, contributed to their relatively easy settlement thanks to this linguistic and colonial commonality. It is also true that the French colonial authorities were more adept at co-opting members of the black intelligentsia in Africa, including those from the francophone Caribbean, through their divide-and-rule policy of assimilation.[96] The British had no such policies, and this more overt blockage contributed to the discontent among the educated in Britain's African possessions.

These, then, I believe, are the fundamental elements that go towards an explanation of the extraordinary character of Caribbean involvement in pan-Africanist projects. There is still need for deeper and further research, but what I have attempted here is the presentation, in broad terms, of the line of continuity between Russwurm's searching in the early nineteenth century and Padmore's dream that culminated in the decolonization and liberation of the African continent.

---

[95] Shepperson, "Pan-Africanism and 'Pan-Africanism'," 355.

[96] See, in particular, G. Wesley Johnson, *The Emergence of Black Politics in Senegal: The Struggle for Power in the Four Communes, 1900–1920* (Palo Alto CA: Stanford UP, 1971); in a pioneering essay, François Manchaunelle has shown that many of those exiled by the French from the Caribbean played important roles in the nationalist struggles on the continent, including North Africa. See Manchaunelle, "Le rôle des Antillais dans l'apparition du nationalisme culturel en Afrique noire francophone," *Cahiers d'études africaines* 32.3 (1992): 375–408. It is interesting to note, however, that the French-speaking black intellectuals who actively supported and sympathized with the pan-Africanist projects before the birth of negritude in the 1930s were Haitian rather than French Caribbean proper. See Shepperson, "Pan-Africanism and 'Pan-Africanism'," 355–56; Geiss, *Pan-African Movement*; Martin Steins, "Black Immigrants in Paris," in *European-Language Writing on Sub-Saharan Africa*, ed. Albert S. Gérard (Budapest: Akadémiai Kiadó, 1986), vol. 1: 354–78; and Oruno Lara, *La Naissance du Panafricanisme: Les racines caraïbes, américaines et africaines du mouvement au XIXe siècle* (Paris: Maisonneuve & Larose, 2000).

WORKS CITED

Abrahams, Peter. *The Black Experience in the Twentieth Century: An Autobiography* (Bloomington: Indiana UP, 2000).

Ayandele, E.A. *The Missionary Impact on Modern Nigeria, 1842–1914* (London: Longmans, 1966).

Bell, Howard, ed. *Search for a Place: Black Separatism and Africa, 1860* (Ann Arbor: U of Michigan P, 1969).

Blackett, Richard. "Martin R. Delany and Robert Campbell: Black Americans in Search of an African Colony," *Journal of Negro History* 62.1 (1977): 1–25.

——. "Return to the Motherland: Robert Campbell, a Jamaican in Early Colonial Lagos," *Journal of the Historical Society of Nigeria* 8.1 (1975): 133–43.

——. "Robert Campbell and the Triangle of the Black Experience," in Blackett, *Beating Against the Barriers: The Lives of Six Nineteenth-Century Afro-Americans* (Ithaca NY: Cornell UP, 1989): 139–82.

Blyden, Nemata. *West Indians in West Africa, 1808–1880: The African Diaspora in Reverse* (Rochester NY: U of Rochester P, 2000).

Brewer, William. "John B. Russwurm," *Journal of Negro History* 13.4 (1928): 413–22.

Burton, Richard. *Wanderings in West Africa: From Liverpool to Fernando Po*, 2 vols. (London: Tinsley Brothers, 1863).

Cassell, C. Abayomi. *Liberia: History of the First African Republic* (New York: Fountainhead, 1970).

Cobley, Alan. "'Far From Home': The Origins and Significance of the Afro-Caribbean Community in South Africa to 1930," *Journal of Southern African Studies* 18.2 (1992): 349–70.

Contee, Clarence. "John Brown Russwurm," in *Dictionary of American Negro Biography*, ed. Rayford Logan & Michael Winston (New York: W.W. Norton, 1982): 538–39.

Dewitte, Philippe. *Les Mouvements nègres en France, 1919–1939* (Paris: L'Harmattan, 1985).

Du Bois, W.E.B. *The Philadelphia Negro: A Social Study*, intro. Elijah Anderson (1899; Philadelphia: U of Pennsylvania P, 1995).

Echeruo, Michael. *Victorian Lagos: Aspects of Nineteenth Century Lagos Life* (London: Macmillan, 1977).

Elkins, W.F. "Hercules and the Society of Peoples of African Origin," *Caribbean Studies* 11.4 (1972): 47–59.

Emmett, Tony. *Popular Resistance and the Roots of Nationalism in Namibia, 1915–1966* (Basel: P. Schlettwein, 1999).

Eschen, Penny von. *Race Against Empire: Black Americans and Anticolonialism, 1937–1957* (Ithaca NY: Cornell UP, 1997).

Foner, Philip. "John Browne Russwurm: A Document," *Journal of Negro History* 54.4 (1969): 393–95.

Fraser, Peter. "British West Indians in Haiti in the Late Nineteenth and Early Twentieth Centuries," *Immigrants and Minorities* 7.1 (1988): 79–94.

Fryer, Peter. *Staying Power: The History of Black People in Britain* (London: Pluto, 1984).

Fyfe, Christopher. *Africanus Horton: West African Scientist and Patriot* (New York: Oxford UP, 1972).

——. *A History of Sierra Leone* (Oxford: Oxford UP, 1962).

——. "The Sierra Leone Press in the Nineteenth Century," *Sierra Leone Studies* 8 (1957): 228–36.

Geiss, Imanuel. "Notes on the Development of Pan-Africanism," *Journal of the Historical Society of Nigeria* 3.4 (1967): 719–40.

——. *The Pan-African Movement: A History of Pan Africanism in America, Europe, and Africa*, tr. Ann Keep (New York: Africana & London: Methuen, 1974).

Green, Jeffrey. *Black Edwardians: Black People in Britain, 1901–1914* (London: Frank Cass, 1998).

Greenfield, Sidney. "Barbadians in the Brazilian Amazon," *Luso-Brazilian Review* 20 (1983): 44–64a.

Gross, Bella. "*Freedom's Journal* and *The Rights of All*," *Journal of Negro History* 17.3 (1932): 241–86.

Hamilton, Holman. *Prologue to Conflict: The Crisis and Compromise of 1850* (Lexington: U of Kentucky P, 1964).

Higman, Barry. "Jamaicans in the Australian Gold Rushes," *Jamaica Journal* 10.2–4 (December 1976): 38–45.

——. *Slave Populations of the British Caribbean, 1807–1834* (Baltimore MD: Johns Hopkins UP, 1984).

Hill, Robert, ed. *The Marcus Garvey and Universal Negro Improvement Association Papers*, vols. 9 & 10 (Berkeley: U of California P, 1995 and forthcoming).

——, & Gregory Pirio. "'Africa for the Africans': The Garvey Movement in South Africa, 1920–1940," in *The Politics of Race, Class and Nationalism in Twentieth-Century South Africa*, ed. Shula Marks & Stanley Trapido (London: Longman, 1987): 209–53.

Hinks, Peter P. *To Awaken My Afflicted Brethren: David Walker and the Problem of Antebellum Slave Resistance* (Philadelphia PA: Penn State UP, 1997).

Hooker, James R. *Black Revolutionary: George Padmore's Path From Communism to Pan-Africanism* (New York: Praeger, 1967).

——. *Henry Sylvester Williams: Imperial Pan-Africanist* (London: Rex Collings, 1975).

Huberich, Charles. *The Political and Legislative History of Liberia*, vol 1 (New York: Central Book Co., 1947).

James, C.L.R. "George Padmore: Black Marxist Revolutionary – A Memoir," in James, *At the Rendezvous of Victory: Selected Writings* (London: Allison & Busby, 1984): 251–63.

James, Winston. *Holding Aloft the Banner of Ethiopia: Caribbean Radicalism in Early Twentieth-Century America* (London & New York: Verso, 1998).

Johnson, G. Wesley. *The Emergence of Black Politics in Senegal: The Struggle for Power in the Four Communes, 1900–1920* (Palo Alto CA: Stanford UP, 1971).

Johnson, Howard. "Barbadian Migrants in the Putamayo District of the Amazon, 1909–11," in *Caribbean Migration: Globalised Identities*, ed. Mary Chamberlain (London: Routledge, 1998): 177–87.

Johnston, Harry. *Liberia*, vol. 1 (London: Hutchinson, 1906).

Kimble, David. *A Political History of Ghana: The Rise of Gold Coast Nationalism, 1850–1928* (Oxford: Clarendon, 1963).

Kolchin, Peter. *American Slavery, 1619–1877* (New York: Hill & Wang, 1993).

Kopytoff, Jean Herskovits. *A Preface to Modern Nigeria* (Madison: U of Wisconsin P, 1965).

Lapp, Rudolph M. *Blacks in Gold Rush California* (New Haven CT: Yale UP, 1977).

Lara, Oruno. *La Naissance du Panafricanisme: Les racines caraïbes, américaines et africaines du mouvement au XIXe siècle* (Paris: Maisonneuve & Larose, 2000).

Lewis, Rupert. *Marcus Garvey: Anti-Colonial Champion* (London: Karia, 1987).

Lynch, Hollis. *Edward Wilmot Blyden: Pan-Negro Patriot, 1832–1912* (London: Oxford UP, 1967).

——. "The Native Pastorate Controversy and Cultural Ehno-Centrism in Sierra Leone, 1871–1874," *Journal of African History* 5.3 (1964): 395–411.

McDaniel, Antonio. *Swing Low, Sweet Chariot: The Mortality Cost of Colonizing Liberia in the Nineteenth Century* (Chicago: U of Chicago P, 1995).

Makonnen, Ras. *Pan-Africanism from Within, as recorded and edited by Kenneth King* (Nairobi: Oxford UP, 1973).

Manchaunelle, François. "Le Rôle des Antillais dans l'apparition du nationalisme culturel en Afrique noire francophone," *Cahiers d'études africaines* 32.3 (1992): 375–408.

Martin, Tony. *The Pan-African Connection: From Slavery to Garvey and Beyond* (Cambridge MA: Schenkman, 1983).

——. *Race First: The Ideological and Organizational Struggles of Marcus Garvey and the Universal Negro Improvement Association* (1976; Dover MA: Majority Press, 1986).

Mathurin, Owen. *Henry Sylvester Williams and the Origins of the Pan-African Movement 1869–1911* (Westport CT: Greenwood, 1976).

Miller, Floyd. *The Search for a Black Nationality: Black Emigration and Colonization, 1787–1863* (Urbana: U of Illinois P, 1975).

Nicol, Abioseh. "West Indians in West Africa," *Sierra Leone Studies* 13 (1960): 14–23.

Okonkwo, Rina. "The Garvey Movement in British West Africa," *Journal of African History* 21.1 (1980): 105–17.

——. *Heroes of West African Nationalism* (Enugu: Delta Publications, 1985).

Olusanya, G.O. "Garvey and Nigeria," in *Garvey: Africa, Europe, the Americas*, ed. Rupert Lewis & Maureen Warner–Lewis (Trenton NJ: Africa World P, 1994): 121–34.

Omu, Fred. "The *Anglo-African*, 1863–65," *Nigeria Magazine* 90 (1966): 206–12.

——. "The Dilemma of Press Freedom in Colonial Africa: The West African Example," *Journal of African History* 9.2 (1968): 279–98.

——. "The *New Era* and the Abortive Press Law of 1857," *Sierra Leone Studies* 23 (1968): 2–14.

——. *Press and Politics in Nigeria, 1880–1937* (London: Longman, 1978).

Padmore, George. *Pan-Africanism or Communism? The Coming Struggle for Africa* (London: Dennis Dobson, 1956).

Patterson, William. *The Man Who Cried GenociAn Autobiography* (New York: International Publishers, 1971).

Rainy, William. *The Censor Censured, or the Calumnies of Captain Burton on the Africans of Sierra Leone* (London: Geo. Chalfont, 1865).

Rich, Paul. "The Black Diaspora in Britain: Afro-Caribbean Students and the Struggle for a Political Identity, 1900–1950," *Immigrants and Minorities* 6.2 (1987): 151–73.

Richardson, Bonham. "Caribbean Migrations, 1838–1985," in *The Modern Caribbean*, ed. Franklin Knight & Colin Palmer (Chapel Hill: U of North Carolina P, 1989): 203–28.

Russwurm, John B. "The Condition and Prospects of Hayti," *Journal of Negro History* 54.4 (1969): 395–97.

Schuler, Monica. *"Alas, Alas, Kongo": A Social History of Indentured African Immigration into Jamaica, 1841–1865* (Baltimore MD: Johns Hopkins UP, 1980).

Shepperson, George. "Notes on Negro American Influences on the Emergence of African Nationalism," *Journal of African History* 1.2 (1960): 299–312.

——. "Pan-Africanism and 'Pan-Africanism': Some Historical Notes," *Phylon* 23.4 (1962): 346–58.

Steins, Martin. "Black Immigrants in Paris," in *European-Language Writing on Sub-Saharan Africa*, ed. Albert S. Gérard (Budapest: Akadémiai Kiadó, 1986), vol. 1: 354–78.

Thompson, Dudley. *From Kingston to Kenya: The Making of a Pan-Africanist Lawyer* (Dover MA: Majority Press, 1993).

Walker, David. *David Walker's Appeal to the Colored Citizens of the World*, ed. & intro. Peter P. Hinks (1829; University Park PA: Penn State UP, 2000).

Woodson, Carter G., ed. *The Mind of the Negro as Reflected in Letters Written During the Crisis, 1800–1860* (Washington DC: Association for the Study of Negro Life and History, 1926).

Zachernuk, Philip. *Colonial Subjects: An African Intelligentsia and Atlantic Ideas* (Charlottesville: UP of Virginia, 2000).

❖

❖ LITERARY WRITINGS OF DIASPORA

Modernity and Historical Consciousness in the "New Negro" Novel at the Nadir (1892–1903)

CARLA L. PETERSON

The movement of the Negro [is] more and more a mass movement toward the larger and the more democratic chance – [...] a deliberate flight [...] from medieval America to modern.[1]

The American Negro must remake his past in order to make his future. Though it is orthodox to think of America as the one country where it is unnecessary to have a past, what is a luxury for the nation as a whole becomes a prime social necessity for the Negro. For him, a group tradition must supply compensation for persecution. [...] History must restore what slavery took away. [...] We find the Negro thinking more collectively, more retrospectively than the rest, and apt out of the very pressure of the present to become the most enthusiastic antiquarian of them all.[2]

T HESE QUOTATIONS come from essays by Alain Locke and Arthur Schomburg; each statement offers us a vision of the American Negro who looks toward the future in anticipation of becoming modern. The second passage further emphasizes how this movement toward modernity can occur only by looking back to the past in a collective retro-

---

[1] Alain Locke, "The New Negro," in Locke, *The New Negro*, intro. Robert Hayden (1925; New York: Atheneum, 1968): 6.

[2] Arthur Schomburg, "The Negro Digs Up His Past," in Locke, *The New Negro*, 231.

spection designed to "supply a group tradition." And it insists that this group tradition is not simply given or found; it is created by the Negro through a process of "remaking."

I offer yet another quotation, the comment "we are a new people," which John Walden, a character in Charles Chesnutt's novel *The House Behind the Cedars*, addresses to his sister Rena.[3] But, even as Walden seeks to constitute himself as new and obliterate the old, he is simultaneously drawn to his past by "a thousand chords of memory and affection."[4] Comments such as these suggest that African-American writers at the turn of the century were equally preoccupied with the creation of a New Negro, but also recognized that to achieve this goal they needed to face rather than suppress their past. If the contributors to *The New Negro* insisted on interpreting the past – both in its African and African-American manifestations – primarily from the point of view of aesthetic and cultural production, these earlier writers turned back to the past in order to confront the historical experience of slavery itself. Their narratives focus foremost on the ways in which family lineages have been disrupted by slavery and its legacy. When such histories become too painful for narrators and characters alike to bear, the narratives recast secular history as sacred history; from a Christian perspective that interprets time as an everlasting present, American slavery is seen both to repeat earlier events and to anticipate later ones that together constitute a history of providential design.

Mainstream ideologies of the Gilded Age believed history to be readily apprehensible and, following this rationalist outlook, articulated an optimistic vision of historical progress: humankind's destiny is seen to unfold within a positivistic evolutionary framework of material and moral progress embodied in the figure of the self-made man whose behavior and values have been formed within the bosom of the modern patriarchal bourgeois family. Yet a sense of unease underlay such complacent thinking, an unease that would only intensify in the era with increasing social and political turmoil.[5] Modernist thought came to question traditional values of historical knowledge and to re-think both historians' interpretations of history as continuous and progressive, and their methods of interpretation as grounded in objective and rational modes of thought; history could no longer be

---

[3] Charles W. Chesnutt, *The House Behind the Cedars* (1900; Athens: U of Georgia P, 1970): 83.

[4] Chesnutt, *The House Behind the Cedars*, 12.

[5] T.J. Jackson Lears, *No Place of Grace: Antimodernism and the Transformation of American Culture, 1880–1920* (1981; Chicago: U of Chicago P, 1994): 7–26.

envisaged as seamless continuity nor especially as progressive development. In *The Uses and Abuses of History*, Nietzsche, for example, counseled the historian to "keep away from all constructions of the world-process, or even of the history of man."[6] Yet he recognized that "man" cannot forget the past and believed historical consciousness to be an essential feature of human life. According to Nietzsche, we can explain the past only from the point of view of our present and what is most "powerful" in it;[7] in this sense, the present redeems the past. In the process, however, we are emboldened to create images of the past that will serve our present and future; the past redeems the present. The historian has now become a self-interested artist rather than a disinterested scientist, and the writing of history artistic composition.

From the vantage point of African Americans, however, the Gilded Age was the "nadir" of black historical experience, characterized by the emergence of increasingly virulent racist ideologies, black disfranchisement, the denial of state services to African Americans, and white mob violence.[8] Hence, the response of black intellectuals to the questioning of historical value was both complex and ambivalent. On the one hand, they applauded the challenge to dominant notions of historical continuity and evolutionary progress. They themselves had long recognized the extent to which their own history could be perceived as discontinuous, leading them to rely on ideas of providential design to make sense of their past. They were equally aware of the degree to which African-American history could be seen to disrupt the dominant historical national narrative, a disruption that was repeatedly rationalized by a negative positioning of Africans and their descendants: romantic racialists held them to be incapable of progress because of an immutable nature that fixed them in the stage of childhood; Hegel asserted that Africans lacked any awareness of an objective existence outside of themselves, hence had created no culture and possessed no history; finally, in the 1890s, men like Frederick Hoffman located African Americans on the darker side of progress – on the side of degeneration.

On the other hand, African-American intellectuals clung to ideologies of progress in the hope that, with the advent of freedom and citizenship, they would finally be able to position themselves on the side of progress and

---

[6] Friedrich Nietzsche, *The Uses and Abuses of History*, tr. Adrian Collins (1874; Indianapolis: Bobbs–Merrill, 1957): 59.

[7] Nietzsche, *The Uses and Abuses of History*, 40.

[8] Rayford Whittingham Logan, *The Negro in American Life and Thought: The Nadir, 1877–1901* (New York: Dial, 1954).

become full participants in Western civilization; they aspired to become New Negroes. According to Henry Louis Gates, Jr., the New Negro agenda was to project the image of a Public Negro Self created out of a willful act of self-negation, of a complete rupture with the past.[9] Yet, no differently from Nietzsche's "man," New Negroes were endowed with historical consciousness and could not forget the past. Instead, under the "pressure of the present," of post-Reconstruction policies that were rapidly eroding the promises of citizenship made by Reconstruction, African Americans understood that they needed to "remake their past" and supply themselves with a group tradition that would enable them to confront the dilemmas of the present and successfully enter the future as modern American subjects. The result was a complex and often problematic vision of the past – of slavery, of the Middle Passage, of Africa – and of the future as well.

Given this scenario, we can begin to see how the postbellum period was an age of retrospection. It gave impetus to the writing of African-American history – in the works of William Wells Brown, William Still, and George Washington Williams – to the sociological studies of W.E.B. Du Bois, and to the beginning of serious investigation into African-American folklore in Hampton Institute's journal, *The Southern Workman*. This is also a period in which African Americans insisted on their presence in the contemporary world, in, for example, their efforts to participate in World Expositions, their ongoing commemoration of historically significant events such as US and West Indian Emancipation Day celebrations, as well as their innovation of other commemorations like Juneteenth. Beyond this body of writings and practices, I want to suggest that if "remaking the past" is indeed an act of artistic invention rather than scientific study, then the writing of historical fiction may be implicated in commemorative processes as well.

Far from being a literary nadir, the period 1892–1903 represents a second flourishing of the African-American novel, breathing new life into a form born forty years earlier with the appearance of William Wells Brown's *Clotel* in 1853. This later period witnessed among others the publication of Frances Harper's *Iola Leroy* (1892), Charles Chesnutt's *The House Behind the Cedars* (1900) and *The Marrow of Tradition* (1901), and Pauline Hopkins's *Contending Forces* (1900), *Hagar's Daughter* (1901–02), *Winona* (1902), and *Of One Blood* (1902–03). The paradox of the birth of the African-American novel in the 1850s and its rebirth at the turn of the century becomes fully comprehensible in the light of Mikhail Bakhtin's conten-

---

[9] Henry Louis Gates, Jr., "The Trope of the New Negro and the Reconstruction of the Image of the Black," *Representations* 24 (Fall 1988): 132.

tion that the novel tends to make its appearance at moments of social crisis. Aptly portraying such critical moments, the novel may be seen as "inseparable from social and ideological struggle, from processes of evolution and of renewal of society and the folk."[10] One important aspect of this renewal is the "remaking" of the past – whether recent or distant – in order to supply a group tradition that could serve African Americans' present and future.

What I want to emphasize is the similarity of the premise of the fictional plots from novel to novel; I suggest that this similarity invites us to consider the texts themselves as ceremonies that commemorate an unknown, suppressed, or forgotten past. Indeed, these novels thematize the Nietzschean dialectic of historical forgetting and remembering as the characters vacillate between the desire to forget the "mournful past" and the compulsion to recall it. The novelists build on this need to remember by constructing their texts as sites of memory which, in Pierre Nora's words, are established at particular historical turning points when "consciousness of a break with the past is bound up with the sense that memory has been torn – but torn in such a way as to pose the problem of the embodiment of memory in certain sites where a historical continuity persists."[11]

To counter this break with the past, this tearing of memory, these novels constitute themselves as what Eric Hobsbawm has termed "invented traditions." According to Hobsbawm, social groups invent traditions at moments of crisis when rapid changes weaken social patterns that had until then been held together by old traditions. The invention of new traditions re-establishes continuities with the old, with a historic past that the group deems worthy of preservation, and in the process reaffirms critical values and norms of behavior. Invented traditions are designed, then, to ensure the social cohesion of the group, the legitimation of its social institutions and authority, and the socialization of members into a particular value system. Hobsbawm terms the invention of traditions a response to "novel situations."[12] Yet, for African-American writers, not only is such invention a response to the newness of life at the nadir, but the response itself is novel; the narratives work to reconstruct continuity with the ruptured past and chart a direction for the future.

---

[10] Mikhail Bakhtin, *The Dialogic Imagination*, ed. & tr. Michael Holquist (Austin: U of Texas P, 1981). 259.

[11] Pierre Nora, "Between Memory and History: Les Lieux de Mémoire," in *History and Memory in African-American Culture*, ed. Geneviève Fabre & Robert O'Meally (New York: Oxford UP, 1994): 284.

[12] Eric Hobsbawm & Terence Ranger, ed. *The Invention of Tradition* (Cambridge: Cambridge UP, 1983): 2.

In constructing their texts as sites of memory that encourage the invention of traditions, African-American novelists of the nadir appropriated the form of the historical romance but subverted many of its values in order to remake a past that would serve their future. I invoke the term 'historical romance' because the genre is in fact preoccupied with the fate of entire societies and perceives their members to be shaped by large historical forces; it is a form pervaded by historical consciousness, by a sense of the importance of the past to the present.[13] The romance plot typically pits a primitive people against a more technologically advanced one, forces of reaction against those of progress. But the African-American novels I consider all ask the question: who is primitive and who is civilized; what constitutes the old, the new, the modern? In response, many of them present southern aristocracy as a backward and reactionary people while the North represents the forces of progress and the New Negro embodies progressive potential. In some of the texts, the mulatto figures specifically as what Chesnutt boldly referred to in his journalism as "the future American."[14] Finally, several of the novels indict the nation itself as a primitive society and suggest that modern civilization exists only on the other side of the Atlantic, in Europe or in Africa.

If the endings of the historical romance traditionally point to the inevitable triumph of forces of progress, even when accomplished at great cost, these African-American novels question whether such forces have, in fact, or can ever, triumph. And if these same traditional endings generally gesture towards a reconciliation between the old society and the new – a reconciliation which often takes the form of a marriage – the African-American novels once again question whether such reconciliation is at all possible. Yet almost all of the novels invoke the possibility of reconciliation

---

[13] George Dekker, *The American Historical Romance* (Cambridge: Cambridge UP, 1987): 38–46. Given my interest in the function of genre here, I use the term "historical romance" in contrast to Susan Gillman's preference for "melodrama" as a literary mode designed to call attention to "the colloquial, popular cultural world" that defined an important aspect of late nineteenth-century life; Gillman, "The Mulatto, Tragic or Triumphant? The Nineteenth-Century American Race Melodrama," in *The Culture of Sentiment: Race, Gender, and Sentimentality in Nineteenth-Century America*, ed. Shirley Samuels (New York: Oxford UP, 1992): 223.

[14] Charles W. Chesnutt, "The Future American: What the Race is Likely to Become in the Process of Time" (1900), in *Stories, Novels, & Essays*, sel. Werner Sollors (The Library of America 131; New York: Literary Classics of the United States, Inc., 2002): 845–63.

by depicting an interracial union at some point in the plot and tracing its familial consequences.

Family is indeed central to the romance, as its plot often unfolds by tracing the history of families over generations. Family members are bound to one another through emotional ties and feelings of commonality. But, just as importantly, the family constitutes a dynastic line that defines itself through linear succession (one generation succeeds another), which itself produces a sense of causality and genealogical destiny (succession proceeds by means of cause and effect). The dynastic line is initiated by a founding father whose authority, derived from being first, goes unquestioned; his descendants achieve identity and legitimacy through succession and inheritance of his legacy. Genealogical succession proceeds toward a teleologically determined end that validates notions of historical progress.[15] It is primarily through this process that family members achieve historical consciousness; they think through the family to history and identity.

In the African-American romance, the family functions as a site of memory as individual family members recall a suppressed or forgotten past and the narrative then reconstructs this history from generation to generation.[16] It is by re-enacting or even inventing traditions that families and narrators alike work to restore a sense of historical continuity where slavery and its legacy have caused a break with the past, a tear in individual and collective memory. The novels' premise posits a white man – slaveholder or at least substantial man of property – as the founding father: Eugene Leroy in *Iola Leroy*, Judge Straight's unnamed friend in *The House Behind the Cedars*, Samuel Merkell in *The Marrow of Tradition*, Charles Montfort in *Contending Forces*, Ellis Enson in *Hagar's Daughter*, Henry Carlingford in *Winona*, and Aubrey Livingston in *Of One Blood*. But here, too, conventional terms and values are challenged once again as the novels proceed to reconstruct the genealogical destiny not so much of the father's white descendants but of the mixed-bloods produced by the sexual union of the father and a black woman: the slave mother and daughter, Hannah and Mira, in *Of One Blood*; the freed slave women, Marie Leroy in Harper's novel and Julia Merkell in *The Marrow of Tradition*; the free women, Molly Walden in *The House Behind the Cedars* and Hagar Enson in *Hagar's Daughter*; and the woman rumored to have black blood, Grace Montfort in *Contending Forces*.

---

[15] Patricia Drechsel Tobin, *Time and the Novel: The Genealogical Imperative* (Princeton NJ: Princeton UP, 1978): 3–16.

[16] In her essay "The Mulatto," Gillman also underscores the importance of family structures in the "race melodramas" of this period.

The novels ask whether it is possible for these characters' descendants –
Iola and Harry Leroy; Rena and John Walden; Merkell's daughter, Janet
Miller; Hagar and her daughter Jewel; Winona; the Montfort children, Will
and Dora Smith; and finally Aubrey Livingston's three children, Aubrey,
Reuel Briggs, and Dianthe Lusk – to think through the family to claim a
modern identity, given the way genealogical destiny has been disrupted by
the slave system. These descendants start with different degrees of self-
knowledge concerning their genealogical line, hence with different subject-
positions. Unaware that their mother possesses black blood, Iola and Harry
Leroy engage in unconscious passing, as does Jewel in *Hagar's Daughter*
and Aubrey Livingston in *Of One Blood*. By contrast, John and Rena Walden, as well as Reuel Briggs in *Of One Blood*, are conscious passers. Will
and Dora Smith openly identify as African-American, as does Winona, but
the history of their ancestry is shrouded in mystery. Janet Miller, finally, is
also aware of her parents' identity but is ignorant of the legal status of their
relationship.

The plots then seek to untangle these dynastic lines, to question conventional notions of genealogical destiny, and to examine the consequences of
such questioning for both family and nation. They ask: how legitimate is the
white founding father's authority? May his authority be usurped by that of
another founding parent, perhaps a black foremother? What legacies are
passed on to their mixed-blood descendants? Can these descendants inherit
the tangible assets of estate? What about family traits? Blood? Are these
mixed-blood descendants themselves slavery's legacy – whether as sin or as
salvation – to the nation? In creating their own families, finally, can they lay
claim at last to the status of modern American citizen? African Americans
were, in fact, fully aware of the degree to which claims of citizenship lay
not only in public but in private rights as well. As early as 1859, for
example, James McCune Smith had written an essay in the wake of the
Dred Scott decision titled "Citizenship." In it he argued that the Constitution of the USA nowhere defines the word 'citizen', hence we must look
to Roman law for its definition. In its codes, Roman law properly spelled
out both the public rights (*jus civitatis*) and the private rights of citizens (*jus
quiritium*), which include "the right of family, of marriage, of a father, of
legal property, of making a will and succeeding to an inheritance."[17] The
familial household is foundational to national belonging.

---

[17] James McCune Smith, "Citizenship," *The Anglo-African Magazine* (May 1859):
143.

At its most fundamental level, the African-American historical romance of the nadir challenged contemporary notions of degeneracy and progress. In all the texts, the white slaveholding families are characterized by lineage, succession, legacy, and inheritance. Yet several – most especially *Iola Leroy*, *The Marrow of Tradition*, and *Of One Blood* – emphasize the degeneration of southern aristocracy in the wake of the Civil War: men die in battle or return to fall prey to alcoholism; couples have difficulty procreating; heirs exhibit criminal tendencies, or are sickly and their survival doubtful. To shore up the decaying order, this class often resorts to the invention of traditions under the guise of restoring the ways of the past. In *The House Behind the Cedars*, for example, the white social elite to which Rena is introduced revives the medieval chivalric tournament as the sign of a South Carolinian renaissance; in *The Marrow of Tradition*, Major Carteret and his colleagues invent a white-supremacist ideology that they deem to be their class's very marrow. Both this degeneracy and its compensatory acts affirm that it is whites, not blacks, who cannot function as proper citizens.

Of these novels, it is the earliest written, *Iola Leroy*, that most radically challenges the authority of the white founding father. At the outset, slave-holding and slave families alike adhere to the social paradigms set by the dominant culture. While the former follow the laws of succession and inheritance, the latter are marked by silences and ruptures: female slaves cannot procreate, slave mothers and fathers are separated from their children; the former slave woman, Marie Leroy, withholds from her children the fact of their black blood; after his death, Leroy's relatives ensure that these same children cannot inherit his estate. But the novel's plot enacts a gradual shift in family fortunes. Even before the end of the Civil War, slave masters start to exhibit signs of degeneracy, and it is slave men who take on the role of surrogate father to their heirs. Furthermore, after the Civil War it is the black family that is reunited. For example, Iola is able successfully to reconnect "the once-severed branches of our family."[18] Refusing to repeat her mother's decision to marry a white man and silence the secret of her slave past, Iola rejects the whiteness of blood and estate derived from her father and promised by her white lover, and reclaims her "blackness."

Blackness here signifies neither color nor blood but lived experience. As Iola's uncle Robert insists, "when a man's been colored all his life it comes a little hard for him to get white all at once."[19] The novel, then, traces the ways in which the "white" Iola and her brother Harry become "colored,"

---

[18] Frances E.W. Harper, *Iola Leroy* (1892; Boston MA: Beacon, 1987): 215.

[19] Harper, *Iola Leroy*, 43.

first through a reinterpretation of the silences in their white family past, and secondly through a new appreciation of the slave past – a past that is "mournful" but whose "Darkness shows us worlds of light / We never saw by day."[20] Marked by darkness (as the only family member who cannot pass for white) and emblematic of slave resistance and agency, it is grandmother Harriet who above all embodies this "light in darkness." At the novel's conclusion, the Leroys become part of a self-contained southern community composed of former slaves. They are also reconstituted, however, as a New Negro family in which the men are self-made entrepreneurs and professionals, and the women agents of benevolence. Yet, to the very end, the family remains centered on Harriet, and we sense that if she must soon pass on, her memory will survive in future generations to provide the core values of African-American modernity.

In striking contrast to *Iola Leroy*, the later novels of Pauline Hopkins and Charles Chesnutt seem more conflicted about the value of the past and look forward instead to the creation of future Americans. If these texts fully acknowledge the ways in which African Americans have been shaped by the historical experiences of slavery and racial prejudice, they also embrace the white founding father's authority and lay claim to his inheritance. Such a strategy is fully comprehensible in the light of the particular "pressures of the present" in which events such as the Plessy v. Ferguson decision, Booker T. Washington's Atlanta Compromise speech, black disfranchisement, and US expansionism abroad, all designed to subjugate peoples of color, forced African Americans to acknowledge the enormous challenges to their right to full citizenship. Much as in *Iola Leroy*, in these novels New Negro modernity is rooted in large measure in progressive ideology, whereby the self-made male protagonists have successfully worked their way into the professions of law, education, and medicine. But, even more significantly, these novels seek to locate modern identity in concepts of race by upholding notions of racial *in*difference.[21] In one way or another, the texts all embrace theories of "of one blood" that either emphasize the common origins of a racially diverse family, point to the invisibility of black blood and the skin's refusal to reveal its presence, or, finally, promote Chesnutt's "future American," the product of racial mingling whose white appearance offers particular privileges:

---

[20] *Iola Leroy*, 273.

[21] Walter Benn Michaels, *Our America: Nativism, Modernism, and Pluralism* (Durham NC & London: Duke UP, 1995): 53–60.

> If it is only by becoming white that colored people and their children are to enjoy the rights and dignities of citizenship, they will have every incentive to 'lighten the breed,' to use a current phrase, that they may claim the white man's privileges as soon as possible.[22]

Hopkins's *Contending Forces* exhibits a much greater ambivalence toward the past than did *Iola Leroy*, as its narrative impulses are directed at the uncovering of the "black" protagonists' British heritage. Through the figure of Ma Smith, who is the repository of the family's collective memory, the text both remembers and forgets. As she retells her life history, Ma Smith silences her mother's African-American family history, which Hopkins had in fact adapted from her own; in the text, Ma Smith's maternal grandfather is James M. Whitfield, Hopkins's own great-uncle. In the 1850s, Whitfield had broken with Frederick Douglass to side with African emigrationists like Martin Delany, arguing that black peoples too had a "manifest destiny" and proposing the creation of a black republic in the Caribbean and Central America. Hopkins's own narrative colludes in Ma Smith's silencing of her maternal history in favor of the "romantic" story of her father's origins in the British Montfort family. In the process, Hopkins (through Ma Smith) invents history: the Montfort wealth is said to derive from a vibrant colonial plantation economy in Bermuda, as the founding father is portrayed as an "exporter of tobacco, sugar, coffee, onions, and other products so easily grown in that salubrious climate."[23] This account, in fact, both conflates and distorts the history of Bermuda's economy: while the onion did become a specialized export in the 1880s, attempts to plant tobacco and sugar during the earlier colonial period failed because of the aridity of the island's soil.

Yet Hopkins's fictional history of a Bermudan sugar and tobacco economy carries tremendous symbolic weight in the novel. It invents both a wealthy plantation and a dependent servile class that, generations later, provide both the Smith family and the villainous John Langley with a legacy of conspicuous consumption (which replaces slave production). Following Fernando Ortiz's paradigm, tobacco in Hopkins's novel is wild and masculine; it is also devilish, given its particular association with Langley, who ostentatiously smokes a cigar as he betrays his race to the southern sympathizer, the Hon. Herbert Clapp. By contrast, sugar is feminine, civi-

---

[22] Chesnutt, "The Future American," 861.

[23] Pauline E. Hopkins, *Contending Forces: A Romance Illustrative of Negro Life North and South*, ed. & intro. Richard Yarborough (1900; The Schomburg Library of Nineteenth-Century Black Women Writers; New York: Oxford UP, 1988): 22.

lized, and indicative of elite social status. It is linked to Ma Smith and her daughter Dora, whose creation of the rituals of tea parties and evening receptions around the consumption of sweets reflects their economic ability and status right – in short, of their New Negro identity.[24]

At the novel's end, the family departs for England to reunite with British relatives and recover their Montfort inheritance. Yet this ending remains ambiguous as a foundation for New Negro modernity. Does it reaffirm the authority of the white founding father and legitimate the genealogical destiny of his mixed-blood descendants through an acceptance of his estate, which is predicated on both the suppression of the slave past as the basis of the family's wealth and an alternative African-American history embodied in the figure of James Whitfield? Does it offer a vision of racial unity by emphasizing the common origin of the black and white Montforts? Or does it represent a return to origins preparatory to a new departure that will in turn enable the mulatto characters to re-create themselves as New Negroes in America?

Hopkins's later novels, *Hagar's Daughter* and *Winona*, as well as Chesnutt's *The House Behind the Cedars* and *The Marrow of Tradition*, push the development of the mulatto figure even further. All four novels emphasize the degree to which interracial liaisons are a fact of American history and reflect an already miscegenous nation; at least two of them further posit that such legalized unions could in fact be the means of achieving national racial reconciliation and unity. In *The House Behind the Cedars* and *Hagar's Daughter*, interracial marriage is both thwarted and actualized. But marital union is made possible only by suppressing the past, through acts of conscious or unconscious passing that result, not in intact families, but in truncated or constructed ones. In the former, family members disappear by crossing the color line; in the latter, individuals from the outside are incorporated into the immediate nuclear family. More importantly, the formation of such families poses the question of whether it is possible for their mixed-blood progeny, as future Americans, to inherit the founding father's estate and enjoy the privileges of whiteness; yet even when the answer is in the affirmative, the conditions of inheritance are qualified and "blackness" is never fully assimilated or legitimated.

To become "new people" and create new families, John and Rena Walden, the protagonists of *The House Behind the Cedars*, suppress their

---

[24] Fernando Ortiz, *Cuban Counterpoint*, tr. Harriet de Onís (New York: Alfred A. Knopf, 1947): 3–46; Sidney W. Mintz, *Sweetness and Power: The Place of Sugar in Modern History* (New York: Viking, 1985): 173.

African-American past by passing; to the extent that they do claim a past, it is based on invented traditions. John adopts his dead white wife's ancestors as his own, and both he and Rena participate in rituals appropriated by the southern white aristocracy from European medievalism by way of Scott's historical romances: they adopt the surname Warwick; Rena is named after *Ivanhoe*'s heroine, Rowena, and, finally, she meets her white lover Tryon at a tournament that consciously re-enacts scenes from Scott's chivalric romances. Yet Rena cannot forget the memories that bind her to her African-American familial and historical past; she returns to her mother and dies soon after. John, by contrast, remains unwavering in his conviction that his identity is inherited from his white father. Midway through the novel, he and his son vanish anonymously into white society. Their disappearance is ambiguous; if it suggests the permanent truncation of John's family, it also leaves open the possibility that, as a "white" man, John's mixed-blood son will inherit his mother's estate.

To an even greater extent than John Walden, it is *Winona*'s heroine who perhaps best represents Chesnutt's ideal of the future American. Winona inherits both her mother's blackness and her father's whiteness (and eventually his estate as well), and she is also acculturated into Native-American traditions; moreover, the novel concludes with her marriage to a British gentleman. To achieve this union, however, Winona must not only reject her mother's "primitive" African-American heritage, but also sever her ties with "barbaric" America, and move to civilized England. There, much like the Smith family of *Contending Forces*, she is reinstated into her father's family's lineage as the legitimate heir to his fortune.

Unlike *Winona, Hagar's Daughter* envisions the possibility of interracial marriage within the nation's borders. Hagar's marriage to Ellis Enson is made possible by her unconscious suppression of her childhood in slavery. The subsequent discovery of her slave past and reconstruction of her true family history initially alienate her from her husband, but at the book's conclusion the couple are reunited both with one another and with their daughter Jewel. Yet the novel's plot and conclusion consistently privilege the values of whiteness. Both Hagar and Jewel are culturally constructed as white; when their "black" blood is discovered, they, unlike Iola and Harry Leroy, lack the ability to appreciate the value of slavery's "mournful past" and more generally the experience of being "colored." And when Jewel is rejected by her white lover, she cannot, unlike her mother, withstand the shock and so dies. The family that emerges at the novel's end is indeed modern in the sense that it is a constructed biracial family: the "black" Hagar becomes mother to her husband's orphaned nephew; yet, in a concession to white privilege, it is this boy who is heir to the family's estate.

In contrast to these novels, in *The Marrow of Tradition* interracial unions are associated with the slave past rather than with the modern present. The novel then seeks to unravel the mysteries that surround them. To what degree have such unions been legitimate? What is their legacy? May their mixed-blood progeny inherit? If so, what is their inheritance? The novel's New Negro representative, Dr Miller, works to establish a modern professional identity based on legacies left him by his black parents. His wife Janet, however, craves familial recognition from her white half-sister. Given the many references to the sisters' exact resemblance, the book repeatedly gestures at ideas of racial *in*difference. But the race riot that occurs midway through the novel clarifies for characters and readers alike just "how inseparably the present is woven with the past."[25] By the close, the traditions of white supremacy are fully exposed and Janet rejects the privileges of "whiteness" offered to her in the form of her sister's recognition of kinship and acknowledgement of her rights to their father's estate.

The motivating force that propels all these plots forward, then, is the legitimation of the genealogical destiny of New Negro or future American characters and the families they have created. Yet the novels are equally inhabited by solitary Old Negro figures, who either do not belong to the newly constituted New Negro household or whose relationship to it is marginal. Unlike *Iola Leroy's* Harriet, they lurk on the periphery of the text, but cannot entirely be discarded. Positioned against the New Negro protagonists, these Old Negroes – former slaves or Africans whose ties to the continent remain intact – appear backward and primitive, characterized by dialect speech, superstitious beliefs, and visionary religious practices. They are variously portrayed by the novelists in negative or positive terms, yet all of them speak important racial truths.

Chesnutt's characterization of such Old Negro figures is infused with an ambivalence that acknowledges African Americans' position at the nadir as existing "on the borderline between two irreconcilable states of life."[26] In *The House Behind the Cedars*, the self-acceptance of Rena's childhood friend and admirer, Frank, is contrasted to her mother's inability to abandon outdated distinctions of color, caste, and class. In *The Marrow of Tradition*, Aunt Jane and her son Jerry are portrayed as self-hating Old Negroes, who derive their identity from their status as former slaves and current servants to the Carteret family. Jerry applies bleacheners to his skin in hope of be-

---

[25] Charles W. Chesnutt, *The Marrow of Tradition* (1901; Ann Arbor: U of Michigan P, 1969): 112.

[26] Chesnutt, *The Marrow of Tradition*, 42.

coming white, while Jane subsumes her identity under that of the Carterets, holding the family's collective memories, preserving their health, and finally giving her life for them. Jerry, however, is shown fully to understand the workings of white privilege, whereas Mammy Jane's belief in the efficacy of conjure is never fully discredited.

Much less ambivalently, Hopkins's novels all invoke an ancestral black mother who embodies the collective memory of African-American as well as African history, thus foreshadowing the novelist's direct evocation of Africa in *Of One Blood*; she is invariably a figure of wisdom and of prophecy. In *Contending Forces*, Sappho's aunt, Madam Frances, is said "to be skilled in the occult arts which were once the glory of the freshly imported African";[27] she foresees John Langley's death in the Arctic ice. In *Of One Blood*, the slave girl, Mira, who turns out to be the mother of the two protagonists, Dianthe Lusk and Reuel Briggs, is given the capacity to enter into a trance and predict the future; after her death, she appears in spirit to her children to warn them of events unknown to them; and the narrative suggests that these abilities are a legacy inherited from ancient African sources. Somewhat less mystically, their grandmother, Aunt Hannah, unravels the tangled skein of genealogy in the Livingston family to reveal that they and Aubrey as well are indeed "of one blood." In *Winona*, finally, Aunt Vinnie appears at the very end of the novel to predict the end of slavery: "Dis is de year of Jubilee, / Send dem angels down. / De Lord has come to set us free, / O, send dem angels down."[28] These peripheral black mother figures turn back to the text's center to question the authority of the white founding father. Their intrusion problematizes traditional notions of historical continuity and progress, challenging the values that have been attached to the Old and the New.

Yet, given the appalling conditions of life at the nadir, these characters underscore the enormous difficulties facing African Americans in their efforts at incorporation into the American body politic. Indeed, even though the novels' newly created families seem to promise the birth of New Negroes and "future Americans," from the viewpoint of the dominant culture the Old Negro figures contest the anticipation of modernity. The narratives seek, then, to reconsider the very basis of citizenship by charting a movement from secular to sacred history. From this perspective, collective

---

[27] Pauline E. Hopkins, *Contending Forces*, 200.

[28] Pauline E. Hopkins, *Winona* (1902), in *The Magazine Novels of Pauline Hopkins* (The Schomburg Library of Nineteenth-Century Black Women Writers; New York: Oxford UP, 1988): 437.

memory is transmitted not only through family history but through the re-reading of scripture and the re-enactment of rituals as well. National belonging is redefined as belonging to the kingdom of God on earth established according to His scheme of salvation; and chronological time gives way to an indivisible present: current events, prefigured in the biblical past, are at the same time yet to come.

Hopkins's novels in particular struggle against chronological order and work to transcend historical time. In accord with emerging modernist ideology, Hopkins turned to concepts of mythic time – or what Nietzsche called the "superhistorical" – whereby human experience is viewed *sub specie æternitatis* rather than *sub specie sæculi*. For Hopkins, the particular form taken by mythic time is that of religion, specifically the Judaeo-Christian tradition. As Nietzsche himself noted, the "superhistorical" consists of the power to turn "the eyes from the process of sheer becoming to that which gives existence an eternal and stable character – to art and religion."[29]

In Hopkins's novels, Judaeo-Christianity functions as a form of remembrance, as yet another site of collective memory and invented tradition. On the level of character, individuals remember not only through the family but also through commemorative religious practices – the enactment of ritual, the reading or reciting of Scripture, the singing of hymns (such as Aunt Vinnie's Jubilee hymn). On the level of narrative, the plots suggest typological readings that work against structures of genealogical succession and toward the collapse of chronological time. These plots are both recapitulative (as they re-enact events from the biblical past) and adumbrative (as these events are seen as yet to come). From this perspective, time becomes an everlasting present, the Old is identical to the New, and history holds out the promise of redemption.[30] Such commemorations offer new possibilities for the remaking of African-American history and suggest that citizenship might lie, finally, not in the American nation but in an earthly kingdom established according to God's plans.

In *Hagar's Daughter* and *Winona*, the narratives re-enact different aspects of the history of Canaan. The first novel rewrites the family history of Israel's founding father, such that Abraham and Hagar give birth to a daughter rather than a son; Egypt's curse on Israel is the curse of those mixed-blood women whose presence so troubles the house of the white founding father; yet the novel's ending holds out hope for a reconciliation

---

[29] Nietzsche, *The Uses and Abuses of History*, 69.

[30] Sacvan Bercovitch, *The American Jeremiad* (Madison: U of Wisconsin P, 1978): 40–44, 75–80.

between the two nations. In *Winona,* the war between abolitionist and pro-slavery forces in Kansas explicitly re-enacts the Holy War between Israel-ites and Philistines in Canaan. John Brown, Parson Steward, and Ebenezer Maybee are all prophet figures derived from 1 Samuel, and Winona's step-brother Judah is the very embodiment of the kingdom established by David.

I turn now to Hopkins's last novel, *Of One Blood,* whose plot neatly recapitulates all the themes analysed above, revealing tensions that the novelist ultimately could not resolve.[31] The novel invokes, only to reject, the conciliatory possibility of the future American, that racially mixed figure empowered "to claim the white man's privileges"; it emphasizes instead the racial nightmare of the genealogical destiny of slave descendants as two brothers end up marrying their sister. Passing for white in Boston's medical community but disillusioned with his prospects for the future, Reuel Briggs travels to the Old Continent, Africa. At this point, the ideo-logy of the future American gives way to that of Ethiopianism: the African American Reuel asserts his common heritage with Africa, which, despite its supposed obscure present, is revealed to have had a brilliant past. Adapting the historical accounts of William Wells Brown and George Washington Williams to her fictional narrative, Hopkins leads Reuel to the discovery of the ancient Ethiopian civilizations of Meroë and Telessar. Here the Old is equated neither with the past nor with the primitive, as these civilizations are represented as both present and proto-modern.

It would seem that, in this return to Africa, Reuel turns from embracing whiteness to embracing blackness. Yet the novel does not promote essen-tialist notions of race; instead, it continues to validate concepts "of one blood," as Ethiopians are asserted to be humankind's original source; whites have simply evolved away from black skin color and Ethiopians themselves range from "creamy tint to purest ebony."[32] Hopkins's novel, then, dis-misses the significance of the visible signs of skin to concentrate on culture and cultural formation as the true measure of progress. It envisions the creation of a syncretic culture that offers readers a mythic version of

---

[31] For a more detailed analysis of *Of One Blood,* see also Gillman, "Pauline Hop-kins and the Occult: African-American Revisions of Nineteenth-Century Sciences," *American Literary History* 8 (Spring 1996): 57–82, Thomas J. Otten, "Pauline Hop-kins and the Hidden Self of Race," *English Literary History* 59 (1992): 227–56, and Cynthia D. Schrager, "Pauline Hopkins and William James: The New Psychology and the Politics of Race," in *The Unruly Voice: Rediscovering Pauline Elizabeth Hopkins,* ed. John Cullen Gruesser (Urbana: U of Illinois P, 1996): 182–209.

[32] Pauline E. Hopkins, *Of One Blood* (1903), in *The Magazine Novels of Pauline Hopkins,* ed. & intro. Hazel V. Carby (New York: Oxford UP, 1988): 545.

modernity – what Paul Gilroy has called a "counterculture of modernity": to the ancient civilization of Telessar, Reuel adds Western knowledge, the cultural legacy of American slavery (in the figure of Aunt Hannah), and Christian doctrine, specifically the teachings of Jesus and the concept of the Trinity. Taken together, this "counterculture" enacts the Ethiopianist promise that Africa shall rise once again.

Even more significantly, however, the narrative attempts to present itself under the aegis of mythic Christian time. Indeed, in it Hopkins sought to transcend secular chronological time by portraying Reuel as the reincarnation of Philip the evangelist, who, according to Acts 8, was the first to send Christianity to Ethiopia's Queen Candace. Consequently, her representation of Reuel is both recapitulative and proleptic. As is engraved on Telessar's sphinx, "That which hath been, is now; and that which is to be, hath already been; and God requireth that which is past."[33] Yet a tension persists in the text between the eternal and the secular. Structures of genealogical succession still prevail: Reuel is inserted into a royal lineage which originates with King Ergamenes and continues through his grandmother Hannah and his mother Mira, and which he himself will perpetuate through his marriage to Queen Candace. Hopkins's last novel, then, embodies the very tension between progressivist and modernist tendencies that characterizes New Negro thinking at the nadir.

Such tensions inhabit not only the historical romances of the nadir but other texts as well. By way of conclusion, I turn to a brief consideration of Du Bois' *The Souls of Black Folk*, a multigeneric text that is part-autobiography, part-history, part-sociology, and part-fiction. Like the historical romance, *The Souls of Black Folk* simultaneously looks back to the past in an effort to make sense of the history of African Americans and forward to the future to consider how African Americans may enter modernity and become citizens of the modern American nation. Like the historical romance again, *The Souls of Black Folk* insists on apprehending African-American life from the perspective of both the secular and the sacred. In demanding opportunities for education, access to jobs, and the right to vote – and thus coming into direct conflict with the more accommodationist stance of Booker T. Washington – Du Bois embraced a progressivist discourse. Recognizing the degree to which religious thought has shaped African-American cultural traditions, however, Du Bois also insisted in

---

[33] Hopkins, *Of One Blood*, 552.

placing African-American history within the realm of sacred time. Thus, the political history of slavery, abolition, and emancipation that Du Bois outlined in chapters 2 and 3 is rewritten in chapter 10, "The Faith of the Fathers," from the point of view of the sacred: the "dream of Abolition" was "a religion to the black world" and the coming of Emancipation seemed "to the freedman a literal Coming of the Lord."[34] Finally, in the turbulent present that is the nadir, Du Bois envisions African Americans "in the great night a new religious ideal," and promises that "some day the Awakening will come."[35]

WORKS CITED

Bakhtin, M.M. *The Dialogic Imagination*, ed. & tr. Michael Holquist (Austin: U of Texas P, 1981).

Bercovitch, Sacvan. *The American Jeremiad* (Madison: U of Wisconsin P, 1978).

Brown, William Wells. *The Rising Son; or The Antecedents and Advancement of the Colored Race* (1874; Miami FL: Mnemosyne, 1969).

Chesnutt, Charles W. *The House Behind the Cedars* (1900; Athens: U of Georgia P, 1970).

——. *The Marrow of Tradition* (1901; Ann Arbor: U of Michigan P, 1969).

——. "The Future American: What the Race is Likely to Become in the Process of Time" (1900), in *Stories, Novels, & Essays*, sel. Werner Sollors (Library of America 131; New York: Literary Classics of the United States, 2002): 845–63.

Dekker, George. *The American Historical Romance* (Cambridge: Cambridge UP, 1987).

Du Bois, W.E.B. *The Souls of Black Folk* (1903; New York: New American Library, 1969).

Gates, Henry Louis, Jr. "The Trope of the New Negro and the Reconstruction of the Image of the Black," *Representations* 24 (Fall 1988): 129–55.

Gillman, Susan. "The Mulatto, Tragic or Triumphant? The Nineteenth-Century American Race Melodrama," in *The Culture of Sentiment: Race, Gender, and Sentimentality in Nineteenth-Century America*, ed. Shirley Samuels (New York: Oxford UP, 1992): 221–43.

——. "Pauline Hopkins and the Occult: African-American Revisions of Nineteenth-Century Sciences," *American Literary History* 8 (Spring 1996): 57–82.

Gilroy, Paul. *The Black Atlantic: Modernity and Double Consciousness* (London: Verso & Cambridge MA: Harvard UP, 1993).

---

[34] W.E.B. Du Bois, *The Souls of Black Folk* (1903; New York: New American Library, 1969): 220.

[35] Du Bois, *The Souls of Black Folk*, 225.

Harper, Frances E.W. *Iola Leroy* (1892; Boston MA: Beacon, 1987).

Hobsbawm, Eric, & Terence Ranger, ed. *The Invention of Tradition* (Cambridge: Cambridge UP, 1983).

Hopkins, Pauline E. *Contending Forces: A Romance Illustrative of Negro Life North and South*, ed. & intro. Richard Yarborough (1900; The Schomburg Library of Nineteenth-Century Black Women Writers; New York: Oxford UP, 1988).

——. *The Magazine Novels of Pauline Hopkins*, ed. & intro. Hazel V. Carby (The Schomburg Library of Nineteenth-Century Black Women Writers; New York: Oxford UP, 1988).

Lears, T.J. Jackson. *No Place of Grace: Antimodernism and the Transformation of American Culture, 1880–1920* (1981; Chicago: U of Chicago P, 1994).

Locke, Alain. *The New Negro*, intro. Robert Hayden (1925; New York: Atheneum, 1968).

Logan, Rayford Whittingham. *The Negro in American Life and Thought: The Nadir, 1877–1901* (New York: Dial, 1954).

Michaels, Walter Benn. *Our America: Nativism, Modernism, and Pluralism* (Durham NC & London: Duke UP, 1995).

Mintz, Sidney W. *Sweetness and Power: The Place of Sugar in Modern History* (New York: Viking, 1985).

Nietzsche, Friedrich. *The Uses and Abuses of History*, tr. Adrian Collins (1874; Indianapolis IN: Bobbs–Merrill, 1957).

Nora, Pierre. "Between Memory and History: Les Lieux de Mémoire," in *History and Memory in African-American Culture*, ed. Geneviève Fabre & Robert O'Meally (New York: Oxford UP, 1994): 284–300.

Ortiz, Fernando. *Cuban Counterpoint*, tr. Harriet de Onís (New York: Alfred A. Knopf, 1947).

Otten, Thomas J. "Pauline Hopkins and the Hidden Self of Race," *English Literary History* 59 (1992): 227–56.

Schrager, Cynthia D. "Pauline Hopkins and William James: The New Psychology and the Politics of Race," in *The Unruly Voice: Rediscovering Pauline Elizabeth Hopkins*, ed. John Cullen Gruesser (Urbana: U of Illinois P, 1996): 182–209.

Smith, James McCune. "Citizenship," *The Anglo-African Magazine* (May 1859): 144–50.

Tobin, Patricia Drechsel. *Time and the Novel: The Genealogical Imperative* (Princeton NJ: Princeton UP, 1978).

Williams, George W. *History of the Negro Race in America* (New York: G.P. Putnam's Sons, 1883).

❖

Notes From Underground
William Demby's *The Catacombs* and the Diasporic Roots of African-American Modernism

KLAUS BENESCH

"I think you've been in Europe too long [...]" "Original! Original! An original thought! Someone says that to me at least once a month. What makes you think so?" "The way you make love. Don't laugh [...]. A woman can tell. You've damn sure been in Europe too long!" (William Demby, *The Catacombs*)

"Call it spadework!" (Charles Johnson, *Oxherding Tale*)

W HEN CRITICS DUBBED his debut novel *Beetlecreek* (1950) "naturalistic" in form and content, the African-American writer William Demby claimed that it should, rather, be called "existentialist," because "black experience is itself and has been historically in this country existentialist; that is, precarious, tied to the moment, history-conscious, and history-making without possessing a constant, solid historical framework."[1] Demby's statement, whatever it might reveal about the triangular constellation of writer, critic, and text, offers a basic interpretation of African-American history and identity. Just consider such landmark texts as Claude McKay's "If We Must Die" (1919), Nella Larsen's *Passing* (1929), Richard Wright's *Native Son* (1940), Ralph Ellison's *Invisible Man*

---

[1] Margaret Perry, "William Demby," in *Dictionary of Literary Biography*, vol. 33: *Afro-American Fiction Writers after 1955*, ed. Thadious M. Davis & Trudier Harris (Detroit MI: Gale Research, 1984): 61.

(1952), James Baldwin's *Nobody Knows My Name* (1961), John A. Williams's *The Man Who Cried I Am* (1967), or Alex Haley's *Roots* (1976); what all of these important documents of the African-American literary tradition try to negotiate is a central crux of black writing: "how envision and name a people whose very existence was predicated upon expropriation of land, culture, and the binding imperatives and designations of what Ellison terms the 'familial past'."[2] As the titles of the above texts readily suggest, the ongoing precariousness of black identity and its troubled relations with history loomed large in the literary imagination of African Americans.[3] Insofar as African-American fiction often highlights the quest for a meaningful vision of the past and, simultaneously, the innate futility of that quest, it must indeed be viewed as a forerunner and laboratory of existentialism and literary modernism generally.

In Albert Camus' novel *L'Étranger* (1942), which Demby reviewed for a student literary magazine when studying at Fisk University, the search for historical causality, for a reasonable cause of human action, fails utterly. While investigating the circumstances that led to the killing of a young Arab, this programmatic existentialist text mingles the past with the present, the reveries of the accused murderer with the testimonies of witnesses, the accidental, momentary event with the mechanistic processes of jurisdiction, without ever providing a compelling motive for the crime itself. For Camus, human life consisted of a mere patchwork of isolated moments, an endless series of unrelated incidents interrupted solely by the desperate act of the individual.[4] The lack of historical causality that characterizes much existentialist writing is equally prominent in *Beetlecreek* and to an even greater extent in Demby's second novel, *The Catacombs* (1965). By dramatizing a constant flow of seemingly independent events (both fictional and factual),

---

[2] Kimberly W. Benston, "'I Yam What I Am': Naming and Unnaming in Afro-American Literature," *Black American Literature Forum* 16.1 (1982): 3.

[3] "Book titles," as Ishmael Reed reminds us in *Flight to Canada*, "tell the story." By juxtaposing the original subtitle of Harriet Beecher Stowe's *Uncle Tom's Cabin* ("The Man Who Was a Thing") and John A. Williams's *The Man Who Cried I Am*, this stunningly postmodern slave narrative evokes the long, painful history of "all of the changes that would happen to make a 'Thing' into an 'I Am'"; Ishmael Reed, *Flight to Canada* (New York: Avon, 1976): 93.

[4] In his novel *La Peste* (1947), Camus later adjusted his bleak portrayal of the isolated, uncommitted individual. Although Demby points to the lasting influence of existentialism on his writing, he is more likely a literary heir to the late than to the early Camus. See also John O'Brien, *Interviews with Black Writers* (New York: Liveright, 1973): 37–39.

The Catacombs creates an ambience of timelessness and continuous present which has become by now synonymous with the literary aesthetics of existentialism and its popular cinematic offspring, *film noir* and postwar neo-realism.[5]

In an interview with John O'Brien, Demby defined his own approach to existentialism as an attempt to pin down the universal importance of all human action, to show that even the most trivial gesture contributes to the "great tapestry" of what we call reality and that, therefore, it cannot be rightfully severed from the larger events of history. "In revolutionary periods," he argues, "people think that a revolution happened when the cannon knocked over a certain wall, when the troops ran in. This is not true. That gesture was the fruit of who knows how many gestures."[6] Even if we take into account the multiple agents involved in bringing about the actual event, this would by no means enable us to resolve the problem of responsibility or to decide what steps should be taken next. In contrast with the naturalist's world of sociobiological forces, Demby's fictional universe appears to be solely determined by the movement of individuals. Many of his characters (black and white) are trapped in a moral and spiritual dilemma, a conflict between instinct and civilization that leaves unanswered the question of personal and collective responsibility for their often desperate, violent acts.

If Demby's first two novels can thus be called distinctly existentialist, they thoroughly differ in terms of style and thematic scope. In *Beetlecreek*, the core issues, alienation, unfulfilled desire, and violent death, still evolve against the limited backdrop of a little coal-mining town in West Virginia, where Demby had spent much of his youth. The second novel shifts the scene of tragic conflict to Europe and, by implication, to world history. Steeped in the author's experience as a black expatriate living in Rome, *The Catacombs* adds to the existentialist undercurrent a sense of diaspora and, simultaneously, sets out to undo the limitations of time and place at large.[7]

---

[5] In Demby's third novel, *Love Story Black* (1978), though largely determined by its satirical take on black militancy and the vagaries of romance in New York City during the late 1960s, the issue of historical causality is finally moved from the level of existentialism to discourse theory. As one of the principal characters claims at the end of the novel, "history is what people *say* about you [...] Not what you say about yourself. History is what people *say* you do, not what you do yourself" (*Love Story Black* (New York: Reed, Cannon & Johnson, 1978): 137.

[6] O'Brien, *Interviews with Black Writers*, 45.

[7] Throughout this essay I use the term "diaspora" *metaphorically*, not in a political or historical sense. Although diaspora has been variously applied as a heuristic tool

Unlike other African-American expatriates who often pitted the loss of
center and subsequent isolation against the personal freedom regained
abroad, Demby is not repelled by the European environment.[8] Rather than
engaging in a discourse on cultural difference, he skillfully conjoins the
various intellectual traditions available to the writer in exile in a multi-
layered narrative about life and art. In its amalgamation of divergent cultural spheres, Judaeo-Christian mysticism, the history of modern art and,
finally, Demby's African-American heritage, *The Catacombs* transcends the
restrictive definition of diaspora as 'homelessness', thereby offering a more
positive view of the expatriate condition.

   Moreover, by accepting the imminent social, political, and military crises
of the present as a necessary stage in the continuing cycle of catastrophe
and renewal, Demby's experimental novel also defies the modernist stance
of the poet's alienation from contemporary society that has become a trade-
mark of major expatriate writers such as T.S. Eliot, Ezra Pound, and Ernest
Hemingway. Unlike, say, Eliot's abhorrence of the lower regions of human
life in *The Waste Land*, *The Catacombs* offers a more promising account of
what might lurk beneath the surface of both being and race. Hence Demby
is by no means a "latecomer" to modernism[9] but the wandering/wondering

---

for the study of the slave trade and the forced mass migration of Africans to the New
World and, after the end of colonialism, as immigrants to Europe, its restrictive,
biblical origins seemed to disturb even those critics who, like Stuart Hall, fervently
welcome it as a new postcolonial paradigm. See Hall, "Cultural Identity and Diaspora," in *Identity: Community, Culture, Difference*, ed. Jonathan Rutherford (London: Lawrence & Wishart, 1990): 235. The most influential adaptation of diaspora as
a critical tool is Paul Gilroy, *The Black Atlantic: Modernity and Double Consciousness* (Cambridge MA: Harvard UP, 1993); for a critical comparison of the
Jewish and the African diaspora, see Glissant, *Le Discours antillais* (Paris: Seuil,
1981): 29.

   [8] As James Baldwin insisted, to most expatriate African Americans France and,
especially, its cultural and political center Paris, remained a legend rather than a
tangible reality. "Through [his] deliberate isolation, through lack of numbers, and
above all through his own overwhelming need to be, as it were, forgotten, the
American Negro in Paris is very nearly the invisible man. [...] He has come, in
effect, to a city which exist only in his mind" (*Notes of a Native Son* (1955; Boston
MA: Beacon, 1990): 118–27. The most comprehensive study of African American
writers in France is Michel Fabre, *From Harlem to Paris: Black American Writers
in France, 1840–1980* (Urbana & Chicago: U of Illinois P, 1991).

   [9] Klaus P. Hansen, "William Demby's *The Catacombs* (1965): A Latecomer to
Modernism," in *The Afro-American Novel Since 1960*, ed. Peter Bruck & Wolfgang
Karrer (Amsterdam: Grüner, 1982): 123.

'outsider' and deconstructor within its rigidly formalist tradition. Ostensibly a modernist text in terms of style and form, *The Catacombs* should, rather, be read as a philosophical inquiry that shares important insights, as well as its central metaphor, with such radically epistemological texts as Thoreau's *Walden* (1854), Ralph Ellison's *Invisible Man* (1952), and Charles Johnson's *Oxherding Tale* (1982).

In what follows, I therefore establish a topical and structural lineage that runs parallel, if not counter, to the isolationist mood of literary modernism. I am not referring here, to be sure, to a comprehensive and exclusively African-American tradition, the kind of "counterculture of modernity" that Paul Gilroy sees at work in the cultural production of the black Atlantic. Rather, I want to show that the particular status of the 'outsider', the traveler, the expatriate, etc., ideally allows for the crossing of racial/cultural borders and the abandoning of fixed ideological positions. As Edward Said has keenly observed,

> the image of the traveler depends not on power, but on motion, on a willing-
> ness to go into different worlds, use different idioms, and understand a variety
> of disguises, masks, and rhetorics. Travelers must suspend the claim of cus-
> tomary routine in order to live in new rhythms and rituals. Most of all, and
> most unlike the potentate who must guard only one place and defend its fron-
> tiers, the traveler *crosses over*, traverses territory, and abandons fixed posi-
> tions, all the time.[10]

Cut loose, if only temporarily, from the relative security of their traditional cultural environment, travelers thus figure as ideal deconstructors: they constantly negotiate the tension between the known and the unknown, between essence and appearance, between their own status as minority and the cultural dominant.

As an African-American writer living abroad, Demby, too, is charting foreign territory. His vision, like Ellison's, is marked by invisibility and Otherness. If "the voice of invisibility," as Ellison has said, "issued from deep within our complex American underground"[11] and the black writer's challenge is therefore to overcome the difficulty in seeing *himself*, Demby seems to project that idea onto the larger plane of world-historical events.[12]

---

[10] Edward W. Said, "Identity, Authority, Freedom: The Potentate and the Traveler," *Boundary 2* 21.3 (Fall 1994): 17.

[11] Ralph Ellison, "Introduction" to *Invisible Man* (New York: Vintage, 1995): xviii.

[12] Richard Wright's "The Man Who Lived Underground" (1961) and LeRoi Jones's *The System of Dante's Hell* (1963) also come to mind here. Though both

Whereas Ellison's invisible man "descended, like Dante, into [the] depths" of the psychological foundations of racism in America,[13] Demby's writer-protagonist is held in thrall by the Roman catacombs as a symbolic site where history and the present meet. To unearth the invisible layering of human existence, to connect the suffering, hope, and, redemption of the martyrs buried in the ancient tombs to the living and their ongoing search for identity thus becomes a major driving force for the exiled black author.

Yet Demby is not merely interested in the past and its ramifications in the present. In *The Catacombs* he also explores the role of art, especially the art of the novel, as a preeminent tool for the writing and recording of history. If it is true, according to the German theologian Karl Barth, that "the goal of human life is not death, but resurrection,"[14] then it is most likely the realm of art where resurrection, that is, the transference of human life to a higher level of consciousness, can be effected. For it is the task of the writer to concoct out of the diversity of human experience a unified piece of art. To highlight the redeeming, synthesizing capacity of art, Demby probes deep into the history of visual representation and creative writing. "I am beginning to have the strangest feeling," he muses at a crucial turning point of the novel, "that we are all nothing more than shadows, spirits, breathed into life and manipulated by Pirandello's fertile mind."[15] An expatriate African American in Rome, the writer-protagonist of *The Catacombs* decidedly uses his writing as an antidote to his notorious Otherness, thereby proffering the novel as an important cultural link that unites people across the boundaries of both time and race.

Although mostly written after his return to America, *The Catacombs* clearly sprang from Demby's experience as a black intellectual who has

---

adopt the idea of "going underground" to a different purpose, they engage the under-world as an epistemological tool, a means to lay bare the existential "angst" (Wright) and racial stereotyping (Jones) buried deep within black–white relations in America. Here is how Wright describes the subterranean vision of his Dostoevskian black protagonist: while groping his way through the sewers of an American city, it finally dawned on him that the items he has seen hovering before his eyes are "by some dime meaning" linked together, "that some magical relationship made them kin. He stared with vacant eyes, convinced that all of these images, with their tongueless reality, were striving to tell him something"; Richard Wright, "The Man Who Lived Underground," in Wright, *Eight Men* (1961; New York. Thunder's Mouth P, 1987): 59.

[13] Ellison, *Invisible Man* (New York: Vintage, 1995): 9.

[14] Demby, *The Catacombs* (1965; New York: Harper & Row, 1970): 40.

[15] *The Catacombs*, 45.

been living abroad for the better part of twenty years. Demby had initially left the USA after his graduation at Fisk to study art history in Italy. From the late 1940s to the late 1960s he lived and worked in Rome, where he became a well-known writer and translator for the Italian film industry. It is worth noting, however, that Demby, who was married to a native and spoke fluently Italian, does not refer to himself as an "expatriate." Whereas writers of the "lost generation," who went abroad after World War I, often expressed their isolation and cultural estrangement, Demby never actually felt cut off from what was going on at home. Having regular access to the now widespread means of electronic communication, he has always retained a strong sense of 'being there' even while living in a foreign environment. As he told John O'Brien,

> now nothing could happen, police dogs would attack people in a church in Alabama and we would know about it in Rome immediately. So I don't think any of us were really expatriates. It always embarrasses me when people say, "Oh, you've come back." But you've never gone. You've been there for twenty years, but you haven't changed your language, you haven't changed your personal history ....[16]

In *The Catacombs*, a text glutted with newspaper clips and references to electronic media, this idea of mediated simultaneity, an encompassing technological lifeworld in which everything seems to happen at once, becomes an important structural device; it spawns a transatlantic, border-crossing narrative that freely shuttles back and forth in time (from ancient Rome to the present and, occasionally, even to an envisioned universal future) as well as in space (from Europe to Africa, Asia, and North America).

The characters and plot-line of the novel are explicitly autobiographical. The major events cover a period of roughly two years between the spring of 1962 and 1964. Although the point of view is shifting, most of the story is told by the narrator and protagonist William Demby, an expatriate black American writer who lives with his Italian wife and his son in Rome. Demby is working on a novel that centers on the love affair between Doris, a young African-American dancer who has come to Rome to play a minor role next to Elizabeth Taylor in the film *Cleopatra*, and her aristocratic lover, an Italian count. The ensuing triangular relationship between Demby, who also falls in love with Doris, the young dancer and the count provides the background for the novel's intriguing pastiche of historical and fictional events. Significantly, the ill-fated encounter of these three characters is

---

[16] O'Brien, *Interviews with Black Writers*, 43.

embedded in images of death and resurrection. Set against the lethal dynamics of world history, from the decline of the Roman empire to the Cuban missile crisis and the assassination of President Kennedy, their feverish, aborted love evokes a sense of tragedy and desolation that perfectly matches with Rome's dissolving, history-laden cityscape. In the end, Doris, who has been pregnant but did not know whether the white or the black man was the father, meets with the count for a last supper in a little restaurant in front of the ancient catacombs. After the meal, they climb down the labyrinthine structure and Doris, whose child has not yet been born, disappears among the moldy recesses where millions of bodies," of all races and colors" had been laid to rest.[17]

Its bleak, melancholy undercurrent notwithstanding, the novel finally dramatizes, in Robert Bone's apt phrase, "the triumph of the life force."[18] Yet, if *The Catacombs* has recourse to the reinvigorating power of myth and religion, as critics often assume, it also issues in a celebration of art over life. As the three major characters await the birth of Doris's child, the unborn baby symbolically stands for the life-giving force of artistic creation: the time of biological gestation coincides with the laborious process of turning life into art or, put in a different way, it represents Demby's pains in giving birth to an experimental novel, in which the act of writing takes center-stage.

Even though the text is layered with Christian images of rebirth and renewal, its most conspicuous features are the manipulation of narrative time and the continuous blurring of different planes of reality. Nowhere does this modernist technique become more apparent than in the following monologue by the author/narrator that occurs halfway through the novel:

> This is a dark depressing time for the novel, a strangely critical time in my life. It is a Janus-time of looking back and forward, looking forward toward Birth, looking backward toward Death. [...] I am moving over a landscape of time and reality totally unlike the dream world I had been living in up to now. The trees and mountains, these rivers and strange fish, these utensils and flowers, these streets and noises are unfamiliar to me. I am here and *there* [...] and now saying this, I am no longer afraid, nor do I feel divided.[19]

---

[17] Demby, *The Catacombs*, 244.

[18] Robert Bone, "William Demby's Dance of Life," *TriQuarterly* 15 (Spring 1969): 134.

[19] Demby, *The Catacombs*, 135.

What is celebrated in this and other discursive passages is the cathartic, soothing capacity of creative language. On one level, the speaker is able to regain control over his life only by turning it into the literary text he is about to write. Significantly, if also somewhat paradoxically, the fusion of real time and narrative time epitomizes and, simultaneously, transcends the author's anxiety and dividedness vis-à-vis the cataclysmic events of modern history. By subverting the epistemological order of 'true' and 'fictional' facts, *The Catacombs* thus provides a strong counterpoint to Western rationalism and its corollary, the juxtaposition of mind and matter.

On yet another level, however, the above passage also illustrates the ability of the literary text to overcome the alienating effects of diaspora. By lending the foreign culture his authorial voice, Demby finally manages to leave the "dream world" of a life in exile, to cross the border between "here and *there*," between one's own culture and the universal truth that connects the lives of all human beings. Hence the division that separates blacks from whites, Italians from Americans, the sufferings of ancient Christians from the predicament of modern man or, for that matter, the writer's life from the life of his fictional characters – all this becomes obsolescent. Quoting from an (authentic) introduction he wrote for the exhibition of a young Roman artist, Demby highlights the interconnectedness and mutual dependency of both "animate" and "inanimate" objects:

> Inanimate objects, be they tables or chairs, typewriters or pillows, Michelangelo's "Pietà," are formed of invisible universes of matter and energy: in this sense they are alive. Enclosed in a room, church or museum, house or castle, they influence one another – condition one another's existence (just as the "animate objects," the human members of a family, influence one another, condition one another's existence, in a house or a castle).[20]

This, then, is the overarching paradox of *The Catacombs*: while both its author and its major characters strive to become "alive" by searching for a place of their own, they always only find themselves conditioned by a space (Rome) or text (art) larger than their individual lives. "This is the kind of thinking you do here in Rome," Doris writes to her mother in America, "I mean, here in Rome you get a historical perspective about things, you take the long view of history but you can't find out anything about your own place in current history."[21] In the end, she will find that place only by going underground: ie, by leaving the surface plane of reality and, symbolically,

---

[20] Demby, *The Catacombs*, 92.

[21] *The Catacombs*, 100.

becoming entombed in the catacombs (which stand for both here, the historical site, and the novel in which she plays a leading role). As Demby announces earlier, "I must save her, though we are not yet in those final chapters when all this is happening."[22]

The act of going underground, of "unearthing" the hidden connections and universal relatedness of all human life, is strongly reminiscent of what the African-American writer Charles Johnson has dubbed "cross-cultural fertilization." Johnson, who was trained as a philosopher and is strongly influenced by both the French phenomenologist Merleau–Ponty and Zen Buddhism, believes that all cultures share some common ground, a space of connection and interrelatedness that is deeply encoded – "as the very stuff of our lives"[23] – in all forms of cultural representation. Expounding on the black writer's task to overcome the relativism of his/her social position, he argues that

> if we go deeply enough into a relative perspective, black or white, male or female, we encounter the transcendence of relativism [...] Because what we have, from the standpoint of phenomenology, are not different worlds but instead innumerable perspectives on one world; and we know that, when it comes to the crunch, we share, all of us, the same cultural Lifeworld – a world layered with ancestors, predecessors, and contemporaries. To think of this world properly is to find that all our perspectives take us directly to a common situation, a common history in which all meanings evolve.[24]

Accordingly, Johnson conjures up the liberating power of "spadework," of laying bare the long pedigree of ancestors, who conjoined in shaping the world as it is. "No form," he writes in his prize-winning novel *Oxherding Tale*, "*loses* its ancestry; rather, these meanings accumulate in layers of tissue as the form evolves."[25] If Johnson's attempt to dodge the pitfalls of

---

[22] Demby, *The Catacombs*, 86.

[23] Charles Johnson, *Being and Race: Black Writing Since 1970* (Bloomington & Indianapolis: Indiana UP, 1988): 52.

[24] Johnson, *Being and Race*, 44.

25 Charles Johnson, Oxherding Tale (1982; New York: Grove, 1984): 119. For a detailed discussion of Johnson's philosophical ideas, see Klaus Benesch, "Slavery as Metaphor: Charles Johnson's Cross-Cultural Slave Narratives," in *Parcours identi-taires*, ed. Geneviève Fabre (Paris: Publications de la Sorbonne Nouvelle, 1994): 127–38, and Ashraf H.A. Rushdy, "The Phenomenology of the Allmuseri: Charles Johnson and the Subject of the Narrative of Slavery," *African American Review* 26.3 (1992): 373–94.

what he calls "relative being"[26] – being wholly defined by the color of
one's skin and the excesses of racial discrimination – is closely connected
to his Zen-induced, universalist world-view, it can also be linked to the
obsessive awareness of "roots," another earthly metaphor, within African-
American history and culture. From this perspective, then, it could well
have been the lack of a "usable" past, the absence of a fixed, monolithic
cultural lineage associated with the African-American odyssey, that has
driven both writers to explore the complexity of human life by "unearthing"
its hidden layering of diverse, multicultural tissue.

In his provocative discussion of contemporary African-American fiction,
Johnson insists that "all presuppositions, all theories, must be suspended
before experience and meaning can be brought forth in black literary art."[27]
Not only does this statement ring with Johnson's outspoken resistance to
black cultural nationalism and politicized writing in general, it also brings
to mind the rebellious philosophy of another American writer and, in his
own way, "outsider" among the hard-working, practical-minded citizens of
Concord, Massachusetts. "What everybody echoes or in silence passes by as
true to-day," Thoreau writes in *Walden*, "may turn out to be falsehood tomorrow, mere smoke of opinion, which some had trusted for a cloud that
would sprinkle fertilizing rain on their fields."[28] Thoreau, like his black
literary heirs Ellison, Demby, and Johnson, worked hard to deconstruct the
shams and illusions that are taken by the majority for the soundest truth.
"We inhabitants of New England," he admonishes his fellow citizens, "live
this mean life that we do because our vision does not penetrate the surface
of things."[29] Consequently, Thoreau set out on his famous journey to
Walden Pond, where, in accordance with Emersonian transcendentalism, he
plowed the fertile grounds of rural Massachusetts for an essential truth that
reaches beyond or, rather, beneath the surface of mere appearances. As he
declares at the beginning of his life in the wilderness, "my head is an organ
for burrowing, as some creatures use their snout and fore paws, and with it I
would mine and burrow my way through these hills."[30]

Demby's text also represents a sophisticated literary 'mining' operation.
What is more, *The Catacombs* propagates the act of 'burrowing' and
'mining' as an intrinsic part of the writer's life in exile. Whereas Thoreau

---

[26] Johnson, *Being and Race*, 14.

[27] *Being and Race*, 29.

[28] Henry David Thoreau, *Walden* (1854; Princeton NJ: Princeton UP, 1971): 8.

[29] Thoreau, *Walden*, 96.

[30] *Walden*, 98.

retreated to an abandoned patch of land at Walden Pond to do the burrowing, Demby, sitting in the middle of the congested Piazza del Populo, finds
himself groping with a novel that is meant "to cast light on the reality of
human existence."[31] Yet like his Romantic predecessor, he, too, has to go
underground in order to realize that, in Thoreau's compelling words, we
have to

> work and wedge our feet downward through the mud and slush of opinion,
> and prejudice, and tradition, and delusion, and appearance, that alluvion which
> covers the globe, through Paris and London, through New York and Boston
> and Concord, through Church and State, through poetry and philosophy and
> religion, till we come to a hard bottom and rocks in place, which we can call
> *reality*, and say, This is, and no mistake.[32]

WORKS CITED

Baldwin, James. *Notes of a Native Son* (1955; Boston MA: Beacon, 1990).

Benesch, Klaus. "Slavery as Metaphor: Charles Johnson's Cross-Cultural Slave Narratives," in *Parcours identitaires*, ed. Geneviève Fabre (Paris: Publications de la
Sorbonne Nouvelle, 1994): 127–38.

Benston, Kimberly W. "'I Yam What I Am': Naming and Unnaming in Afro-
American Literature," *Black American Literature Forum* 16.1 (1982): 3–11.

Bone, Robert. "William Demby's Dance of Life," *TriQuarterly* 15 (Spring 1969):
127–41.

Demby, William. *Beetlecreek* (New York: Rinehart, 1950).

——. *The Catacombs* (1965; New York: Harper & Row, 1970).

——. *Love Story Black* (New York: Reed, Cannon & Johnson, 1978).

Eliot, T.S. *Collected Poems, 1909–1935* (New York: Harcourt, Brace, 1936).

Ellison, Ralph. "Introduction" to *Invisible Man* (New York: Vintage, 1995): vii–xxiii.

——. *Invisible Man* (New York: Vintage, 1995).

Fabre, Michel. *From Harlem To Paris: Black American Writers in France, 1840–
1980* (Urbana & Chicago: U of Illinois P, 1991).

Gilroy, Paul. *The Black Atlantic: Modernity and Double Consciousness* (London:
Verso & Cambridge MA: Harvard UP, 1993).

Glissant, Édouard. *Le Discours antillais* (Paris: Seuil, 1981).

Hall, Stuart. "Cultural Identity and Diaspora," in *Identity: Community, Culture, Difference*, ed. Jonathan Rutherford (London: Lawrence & Wishart, 1990): 222–37.

---

[31] Demby, *The Catacombs*, 39.

[32] Thoreau, *Walden*, 97–98.

Hansen, Klaus P. "William Demby's *The Catacombs* (1965): A Latecomer to Modernism," in *The Afro-American Novel Since 1960*, ed. Peter Bruck & Wolfgang Karrer (Amsterdam: Grüner, 1982): 123–44.

Jones, LeRoi. *The System of Dante's Hell* (1963; New York: Grove, 1965).

Johnson, Charles. *Being and Race: Black Writing since 1970* (Bloomington & Indianapolis: Indiana UP, 1988).

——. *Oxherding Tale* (1982; New York: Grove, 1984).

O'Brien, John. *Interviews with Black Writers* (New York: Liveright, 1973).

Perry, Margaret. "William Demby," in *Dictionary of Literary Biography*, vol. 33: *Afro-American Fiction Writers after 1955*, ed. Thadious M. Davis & Trudier Harris (Detroit MI: Gale Research, 1984): 59–64.

Reed, Ishmael. *Flight to Canada* (New York: Avon, 1976).

Rushdy, Ashraf H.A. "The Phenomenology of the Allmuseri: Charles Johnson and the Subject of the Narrative of Slavery," *African American Review* 26.3 (1992): 373–94.

Said, Edward W. "Identity, Authority, Freedom: The Potentate and the Traveler," *Boundary 2* 21.3 (Fall 1994): 1–18.

Thoreau, Henry David. *Walden* (1854; Princeton NJ: Princeton UP, 1971).

Wright, Richard. "The Man Who Lived Underground," in Wright, *Eight Men* (1961; New York. Thunder's Mouth P, 1987): 27–92.

The Conundrum of Home
The Diasporic Imagination
in *The Nature of Blood* by Caryl Phillips

KATHIE BIRAT

T HE FICTION OF CARYL PHILLIPS, as can be seen from the
titles of certain of his novels – *The Final Passage, Cambridge,
Crossing the River, Higher Ground* – turns on the displacement of
Africans within the context of the slave trade and the multiple forms of
dislocation and fragmentation that have been the consequence of this initial
phenomenon. Phillips has used fictional narrative to create a dynamic
interaction between the historical fact of loss and dispersion and the need
for diasporic communities to refigure the past as a way of imagining and
constructing the future. While his first novel, *The Final Passage*, was concerned with the relationship between an island in the Caribbean and
England, representing one side of "the triangular trade," his subsequent
novels have gradually expanded that space to include a complex network of
relations between different groups of people living in diverse periods.
Beginning with *Higher Ground* in 1989, Phillips extended his vision of the
diaspora to include the Jewish diaspora and the effects of the Holocaust.
While he was widening the span of his thematic preoccupations, he began
using a polyphonic technique, allowing his characters either to speak for
themselves or viewing the world through their eyes. He has used an essentially historical awareness of the impact and meaning of the diasporic
experience to deepen and enrich the representation of the lives of his characters. At the same time, he has sought fictional techniques that would

make it possible to express the effects of displacement as they are felt by people who did not experience the initial loss of a homeland themselves.[1]

Within the historical and critical context of the late twentieth century, it is clear that Phillips's fictional approach to the question of the diaspora is part of a larger debate about the fate of displaced peoples and the ways in which displacement should be viewed and treated. During a seminar on multicultural writing organized by the British Council in Paris in April 2000, Phillips and Raphaël Confiant expressed different opinions concerning the role to be played by writers belonging to the African diaspora.[2] Phillips's attitude toward the idea of 'home' clearly echoed his fictional approach to the diaspora. As a West Indian growing up in England, he had experienced the effects of a racism which left him divided between his physical presence in England and his West Indian origins. He talked about being persistently reduced to a racial identity by the question "Where are you *really* from?" Phillips's artistic response to this background has been a desire to uncouple nationality from race and to explore the diasporic experience within the context of what he defines as his "triangular" Atlantic home. This is a way for him to give himself an imaginary space in which to explore the complex nature of his own experience within a larger frame suggested by the historical context of the slave trade.[3] Raphaël Confiant disagreed with this imaginative expansion of the notion of home beyond the Caribbean. Clearly, for Confiant, who explained that he had refused an invitation to teach in an American university, people of the African diaspora living in the Caribbean need to speak from a position that is both literally and figuratively identified with the Caribbean space. To step out of that space is to run the risk of an even greater dispersion and the loss of a hard-won sense of cultural identity.

The confrontation between Confiant and Phillips reflects two different approaches to the diasporic experience. On the one hand, the exploration of

---

[1] Bénédicte Ledent discusses the use of polyphony and dialogics by Caryl Phillips and Fred D'Aguiar to represent "the ternary topography of slavery" in "Remembering Slavery: History as Roots in the Fiction of Caryl Phillips and Fred D'Aguiar," *The Contact and the Culmination*, ed. Marc Delrez & Bénédicte Ledent (Liège: U of Liège, 1996): 271–80.

[2] "L'Ecriture Multicolore: Multiculturalism in French and British Writing"; seminar organized by the British Council in Paris, 28–29 April 2000, and chaired by Caryl Phillips and Raphaël Confiant.

[3] Phillips clearly expressed the connection between his own experience and the exploration of historical themes by saying: "I am writing about myself in some oblique way."

specific forms of cultural expression in the Caribbean has made it possible to see these forms as a response to and compensation for the loss of an African past. The artistic innovation that has accompanied this search has, in addition, enabled writers to counteract the lingering effects of cultural colonialism. To the extent that this search for cultural roots has been linked to an active quest for both appropriate and innovative artistic techniques, it has escaped the threat of what Phillips refers to as "the pressure to be conservative in a threatened culture."[4] However, the need felt by writers like Phillips to remain in touch with the artistic and cultural debates taking place in an increasingly international context has led them to view the Caribbean experience in terms of a broader discussion which to some extent is 'located' outside the Caribbean, either in Europe or in North America.[5]

These are the two sides of the paradox to which Phillips refers in talking about "the conundrum of home."[6] Home can never be a simple notion for someone who has been displaced both directly in his own life and indirectly through the history of the group to which he belongs. This is the dilemma underlying all forms of artistic expression which seek to capture the experience of diasporic populations. Caught in a paradox with Orphic echoes, they can only bring the past to bear on the present by refusing to look back, thus escaping the pitfalls of nostalgia. Their pertinence in a changing world depends on their ability to reshape the past in terms which make it relevant to the context of the present. This can be done, of course, without stepping outside the Caribbean as the framework for narrative. However, the specificity of Caryl Phillips lies in his desire to explore "the conundrum of home" within an imaginative framework which seems to be increasingly removed from his own experience.

---

[4] This remark was also made during the debate with Confiant.

[5] Michael Dash expresses the irony of this theorizing of the Caribbean experience when he says: "It seems almost as though after not knowing what to do with the Caribbean, everyone now wants to be Caribbean"; *The Other America: Caribbean Literature in a New World Context* (Charlottesville: UP of Virginia, 1998): 6. He identifies the critical context on which this expansion of the Caribbean paradigm relies: "In championing a poetics of multiplicity and heterogeneity as opposed to exclusivity and opposition, postmodernism put the emphasis on liminality and indeterminacy, perhaps allowing for a proper theorizing of that 'delicate tenuity' that Césaire saw as the Caribbean's defining characteristic."

[6] Remark made during the Paris seminar, in relation to the difficulty of defining the idea of home for diasporic populations.

In his recent novel *The Nature of Blood*,[7] Phillips renews the meaning of the diasporic experience of African populations by relating it directly to the paradigmatic diaspora represented by the Jews. Whereas in *Higher Ground* only the final section of the novel involves a Jewish refugee, in *The Nature of Blood* it is the Holocaust and the creation of the state of Israel that forms the narrative core. The story of Othello is introduced as a narrative counterpoint, allowing the confinement of the Jews in the ghetto of Venice to function as a mirror in which the reader views the future destiny of the African slaves. The preservation of one's own past is thus pictured as being dependent on a capacity to see its relevance to other pasts.

While this reliance on the metafictional potential of narrative is a characteristic of Phillips's fictional technique, he has never used it as extensively as he does in *The Nature of Blood*. On the one hand, this deliberate displacement of the African experience into the framework of another diaspora could be read as a reluctance to make use of the critical paradigms which writers of the African diaspora have so painstakingly elaborated over the course of the twentieth century. On the other, it could be seen as the desire to avoid the pitfalls of reference to specific worlds while expressing the tension between the opposing visions that underlie all worlds. Viewed in this light, Phillips may be moving away from specific reference to the African diaspora as a way of capturing all the more clearly the experience of loss which is the essence of all forms of uprooting. Furthermore, the dichotomies with which he is concerned are not only those which oppose past and present, Africa and America, but also the representational one which distinguishes fiction as process from the referential frames in which it sometimes finds itself trapped.

That the novel is concerned with the competing claims of the past and the future, of memory and desire, is explicitly stated in one of the fragments in which an anonymous narrator evokes the psychological horror of the Holocaust and its effect on the survivors:

> Their condition serves a commemorative function, suggesting a loyalty to the dearly departed. Naturally, their suffering is deeply connected to memory. To forget is a crime. How can they both remember and move on?[8]

---

[7] He has since published the novel *A Distant Shore* (New York: Alfred A. Knopf, 2003).

[8] Caryl Phillips, *The Nature of Blood* (London: Faber & Faber, 1997): 157. Further page references are in the main text.

This is, of course, the dilemma to which Phillips gives fictional expression. How can peoples affected by displacement and dispersion preserve a living connection to the past without being paralyzed by their memories? Fiction can only be seen as preserving this living connection if it brings the past to life in the present. Fictional narrative is called upon to transform the revisiting of the past into a dynamic process, a re-enactment of the forces underlying its thematic concerns.

The pertinence of Phillips's fictional treatment of memory becomes particularly clear if examined in the light of Paul Ricoeur's study of history and memory in his latest work, *La Mémoire, l'histoire, l'oubli*. Ricoeur is concerned with the collective suffering represented by the Holocaust and the question of whether it is possible for history to provide a narrative version of that suffering capable of transforming it from experience into meaning. While Phillips calls on memory to bring history to life as personal experience, Ricoeur explores the ways in which memory serves as the "womb" of history.[9] Both are interested in memory as the vital link between a personal experience of the past and the discursive shapes through which that past becomes available for communication as narrative. And both are aware of the dangers involved in any attempt to establish a connection between personal memory, collective memory and history. Each one can be seen as adopting a specific position in a debate concerning the representation of the past. Raphaël Confiant's disagreement with Phillips is based on his criticism of the distance which the latter seems to have placed between himself and the diasporic population of which he is a member; in the same way, certain criticisms of the first form of Ricoeur's work, presented as a lecture in honor of Marc Bloch, revolved around what some people saw as a willingness on the part of Ricoeur to minimize the importance of the Holocaust through a distancing based on questions of historical representation.[10]

---

[9] Paul Ricoeur, *La Mémoire, l'histoire, l'oubli* (Paris: Seuil, 2000): 106. "Commanding someone to remember may be understood as an invitation to use memory to short-circuit the work of history. I am all the more aware of this danger as my book constitutes a plea to consider memory as the womb of history, to the extent that it remains the guardian of the relationship of representation by which the present is linked to the past" (translation mine).

[10] Rainer Rochlitz, "La mémoire privatisée," *Le Monde*, 25–26 June (2000): 14–15. In his response to Ricoeur's lecture, Rochlitz criticizes him for considering the historian as someone who is able to dissociate his scholarly role from his duty as a citizen. He says: "Paul Ricoeur presents the historian as a solitary consciousness faced with his object of study or his text. This conception is not realistic. The func-

The most interesting aspect of Ricoeur's work is the attention that he gives to personal memory as the root of collective representations of the past. In a lengthy discussion of the terms used by Plato and Aristotle to describe memory, he examines the ambiguous status of memory as a form of imagination which makes specific claims to truthfulness. He tries to push the paradoxes he unearths in the course of his investigation to their ultimate limits in order to understand in what terms they may eventually be bridged, and at what cost. The first paradox to be confronted in dealing with memory from a philosophical point of view is the distinction between imagination and memory, as both take the form of images in the mind. It is in the gap between memory and imagination that Ricoeur perceives what he calls the "vulnerability" of memory. Memory may be hindered or blocked by grief; it may be manipulated for reasons of ideology; it may be transformed into an obligation, by which it is redirected from the past toward the future. All three of these potential abuses of memory run the risk of compromising its capacity to be truthful.[11] The second major obstacle to be overcome in understanding the link between memory and history is the passage from individual to collective memory. Ricoeur attempts to assign a specific place to collective memory, as distinct from history, by speaking of it in terms of the ascription of actions to a singular or plural subject.[12] However, he recognizes that it is difficult to avoid considering history as a way, perhaps the only way, of gaining access to collective memory. The originality of his approach lies in the way in which he attempts to preserve the specificity of memory throughout his investigation. As in *The Rule of Metaphor*, it is his way of attempting to preserve the connection between a direct experience of the world and the intellectual constructs to which that experience gives rise.[13] This explains, for instance, the importance that he attaches to the role of live testimony in the process through which memory is transformed into historical understanding and representation.

It is the idea of memory as a living link between past and present that allows Ricoeur's text to shed light on the way Caryl Phillips treats the problem of memory in relation to diasporic populations. The importance of memory in the works of writers belonging to diasporas is to a great extent a

---

tion of the debate among historians is precisely to rectify the partisan and partial dimensions of '*the representations of the past*'. History, above all that history, cannot be written in an ivory tower, far from the public debates."

[11] Paul Ricoeur, *La Mémoire, l'histoire, l'oubli*, 67–111.

[12] Ricoeur, *La Mémoire, l'histoire, l'oubli*, 152–63.

[13] It is the French title *La Métaphore vive* that expresses this perspective. In *La Mémoire, l'histoire, l'oubli*, Ricoeur refers to what he calls "la mémoire vive."

recognition of the impact on the present of events that belong to the past. In American literature, William Faulkner has dealt with the obsessional nature of memory as a way of talking about the inability of Southerners to give up a mythical past which they see as being the core of their identity. Although American Southerners were never dispersed, the political and economic dismantling of the Southern states after the Civil War was experienced as an invasion which severed the South from its own past. In the novels of Faulkner, this distorted relation between memory and history takes the form of an endless repetition of obsessional behavior. It reflects the inability to bury the past, which Ricoeur identifies as one of the potential abuses of memory. That Toni Morrison, who has been greatly influenced by Faulkner, should have used personal trauma as a way of approaching a troubled collective past in *Beloved* is not at all surprising. She makes it quite clear that there can be no future for her characters, either individually or collectively, until grief has been allowed to do its work. In the same way, Richard Wright's representation of his childhood in *Black Boy* owes much of its impact to the way in which the author forces the reader to confront the devastating effects on personal memory of a collective trauma.

Phillips is also concerned with memory as the living sign of the relation between past and present. He uses memory, or its loss, to explore the way in which a fictional character experiences a past from which he has been separated, or which he has never known directly. In *Cambridge*, the African slave transported to the Caribbean talks of the loss of his African home at the moment of his capture by saying: "Our history was truly broken."[14] In his novels, Phillips tends to treat memory as something that is inaccessible, cut off by the initial displacement which has erased all traces of the past. Thus he tends to approach the loss of the past historically and textually, relying on the patterns of discourse itself to make the past accessible by relating it to the distancing involved in all forms of representation. His characters are generally creatures of language and discourse, who become perceptible only through their entry into language. Thus the narrator of the first section of *Higher Ground* is a native interpreter in a fort on the west coast of Africa. The narrator of the first section of *Crossing the River* is a former slave sent back to Africa, who expresses himself through letters sent to his master. In each of these cases, language serves as a mirror reflecting not the past, but the process through which it has been lost.

Phillips uses three principal techniques in attempting to transform his fictional treatment of the Holocaust into the locus of an examination of the

---

[14] Caryl Phillips, *Cambridge* (London: Bloomsbury, 1991): 137.

relationship between memory and history in the lives of diasporic populations. He has, first of all, chosen to situate his story in a transitional period,
in which the impact of public events on private memory is acutely felt.
Secondly, he uses interior monologue as a means of reproducing the fluidity
and formlessness that characterizes direct experience and personal memory
as opposed to clearly organized narrative representations. Thirdly, as in his
other novels, he avoids giving the novel an overall narrative frame, in terms
either of an omniscient narrator or of a story capable of integrating and including all the others. He thus problematizes all of the steps involved in
making sense of personal experience in terms of broader narratives. More
importantly, the constituting of those narratives ultimately depends on the
reader's perception. However, as the ominous title of the novel suggests,
Phillips is not trying to suggest that the recovery of personal memory can
stave off or counteract the effects of history. Something that by general con-
sensus is called 'history' does ultimately emerge from the assembling of
individual memories into collective narratives. But a re-examination of the
ways in which those narratives are constituted can re-open history by
revealing it to be a process always at work in the present moment. Seen in
this perspective, the fictional text becomes the site of a confrontation between the fluid images of personal experience and the narrative frames, both
personal and collective, through which we make sense of them. Phillips's
purpose is not to re-write history, but to re-examine its roots in memory.

Ricoeur, like others who have discussed the place of the Holocaust in
terms of historical consciousness, points out that the present period is a
watershed, to the extent that living witnesses of the experience, both victims
and aggressors, will soon disappear. In this respect, the beginning of the
twenty-first century represents the transition between memory and history,
the moment when the Holocaust vanishes from memory to survive only as
history. Caryl Phillips situates the main narrative thread of *The Nature of
Blood* at another transitional moment, the end of the Second World War,
when the awareness of what had been done to the Jews was still a lived
experience. Those who had been affected by the deportation were just
beginning to try to come to terms with it as a describable, historical phenomenon. Eva, the young woman living in a camp for refugees on Cyprus
organized by the British, has temporarily lost all sense of personal and
collective identity. The binary relation between refugee camp and homeland
is broken down in the loss of the essential distinction between self and
other, self and world. In this situation, all positions become relative; an
orderly, rational world can re-emerge only as one pole of a relation with the
self. In the camp, Eva thinks:

> Those of us who have lasted until the arrival of these Englishmen, we have
> forgotten how to think of tomorrow. On this first night, I try to channel a
> course in my mind which might lead to the future. But it is not easy. I simply
> cling to the image of my sister.[15]

The island of Cyprus provides an ironical link with another story, that of
Othello, who finds himself in Venice when the city-state is trying to defend
itself against the Turks. In both cases, Cyprus appears as a point in a web of
shifting relations between rival civilizations. While Eva has been rescued by
the English from the Germans, Othello is an auxiliary in the struggle
between the Venetians and the Turks:

> The Turks, so intelligence had informed the doge, having already reddened
> their scimitars with much Christian blood, were now planning to attack the
> Venetian island of Cyprus. My commission was to revisit an island with
> which I was already familiar, this time at the head of the Venetian army, and
> to subdue the infidel usurper who was forever laying claim to this perilously
> situated outpost of Christian civilization. (137)

In both cases, the characters are dissociated from the places which will
define their future historical identities: ie, Israel and America. The ghetto in
which Eva had been confined before the war appears in the story of Othello
as an area of Venice which is in the process of becoming a separate space
for the Jews. More importantly, the racial status of Othello as a black man
can be observed as it emerges from the reactions of the people around him.
Thus the dichotomies created by historical representations of the Jewish and
African diasporas are subordinated to a narrative logic that temporarily
blurs the conventional polarities. This makes it possible for the reader to
perceive the formation of diasporas in new ways. By focussing on the end
of the Second World War in the narrative of Eva, Phillips views the Holocaust as a repetition of the initial paradigmatic scattering of the Jews. But
by interweaving this narrative thread with the story of Othello, he broadens
the application of the term diaspora to include other populations.

    It is primarily through the use of first-person narration and interior
monologue that Phillips explores the borderline between personal experience and its historical representation. Eva's narration, presented as short
passages recounted in the present tense, usually outside of any dialogue
with people from the real world, reflects the workings of a mind unable to
give narrative shape to the past and the future. She is not, or not yet, a

---

[15] Caryl Phillips, *The Nature of Blood* (London: Faber & Faber, 1997): 17–18.
Further page references are in the main text.

witness of the Holocaust, for she does not appear to have established a causal relation between her past experience and her present condition. Her condition, on the contrary, seems to depend on the situation in which she finds herself, from moment to moment:

> The small park is surrounded by elm trees. I sit on a bench in the shade of these trees and stare at the fountain. [...] There is a kind of silence that convinces me that all around there are people. Watching and waiting to see what I will do. And then an elderly couple appear. They walk arm in arm towards me. They stare directly at me, then the woman looks from me and glances across at her husband. I know what he is thinking, but I do not care. (31)

The thoughts of Othello are likewise presented as an interior monologue. Thus, as Othello waits to be called to lead the Venetian campaign against the Turks, his thoughts, like Eva's, reflect the perplexity of someone who, because he does not understand the exact nature of his surroundings, is not sure who he is:

> Venice remains silent, and my mind continues to wrestle with difficult thoughts. I look again to the bed and gaze upon the sight of my wife's body. If only I were privy to her Venetian thoughts, I might begin to help her make sense of her new circumstances. (149)

The effect of this use of interior monologue is to problematize the relation between the voice of the characters and the historical context which would permit them, and the reader, to make sense of their predicament. This is, of course, a common strategy in twentieth-century fiction. It can be used for different purposes, but essentially expresses a questioning of the relation between personal consciousness and social context. In *The Nature of Blood*, it becomes a way of exploring the effects of the diasporic experience on individuals.

By revisiting crucial moments in the formation of diasporic consciousness, Phillips questions the functioning of the diaspora as a frame through which personal experience takes on collective meaning. This explains why writers like Confiant can see his treatment of the question as a betrayal of collective consciousness. But for Phillips, an imaginative return to the roots of the diasporic experience constitutes the only way of understanding its real nature. It is precisely by modifying the relation between perception, which is personal, and narrative, which organizes perception into communicable sequences, that fiction opens the historical past to re-examination.

In *The Nature of Blood*, interior monologue, interspersed with passages narrated by an anonymous voice, makes it possible to observe the relation between personal perception and collective narrative, a relation that is often masked in fiction by the use of an omniscient narrator. Such narrators blend their own perception with an overall, controlling view in ways that hide, precisely, the workings of collective consciousness. It is for this reason that they have come to be seen as the purveyors of hidden ideologies. By separating the personal and collective functions of his narrators, Phillips allows the reader to examine the diasporic experience from both sides of the process through which collective narratives emerge. This approach can be seen, for instance, in a passage near the end of the first section of the novel, in which Eva is trying to recover a coherent sense of self. At one point, she is given a tube of lipstick by another woman. Unwilling to use this lipstick, which represents a social connection to the world, she looks at herself in the mirror:

> She has a present for me. She slips it into my hand and then leaves the room. I know what I have to do. I wait for a few moments and then move across to the mirror. A stranger's face, with large puffy eyes. I do not want this anguished expression. How can this stranger be me? [...] I smear the lipstick around my mouth. A jagged slash, red like blood. [...] How can she give me this useless lipstick? How can she give me such a present? I am not like them. I am not. (48)

By refusing the lipstick, Eva invests it with a personal meaning, as the sign of loss and pain. She thus opens a breach between herself and the collective narratives of seduction and social acceptance which could potentially put an end to her isolation. In the following paragraph, the narration shifts from Eva's thoughts to the words of a third-person narrator, who tells the story of a Jewish boy who disappears in the town of Portobuffole in 1480. The gap between the end of Eva's speech and the beginning of the following paragraph is more than one of time and space. It is the distance that separates an interior, personal voice from the anonymous voice of the historian.

Ricoeur points out that the writing of history involves the passage from an individual voice that remembers to a representation of collective experience through a voice that attempts to be impersonal. It is the transition from the individual to the collective, from the personal to the impersonal, that is the most problematic aspect of constructing historical representations on the basis of individual experiences. In examining the way in which personal memory becomes history, Ricoeur recognizes the importance of what he calls "the declarative phase of memory," in which images are given verbal form.[16] Rather than taking this declarative phase for granted, which would amount to suppressing the most crucial phase in the passage from memory to history, he pays close attention to the ways in which this transition can be effected, particularly through the use of oral and written testimony. He points out two important dimensions of testimony: he underlines the fact that it relies on the linking of an assertion to its source in the speaking subject and that it creates a situation of dialogue between the witness and the person who receives and accepts the testimony.[17]

The fictional strategy of Phillips relies to a great extent on the use of dialogic relations established at different levels of the narration. While, on a first level, they concern the connections between the characters, these relations are extended outward in a complex pattern of echoes to suggest hidden links between seemingly disparate destinies. In this way, the apparently binary opposition between past and present, and between self and Other, which underlies the diasporic experience is shown to be a broad spectrum of compromises involving many different people, in different times and places. While the reader may temporarily lose sight of the historical forces impelling the displacement of diasporic populations, he acquires a deeper sense of what constitutes the core of the experience and thus becomes a potential witness himself.

It is through Eva's evocation of her family and their sometimes conflictual relations that the reader comes to understand the effect of the Holocaust on her personal development. A pattern of collective betrayal gradually becomes perceptible through the minute cracks in family and social relations which signal other potential forms of abandonment. The reader discovers that Eva's mother, like the girl Rosa, whose husband has disappeared, married "outside her people" in choosing a husband from a different

---

[16] Ricoeur, *La Mémoire, l'histoire, l'oubli*, 158. "In its declarative phase, memory enters the region of language: a remembered event which is given verbal expression, which is pronounced, is already a kind of discourse through which the subject speaks with itself."

[17] *La Mémoire, l'histoire, l'oubli*, 204–205. "Self-designation takes place in an exchange which creates a situation of dialogue. It is in front of someone that the witness attests to the reality of the scene at which he claims to have been present, either as actor or as victim, but, in either case, at the moment of witnessing, in the position of a third party in relation to all the protagonists of the event. [...] The certification of the testimony becomes complete only through the parallel response of the person who receives and accepts it."

social class against the will of her parents.[18] In one particularly revealing passage, Eva remembers that when she was harassed by people on the way to school, her mother retreated into her private memories, temporarily abandoning her:

> As the candles burnt low, and Mama began to revel in the warm glow of her private memories, it began to upset me that she never once referred back to the fact that I had just been beaten. Finally, after Mama's anecdotes and advice had run their course, and as Margot and I began to make our way to bed, she looked at me and confirmed that, from tomorrow, she would be accompanying me on both the journey to school and the journey back home at the end of the day, but she mentioned this as though it were an afterthought. (89)

It is Eva's father who explicitly refers to the narrative of the Jews as an explanation of their fate:

> According to Papa, we had followed the advice of our prophets. 'Come, my people, enter thou into thy chambers, and shut thy doors about thee: hide thyself for a little moment, until the indignation be overpast.' But it appeared that there would be no end to the indignation. (71)

Both personal anecdote and public narrative emerge in situations of dialogue. At the initial level represented by the passages quoted above, it is the characters themselves who serve as witnesses, gradually giving their personal lives the shape of the diasporic experience referred to by Eva's father.

In reading the narrative of Othello, in which he recounts his arrival in Venice and his growing awareness of the difference between himself and the Venetians, the reader discovers the ways in which Eva's narration serves as a counterpoint to Othello's. Eva is a young Jewish girl whose life has been shattered both on a personal and a historical level by the Holocaust. Othello is a mature man living in a period preceding the historical events which will disperse his people. Both are members of diasporic populations. However, their stories are not meant to be simply superimposed. Nor is one meant to fill, on a purely historical level, the gaps created in the other. The essential borderline, both within and between their lives, is that which separates experience from the narrative forms through which it is given

---

[18] Eva and her parents share an apartment with a young woman named Rosa, who explains to Eva that her husband is fighting outside, in the underground. He comes to see her occasionally, but less and less often as the situation worsens. Eva's mother, who does not want her to speak to Rosa, explains enigmatically that "'she married outside of her people'" (70).

meaning. It is in this way that Phillips examines the nature of historical memory by re-imagining it as individual consciousness. At the same time, this technique becomes a way of revealing the potentially paralyzing power of the cultural narratives through which personal experience is given collective meaning.

Both Eva and Othello are seen as isolated figures placed in situations in which they must use their imagination to provide the missing links between themselves and the world. Eva goes to a café with her father and finds herself imagining a story to explain the connection between an older man and a woman seated facing them:

> I looked at Papa and nodded. I could see that he was embarrassed that the lovers were making no allowance for my presence, but I was thrilled with this development. I began to imagine this woman as the most glamorous person in the world: a French cabaret star who had travelled from Paris and deposited herself in our country, in a café in our city, at our table. (83)

In the same way, Othello's imagination is stimulated by the mysterious quality of the Jewish ghetto in Venice, and he finds himself imagining the beauty of their women: "I longed to catch a glimpse of one of their beautiful black-eyed women, but the inhabitants of this region appeared to be sleeping peacefully" (130). For both Eva and Othello, imagination becomes a way of appropriating experience, of making it their own. While Eva refers to the strange woman as "my glamorous woman" (87), Othello describes Venice at night as "a sleeping babe upon whom one might spy with proprietorial glee" (121).

It is, of course, the similarities between the two stories that suggest the ironical ways in which the gaps in one may be echoed in the incidents of the other. The asymmetry in the relation between Othello and Desdemona reflects the incongruity of the relation between the mysterious woman and the older man. Young Rosa's abandonment by her husband is mirrored in Othello's abandoning of his African wife in favor of Desdemona. As Othello puts on the costumes of Venice, assuming that this will make him resemble the Venetians, Eva looks out into the street and realizes that the persecution of the Jews is erasing all the distinctive traces of their wealth, education, and social status: "From this precarious position, I looked down into the streets. It had been some time now since anyone in our community had witnessed splendid decorative hats upon women's heads, or gentlemen walking with canes" (60). For both Eva and Othello, the answers to the dilemmas which puzzle them lie beyond the scope of their understanding, in narratives that exceed the boundaries of their individual lives. The reader, as he recognizes parallels and contrasts between the two stories, inevitably establishes connections which the characters themselves are unable to perceive. The very need to make sense of what is given as perception, but withheld as explanation, within the individual stories, incites him to create links at another level. While some of these links are suggested by elements within the stories themselves, like those mentioned above, others are found in passages presented in a third-person narration which cannot be traced to any specific source. The tragedy of Eva's life is incorporated into the more general narrative of the Holocaust by a voice that seems to belong to someone doing research on victims of deportation:

> What I now know of the condition I've learnt largely because of Eva Stern. Not because I possess any intimate knowledge of her case history. I hardly knew her. I interviewed her just once. But it was she who started me thinking about the problem in general. (173)

The future destinies of Othello and the city of Venice are presented in a form resembling entries in an encyclopedia:

> OTHELLO: A play by William Shakespeare. Probably written between 1602 and 1604, and first performed in 1604. The principal source for the play is Giraldi Cinthio's *Hecatommithi*, a collection of Italian stories first published in Venice in 1566. (166)

In each of these cases, the gap between personal memory and the form it takes in someone else's words expresses the tenuous nature of the relation between private and public history. Much can be lost in the spaces that Phillips leaves blank, but much can also be found and rebuilt in those openings. Ultimately, to return to Ricoeur's idea of the importance of testimony, it is the reader who receives and certifies the testimony which Phillips's characters offer in what is essentially a private gesture, as they often seem to be speaking to themselves. However, this dialogic relation with the reader involves a different type of participation on his part from that often found in the writings of people belonging to diasporic populations.

Many African-American and Caribbean writers see the interconnection between the individual and the group as a way of compensating for the disruption and fragmentation caused by the diasporic experience. Caryl Phillips, for his part, uses the space between individual trauma and collective narratives as a way of imagining new relations between histories that have often been viewed as separate. Rather than using the collective consciousness of the racial or ethnic group as a means of recovering and preserving the lost past of the individual, he shows how all pasts are interconnected. His main concern seems to be with exploring the ways in which narratives functioning at different points in a range of possible relations between individual consciousness and historical explanation help diasporic populations survive, while at the same time putting them at greater risk.[19] In this respect, the use of the Jewish diaspora as the frame for *The Nature of Blood* points up the irony implicit in any desire to use narrative to preserve the purity of experience. It is the Jewish diaspora, more than any other, that has retained its sense of group identity by the transmission from generation to generation of a founding narrative meant to both explain and justify their separateness and their dispersal: "Their feast was designed to celebrate the moment in their history when they claimed that the Red Sea turned into blood and destroyed the Egyptian army … " (52).

By interweaving the story of the Jewish diaspora with that of the Africans, Phillips confronts the different destinies of two peoples: one of them has maintained its sense of collective identity through the preservation of a cultural narrative with scriptural roots; the other, having no such narrative, finds itself fragmented and reproduced partially in the narratives of others. His purpose is not to question the validity of the claims made by the Jewish diaspora on the basis of their cultural narratives, just as Paul Ricoeur is not questioning the exceptional status of the Holocaust by trying to dilute it in historical narrative. Phillips is, rather, using his own position as a member of a diaspora without a founding story in order to examine the role played by such cultural narratives in the lives of other diasporic populations. He sees the narratives of diasporic populations as taking shape in a space that is shared. Their stories become their own only by becoming someone else's. This is, indeed, for him the nature of the "conundrum of home," which fiction can only explore but never resolve.

WORKS CITED

Dash, J. Michael. *The Other America: Caribbean Literature in a New World Context* (Charlottesville: UP of Virginia, 1998).

Ledent, Bénédicte. "Remembering Slavery: History as Roots in the Fiction of Caryl Phillips and Fred D'Aguiar," in *The Contact and the Culmination: Essays in Honour of Hena Maes–Jelinek*, ed. Marc Delrez & Bénédicte Ledent (Liège: U of Liège, 1996): 271–80.

---

[19] In the story concerning the Jews of Portobuffole in the fifteenth century, the anonymous narrator shows how a misinterpretation of the ritual of the Passover, which commemorates the story of the flight from Egypt, leads the Christians of the town to accuse the Jews of sacrificing a Christian child. Phillips, like Ricoeur, seems to be aware of the potential dangers of an excessive attachment to the past.

Phillips, Caryl. *Cambridge* (London: Bloomsbury, 1991).
——. *A Distant Shore* (New York: Alfred A. Knopf, 2003).
——. *The Nature of Blood* (London: Faber & Faber, 1997).
Ricoeur, Paul. *La Mémoire, l'histoire, l'oubli* (Paris: Seuil, 2000).
Rochlitz, Rainer. "La Mémoire privatisée," *Le Monde* (25–26 June 2000): 14–15.

❖

Modernism in the Black Diaspora

Langston Hughes
and the "broken cubes of Picasso"[1]

SETH MOGLEN

I N THE SPRING OF 1934, Langston Hughes published a poem called "Cubes" in *New Masses*, the premier literary journal of the American anti-capitalist Left. Hughes had recently returned home from a year spent in the Soviet Union and, at the time of the poem's publication, he was at the height of his commitment to the revolutionary socialist movement. He was also thinking with particular intensity about the relationship between the expansion of capitalism and the spread of a racially based European imperialism. Like many of Hughes's poems from the mid-1930s, "Cubes" is centrally concerned with this connection between capitalism and empire – with the global system that had, over several centuries, produced the African diaspora. Within the context of these political concerns, "Cubes" offers a revelatory exploration of the international aesthetic transformation that we have come to call modernism. The poem is at once an innovative modernist experiment and a powerful critique of modernism

---

[1] I would like to thank the following friends and colleagues who commented on earlier drafts of this essay: Charles Altieri, Greg Forter, Kristin Handler, Lawrence Levine, Helene Moglen, Fred Moten, Ben Nathans, Carolyn Porter, the late Michael Rogin, and Susan Schweik. I would also like to thank Geneviève Fabre, who invited me to present an earlier version at the international conference "Diasporas africaines: Conscience et Imaginaire" at the University of Paris, Charles V in October 2000, as well as the colleagues who responded to my work there. This essay is dedicated to the memory of my father, Sig Moglen (1936–2001).

from a black diasporic perspective. "Cubes" suggests that the revolutionary
aesthetic practices of the early twentieth century were symptomatic expressions of an expanding system of racial and economic exploitation. But the
poem demonstrates that these practices could also provide artists in the
African diaspora with an indispensable means of understanding, and thereby resisting, that system of exploitation. Before developing this argument, I
want to contextualize my reading by describing briefly some of the idiosyn-
cracies of the scholarship on Langston Hughes and American modernism.
As we will see, this history tells us important things about the ways in
which this literary field has been structured – and how a reading of "Cubes"
can alter our understanding of modernism itself.

As far as I know, "Cubes" has never been written about: it has been
ignored equally by Hughes scholars and by students of modernism. The
poem's neglect reflects the peculiar history of American scholarship about
the artistic revolutions of the early twentieth century. As critics now widely
recognize, modernism was canonized in the USA during the Cold War in
ways that were politically narrow and racially exclusionary. When an influential version of the movement was consolidated in the 1940s and 1950s,
scholars generally assumed that African Americans had not contributed to
its development.[2] This racially exclusionary view was so entrenched that,
when African-American literary studies blossomed in the 1960s, most
students of black culture accepted the notion that modernism's formal practices and social concerns were largely alien to black writers of the earlier
twentieth century. Indeed, they frequently defined the distinctive features of
African-American culture in express opposition to an artistic movement that

---

[2] The exclusion of African Americans from the emerging canon of modernism
reflected, of course, a racial myopia that has pervaded US literary studies more
generally. Documenting silence or exclusion is a difficult task, but a couple of significant examples should indicate the racial bias of earlier modernism scholarship.
When Richard Ellman and Charles Feidelson, Jr. assembled the impressive and
influential anthology that helped to define the modernist canon as it emerged from
the New-Critical generation, *The Modern Tradition: Backgrounds of Modern Literature* (New York: Oxford UP, 1965), they included no African-American writers.
The persistence of this exclusion into the next critical generation is illustrated by the
fact that the best single-volume overview of the international modernist literary
movement from the 1970s, *Modernism, 1890–1930*, ed. Malcolm Bradbury & James
McFarlane (Harmondsworth: Penguin, 1976), does not include a single African-
American author in its biographical list of 100 modernist writers, nor does its 1300-
item bibliography contain a single reference to a black author or work.

was presumed to be inherently racist and primitivist.[3] Into the 1980s, the scholarship on Langston Hughes generally reflected these oppositions. Those critics who rightly celebrated Hughes as a writer working in the black vernacular tended to assume that his commitment to the idioms of black working-class speech and to the popular musical forms of jazz and the blues must place him outside the modernist tradition.[4] Similarly, the relatively small number of scholars who acknowledged and celebrated Hughes's socialist politics generally assumed that the poet's radicalism put him at

---

[3] For example, the opposition between modernism and African-American culture can be seen at work in typically complex ways in Nathan Huggins's important early study, *The Harlem Renaissance* (New York: Oxford UP, 1971). On the one hand, Huggins criticized the literature of the Renaissance for failing to achieve the sophistication of the 'formalist' 'high art' associated with canonized modernism. On the other, he singled out for praise a few vernacular currents of early twentieth-century black culture, especially jazz, which he viewed as lying outside this 'high culture'. It is striking that the first sustained polemical effort to break down the opposition between modernism and African-American culture, Houston Baker Jr.'s *Modernism and the Harlem Renaissance* (Chicago: U of Chicago P, 1987), was still so deeply influenced by this binary that Baker insisted on defining African-American modernism as a separate tradition opposed to a racist and primitivist Euro-American modernism.

[4] The distinction between Hughes's commitment to 'folk culture' and the 'high art' associated with canonized modernism has structured a great deal of the Hughes scholarship. Nathan Huggins, for example, argues that Hughes chose to reject "serious 'high culture'" and "formalism" in the name of black "folk art" (*The Harlem Renaissance*, 227). In a more recent example, Karen Jackson Ford celebrates Hughes's "aesthetics of simplicity," claiming that Hughes embraced "folk materials rather than high art"; "Do Right to Write Right: Langston Hughes's Aesthetics of Simplicity," *Twentieth Century Literature* 38.4 (Winter 1992): 446. Arnold Rampersad argues similarly that in his "loyalty to the forms of black culture," Hughes rejected "modernism as defined by elitism, hyper-intellectualism, and a privacy of language"; *The Life of Langston Hughes*, vol. 1: *1902–1941: I, Too, Sing America* (New York: Oxford UP, 1986): 102 (cited hereafter as *Life*). Rampersad's invaluable two-volume biography was actually poised at the turning-point of current thinking about modernism, and about Hughes's relationship to it. Early in the first volume, Rampersad does seem to acknowledge that modernism might be a complex and contested phenomenon, and that Hughes was pursuing "a version of modernism" that was "populist in nature" and "quite unlike" the modernism of Ezra Pound and T.S. Eliot, "whose elite standards would soon define the term" (*Life*, vol. 1: 29). During the remainder of his study, however, Rampersad is generally content to abandon the term "modernism" to the "elite standards" he associates with Pound and Eliot, and to define Hughes's poetry as a repudiation of modernism itself.

odds with a literary tradition understood to be apolitical or actively conservative.[5] In this context, critics inevitably had difficulty making sense of
a poem like "Cubes" – a poem that clearly reflects Hughes's militantly anti-
capitalist and anti-imperialist sensibility but that also stands as a manifesto
of black modernism.

In more recent years, an emergent 'new modernism studies' has expanded and diversified our understanding of this complex literary movement, dissolving some of the misconceptions that prevented critics from
grasping the modernism of writers such as Langston Hughes. This revisionary scholarship has had a number of goals, but canon expansion has been
the most central. Critics have sought to explore the meanings and uses of
modernism for women writers, for working-class authors and writers on the
Left, and for writers from racially subordinated groups.[6] In this altered context, some recent criticism has started to consider how Hughes's political

---

[5] Adrien Oktenberg, for example, expresses this view particularly clearly, arguing
that Hughes's commitment to 'proletarian' writing must be understood as directly
"opposed" to the "art for art's sake" "doctrine" of "the modernist faction" represented by "Pound, Eliot, Williams, Stevens, Moore, Crane"; "From the Bottom Up:
Three Radicals of the Thirties," in *A Gift of Tongues: Critical Challenges in Contemporary American Poetry*, ed. Marie Marris & Kathleen Aguero (Athens: U of
Georgia P, 1987): 86, 93–99.

[6] The phrase "new modernism studies" has come into common usage relatively
recently to identify the substantial changes that have taken place in the field over the
last two decades. Many scholars have participated in the welcome expansion of the
modernist canon, but a few of the most influential general interventions are these: on
female modernists, see Shari Benstock, *Women of the Left Bank, Paris 1900–1940*
(Austin: U of Texas P, 1986), Suzanne Clark, *Sentimental Modernism: Women
Writers and the Revolution of the Word* (Bloomington: Indiana UP, 1991), and Bonnie Kime Scott's influential revisionary anthology *The Gender of Modernism: A
Critical Anthology* (Bloomington: Indiana UP, 1990); on working-class and left
modernism, see esp. Cary Nelson, *Repression and Recovery: Modern American
Poetry and the Politics of Cultural Memory, 1910–1945* (Madison: U of Wisconsin P,
1989), Michael Denning, *The Cultural Front: The Laboring of American Culture in
the Twentieth Century* (New York: Verso, 1996), and Walter Kalaidjian, *American
Culture Between the Wars: Revisionary Modernism and Postmodern Critique* (New
York: Columbia UP, 1993); on African-American modernism, Houston Baker's
Modernism and the Harlem Renaissance was a pathbreaking study and, more
recently, George Hutchinson's *The Harlem Renaissance in Black and White* (Cambridge MA: Harvard UP, 1995) has dramatically shifted the debate by emphasizing
the interracial character of American modernism, including the formation called the
"Harlem Renaissance."

radicalism and his commitment to the black vernacular carried him, not outside this artistic movement but, rather, into the development of a distinctive populist and revolutionary version of modernism.[7]

While the new modernism studies has valuably prised open an exclusionary canon, however, the gain in critical breadth has sometimes come at the cost of analytical precision. One strong impulse in recent scholarship has been the tendency to employ 'modernism' as a period term: many recent critics have come to use the word 'modernism' to mean 'modern' literature, the literature corresponding to the period of 'modernity'. According to this usage, all writers working in the early twentieth century, for example, seem to become 'modernists'.[8] This terminology has the obvious appeal of inclusiveness: it encourages us to tear down the partitions that have often separated consideration of those writers traditionally recognized as participants in the avant-garde from their contemporaries. But there are serious disadvantages to this usage as well. Above all, it obscures the formal particularities that distinguish the revolutionary experiments that some (but not all) early twentieth-century writers understood themselves to be collectively engaged in and that the word 'modernism' has sought, retrospectively, to

---

[7] See especially James Edward Smethurst's astute account of what he calls Hughes's "popular neomodernism" in *The New Red Negro: The Literary Left and African-American Poetry, 1930–1946* (New York: Oxford UP, 1999), particularly ch. 3 and 5.

[8] This tendency to use modernism as a period term, without concern for the formal particularities that distinguish 'modern*ist*' from other 'modern' literature has been especially pronounced in some of the most daring and valuably revisionary work of recent years. The problems raised by this terminology become particularly acute in the case of scholars who use a sociological definition of 'modernity' as a period stretching over two or more centuries. Marshall Berman, for example, in his influential and evocative study *All That Is Solid Melts Into Air: The Experiences of Modernity* (New York: Simon & Schuster, 1982), uses the term modernism to describe all the cultural formations since the rise of modern capitalism, from Goethe onwards. In *The Black Atlantic: Modernity and Double Consciousness* (Cambridge MA: Harvard UP, 1993), Paul Gilroy uses 'modernism' to mean the 'culture' (and 'countercultures') of 'modernity', where modernity seems to mean the period since the rise of the Enlightenment and the African slave trade. Among revisionary scholars working with a narrower periodization (the early twentieth century), similar though less extreme problems emerge. In *The Harlem Renaissance in Black and White*, George Hutchinson blunts the precision of his invaluable intervention by using the word 'modernism' as roughly synonymous with the entire "American literary field," which results, for example, in figures like Theodore Dreiser being identified as 'modernist'.

identify. This inattention to form is not, of course, accidental. Many revisionary scholars today associate a careful consideration of form with an
older critical 'formalism' that did indeed often mask elitist social attitudes.
To ignore the formal considerations that distinguish modernist writing from
other literary practices is thus often imagined to be politically progressive
because it enables the inclusion of writers who have been marginalized on
the basis of such 'formalist' arguments.

This view – let us call it 'anti-formalist' – rests on assumptions that are
highly problematic in literary-historical and political terms. In many cases,
the anti-formalist view stems, implicitly or explicitly, from the false presumption that left writers or authors from socially marginalized groups were
less concerned with formal experimentation in general – and with modernist
experiments in particular – than their traditionally canonized peers. (This
presumption has, for example, characterized the scholarship on Langston
Hughes, as I have suggested – and I will be showing the inadequacy of this
perspective.) Alternately (or sometimes simultaneously), the anti-formalist
view rests on the presumption that the formal practices that distinguish
modernism from other literary traditions can be ignored because they are
socially and politically inconsequential, mere superficial changes in literary
fashion. This seems to me a serious error. These formal experiments were
the urgent efforts of men and women to find strategies to represent and
respond to the social forces that were – often catastrophically – transforming their lives. This was no less true for committed and self-conscious left
modernists like Langston Hughes or Tillie Olsen than it was for more conservative and traditionally recognized figures like Eliot and Pound.

Of course, modernist formal practices are not inherently politically progressive (feminist, anti-racist, non-homophobic, anti-capitalist), any more
than they are inherently conservative. What I am suggesting is that these
formal practices are *politically significant*, although that significance varies.
To ignore the particular technical experiments of previously marginalized
writers is to ignore their understanding of the social crises that they faced –
crises that they believed required enormous effort and ingenuity to represent. It is also to ignore the political alternatives – the social aspirations and
yearnings – that were articulable for writers like Langston Hughes only
through modernist forms. To grasp the distinctive representational experiments of writers recently incorporated into an expanded modernist canon is
thus a precondition for fully grasping the political visions that had, until
recently, been excluded from our literary tradition.

In a brief but evocative essay called "Cognitive Mapping," Fredric Jameson has offered a particularly fruitful starting-point for thinking about the
historical conditions and political implications of modernist form. He

proposes that modernism can best be understood as the effort to invent
formal strategies adequate to representing the social order that comes into
being with the transition from "market" to "monopoly capitalism." In this
new stage of capitalism, there emerges an increasingly bewildering gap
between individual "lived experience" and the vast new "economic and
social form[s]" that structure the "social totality." This gap is produced in
large measure by the staggering scale on which economic activity takes
place in an era of expanding and intensifying imperialism. Jameson illustrates the cognitive difficulty faced by individual subjects by pointing to the
discrepancy between a person's experience of "a certain section of London," for example, and the vast "colonial system of the British empire that
determines the very quality of the individual's subjective life" but is neither
"accessible to immediate lived experience" nor "even conceptualizable for
most people." Our "various modernisms" cohere, according to Jameson, in
their attempt to invent new formal strategies capable of figuring this global
economic and social system – a system that shapes every aspect of individuals' lives, even as it eludes their immediate lived experience and therefore defies earlier strategies of literary representation.[9]

Jameson's formulations provide a valuable way of approaching "Cubes"
because they resonate so powerfully with the vision of modernism that
Hughes himself develops in this poem. Like Jameson, Hughes insists that
this artistic movement cannot be understood outside the context of an
expanding capitalist economic system that had become, in an age of intensifying imperialism, ever more global in scale. The interlocking systems of
capitalism and empire were, according to Hughes, responsible both for the
emergence of avant-garde aesthetic practices and for the enforced migrations and oppressions of the African diaspora. Hughes's assessment of
modernism in "Cubes" is, accordingly, ambivalent. At one level, the poet
offers a trenchant critique of modernist art as a "disease." The poem suggests that the revolutionary aesthetic practices of his generation – practices
for which Picasso's cubism stands as symbol and model – should be recognized as symptomatic expressions of a global system of exploitation that
was deforming the lives of people around the world. But this critique is
offered from within this aesthetic movement itself, by a poet who clearly
perceives himself as a participant in its formal revolution. For "Cubes" is
not only a meditation on modernism: it is also a demonstration of its power.

---

[9] Fredric Jameson, "Cognitive Mapping," in *Marxism and the Interpretation of
Culture*, ed. Cary Nelson & Lawrence Grossberg (Urbana: U of Illinois P, 1988):
347–57.

Through the development of what I will call a black vernacular literary cubism, Hughes provides in this poem a "cognitive map" – a "figuration," in Jameson's sense – of a system of exploitation so vast that individuals could perceive it only in fragments. In doing so, Hughes suggests that modernism is a "gift" as well as a "disease": that its formal practices may be uniquely capable of representing – and thereby enabling us to resist – the global economic and social order that has produced them.

In the opening stanza of "Cubes," Hughes offers a 'cubist' portrait of the modernist moment:

> In the days of the broken cubes of Picasso
> And in the days of the broken songs of the young men
> A little too drunk to sing
> And the young women
> A little too unsure of love to love –
> I met on the boulevards of Paris
> An African from Senegal.[10]

The stanza confronts us with a cluster of fragments whose relations to one another are initially obscure. Hughes calls our attention, first, to the distinctive representational practice of modernism – to "the broken cubes of Picasso" – and to the specific historical moment ("the days") in which that modernist technique was born. Second, he suggests that the revolutionary representational technique of avant-garde modernists like Picasso is somehow related to a widespread popular crisis in self-expression and affective connection. (This crisis is evocatively figured as a mixture of desire and impotence: while the "young men" are moved to sing and the "young women" want to love, intoxication makes their songs "broken" and insecurity breeds emotional incapacity.) Third, both modernism and this affective crisis are associated with the enigmatic encounter "on the boulevards of Paris" between the African-American poet and the "African from Senegal." Like the viewer of a cubist painting, or a pedestrian in the modern metropolis, we are confronted by Hughes with a problem of relation, with the task of mapping or cognitively assimilating a set of abruptly juxtaposed

---

[10] "Cubes" was originally published in *New Masses* (13 March 1934); repr. in *Good Morning Revolution: Uncollected Writings of Langston Hughes,* ed. Faith Berry (New York: Citadel, 1973): 14–15 and in *The Collected Poems of Langston Hughes*, ed. Arnold Rampersad & David Roessel (New York: Alfred A. Knopf, 1994): 175–76. Because many readers will be unfamiliar with "Cubes," and because the poem has been out of print until recently, I have reprinted the text in its entirety as an appendix to this essay.

aesthetic, psychic and social realities. The apparent simplicity of Hughes's language should not obscure the ambition of the poet's challenge: how are we to understand the social system that gives rise, at once, to the modernist artistic revolution, to the affective and expressive crisis of the metropolitan imperial subject, and to the confounding modern experience of the black diaspora itself? The remainder of the poem can be understood as a cubist exploration of the elusive relations among these fragments – as an attempt to produce a cognitive map of the modernity thus enigmatically experienced.

At a formal level, Hughes holds together the disparate fragments of the opening stanza through a series of linguistic repetitions. Although we cannot yet understand the substance of the connection, we know that Picasso is associated with the drunken men because his "broken cubes" echo their "broken songs," and because Hughes repeats twice that it is "in the days" of one that the other has also been produced. The men are, in turn, associated with the fearful women because both are "young" and because the men are "*A little* too drunk" just as the women are "*A little* too unsure of love." These repetitions of simple words and phrases are partially responsible for the colloquial feeling of the stanza. This technique, which produces a steadily increasing emotional intensity and conceptual sophistication over the course of the poem, is in fact a carefully controlled formal experiment that draws on two strands of modernist aesthetics: the model of Picasso's cubism and the black vernacular musical sources that pervade Hughes's poetry. The poet employs linguistic repetition here the way a cubist painter employs geometric repetition – in order to establish and emphasize underlying similarities, relations, and resonances among apparently disparate objects. (Just as Picasso might suggest that a guitar, a newspaper and a human form may echo one another geometrically within a given composition, Hughes establishes through linguistic resonances the obscure relations between Picasso's representational practice and the quotidian behavior of the young.) These repetitions also draw on the vernacular practices of jazz and the blues – musical practices that are among the most influential US contributions to the modernist aesthetic revolution.[11] Like the repeated line

---

[11] While I will be suggesting some of the ways in which Hughes's use of repetition in this poem draws on vernacular musical traditions, "Cubes" is not, strictly speaking, a 'blues' or a 'jazz' poem in the sense that its overall poetic structure does not closely follow a single musical form in the way that some other Hughes poems do. For the influence of the blues on Hughes's poetry, the most sustained study is Steven Tracy, *Langston Hughes and the Blues* (Chicago: U of Illinois P, 1998); see

within a blues stanza, the repeated words enable Hughes to explore the multiple meanings and emotional nuances contained within a single phrase. And just as a jazz musician may employ a repeated riff persistently within a single improvisation in order to explore unsuspected paths between one harmonic or melodic point and another, so too the repeated words enable Hughes to trace possible relations between apparently disparate social phenomena without entirely rupturing the continuity of his inquiry. From the outset, then, Hughes's technique here is at once modernist and vernacular: it is, perhaps most precisely, a black vernacular literary cubism.[12]

In the second stanza, Hughes focusses his attention on one of the fragments from his initial portrait: the enigma of the African in Paris. He approaches this enigma by expressing his confusion – at once a moral and cognitive uncertainty – about why this black man has been subjected to such a striking geographical displacement:

> God
> Knows why the French
> Amuse themselves bringing to Paris
> Negroes from Senegal.

The poet's expression of uncertainty contains the fragments of its own clarification. At the most obvious level, Hughes indicates that the African's presence in Paris can only be understood in the context of the bewildering global system of exploitation – and migration – produced by European imperialism. As a member of a colonized people and a subject race, the

---

also David Chinitz, "Literacy and Authenticity: The Blues Poems of Langston Hughes," *Callaloo* 19.1 (1998): 177–92.

[12] By using this formulation, I want to suggest that Hughes's formal experiment in "Cubes" can usefully be understood as a literary equivalent of the vernacular cubisms explored by African-American visual artists during the 1930s, such as Aaron Douglas in his famous "Aspects of Negro Life" murals and Jacob Lawrence in the "Toussaint L'Ouverture" series. On the relationship between black vernacular music and African-American visual art, including cubist experiments, see Richard J. Powell, "Art History and Black Memory: Toward a 'Blues Aesthetic'" (1994), in *The Jazz Cadence of American Culture*, ed. Robert O'Meally (New York: Columbia UP, 1999): 182–95, and Paul Gilroy, "Modern Tones," in *Rhapsodies in Black: Art of the Harlem Renaissance*, ed. Richard J. Powell et al. (Berkeley: U of California P, 1997): 102–109. See also Robert Hughes's comments on Stuart Davis's experiments in the 1930s (and Romare Bearden's in the 1960s) with cubism as a visual equivalent to the musical idioms of jazz improvisation: *American Visions: The Epic History of Art in America* (New York: Alfred A. Knopf, 1997): 430–47, 519–21.

Senegalese man has been "brought" to his current geographical location by those with power over him. This materialist political perspective is psychologically inflected, as Hughes emphasizes that the black man has not simply been 'brought' to Paris, but has been brought specifically so that the French may "*amuse*" themselves through him. The poet suggests here that the global migrations of the African diaspora have not only a *material* cause, but also – and ultimately – a *libidinal* one. This is a quintessentially Hughesian insight and deserves emphasis. As he does throughout his poetic corpus, Hughes insists in "Cubes" that systems of material exploitation – including those of imperialism – stem ultimately from the desire of those with power to extract *pleasure* (in this formulation, "amusement") from their subordinates.

Significantly, the poet's psychological and materialist perception derives from a sense of racial identification with the African. While his encounter with the Senegalese man superficially resembles the long parade of modernist encounters with primitive Others (often in the streets of Paris), the black American poet refuses the distance that usually characterizes these canonical moments of exoticism. On the contrary, he immediately identifies with the Senegalese expatriate, referring to him as a "Negro" – the preferred term of African-American self-designation in the 1930s and a term that could apply equally to all peoples of African descent. By establishing this point of diasporic identification, even as he politicizes the African's situation, Hughes implicitly calls into question the meaning of his own presence as an African-American poet in Paris. Is his own place in the Western metropole truly freer than that of this other black man? As a black modernist who travels the world reading his poems of African-American life, is his task also to "amuse" those in power?[13]

In the third stanza, Hughes explicitly argues that the racial and economic power relations of imperialism – with their libidinal as well as material dimension – lie "behind" the aesthetic practice of modernism:

---

[13] In her important study of African-American anti-imperialism, *Race Against Empire: Black Americans and Anti-Colonialism, 1937–1957* (Ithaca NY: Cornell UP, 1997), Penny von Eschen has emphasized the importance of the politicized identification of African Americans with African colonial subjects. "Cubes" offers here a phenomenological, poetic enactment of this identification on the part of Hughes, an influential early figure in this political tradition. David Chioni Moore has offered the most subtle account to date of the complex racial vision underlying Hughes's anti-imperialist and anti-capitalist politics in the 1930s: see "Local Color, Global 'Color': Langston Hughes, the Black Atlantic, and Soviet Central Asia, 1932," *Research in African Literatures* 27.4 (Winter 1996): 49–70.

> It's the old game of the boss and the bossed
>   boss and the bossed,
>   amused
>   and
>   amusing,
>   worked and working,
> Behind the cubes of black and white,
>   black and white,
>   black and white

Through a succession of three pairings in the first part of the stanza, Hughes emphasizes that the power relations that lie behind modernism – and that define the relationship between the French and the "Negro from Senegal" – are exploitative, but also inherently unstable. The first formulation describes the "old game" of exploitation as a relation in which some people are not merely subjected to the power of another ("the boss"), but are defined by it: they are simply "the bossed." The second reiterates the centrality of pleasure in such relations – but it also complicates the simple distribution of power, suggesting that it may well be the activity of the subordinates (those who *do* the "amusing") that defines the status and identity of the dominant one (the "amused," who has become the *object* of the verb and of the subordinate's action). The third formulation is significantly ambiguous. At one level, this third pairing can be seen to mirror the first two, describing once again the opposition between those who are subordinate (those who are "worked") and those who dominate them (those who are "working" others). But this third formulation has another meaning which explicitly focusses our attention on the instability of the location of agency that I have emphasized in describing the shift from the first to the second opposition. For the third pairing – "worked and working" – also describes two different ways of understanding the complex position of the subordinate, who can be perceived both as the object of exploitation (one who is "worked" by another) and as the active agent of productive labour (the one who is "working"). Through this succession of oppositions, Hughes offers a poetic and libidinally inflected extension of an insight that many will associate with Hegel's famous master–slave dialectic: the poet insists that, in relations of domination, the master's power to compel others to provide for his "amusement" is always tenuously balanced against the latent power of those who perform the work and provide the pleasure.[14] In the final lines of

---

[14] For Hegel's account, which has influenced generations of Marxists, see his "Self-Certainty and The Lordship and Bondage of Self-Consciousness," in *The*

the stanza, Hughes asserts that such complex and unstable power relations lie "Behind the cubes of black and white" – "behind" the expressive practice of modernism.

The sophistication of Hughes's analysis here has been achieved through an extension of his black vernacular cubist technique. Just as a cubist painter can establish the resonances among disparate objects by reducing them to shared and repeated geometric forms, Hughes has successfully schematized various relations of exploitation within a simple series of binary oppositions (boss/bossed; amused/amusing; worked/working). And just as the cubist's geometric "reduction" often involves an increased capacity to represent many perspectives of an object simultaneously, so too Hughes's deceptively 'simple' schematization contains within it a dynamic and subtle account of the multiple ways in which unstable hierarchical power relations should be simultaneously understood. Furthermore, the vernacular technique of linguistic repetition enables the poet to encapsulate formally the central observation that he has asserted conceptually. The repeated phrase at the end of the stanza – "cubes of black and white, / black and white, / black and white" – carries a dual meaning: it refers simultaneously to the "broken cubes" of modernist representation (Hughes's as well as Picasso's) and to the race relations that structure the Great Game of empire. By using the same figurative phrase for modernism and empire, Hughes insists, formally as well as cognitively, that the new expressive practice cannot be separated from the material, social relations in the midst of which it has emerged.[15]

In the fourth stanza, Hughes deepens this analysis, suggesting that if inequitable social relations are to be sustained, those with power must provide some sort of compensation – libidinal or ideological – to those whom they

---

Phenomenology of Mind, tr. J.B. Baille (London: George Allen & Unwin, 1931): 218–40.

[15] The accretive, synthesizing power of Hughes's technique of linguistic repetition is even greater than this compressed analysis suggests. For all the oppositions of the first half of the stanza ("boss and the bossed," "amused / and / amusing," "worked and working") are echoed rhythmically and syntactically by the final repeated phrase ("black and white, / black and white, / black and white"), and the final phrase, by a kind of rhetorical implication, knits together a whole host of phenomena that have been invoked: class hierarchy, racial hierarchy, hierarchies of pleasure and amusement, imperial power relations, and the practices of modernism (in the "black and white" of ink as well as paint). Like a blues singer, or a cubist painter revealing to us additional facets of the same object, Hughes implies a different meaning with each repetition of the phrase "black and white."

exploit. As he explains allegorically, the Europeans have sought to make imperialism palatable by proffering their espoused Enlightenment ideals:

> But since it is the old game,
> For fun
> They give him the three old prostitutes of
>   France –
> Liberty, Equality, Fraternity –

At the most obvious level, this passage deploys a commonplace misogynist trope of the 1930s Marxist Left in order to emphasize the cynical use of Enlightenment ideology to justify imperial exploitation. According to that trope, the immorality of a nation that compromises its political ideals in the name of economic gain is aptly figured by the corrupted woman who sells her sexual virtue as a prostitute. Just as the "boss" may provide the compensatory sexual pleasure of a prostitute to secure the continued participation of the immigrant worker in the "game" of exploitation, so the French provide the ideological compensation of Enlightenment ideals ("Liberty, Equality, Fraternity") which obscure and justify the practice of imperialism itself.

In a remarkable move in the second half of the stanza, however, Hughes resists this misogynist cliché by returning the allegory to its literal level, focussing attention on the prostitutes themselves. He now represents the "old prostitutes" not as the epitome of moral depravity, but as themselves the victims of an institutionalized system of exploitation:

> And all three of 'em sick
> In spite of the tax to the government
> And the legal houses
> And the doctors
> And the *Marseillaise*.

The poet emphasizes here the fact that the legalized system which is supposed to protect the prostitutes is in fact an official mechanism of their oppression. Just as the French seek to justify imperialism by proclaiming their corrupted Enlightenment ideals, so too they have erected a legal and ideological apparatus around prostitution to make it seem safe and compatible with their national self-image. While the government takes its portion of the prostitutes' earnings through taxes, neither the state's regulatory gestures ("the legal houses" and "the doctors") nor its ideological subterfuges ("the *Marseillaise*") actually protect the prostitute from the ravages of her occupation. The prostitute – a recurring figure throughout Hughes's poetry – thus stands here as a perfect symbol of the exploited worker. She performs, most literally and most intimately, the function that he believed pertains always to the worker: providing pleasure to those with power.[16] And the prostitute's "sickness" is the literal embodiment of the toll taken by her exploited labor; it is the price she pays for providing "fun" to men who have money and therefore power over her. Her "sickness" is at once an instance of, and a figure for, the deformation of self that follows from the exploitation of one's capacity to provide pleasure.

The prostitute thus stands in a complex relation to the Senegalese man. On the one hand, she is his double, his sister – the perfect representative of his own exploitation. On the other, he is himself an instrument of her oppression. While her exploitation is parallel to that of the worker, the black man, the colonial, it is also used as a diversionary device that cuts across, palliates, obscures, these other oppressions. Through a kind of careful, colloquial rotation of his subject, Hughes transforms a banal, misogynistic

---

[16] Hughes's emphasis on pleasure is conceptually significant for those interested in theorizations of exploitation. In the 1930s, and throughout his adult life, Hughes was deeply influenced by the Marxist account of exploitation, with its materialist emphasis on the ways in which capitalism involves an intensification of the process by which a minority (those who happen to own capital) are able to extract surplus value from the labor of the great majority, who must work at whatever wages the market will provide. While basically accepting a Marxist analysis, Hughes adds to it a psychological or phenomenological dimension. The poet emphasizes that individual members of the capitalist class personally seek to maximize their capital, in the last analysis, in order to maximize their pleasures, material, psychological, emotional, sensual, etc. (The French bring the African to Paris, ultimately, in order to "amuse" themselves.) Some specialized workers who happen to earn a living by directly providing pleasure to others are immediately aware of the relationship between their exploitation and the pleasures of others: this is true, for example, of those who produce art, knowledge, or entertainment of various kinds, and also those who provide sexual or other forms of physical pleasure. (It is this recognition that underlies Hughes's identification, as a poet, with the African and, throughout his poetic corpus, with the prostitute.) While most workers do not provide pleasure directly in this way, Hughes suggests that this is the ultimate goal of their exploitation, from a psychological or interpersonal standpoint: the surplus value extracted from their labour will, one way or another, increase the commodified pleasures that can be disproportionately consumed by those with capital. Hughes did not abandon a structural, materialist analysis of exploitation (he wrote many poems in the 1930s emphasizing the "impersonal" dynamics driving the processes of economic exploitation), but in "Cubes" and other poems, he emphasizes that the libidinal effects of economic exploitation were among the most important, and damaging, aspects of capitalist society.

political allegory into a multi-layered analysis, insisting that these disparate forms of oppression and exploitation – across lines of gender, class, race, and empire – are structurally homologous but also independent and variably interrelated.[17]

This complex materialist analysis has important ramifications for Hughes's relationship to the Enlightenment values for which the prostitutes allegorically stand. Above all, we must grasp the dialectical ambivalence that the poet introduces through his humanization of the prostitutes. He recognizes the truth of the Marxist critique of Enlightenment ideals as the ideological instrument of an unjust ruling class. (He sees that the proclamations of "Liberty, Equality, Fraternity" are often deployed as cynical deceptions and ideological distractions.) At the same time, however, he refuses to engage in a simple repudiation of Enlightenment values, just as he refuses the vulgar misogyny of the prostitution cliché. The prostitute's "sickness" is the result of her exploitation rather than her depravity; so too these Enlightenment values are seen not as innately meretricious, but as deformed by a system of interlocking power relations.[18]

---

[17] The Marxist tradition has been widely (and, in some of its incarnations, appropriately) criticized for promoting a totalizing vision that minimizes the significance of racial and gender oppression or that seeks to reduce these to mere epiphenomenal effects of capitalism. I want, therefore, to emphasize the flexibility and dynamism of Hughes's figuration of the global system in "Cubes." It is, in my view, emblematic of the African-American Marxist tradition at its best: a tradition that has placed a priority on developing a materialist analysis that grasps the relative autonomy of racial (and often gender) oppression, as well as their systematic incorporation into a capitalist economic structure. This tradition remains under-studied. Relatively recent books by Robin D.G. Kelley, *Hammer and Hoe: Alabama Communists During the Great Depression* (Chapel Hill: U of North Carolina P, 1990), and Penny von Eschen, *Race Against Empire*, have added to the pathbreaking work of Cedric J. Robinson, *Black Marxism: The Making of the Black Radical Tradition* (London: Zed, 1983) and Mark Naison, *Communists in Harlem During the Depression* (Urbana: U of Illinois P, 1983) and to Nell Irvin Painter's oral history *The Narrative of Hosea Hudson: The Life and Times of a Black Radical* (Cambridge MA: Harvard UP, 1979). Two recent studies of the African-American Marxist literary Left are James Smethurst's *The New Red Negro* and William J. Maxwell's *New Negro, Old Left: African-American Writing and Communism Between the Wars* (New York: Columbia UP, 1999).

[18] It is also worth noting an additional implication of this underlying metaphor for Hughes's relationship to Enlightenment values. Throughout his career, the poet persistently returned to the parallel between sexual desire and the longing for freedom. Hughes clearly believed that people did indeed yearn for "Liberty, Equality,

The last stanza follows the Senegalese expatriate back to Africa, and anatomizes the legacy he carries with him in his migrations through the black diaspora – a legacy of injury caused by these systems of exploitation, which are entangled with Enlightenment politics and modernist aesthetics.

> Of course, the young African from Senegal
> Carries back from Paris
> A little more disease
> To spread among the black girls in the palm huts.
> He brings them as a gift
>   disease –
> From light to darkness
>   disease –
> From the boss to the bossed
>   disease –
> From the games of black and white
>   disease
> From the city of the broken cubes of Picasso
>   d
>   i
>   s
>   e
>   a
>   s
>   e

At the literal level, the Senegalese man carries home a sexually transmitted disease that he has contracted from the French prostitutes. But the "disease" he carries also has a series of metaphorical meanings. First, he has fallen ill, like the prostitutes, because he has suffered the same deformation of self that results from undergoing the exploitation of one's capacity to produce, to amuse, to give pleasure. It is worth emphasizing that the "young African" now "spread[s]" the disease among "the black girls" – not as a result of

---

Fraternity" as fundamentally as they longed for sexual fulfillment, and his verse (including "Cubes") implies that these desires may share a common libidinal source. For this reason, people's political ideals (like their sexual desires) are easily manipulated; and for this reason, such manipulation has particularly damaging effects. Ann Borden has touched on this nexus of political and erotic concerns in Hughes: see "Heroic 'Hussies' and 'Brilliant Queers': Genderracial Resistance in the Works of Langston Hughes," *African American Review* 28.3 (Fall 1994): 342–44.

domination, but simply through his acts of sexual connection.[19] The disease is now internalized: the deformation of self cannot be limited to exploitative relationships, but rather makes itself felt in all relations. The capacity to give and receive pleasure has itself become infected. As the structures of domination expand ever-outward, with the extension of empire and of an increasingly global capitalism, the effects of exploitation, intimate as well as public, expand: the damage cannot be contained to the actual sites of instrumental material appropriation (the brothel, the workplace, the urban industrial metropole) – rather, they migrate, permeating more and more relations.[20]

At another level, the disease that the African carries home is also the internalized result of his encounter with the universalizing Enlightenment ideals, "Liberty, Equality, Fraternity." The final sentence of the poem offers a reprise of the bitter ironies of this encounter with an Enlightenment idealism that is at once the hypocritical instrument of exploitation and also a

---

[19] While there is no explicit indication that the young African's relationship to the "black girls" is exploitative (as his relationship to the prostitutes is), Hughes does emphasize here the added vulnerability of women in the colonial situation. Current gay readings of Hughes might be supplemented by the critique of heterosexuality contained in this poem. Put simply, "Cubes" suggests that the hierarchical structures embedded in normative heterosexuality are inevitably drawn into the expanding systems of economic, racial and imperial exploitation. This critique of heterosexuality is, like his critique of modernism and Enlightenment politics, a richly ambivalent one. Here, as throughout his career, Hughes invokes sexuality as a central aspect of and metaphor for the positive human potentialities that are deformed by oppressive power relations. For two accounts that offer fragmentary gay readings of Hughes, see Borden, "Heroic Hussies," and bell hooks, "Seductive Sexualities: Representing Blackness in Poetry and on Screen," in *Yearning: Race, Gender and Cultural Politics* (Boston MA: South End, 1990): 193–201. See also David Jarraway's argument that, in his life and work, Hughes was committed to an ambiguous "deferred" sexual "subjectivity": "Montage of an Otherness Deferred: Dreaming Subjectivity in Langston Hughes," *American Literature* 68.4 (December 1996): 834–40.

[20] Hughes suggests here that the psychological deformities that accompany the experience of exploitation spread steadily across society in much the same way that the psychological effects of commodification and reification permeate capitalist societies, according to Marx and Lukács respectively. See Karl Marx, "The Fetishism of Commodities and the Secret Thereof," *Capital*, vol. 1, tr. Samuel Moore & Edward Aveling (New York: International Publishers, 1967): 71–83, and Georg Lukács, "Reification and the Consciousness of the Proletariat," in Lukács, *History and Class Consciousness: Studies in Marxist Dialectics*, tr. Rodney Livingstone (Cambridge MA: MIT Press, 1982): 83–223.

liberatory tradition that is being daily more deformed – like the prostitute and the African himself. The sarcasm of the first proposition here – that the African has brought this disease home as a "gift" – is compounded by the second assertion, so resonant with the complacent racism of an Enlightenment-justified imperialism, that this "gift" has traveled "from light to darkness." In the final three propositions, Hughes retraces the larger terrain covered by the poem, insisting that this disease has been transmitted not only through hierarchically organized class relations ("From the boss to the bossed") and imperialistic race relations ("From the games of black and white"), but also through the expressive practices of modernism that emerged in the metropolitan imperial centers ("From the city of the broken cubes of Picasso"). With its call-and-response structure, the stanza again deploys the poet's vernacular cubist technique: with every repetition of the word "disease," Hughes adds and links together another determinant of the crisis of modernity, so that by the end he has enabled us to see that capitalism and empire, modernism and Enlightenment, are tightly interwoven features of a common and corrosive system.

Finally, in its concluding gesture, the poem's last (and most densely coded) word – disease – is typographically broken, fractured, denaturalized, spacialized. Having turned the image over and over, teasing out and accreting its many meanings, Hughes subjects the word itself – a physical assemblage of letters – to a cubist rendering, a modernist representation. While the poem's final proposition declares that the "disease" of modernity comes "*from the city* of the broken cubes," Hughes formally asserts that we cannot understand the disease without representing and recognizing it as itself *one of* those "broken cubes." Modernism and the disease are, he insists, inseparable – cognitively, representationally, politically.

In the end, "Cubes" articulates an ambivalent vision of modernism. The poet insists that modernism is part of the "disease" being spread by a vicious modernity – a direct expression of an expanding system of economic, racial and gender exploitation. "Behind the cubes of black and white" lay "the old game of the boss and the bossed" – a game being conducted on an unparalleled scale in an age of intensifying imperialism, stretching quite literally from the "boulevards of Paris" to the "palm huts" of Senegal. But Hughes does not reject or separate himself from modernism on this account. On the contrary, "Cubes" is also a self-conscious embrace of modernism as a set of representational practices uniquely suited to capturing and exposing this bewildering system of exploitation, so vast that even as it shattered more and more of the world, it could itself be perceived only in fragments.

The poem is itself an eloquent proof of modernism's representational power. By arranging and re-arranging its fragments, the poem ultimately resolves its opening enigma: in a world in which the human capacity to produce, to amuse, to give pleasure is being exploited ever more extensively, a deepening crisis has emerged in which the young are uncertain about the possibility of love and are unable to sing an unbroken song. Hughes suggests that modernism is a sensibility, a structure of feeling, that corresponds to those broken songs and insecure yearnings – and by the end, he has made it clear why the African in Paris stands as an apt symbol for the material processes that have brought that sensibility into being. The poet demonstrates that modernism is also a specific set of representational strategies that can enable us to produce a cognitive map of these vast, almost unknowable material processes and the subjective experiences that accompany them. In the poem's last word, Hughes offers us a visual synecdoche of this process, this map. For in that simple cubist rendering of "disease" he leaves us with an image of an entire complex process of exploitation, quite literally dissolving – into the lives and the psyches of people around the globe, permeating ever more extensively the relations between women and men, black and white, African and Occidental, the bossed and the bosses, the amusing and the amused. The power of modernist representation to piece together in this way the dissolving fragments of a corrosive modernity – a power at once enacted and analysed in "Cubes" itself – suggests that the poet is not only being sarcastic when he describes the "disease" of modernism as a "gift." Hughes will no more reject a tainted modernism than he would the political ideals of the Enlightenment, entangled though they are with the practice of empire and racism, class exploitation and patriarchy. For modernism, he suggests, can perhaps alone reveal to us the "disease" that has brought it into being.

WORKS CITED

Baker, Houston, Jr. *Modernism and the Harlem Renaissance* (Chicago: U of Chicago P, 1987).

Benstock, Shari. *Women of the Left Bank, Paris 1900–1940* (Austin: U of Texas P, 1986).

Berman, Marshall. *All That Is Solid Melts Into Air: The Experiences of Modernity* (New York: Simon & Schuster, 1982).

Borden, Ann. "Heroic 'Hussies' and 'Brilliant Queers': Genderracial Resistance in the Works of Langston Hughes," *African American Review* 28.3 (Fall 1994): 342–44.

Bradbury, Malcolm, & James McFarlane, ed. *Modernism, 1890–1930* (Harmonds-worth: Penguin, 1976).

Chinitz, David. "Literacy and Authenticity: The Blues Poems of Langston Hughes," *Callaloo* 19.1 (1998): 177–92.

Clark, Suzanne. *Sentimental Modernism: Women Writers and the Revolution of the Word* (Bloomington: Indiana UP, 1991).

Denning, Michael. *The Cultural Front: The Laboring of American Culture in the Twentieth Century* (London & New York: Verso, 1996).

Ellman, Richard, & Charles Feidelson, Jr., ed. *The Modern Tradition: Backgrounds of Modern Literature* (New York: Oxford UP, 1965).

Eschen, Penny von. *Race Against Empire: Black Americans and Anti-Colonialism, 1937–1957* (Ithaca NY: Cornell UP, 1997).

Ford, Karen Jackson. "Do Right to Write Right: Langston Hughes's Aesthetics of Simplicity," *Twentieth Century Literature* 38.4 (Winter 1992): 436–57.

Gilroy, Paul. *The Black Atlantic: Modernity and Double Consciousness* (London: Verso & Cambridge MA: Harvard UP, 1993).

Gilroy, Paul. "Modern Tones," in *Rhapsodies in Black: Art of the Harlem Renais-sance*, ed. Richard J. Powell et al. (Berkeley: U of California P, 1997): 102–109.

Hegel, G.W.F. "Self-Certainty and the Lordship and Bondage of Self-Conscious-ness," *The Phenomenology of Mind*, tr. J.B. Baillie (London: George Allen & Unwin, 1931): 218–40.

hooks, bell. "Seductive Sexualities: Representing Blackness in Poetry and on Screen," in *Yearning: Race, Gender and Cultural Politics* (Boston MA: South End, 1990), 193–201.

Huggins, Nathan. *Harlem Renaissance* (New York: Oxford UP, 1971).

Hughes, Langston. "Cubes," originally published in *New Masses* (13 March 1934); repr. in *Good Morning Revolution: Uncollected Writings of Langston Hughes,* ed. Faith Berry (New York: Citadel, 1973: 14–15, and in *The Collected Poems of Langston Hughes*, ed. Arnold Rampersad & David Roessel (New York: Alfred A. Knopf, 1994): 175–76.

Hughes, Robert. *American Visions: the Epic History of Art in America* (New York: Alfred A. Knopf, 1997).

Hutchinson, George. *The Harlem Renaissance in Black and White* (Cambridge MA: Belknap P/Harvard UP, 1995).

Jameson, Fredric. "Cognitive Mapping," in Jameson, *Marxism and the Interpretation of Culture*, ed. Cary Nelson & Lawrence Grossberg (Urbana: U of Illinois P, 1988): 347–57.

Jarraway, David. "Montage of an Otherness Deferred: Dreaming Subjectivity in Langston Hughes," *American Literature* 68.4 (December 1996): 834–40.

Kalaidjian, Walter. *American Culture Between the Wars: Revisionary Modernism and Postmodern Critique* (New York: Columbia UP, 1993).

Kelley, Robin D.G. *Hammer and Hoe: Alabama Communists During the Great De-pression* (Chapel Hill: U of North Carolina P, 1990).

Lukács, Georg. "Reification and the Consciousness of the Proletariat," in Lukács, *History and Class Consciousness: Studies in Marxist Dialectics*, tr. Rodney Livingstone (Cambridge MA: MIT Press, 1982): 83–223.

Marx, Karl. "The Fetishism of Commodities and the Secret Thereof," *Capital*, vol. 1, tr. Samuel Moore & Edward Aveling (New York: International Publishers, 1967): 71–83.

Maxwell, William J. *New Negro, Old Left: African-American Writing and Communism Between the Wars* (New York: Columbia UP, 1999).

Moore, David Chioni. "Local Color, Global 'Color': Langston Hughes, the Black Atlantic, and Soviet Central Asia, 1932," *Research in African Literatures* 27.4 (Winter 1996): 49–70.

Naison, Mark. *Communists in Harlem During the Depression* (Urbana: U of Illinois P, 1983).

Nelson, Cary. *Repression and Recovery: Modern American Poetry and the Politics of Cultural Memory, 1910–1945* (Madison: U of Wisconsin P, 1989).

Oktenberg, Adrien. "From the Bottom Up: Three Radicals of the Thirties," in *A Gift of Tongues: Critical Challenges in Contemporary American Poetry*, ed. Marie Marris & Kathleen Aguero (Athens: U of Georgia P, 1987): 93–99.

Painter, Nell Irvin. *The Narrative of Hosea Hudson: The Life and Times of a Black Radical* (Cambridge MA: Harvard UP, 1979).

Powell, Richard J. "Art History and Black Memory: Toward a 'Blues Aesthetic'" (1994), in *The Jazz Cadence of American Culture*, ed. Robert O'Meally (New York: Columbia UP, 1999): 182–95.

Rampersad, Arnold. *The Life of Langston Hughes*, vol. 1: *1902–1941: I, Too, Sing America* (New York: Oxford UP, 1986).

Robinson, Cedric J. *Black Marxism: The Making of the Black Radical Tradition* (London: Zed, 1983).

Scott, Bonnie Kime, ed. *The Gender of Modernism: A Critical Anthology* (Bloomington: Indiana UP, 1990).

Smethurst, James Edward. *The New Red Negro: The Literary Left and African-American Poetry, 1930–1946* (New York: Oxford UP, 1999).

Tracy, Steven. *Langston Hughes and the Blues* (Chicago: U of Illinois P, 1998).

❖

Appendix

Cubes

In the days of the broken cubes of Picasso
And in the days of the broken songs of the young men
A little too drunk to sing
And the young women
A little too unsure of love to love –
I met on the boulevards of Paris
An African from Senegal.

God
Knows why the French
Amuse themselves bringing to Paris
Negroes from Senegal.

It's the old game of the boss and the bossed
   boss and the bossed,
 amused
  and
 amusing,
   worked and working,
Behind the cubes of black and white,
 black and white,
  black and white

But since it is the old game,
For fun

They give him the three old prostitutes of
    France –
Liberty, Equality, Fraternity –
And all three of 'em sick
In spite of the tax to the government
And the legal houses
And the doctors
And the *Marseillaise*.

Of course, the young African from Senegal
Carries back from Paris
A little more disease
To spread among the black girls in the palm huts.
He brings them as a gift
    disease –
From light to darkness
      disease –
From the boss to the bossed
 disease –
From the games of black and white
    disease
From the city of the broken cubes of Picasso
   d
    i
  s
   e
    a
     s
   e

❖

❖ VISUAL ART AND PERFORMANCE

Du Bois, *The Crisis*, and Images of Africa and the Diaspora

AMY KIRSCHKE

E ARLY IN HIS CAREER, W.E.B. Du Bois established a con-
suming drive to illustrate the most important aspects of Negro life
in America. As David Levering Lewis writes, "The author of *The
Souls of Black Folk* comforted himself as the avatar of a race whose
traveled fate he was predestined to interpret and direct."[1] With both his
work on *Horizon* magazine and, more importantly, his editorship of *The
Crisis*, Du Bois used art to illustrate the major issues of the day. For Du
Bois, art provided an immediate reference point, since visual representations could make a statement in an instant and underline the importance of
an issue.

Africa was one of the most central concerns for Du Bois. By including
essays and editorials on the major issues involving Africa and supporting
them with visuals, Du Bois sought to create and strengthen a sense of identity with Africa. Over the course of his time at *The Crisis*, he introduced
images largely unfamiliar to his readership. He hoped they would become a
part of their visual vocabulary, increasing a personal connection with Africa, and stimulating interest in the events and circumstances relevant to
African life. This essay examines those visuals in *The Crisis*. By approaching this subject in chronological progression, the greater frequency and
sophistication of the visual images over time becomes obvious. These also
reflect the growth of interest among readers, with their support for these

---

[1] David Levering Lewis, *W.E.B. Du Bois: The Fight for Equality and the American Century, 1919–1963* (New York: Henry Holt, 2000): 2.

images of Africa, and the slow cultivation of a group identity and even a sense of group memory of things 'African'.

African Images and Abstractions in the First Years of *The Crisis*

The Crisis first appeared in November 1910. In the beginning, Du Bois was technically required to submit his work to a board of directors, which consisted of two white men, one white woman, and two black men. The board played little role in restraining or restricting him. Du Bois stated in his introduction that he would set forth "Those facts and arguments which show the danger of race prejudice."[2] He established the format of *The Crisis* early on: "Along the Color Line" would discuss politics, education, social uplift, organizations and meetings, science and art, opinions, editorials; "the Burden," for coverage of civil, economic, political and literal atrocities against African Americans; and "what to read," "talks about women" and "men of the Month" were added respectively in December 1910 and May 1911. Most visuals in this early issue were advertisements, and lacked any political content.

Shortly thereafter, *The Crisis* began to include African images and political commentary, reflecting Du Bois's life-long personal commitment to Africa and her people, his support and development of the pan-Africanist movement, and his own interest in the culture of Africa. His interest was sparked by the work of the anthropologist Franz Boas. In 1906, Du Bois invited Boas to speak at Atlanta University. Boas spoke on the greatness of African culture and urged his audience to reclaim their African heritage. Du Bois never forgot the incident and recalled it in his 1939 book *Black Folk Then and Now*:

> Franz Boas came to Atlanta University where I was teaching history in 1906 and said to a graduating class: You need not be ashamed of your African past; and then he recounted the history of black kingdoms south of the Sahara for a thousand years. I was too astonished to speak. All of this I had never heard and I came then and afterwards to realize how the silence and neglect of

---

[2] David Levering Lewis, *W.E.B. Du Bois: Biography of a Race: 1868–1919.* (New York: Henry Holt, 1993): 411.

science can let truth utterly disappear or even be unconsciously distorted."[3] Du Bois would continue his association with Boas, who served as "virtually the house anthropologist for *Crisis* magazine, and greatly influenced Du Bois's ideas on race.[4]

Boas also spoke at the first Pan-African Congress, and was an ally of Du Bois in trying to generate an anti-racist movement among social scientists.[5]

In March 1911, the first African image appeared in *The Crisis,* an un-signed drawing of "Ra-Maat-Neb" after Lepsius. The caption read, "Egyptian Portrait of One of the Black Kings of the Upper Nile, Ra-Maat-Neb, Builder of Pyramid No. 17." The drawing (Figure 1 at the end of this essay), just a simple profile of the king in full ceremonial garb, is noteworthy because of the use of Egypt as a symbol of Africa. Although Boas focussed his work on sub-Saharan Africa, much more was known about Egyptian art and culture. Europeans had, in fact, appropriated the Ancient Egyptian civilization as part of their heritage and already recognized it as "high culture." Du Bois believed that African-American culture should reflect the same ideas of high culture which Europeans promulgated. For him, it made perfect sense to connect visually to Africa via Egypt. Egypt was geographically part of Africa, even if the connection between its history and sub-Saharan Africa was unclear. Du Bois was determined to re-acquire the 'memory' of Egyptian glory for Africans and their descendants, American blacks.

This attempt to re-connect historical Africa with contemporary blacks also brought with it a political mission, the struggle against European colonialism and exploitation. Egypt was under British dominance, sharing this fate with the rest of Africa. After Tutankhamen's tomb was discovered in 1922 and Americans became fascinated with Egypt, Du Bois reiterated this connection between Egypt and African Americans. A pyramid, a sphinx or an Egyptian king were a large part of the iconography of Africa, a language familiar to *Crisis* readers. The March issue included an essay on "African Civilization," outlining the rich discoveries made by archaeologists, and made a bold suggestion about the connection between Africa and Egypt:

> There existed, of course, until quite recent times a high civilization among the blacks of the upper Nile [...] How far Egypt took its civilization from the

---

[3] Du Bois, *Black Folk Then and Now* (1939; Millwood NY: Kraus–Thomson, 1975): vii, and George Hutchinson, *The Harlem Renaissance in Black and White* (Cambridge MA: Belknap P/Harvard UP, 1995): 63.

[4] Hutchinson, *Harlem Renaissance in Black and White,* 63.

[5] Lewis, *W.E.B. Du Bois: The Fght for Equality,* 472.

black empire and how far the two cultures originated simultaneously, from a common source, will not be decided until all the ruins have been unearthed and their records read, but it looks as if old theories were turning upside down, as if the black nations of certain regions of Africa were not races in their infancy, but the descendants of powerful civilizations broken by the slave trade and by misfortune in successive wars. [...] *The Egyptians always said that their forefathers learned their arts and largely received their laws from the black people further south....*[6]

In the 1910s, *The Crisis* regularly had essays, articles and updates on African political issues. Sometimes, visuals were included, in the form of cartoons, Egyptian reliefs, or photographs, often reprinted from other publications. Monthly essays discussed the new railway from West Africa to the Congo, African education, life in South Africa, and "Moslem Spain." Folktales, poetry and African culture "tidbits" were featured as well. Du Bois included essays on small kingdoms and successful tribes, showing them as an inspirational people surviving despite the worst conditions of poverty and colonization. He presented them as the bearers of the high culture of Africa, and hoped these graphic essays would provide inspiration for American blacks who were trapped under the conditions of racism and segregation in America. Du Bois was very much on the cutting edge in his work in *Crisis*. He had studied in Europe and was familiar with European art and culture. He knew that Europeans and their descendants looked to their ancestors to justify their alleged superiority and status. Why should African Americans not turn to Africa for the same reasons? Africa had a rich culture that had been stolen from African Americans through slavery, and it needed to be reclaimed.

Du Bois also included the rest of North Africa in his understanding of the connection between American blacks and their homeland. Photographs of children learning in an Arab school in North Africa, studying the Koran and royalty, including the seventeen-year old king of Uganda, Daudi Chua, kept the readership informed of events in Africa. *The Crisis* presented photographs of pageants, such as the "Historical Pageant of the Negro Race" at the Emancipation Exposition, a full-page photo of "forty maidens" dancing before the enthroned "Pharaoh Ra, The Negro," and a photograph of an Ethiopian king, in his royal costume, without text. In November 1914, shortly after the beginning of World War I, black soldiers from Senegal were featured in a double-page photograph entitled "Out of Africa Have I called my son!" Here, the soldiers were shown ready to fight "to protect the

---

[6] *The Crisis* (March 1911): 25 (my emphasis).

civilization of Europe against itself."[7] Du Bois felt that if Africans were to fight in Europe for the safety of whites, surely they were entitled to the same rights and privileges as whites. He made this point repeatedly, as he would later with regard to African Americans fighting in World War I.

The cover for December 1915 was a poster for the "Star of Ethiopia" pageant, a "production of artistic and musical value which includes over 1,000 persons in its drama. This pageant portrays the history of the colored race from the time men were equal in the Stone Age, through the glories of the Ethiopian Empire, through slavery and freedom, and up to its present development in science, art, and education."[8] The article refers to the African-American contributions of rhythm, ragtime and the banjo, among other artistic achievements. Photographs of pageant participants, three young women in particular, were included.

Du Bois chose poignant and graphic political cartoons with a view to creating a shared sense of identity between his readers and Africans. In March 1917, E.A. Harleston provided a cartoon showing a Congolese man in tattered garment and sandals, his hands severed, facing a seated white man. The caption read "Voice of Congo: 'If your uncle had left us our hands, Albert, we could be of more use to you now'" (Figure 2). This referred to the brutality suffered by the Congolese at the hands of Belgian colonizers. The atrocities, including the severing of hands and feet, were well documented. A white man in military garb, sitting in front of a portrait of the elderly Leopold, King of the Belgians, looks off, unconcerned with the horror before him.[9]

Du Bois also highlighted those few African states that had preserved the dignity of independence, even if under the indirect rule of a European state. The November 1917 issue included a fine drawing, by John Henry Adams, of the "Empress Tatou, Widow of the late Menelik II, Emperor of Abyssinia, and mother of the present Empress Ouizeros Zeoditu" (Figure 3). These images were a source of education and race pride for the readers of *The Crisis*. Du Bois wanted to show a constant connection to Africa, and the tangible reasons for pride in a contact with African peoples and an attachment to its culture.[10]

---

[7] *The Crisis* (November 1914): 26–27.

[8] *The Crisis* (December 1915): 75.

[9] *The Crisis* (March 1917): 247.

[10] *The Crisis* (November 1917): 25.

Africa: Images after the European War

In January 1919, Du Bois' essay on the "Future of Africa," originally published in the *Atlantic Monthly*, was summarized in the pages of *The Crisis*.
He discussed the aftermath of the war, and what should happen to the
colonies seized by the allies from Germany. Du Bois did not want to see the
colonies subjected to yet another "imperial master." A Pan-African Congress, with Du Bois in attendance, was announced and would be held in
Paris in the winter. The Congress would use Du Bois' statement as a starting point for discussion.

Du Bois discussed in February 1919 the idea that it had been suggested
that the colonies which Germany lost should not be handed over to "any
other nation of Europe, but should, under the guidance of *organized
civilization*, be brought to a point of development which shall finally result
in an autonomous state." The plan had met with much criticism and ridi-
cule. In February 1919, Du Bois wrote "Not Separatism." This essay was a
powerful attack on all forms of racial separatism:

> This is not a separatist movement. There is no need to think that those who
> advocate the opening up of Africa for Africans and those of African descent
> desire to deport any large number of colored Americans to a foreign and, in
> some respects, inhospitable land. [...] It is as absurd to talk of a return to
> Africa, merely because that was our home 300 years ago, as it would be to
> expect the members of the Caucasian race to return to the fastnesses of the
> Caucasus Mountains from which, it is reputed, they sprang.[11]

Although attacking separatism, Du Bois saw an important role for American
blacks in dealing with Africa:

> But it is true that we as a people are not given to colonization, and that thereby
> a number of essential occupations and interests have been closed to us which
> the redemption of Africa would open up. The African movement means to us
> what the Zionist movement must mean to the Jews, the centralization of race
> effort and the recognition of a racial fount. To help bear the burden of Africa
> does not mean any lessening of effort in our own problem at home. Rather it
> means increased interest. For any ebullition of action and feeling that results

---

[11] *The Crisis* (February 1919): 165–66.

in an amelioration of the lot of Africa tends to ameliorate the condition of colored peoples throughout the world. And no man liveth to himself.[12]

David Levering Lewis has described how Du Bois evinced "a tone of unconscious cultural superiority" and came "perilously close to imagining himself a pan-African pro-consul" in his thinking of how American blacks might involve themselves in African development.[13] Although he may have had these colonialist sentiments, Du Bois also remained fiercely critical of any schemes to "return to Africa" as a solution to America's racial problems. He disagreed profoundly with the West Indian leader and founder of the Universal Negro Improvement Association, Marcus Garvey, who advocated a return to Africa, working with the Liberian government and even buying his own cruise line, to transport African Americans back to Africa. Along with the NAACP, Du Bois vehemently opposed this and made sure his readers knew of his views on the matter.

Garvey responded by criticizing Du Bois bitterly both in public speeches and in writings, stating that Du Bois was part-white and part-black in mind as well as blood, and did not know who he was or where he was. To Du Bois, Garvey was an unscrupulous, lower-class man, whose "spinning" dreams frightened "Africans as well as Europeans."[14] Lewis notes:

> Whenever Du Bois wrote or spoke of Garvey there was always the unmistakable hint of a tolerant, well-bred preceptor's exasperation when forced to deal with a gifted, unruly, somewhat gauche parvenu-someone woefully uninstructed in the vicarious and solemn symbolism of responsible black leadership.[15]

Along with these other objections to Garvey, the role of Africa in black America's identity also played a role. Nathan Huggins observes that it was Du Bois' very deep interest in Africa that made him so hostile to Marcus Garvey. Du Bois was searching for a careful balance of "Negro integration" into American society while Garvey was advocating separatism. Du Bois nurtured the image of the intelligent, reasonable, thoughtful black leader, whereas Garvey, Du Bois perceived, was "cutting the fool before the world."[16] Du Bois had a life-long commitment to pan-Africanism; Garvey

---

[12] *The Crisis* (February 1919): 1666.

[13] Lewis, *Biography of a Race*, 119–20.

[14] Nathan Huggins, *Harlem Renaissance* (New York: Oxford UP, 1971): 46.

[15] Lewis, *Biography of a Race*, 73.

[16] *Biography of a Race*, 47.

threatened that vision with his appeal to the common man to return back to Africa.

In the 1920s *The Crisis* reflected a heightened interest in Africa. January 1920 brought more history and culture to its readers with an image captioned "Native of Fumban, German East Africa, Wearing the Ancient Headdress." Almost every month, a photograph of African royalty, or African dignitaries, children, or military people, was included in the pages of *The Crisis*, often accompanied by text, essays, editorials and poetry. Du Bois sought to convince African Americans that they had a royalty and aristocracy that could rival any of the Europeans.

The cover of the January 1921 issue featured a statue entitled "Africa" from the group on the New York Custom House (Figure 4). It showed a somewhat defeated figure, clad from the waist down, her breasts exposed in the Hellenistic tradition, with one arm resting on the head of a sphinx. The classical connotations are strong. The figure appears to be forlorn and exhausted, but still holds herself up, with the aid of the sphinx. Despite her fatigue she is strong: her musculature is emphasized, and her feet are planted firmly on the ground, holding her steady. Even though her head hangs down, and her eyes are closed, the forceful, steady, firm profile of the sphinx remains undaunted. The connotations are clear: "Africa" may be tired from the battle, but she has not lost. The image of the sphinx is the symbol of the long history of Africa in this context, and an affirmation that Africa will finally overcome any adversity.

The Crisis continued to discuss African events and culture, even offering travel suggestions. In the September 1921 issue, it included a report to the Secretary of State, prepared by Captain H.O. Atwood, on "Emigration to Liberia" which told emigrants to bring money, things necessary for community living, and even proper sewing supplies. The October 1921 issue discussed Ethiopian art, stressing its significance for an independent black country in Africa. The cover of the November 1921 issue was entitled "Science" and featured a photograph of a piece of sculpture, heavily Egyptian-influenced. While the caption inside reads "Figure of Africa typifying 'science' in the Palais Mondial, Brussels, where the Second Pan-African Congress was held," the inscription itself declares: "I am the one that was, that is, and that shall be. No mortal may unveil my face." Inside the issue, Jessie Fauset penned a lengthy essay on the second Pan-African Conference. Du Bois offered a manifesto to the League of Nations after Fauset's essay, asking that the International Bureau of Labor set aside a section to deal particularly with the needs of native Negro labor, that self-government be recognized as the ultimate aim of all men and nations, and therefore that black people be represented by a man of Negro descent. Finally, the manifesto stated that the League of Nations should pay careful attention to the treatment of people of Negro descent.[17] Du Bois also regularly included the opinions of Africans in the pages of *The Crisis*, an indication of the high regard for them he wanted American blacks to have.

Laura Wheeler, a frequent contributing artist to *The Crisis*, often created black-and-white drawings of African peoples for Du Bois. Du Bois was a strong believer in women's equality, and women played an important role in *The Crisis*. This role, however, tended to support and amplify the opinions already expressed by Du Bois.[18] The April 1923 cover, "Egypt-Spring," features a young woman, clad from the waist down, her breasts hidden by her arms, playing a harp-like instrument (Figure 5). The instrument is also a piece of sculpture: the base forms the head of a figure, and the signs of spring, trees, birds and flowers (papyrus?) line the composition. An Egyptian-inspired border circles the composition. Again, Egypt was considered to be interchangeable with Africa. In addition to numerous *Crisis* covers, Wheeler also created drawings for the essays and poetry included.

The third Pan-African Conference was reviewed in the January 1924 issue, accompanied by a photograph of three participants, including Du Bois. A photo of the president of Liberia, whom Du Bois was visiting when this issue appeared, also graced the essay. It ended with words that pillory much of the hypocrisy of Western nations who dealt with Africa:

> In fine, we ask in all the world that black folk be treated as men. We can see no other road to Peace and Progress. What more paradoxical figure today fronts the world than the official head of a great South African State striving blindly to build peace and Good Will in Europe by standing on the necks and hearts of millions of black Africans.[19]

In October 1927, *The Crisis* reviewed the history of the pan-African Congresses. The fourth such Congress, held in New York City in 1927, endorsed a declaration that expressed what it called "the legitimate aims and needs of the Negro people." Sounding like Woodrow Wilson's Fourteen Points, the Congress wanted self-determination for Africans, an end to European colonialism, and the radical "reorganization of commerce and industry so as to

---

[17] *The Crisis* (November 1921): 18.

[18] For more and detailed information on Fauset and Du Bois, see Lewis, *W.E.B. Du Bois: The Fight for Equality*, 49–50.

[19] *The Crisis* (January 1924): 122. The article was signed by Hunt, Logan, and Du Bois. Du Bois was referring to the South African leader Jan Smuts.

make the main object of capital and labor to benefit the welfare of the
many, rather than the enriching of the few." The Congress also criticized the
US occupation of Haiti, begun by Wilson in 1916 as a wartime emergency
but resulting in full-scale military occupation. It called on American blacks
to make use of their political power and to keep "their eyes fixed upon the
international problems of the color line and the national problems which
affect the Negro race in the United States. Only independent votes for candidates who will carry out [American blacks'] desire regardless of party will
bring them political and economic freedom."[20]

Along with political activism, Du Bois placed increasing emphasis on
using the growing economic power of African Americans to promote
change:

> The economic situation of American Negroes is still precarious. We believe
> that along with their entry into industry as skilled and semi-skilled workers
> and their growing ownership of land and homes they should especially organ-
> ize as consumers and from co-operative effort seek to bring to bear upon in-
> vestors and producers the coercive power which co-operative consumption
> has already attained in certain parts of Europe and of America. Lynching,
> segregation and mob violence still oppress and crush black America but
> education and organized social political power begin to point the way out.[21]

In Du Bois' world-view, there was an intimate connection between the
treatment of Negro peoples in Africa and the treatment of all people of
African descent. He appealed to his readers to embrace the Pan-African
movement, and to treat all black peoples as their own, to realize that the
problems of Africans were indeed their own, and that their treatment was
reflected in the treatment of Negroes at home. He therefore appealed to the
readership to embrace the woes of Africa and used the art of Africa to stress
this connection. He asked the League of Nations to use their "vast moral
power of world public opinion and of a body conceived to promote peace
and justice among men," and to take a firm stand on the absolute equality of
races and to suggest to the colonial powers connected with the League of
Nations the forming of an International Institute for the study of the Negro
problems, and for the evolution and protection of the Negro Race. [22]

---

[20] *The Crisis* 34 (October 1927): 263.

[21] *The Crisis* 34 (October 1927): 263–64.

[22] *The Crisis* 34 (October 1927): 263–64. The letter was signed W.E. Burghardt
Du Bois, Secretary, Geneva, September 15, 1921.

Du Bois Visits Africa: The Romantic View

In April 1924, Du Bois published selections from his journal chronicling his first trip to Africa from December 1923 through January 1924. The entries were personal and emotional. "When shall I forget the night I first set foot on African soil – I, the sixth generation in descent from my stolen fore-fathers."[23] Du Bois depicted his experience in uncharacteristically dramatic language. He recorded in his journal that "the spell of Africa is upon me. The ancient witchery of her medicine is burning my drowsy, dreamy blood." His first impressions clearly overwhelmed him:

> this is not a country, it is a world – a universe of itself and for itself, a thing Different, Immense, Menacing, Alluring. It is a great black bosom where the Spirit longs to die. It is life so burning, with fire so encircled that one bursts with terrible sound inflaming life.

Africa always had great symbolic importance to Du Bois, and his visit intensified these feelings. He wrote of the continent in utopian language:

> Things move – black shiny bodies [,] perfect bodies, bodies of sleek unearthly poise and beauty. Eyes languish, black eyes – slow, yes, lovely and tender eyes in great dark formless faces. Life is slow here. [...] Life slows down and as it slows it deepens; it rises and descends to immense and secret places.

Africa, in Du Bois' words, "is the Spiritual Frontier of human kind – oh the wild and beautiful adventures of its taming!" Indeed, Du Bois even speculated that Africa would produce a new and different civilization "without coal, without noise, where machinery will sing and never rush and roar, and where men will sleep and think and dance and lie prone before the rising sons, and women will be happy."[24]

This journal selection reveals that Du Bois looked at Africa with the eye of a primitivist, romanticizing the simple, sweet African lifestyle, the slow eyes, the ease of it all. He even sounds like the young Karl Marx with his description of an Africa which could escape the unpleasant changes brought by capitalist development elsewhere. Indeed, in many ways his approach to Africa resembles that of whites to the work of the Harlem Renaissance,

---

[23] *The Crisis* (April 1924): 248.

[24] *The Crisis* (April 1924): 274. This parallels nineteenth-century Marxist imagery of the post-revolutionary world.

which also emphasized primitivism. Du Bois' vision of Africa, with this primitivist spin, would appear on the covers of *The Crisis*, such as Allan Freelon's "Jungle Nymph" in June 1928.

The cover for the June 1924 *Crisis*, "Africa in America," was provided by Laura Wheeler (Figure 6). In her characteristic black-and white-style, with only a few details of the human form, she shows a full-figured woman, clad with a sheer garment that still reveals all the lines of her body as if she were nude, adorned with jewelry including wrist and armbands, earrings, necklaces and a ceremonial headpiece. The woman carries a covered urn on her shoulder. Behind her, the pattern of the swirling ocean is formed, with a ship crossing in full sail, a symbol of the Middle Passage – the long and harrowing journey from Africa to slavery in the Americas. The figure is strong and erect, proud and lovely, as she stands as a symbol of Africa, brought to America against her will, but still retaining her African heritage.

In this issue, Du Bois discussed – free of the hyperbole of Garvey and his followers – the opportunities available to black Americans to migrate to Africa. He noted that *The Crisis* received requests periodically from readers who would like advice concerning migration to Africa. Here Du Bois recognizes the hardships attendant on emigration. He discouraged middle-aged and elderly people from going there, as well as younger people hoping for work, since Africa had an abundance of skilled and unskilled laborers. "There is a magnificent chance for pioneers but the point is, pioneering is a far different thing from going to work in a fully developed land."[25] Liberia needed physicians, dentists and nurses. The "spiritual harvest of practical missionary work would in the end be far greater than we can now dream." Du Bois also noted how polite the "natives" are to each other, both young and old.

> I have often thought, when I see the awkward and ignorant missionaries some-
> times sent to teach the heathen, that it would be an excellent thing if a few
> natives could be sent here to teach manners to black and white.[26]

The text was prefaced by Laura Wheeler's cover, and was accompanied inside by a photograph of an African family, entitled "In the African Bush."

Arnold Rampersad has argued that Du Bois did not lose interest in Africa or pan-Africanism, even if Africa was for Africans and not for foreigners who happened to be black. His visit

---

[25] *The Crisis* (June 1924): 58.

[26] *The Crisis* (June 1924): 58.

confirmed the balance between romance and reality that distinguished the *The Crisis* treatment of race from the excesses of Garveyism. Even so, it was difficult to keep black American interest in pan-Africanism alive. "American Negroes," Du Bois later wrote, "were not interested." That there was resistance from black Americans to find a connection with Africa is not surprising. In the context of the 1920s when most white Americans were isolationists, and saw their ancestral Europe as the place they left, not an inspiration, this attitude is more understandable. Black Americans had been in America longer than whites, their ties from Africa had been severed long before. Du Bois was discouraged, but he also recognized that he may have planted seeds that would flower at a later time. The hastily organized fourth Pan-African Congress, held in New York in 1927, ended the major phase of Du Bois' involvement with Pan-Africanism[27]

– although his interest in Africa would continue till the end of his life.

Additional African Images in *Crisis*: 1920s and 1930s

Du Bois made increasing use of African imagery in the 1920s and 1930s. Another Art Deco-inspired African cover by Laura Wheeler (now Laura Wheeler Waring) appeared in September 1924: "The Strength of Africa" (Figure 7). It shows a muscular (Nubian?) attendant, with an Egyptian-inspired decorative headpiece and ankle bracelets, sheltering a woman (likewise wearing a headpiece and ankle bracelets) with his large peacock-feather fan or shade. He follows behind her as she takes her lion for a walk. The lion is in complete silhouette; she is in profile, with a wrap on her lower body and transparent wrap on her upper body. A rather exotic bustier covers her breasts. She again represents an exotic, primitive, decadent style, she is clearly royalty or someone of importance. The title "The Strength of Africa" forms the base of the composition.

The December 1924 cover of *The Crisis* presents a "North African warrior of the 15th Century." He is a proud, strong man in armor, holding a weapon in his right hand and looking off to the side. The unsigned image is another reminder to the readership of the long history of Africa and the desire to claim all of the continent, including its Arab north, as part of the heritage of American blacks. It is a rare cover for December, with no religious content. Inside the issue, Kantiba Nerouy sketches a brief history of

---

[27] Arnold Rampersad, *The Art and Imagination of W.E.B. Du Bois* (Cambridge MA: Harvard UP, 1976): 155.

Egypt, Ethiopia and Abyssinia, arguing that the people of this region have "as much if not more Negro blood than American Negroes."[28] A map and Egyptian drawings were inserted.

One of the more 'sultry' covers was displayed in the May 1925 issue. An unsigned photograph, "A Moorish Maid," shows a woman wearing a necklace and head wrap, revealing a small part of her nipple, indicating she is at least partly nude. This cover served both to showcase a dark-skinned woman and to lure a readership – undoubtedly male – to open *The Crisis* and read on. Other African-American magazines such as the Urban League's *Opportunity* were using similar images to attract new readers. Du Bois frequently placed beautiful women on his covers. Inside was "Part II" of "Dark Algiers the White," where Jessie Fauset wrote about her wanderings and explorations in the Arab quarter of Algiers. It was not unusual for *The Crisis* to offer travel accounts, including "Impressions of Uganda" in the May 1925 issue, along with Fauset's recollections.

Du Bois also took up the banner for African art, especially its inspiration for the "high culture" of modern art. The May 1925 issue included excerpts from an article by Paul Guillaume, who noted that "the modern movement in art gets its inspiration undoubtedly from African art, and it could not be otherwise." Guillaume had a substantial African art collection, and it was he who provided the art collector Albert Barnes with his African pieces. He and Barnes came to be considered authorities on African art. Guillaume developed the view that African art should be analysed on purely formal grounds, that it was exemplary of "formal perfection," displaying the "highest degree of mastery and civilization," as one of his followers wrote – Guillaume attempted to show how African art differed from European art, that it varied greatly in style depending on where it was made and which 'tribe' made it; "what the new generation should ask from the Negroes is a lesson in sculptural knowledge, no clumsiness, [...] a state of universality and not the exotic and savage."[29] Guillaume listed in his essay artists who take inspiration from Africa, including Picasso. "African art," he maintains,

> the most modern of the arts, by this spirit is also the most ancient. In the dim, distant epochs, the men who were first active in the world after the silence of the centuries were the black men. These men were the first creators, the first warriors, the first poets; they invented art as they invented fire....[30]

---

[28] *The Crisis* (December 1924): 68.

[29] Hutchinson, *Harlem Renaissance in Black and White*, 427.

[30] *The Crisis* (May 1925): 39.

African art had long provided stylistic inspiration to European artists, including Picasso, Braque, Modigliani, and others.

With the beginning of the Harlem Renaissance in the mid-1920s, Du Bois' interest in seeing more artistic renderings of African themes came to fruition. The work of Aaron Douglas appeared regularly in *The Crisis*; Douglas frequently used Egypt to represent Africa, as well as African masks from the Ivory Coast.[31] June 1928 revealed that interest in primitivism was not restricted to white journals, luring in readers, as it did, with "A jungle Nymph" by Allan Freelon (Figure 8), which has a young woman of African descent by a pond, leaning back on her arms to expose her unclothed body, amidst tropical foliage. She has an African hair-style, and her nudity is heightened by the earrings she wears. We observe her, but she, oblivious gazes down in privacy or modesty. The image fits with the description of Africa previously cited: "black shiny bodies, perfect bodies, bodies of sleek unearthly poise and beauty. Eyes languish [...] lovely and tender eyes in great dark formless faces."[32]

Joyce Carrington's September 1928 cover of a woman in an African set-ting, complete with palm tree, pyramid and African necklace (Egypt and Africa are interchangeable here), also sports a very 1920s hair-style (Figure 9). Celeste Smith presents her drawing of "Excelsior" inside the January 1929 issue: has a nude figure, arms overhead, in a style reminiscent of Aaron Douglas, balancing on the world with feet on the continent of Africa (Figure 10).

Du Bois continued to include images of Africa royalty, along with politi-cal statements by the rulers, accompanied by formal state photos, usually in native regalia rather than Western clothing. The June 1932 issue contained a photograph of "His highness, Daudi Chwa, Kabaka of Buganda." Buganda was part of the Uganda protectorate, then the most prosperous of the four Kingdoms:

> After serious thinking they have come to the conclusion that the white man
> intends to keep them in their place of primitiveness, and that he does not wish
> to give them a kind of education that will make them full men and self-reliant,

---

[31] For a full discussion of Douglas and his interest in Africa, see Amy H. Kirschke, *Aaron Douglas: Art, Race, and the Harlem Renaissance* (Jackson: UP of Mississippi, 1995), and Kirschke, "Oh Africa! The Influences of African Art During the Harlem Renaissance," in *"Temples for Tomorrow": Looking Back at the Harlem Renaissance*, ed. Geneviève Fabre & Michel Feith (Bloomington: Indiana UP, 2001): 73–83.

[32] *The Crisis* (April 1924): 274.

because if he (the white man) does so, the darker people will compete with him in all walks of life, and they will occupy all the positions of admini-stration, with the result that the number of the unemployed people in Europe will increase. [...] The darker people have found out that only their personal efforts will bring about their salvation: and they think that to attain this end they must improve their economic conditions.[33]

The text was accompanied by the photo, a map showing the location of Uganda in Eastern Africa, and a note on Uganda by Du Bois. He wanted the message of liberation to come not only from him, but from African royalty as well.

Du Bois also continued to use cartoons to shake the complacency of whites about their superiority towards Africans. A small unattached cartoon by R.O. Berg in the November 1932 issue portrayed the typically ignorant white tourist (Figure 11) – two overweight, overindulged white people, under the shade of a palm, look at a proud black woman who is tall, slim and strong. She is balancing a basket of goods on her head as she walks down the street. The man and woman exclaim: "Ain't she funny!" The irony of this comment by "ugly Americans," as the term would later be used, is obvious.

Du Bois was determined to discuss the suffering of Africans even in the 1930s, despite the dire economic conditions Americans faced at home. He included essays on Liberia, South Africa and other parts of the continent. An Art Deco-inspired muscular figure in the style of a WPA mural featured on the cover of the March 1933 issue: "A flight into Egypt," by Zell Ingram, shows two figures in modern garb, lungeing forward in silhouette, with a barren tree branch behind them. Nothing alludes to the flight of Joseph, Mary and Christ. There is little detailing to their bodies, but their faces, with the 'slit' eyes and full lips of Dan masks from the Ivory Coast, were clearly inspired by the artist Aaron Douglas's use of Egyptian silhouette and African masks. The simple style of the cover was quite effective, the letter-ing, now typeset instead of handwritten, lending the cover a polished, clean appearance.

Images of Africa were placed throughout in the June 1933 issue, where a brief discussion of "Negro Egypt" and the excavations there was accom-panied by a photograph of a relief of black pharaohs. The July 1933 issue gave an outline of the "World History of the Negro, in a Thousand Words" by Alfred Edgar Smith. This issue included several essays on Africa, as did most issues in 1933. Great attention was devoted to Liberia, where Du Bois

---

[33] *The Crisis* (June 1932): 183.

had made his first trip, and to South Africa, which was already displaying features of what would later be called "apartheid." A discussion of Haiti and US policy there was also included as a case-study of the treatment of African peoples, demonstrating how Du Bois saw the connection between the US occupation of this diaspora country and European colonialism in Africa.

Conclusion

Among the many passions or causes that Du Bois championed as editor of *The Crisis*, issues surrounding Africa and the diaspora were his highest priority. His lifelong passion for Africa developed and flourished in the pages of the periodical; it was here that he found a home for his opinions, articles and essays, and for his choice of art work. It was a place where he had ample opportunity to advance his causes. He used art as an emotional, visceral instrument in this endeavor, to tie his readers to their heritage, a heritage that had been lost through the ravages of slavery and racism. His use of art was not always consistent. Sometimes he turned to actual pieces of African art, and to Egyptian-inspired pieces, as a tangible connection with Africa's rich culture. He used photographs of ordinary people living their daily lives in Africa, as well as photos of dignitaries and royalty. But he also included somewhat exotic or fantastic renderings of Africa, almost echoing the primitivism that he cautioned against. His own description of his time in Liberia paralleled Laura Wheeler's exotic view of Africa more than it did the serious and practical African art with which he was familiar. Du Bois also used art to develop his own concept of the black diaspora.

By insisting that African Americans recognize their shared racial identity with Africans of all regions – not just sub-Saharan but also Egyptian and North African – and by including the Caribbean but also African diasporic nation of Haiti, Du Bois fashioned an extraordinarily expansive concept of the African diaspora. Du Bois' vision – confirmed and amplified by artistic creations – possessed a more vigorous vector than the intellectual currents of his own time, challenging the somewhat provincial notions of many African Americans, and laying the groundwork for future developments in the worldwide struggle for racial equality.

Du Bois was determined to introduce Africa in any way possible, through African art, through photos of African peoples, and through drawings and paintings that offered an exotic and even romantic view of life in Africa. His diary, chronicling his visit to Liberia in 1924, said it best:

"Africa is the Spiritual Frontier of human kind – oh the wild and beautiful adventures of its taming!"[34]

WORKS CITED

Du Bois, W.E.B. *Black Folk Then and Now* (1939; Millwood NY: Kraus–Thomson, 1975).

Huggins, Nathan. *Harlem Renaissance* (New York: Oxford UP, 1971).

Hutchinson, George. *The Harlem Renaissance in Black and White* (Cambridge MA: Belknap P/Harvard UP, 1995).

Kirschke, Amy H. *Aaron Douglas: Art, Race, and the Harlem Renaissance* (Jackson: UP of Mississippi, 1995).

——. "Oh Africa! The Influences of African Art During the Harlem Renaissance," in *Temples for Tomorrow: Looking Back at the Harlem Renaissance*, ed. Geneviève Fabre & Michel Feith (Bloomington: Indiana UP, 2001): 73–83.

Lewis, David Levering. *W.E.B. Du Bois: Biography of a Race: 1868–1919* (New York: Henry Holt, 1993).

——. *W.E.B. Du Bois: The Fight for Equality and the American Century 1919–1957* (New York: Henry Holt, 2000).

Rampersad, Arnold. *The Art and Imagination of W.E.B. Du Bois* (Cambridge MA: Harvard UP, 1976).

---

[34] *The Crisis* (April 1924): 274.

FIGURE 1. "Egyptian Portrait of One of the Black Kings of the Upper Nile, Ra-Maat-Neb, Builder of Pyramid No. 17," unsigned drawing of "Ra-Maat-Neb" after Lepsius, *The Crisis* (March 1911).

FIGURE 2. Cartoon by E.A. Harleston, "Voice of Congo: 'If your uncle had left us our hands, Albert, we could be of more use to you now'," *The Crisis* (March 1917).

FIGURE 3. Drawing by John Henry Adams, of the "Empress Tatou, Widow
of the late Menelik II, Emperor of Abyssinia, and mother of the present
Empress Ouizeros Zeoditu," *The Crisis* (November 1917).

FIGURE 4. Cover picture featuring the statue of "Africa" from the group on
the New York Custom House, *The Crisis* (January 1921).

FIGURE 5. "Egypt-Spring," cover drawing by Laura Wheeler for *The Crisis* (April 1923).

FIGURE 6. "Africa in America," cover drawing by Laura Wheeler, *The Crisis* (June 1924).

FIGURE 7. "The Strength of Africa," cover drawing by Laura Wheeler Waring, *The Crisis* (September 1924).

FIGURE 8. "A jungle Nymph," drawing by Allan Freelon, *The Crisis* (June 1928).

FIGURE 9. Cover drawing by Joyce Carrington, *The Crisis* (September 1928).

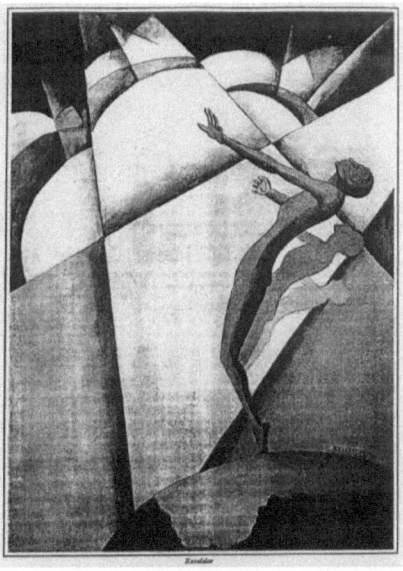

FIGURE 10. "Excelsior," drawing by Celeste Smith, *The Crisis* (January 1929).

FIGURE 11. "Ain't she funny!" – cartoon by R.O. Berg, *The Crisis*
(November 1932).

"Ethiopia shall soon stretch forth her hands"

Ethiopianism, Egyptomania,
and the Arts of the Harlem Renaissance

IRIS SCHMEISSER

And Abyssinia, deep-set in the shoulder of Africa, besieged by the hungry
wolves of Europe? The only nation that has existed free and independent from
the earliest records of history until today! Abyssinia, oldest unconquered
nation, ancient-strange as Egypt, persistent as Palestine, legendary as Greece,
magical as Persia.[1]

M Y ESSAY addresses the diasporic consciousness and imagination articulated by visual artists participating in the cultural
movement known as the Harlem Renaissance. I argue that one
can trace a recurring motive, a renascent diasporic sensibility, in the works
of visual artists such as Meta Vaux Warrick Fuller, Aaron Douglas, Laura
Wheeler Waring, Lois Mailou Jones and Albert Alexander Smith. Ethiopianism and Egyptomania represent two pervasive modalities of cultural pan-
Africanism among artists of the Harlem Renaissance.

The Ethiopianist tradition prophesied an imaginary, culturally achieved
return to a former efflorescence.[2] It originated in New World black thought

---

[1] Claude McKay, *Home to Harlem* (New York: Harper & Brothers, 1928): 135.

[2] This concept is borrowed from James Clifford's cultural analysis of the strategies at work in diasporic imagination; Clifford, "Diasporas," *Cultural Anthropology*
(1994): 302–38.

as far back as the late eighteenth century and translated into modern back-to-Africa movements such as Garveyism. A powerful vision of cultural renewal, it bestowed upon the artistic project of the Harlem Renaissance the task of reconstructing a new "Ethiopian Golden Age."

Apart from the cultural and aesthetic strategy of Ethiopianism, it is Egyptomania that, I will argue, constitutes one of the defining characteristics of the visual culture of the Harlem Renaissance. Egyptomania is not equivalent to a simple obsession with Egyptian style:

> It is not enough to copy Egyptian forms – artists must 're-create' them in the cauldron of their times, or must give them an appearance of renewed vitality, a function other than the purpose for which they were originally intended.[3]

Inspired by, yet different from, Western Orientalist traditions, Egyptomania in the context of black visual culture represents a strategy of signifying on aesthetically ennobled African sources and filling them with contemporary significance.[4]

My essay will analyse the various aesthetic manifestations of African-American visual artists' identification with Ethiopia and Egypt a source of a native tradition, cultural heritage and pride. I show how such a black-centered historicism with a diasporic bent, whether intellectual or populist, endowed the arts with a special missionary and redemptive role in fostering an 'original' art movement which authenticated itself by rehabilitating a transnational pan-African cultural connection.

---

[3] Jean–Marcel Humbert, *L'Egyptomanie dans l'art occidental* (Paris: ACR, 1989): 21.

[4] Stephen Howe considers the notion of 'Egyptomania' to be a self-indulgent by-product of afrocentrism; it thus, he argues, refers to the irrationalist, monumentalist side of an Egyptianism that produces "ego-boosting myths of black Pharaos"; Howe, *Afrocentrism: Mythical Pasts and Imagined Homes* (London & New York: Verso, 1998): 49. In the context of visual culture, however, as I would like to show, 'Egyptomania' has different roots.

African-American Culture
and the Origins of Ethiopianism[5]

'Ethiopianism' represents a key factor in the history of African-American diasporic consciousness. The origins of Ethiopianism in African-American culture are in the times of slavery, when African Americans drew spiritual comfort from the strategic interpretation of the bible's prophetic mentioning of Ethiopia's coming redemption, which promised African Americans deliverance from bondage. Ethiopia thus emerged as a universal symbol in African-American self-awareness, with which a "complex of romantic, spiritual, and political beliefs" was associated.[6] Not only did this "Ethiopia of the Bible" constitute one of the great civilizations of antiquity, it was also classified as a region with considerable economic and military power ruled by a strong (black) people.[7] The essential point, however, was the redemptive eschatology provided by the most prominent biblical evocation of Ethiopia as set forth in the book of Psalms, in which it is predicted that "Princes shall come out of Egypt, Ethiopia shall soon stretch forth her hands." Typically, secular and spiritual ideas that characterized post-revolutionary Ethiopianist thought combined the Christian missionary aspect of black uplift and progress through conversion with the colonial notion of bringing the 'gifts' of Western civilization.[8] The antebellum Ethiopianist tradition was characterized by a distinctly black-centered manifest destiny marked by a call for pan-African nationhood, African redemption, and black messianism.[9] In the course of the post-Civil War era – with the establishment of black colleges, universities, and, especially at the turn of the century, black cultural institutions such as the American Negro Academy – the

---

[5] My historical overview of Ethiopianism and its cultural function in African-American thought and politics is based on James Harris' *African-American Reactions to the War in Ethiopia 1936–1941* (Baton Rouge & London: Louisiana State UP, 1994); William R. Scott's *The Sons of Sheba's Race: African-Americans and the Italo-Ethiopian War 1935–1941* (Blacks in the Diaspora; Bloomington & Indianapolis: Indiana UP, 1993); Wilson J. Moses' *Afrotopia: The Roots of African-American Popular History* (Cambridge: Cambridge UP, 1998), and John Cullen Gruesser's *Black on Black: Twentieth-Century African American Writing About Africa* (Lexington: UP of Kentucky, 2000).

[6] Gruesser, *Black on Black*, 1.

[7] Scott, *The Sons of Sheba's Race*, 14.

[8] *The Sons of Sheba's Race*, 17.

[9] *The Sons of Sheba's Race*, 18.

Ethiopianist prophecy became increasingly secularized. The popularity of 'Ethiopian symbolism' and cultural identification, which was to reach into the Harlem Renaissance, received a boost at the end of the century when 'real' Ethiopia captured the interest of African Americans, including the key historical event of Ethiopians warding off the Italian invasion at Adwa in 1896. From this historic incident onward, "Ethiopia replaced Haiti and Liberia as the master symbol of Black Power and Black Nationalism."[10] It was the first time in the era of colonialism that an indigenous population had resisted and successfully subdued a European power. The event was extensively covered and celebrated by the African-American press as a event heralding the rise of the oppressed colored nations of the world.[11] Garvey, a staunch reviver of Ethiopian millennialism, popularized the Ethiopian rhetoric and transformed it into a cultural ideology. The cultural identification of the black diaspora with Ethiopia – especially in African America and the Caribbean – once again surged with the coronation of Ras Tafari Makonnen in 1928 and his subsequent emperorship as Haile Selassie I from 1930. Ethiopia had a special significance in the black diasporic imagination, since it was the only African entity apart from Liberia that had managed to maintain its independence on an otherwise colonized African continent. Another defining incident which promoted the heightened participation of African Americans in the making of a politics of the diaspora was the Italian invasion of Ethiopia in 1935.[12] The "Abyssinian crisis" was a singular event in the history of the modern black diaspora's response to Africa – it was the first time that affirmations of black identity were expressed over a major concrete issue that served "to rally a large and internationally receptive constituency."[13] The Italian invasion was the major factor in the resurgence of Ethiopianism with its program of redemption of Africans – Abyssinians

---

[10] St. Clair Drake, *The Redemption of Africa and Black Religion* (Chicago: Third World P, 1970): 73.

[11] Scott, *The Sons of Sheba's Race*, 21.

[12] The invasion of Mussolini's fascist army on 3 October 1935 and the resulting campaign was extremely violent. Ethiopia, a member of the League of Nations since 1923, made a plea to the organization for international intervention, yet the French and British colonial empires – due to their stake in Africa – recognized the Italian occupation and thus impeded a unanimous international reaction. Haile Selassie, the cultural icon of this resurgent political Ethiopianism in the diaspora, fled to Geneva in 1936 and later to London, where he remained in exile until 1941. It was not until January 1942 that Ethiopia was liberated.

[13] James Harris, *African-American Reactions to the War in Ethiopia 1936–1941*, 155.

on the continent, and the oppressed peoples of African descent in the New World. It fostered unity among descendants of Africans around the world concerning the Ethiopian cause and thus strengthened greatly pan-African awareness and mobilization of black consciousness in general.[14]

The interest of the Harlem Renaissance in Ethiopianism is an all-too-natural consequence, if one considers that one of the cultural movement's defining vectors was a decidedly black-centered historicism. John Gruesser, who traces Ethiopianism through twentieth-century African-American literature, classifies Ethiopianism as a "teleological and uniquely African-American view of history"[15] that greatly influenced early twentieth-century pan-Africanism. He extracts a set of identifiable Ethiopianist elements from the discourse of nineteenth-century black-nationalist rhetoric. This discourse also created an Ethiopianist iconography in the works of modern black visual artists. First, the Ethiopianist tradition asserts a common heritage shared by people of African descent. It links displaced New World blacks with an – albeit imagined – African homeland and its ancient civilization. Second, it is embedded in a cyclical view of history grafted onto the biblical rhetoric of a divinely ordained historical fate and destiny. Many black artists and intellectuals of the Harlem Renaissance were particularly drawn to an aesthetic exegesis of the Ethiopian prophecy which envisioned the dawning of a new age. African redemption, as the antithesis to the myth of the "decline of the West," hence mirrored and threatened then-prevalent Euro-American cultural anxieties about the "passing of a great (white) race."[16] It considerably influenced the New Negro ideal of cultural elevation through black self-education.

---

[14] Harris, *African-American Reactions to the War in Ethiopia 1936–1941*, 34. Harris also mentions references by Ras Tafari Makonnen to the African-American "Ethiopian heritage" in the context of diplomatic relations between the two countries to substantiate the connection between pan-African politics and cultural identity: On 7 June 1922, Ras Tafari Makonnen pointed out to a consul-general in New York representing Ethiopia's interests that "we would welcome [black Americans] back to Abyssinia, their fatherland. [...] There is plenty of room for them here and we are certain they would be of the greatest aid in restoring their ancient land to its pristine glory"; quoted in Harris, *African-American Reactions to the War in Ethiopia*, 6.

[15] John Cullen Gruesser, *Black on Black: Twentieth-Century African American Writing About Africa*, 1.

[16] Gruesser, *Black on Black*, 5.

Myths of Racial Origin

As mentioned earlier, Ethiopianism derived from a strategic reading of the bible to claim a specifically black form of providential design. In this context, the construction of the racially significant "Hamitic hypothesis" was, historically, sometimes instrumentalized to further, and sometimes to contradict, the thus divinely ordained fate of enslavement. The "Hamitic hypothesis" is based on the Old Testament story of Noah and his sons, Ham, Shem, and Japheth, which generations of biblical scholars have constructed as a myth of the diversity of nations, combining this genealogy with environmental theories to explain differences in skin color.[17]

This conflict over the race of the descendants of Cush is also deployed by those black vindicationists who used biblical sources to support their claims that the founders of the Mesopotamian civilizations were black.[18] Central to this ethnocentric classification of the origins of people in the Old Testament tradition is the story of "Noah's curse," which was used as a source for the construction of the "Hamitic hypothesis," whose influence can be traced even into the twentieth century and to afrocentric debates on African cultural unity.[19] Biblical exegesis during the course of a complicated history of interpretation and social application to racial difference and subordination has drawn upon "Noah's curse" not only to explain the divinely ordained right to enslave the descendants of Ham, but also, which is the more intriguing hypothesis, to explain the origins of blackness. Well into the nineteenth century, this exegesis of the biblical story served as a justification for the enslavement of Africans, which were thus identified as Ham's descendants, conflating the idea of subordination and skin color.[20]

---

[17] Drake, *The Redemption of Africa and Black Religion*, 13.

[18] Drake, *Black Folk Here and There: An Essay in History and Anthropology* (Los Angeles: Center for Afro-American Studies, U of California P, 1991): 16.

[19] As a consequence of Noah's curse laid upon the descendants of Ham, the Canaanites – of who Canaan, the son of Ham, was the progenitor – lost their right to the land, the area bounded by Syria to the North, Egypt to the south and the Mediterranean sea to the West, which the ancestors of the Hebrew people, descendants of the son of Shem, also claimed. As a result of Noah's curse, the subordination of the Canaanites was considered to be based upon God's will and therefore legitimated enslavement; St Clair Drake, *The Redemption of Africa and Black Religion*, 16.

[20] Drake, *The Redemption of Africa and Black Religion*, 16.

Most intriguingly, the "Hamitic hypothesis," after it had been dissociated from its original meaning (the tenet of Noah's curse legitimating slavery), was exploited by white supremacists and afrocentrists alike to justify their claims.[21] In the late nineteenth and early twentieth century, mostly European archaeologists, ancient historians, and ethnologists perpetuated the scientifically corroborated myth – once more underlining black inferiority – that all African cultural achievement was the result of outside "Hamitic" influence.[22] In 1900, for instance, the colonial ethnologist Maurice Delafosse would publish an article glorifying the Egyptians as civilizers of the black race.[23]

The "Hamitic hypothesis" was also at the center of the debate launched by early twentieth-century black scholars regarding cultural and historical evidence for the black origins of ancient civilizations. It is interesting to see how Ethiopianism was, as a result, revitalized by blacks historians and historicists, by black intellectuals and artists alike.[24] The intellectual and popular resurgence of the Ethiopianist tradition manifested itself in the aesthetic inventory of the Harlem Renaissance for two reasons: one, because of the usability of the "Ethiopian past" as a source of inspiration to authenticate the project for a "racial school of art" as envisioned by Locke; second, because of the need for fashioning black counter-myths against white racist documents speaking of black people's primitive, uncivilized and thus inferior nature. Such a racist discourse, which relegated people of African descent to separate origins and primitivism alike, cemented the popular belief that a people that could not trace its origins back to a great

---

[21] Howe, *Afrocentrism*, 16.

[22] Howe, *Afrocentrism*, 115. In the discourse of scientific racists, "Hamites" were considered light-skinned peoples of ancient Egyptian, Indo-European or, most bizarre, 'Aryan' origin. They held the view these peoples had spread across Africa, where, as Howe writes, "they generally formed a small elite ruling over mentally and physically inferior subject races. All significant cultural achievements could be attributed to their influence" (115).

[23] Maurice Delafosse, "Sur des traces probables de civilisation égyptienne et d'hommes de race blanche," *Anthropologie* 11 (1900): 431–51, 543–68, 677–90; "les anciens Égyptiens [...] étaient des blancs du rameau hamitique mélangés d'éléments sémitiques et, par suite du grand nombre d'esclaves noirs, altérés par des éléments nigritiques" (432).

[24] Examples of that debate would be Pauline Hopkins's 1905 *Primer of Facts Pertaining to the Greatness of the African Race*, John William Norris's *The Ethiopian's Place in History* and James M. Webb's *The Black Man, the Father of Civilization, Proven by Biblical History*, both published in 1916 (Howe, *Afrocentrism*, 35).

civilization was also incapable of producing great art.[25] Black artists'
creative response to the discourse of scientific racism, based on the ideological linkage of race and civilization, thus instrumentalized the counter-
myth of black contributionism as promulgated by twentieth-century cultural
Ethiopianists such as W.E.B. Du Bois, Charles Seifert, Pauline Hopkins and
Drusilla Houston.

In *Our America*, Walter Benn Michaels also challenges the ideological
linkage between race, culture and civilization in discourses of racial origin
in the USA between the wars. Michaels investigates the cultural consequences of such phenomena as the Johnson–Reed Immigration Act of 1924,
which restricted immigration according to the principle of national origins.[26] This meant that eligibility for American citizenship was defined as
dependent on ethnic identity:

> ... linked first to the number of people living in America who had themselves
> been born in that region and, starting in 1927, to the number of Americans
> who could trace their "ancestry" back to that region, the Johnson Act required
> "racial analysis" of the American population.[27]

Lothrop Stoddard's *The Rising Tide of Color*, but also (this is the connection Michaels makes) the aesthetic strategies of black modernists could be
interpreted both as a symptom of or as a response to America's preoccupa-
tion with nativism at the time. Introducing the composite term "nativist
modernism," Michaels tries to embrace the changing conceptions of identity
that were articulated by the white majority's hostility towards a racial Other
in the 1920:

---

[25] As Robin Wiegman writes, "The fascination with Egypt and the question of the
racial category that the Egyptian occupied points toward the ideological linkage
between race and civilization, a linkage that has played a central role in crafting a
variety of racist discourses throughout the Western world. Through the postulation
that those of African descent were incapable of producing anything but the most
primitive of civilizations – those devoid of complex social structures, philosophy,
and high art – the paternalistic function of the slave system was often affirmed";
Wiegman, *American Anatomies: Theorizing Race and Gender* (Durham NC: Duke
UP, 1995): 52.

[26] The principle of national quotas had already been established in 1921 with the
passing of the Immigration Act of that year, which had created quotas based on the
number of foreign born Americans recorded in the 1910 census.

[27] Walter Benn Michaels, *Our America. Nativism, Modernism, and Pluralism*
(Durham NC & London: Duke UP, 1995): 30.

I will argue that nativism in the period just after World War I involved not only a reassertion of the distinction between American and un-American but a crucial redefinition of the terms in which it might be made.[28]

Race emerges as a crucial marker of modern identity.[29] "Nativist modernism" was governed by references to race, heritage and ancestry. It inadvertently constituted the axis of African-American identity constructions during the Harlem Renaissance which negotiated one's cultural and racial belonging to Africa and or/America. Concluding with Michaels, one could extend the notion of such a nativist modernist strategy to the revitalization of Egyptianisms and Ethiopianisms as core themes in the black aesthetic debate during the Harlem Renaissance. Origin and originality were conflated in the narratives of cultural kinship, from which a black aesthetic tradition was derived that reached from an ancient African past to the contemporary African diaspora. Ethiopianism typically projects a creation myth of racial – fused with cultural – origin.

Ethiopianism, Egyptomania and the Black Aesthetic

The following works were influential, if not foundational, in formulating a black aesthetic derived from Ethiopianism – Drusilla Dunjee Houston's 1926 *Wonderful Ethiopians of the Ancient Cushite Empire,* Du Bois' various publications on Africa and its diaspora, Charles C. Seifert's 1938 *The Negro's or Ethiopian's Contribution to Art,* Pauline E. Hopkins' 1905 *A Primer of Facts Pertaining to the Early Greatness of the African Race and the Possibility of Restoration by its Descendants* and 1903 article "Venus and Apollo Modelled from Ethiopians."[30] Garvey also distributed his

---

[28] Michaels, *Our America,* 2.

[29] *Our America,* 13.

[30] That the Ethiopianist tradition was not only based on cultural linkage but that it was also employed to substantiate a black aesthetic tradition or lineage is exemplified by Pauline Hopkins's 1903 essay "Venus and the Apollo Modeled from Ethiopians" published in the *Colored American,* an example of vindicationism in the arts. Hopkins gives scientific proof of her claim that an African origin can be traced from Ethiopia to Egypt to Greece and that classic Greek sculpture was indebted to African models: "Not only have authorities in the art world demonstrated that those most famous examples of classic beauty in sculpture – the Venus de Milo and the Apollo Belvedere – were chiseled from Ethiopian slave models, but Dr. Dudley Allen

Ethiopianist propaganda through pamphlets, essays, poetry and art.[31] These narratives; academic and populist; were united over the search for black origins and how a black aesthetic might be constructed via an ancestral legacy. They surfaced in the arts and aesthetics of the Harlem Renaissance and were characterized by the following themes:

> identification with an ancient Egypt that was "at least partly the creation of 'Ethiopians', 'Negroes', 'Cushites' or 'sons of Ham';
> the conviction that Africa was the cradle of civilization which then translated into Greece;
> the belief in a past African "golden age" as a symbol of racial pride and future redemption.[32]

Early twentieth-century Ethiopianist scholarship focussed not only on the racial character of the "Hamites" and the cultural linkage between Ethiopia and the diaspora, but also on Ethiopian and Egyptian influence throughout Africa. Houston's popular Ethiopianist treatise *Wonderful Ethiopians* was inspired by Du Bois and formulated a strong pan-African awareness of cultural unity between Africa and the diaspora.[33] As Houston notes in her preface to the first volume,

> the minds of men today are stirred with eager questionings about the origin of civilization and about the part the different races of mankind played in its development from primititive ages. The remains that archeologists are uncovering in Egypt, old Babylonia, and South America, reveal that there were significant factors in the first development of the arts and sciences that history has failed to make clear.[34]

What I find intriguing about Houston's work is that she combines the teleology of Ethiopianism and the redemption of Africa and its diaspora it envisions with a critique of colonial domination. It furthermore underscores

---

Sargent, director of physical culture in Harvard University, now announces the finest knowing [sic] living example of symmetrical physical development in a human being to be a young mulatto named Thomas E. White"; Hopkins, "Venus and Apollo Modelled from Ethiopians," *Colored American Magazine* 6 (May–June 1903): 465.

[31] See Tony Martin, *Literary Garveyism: Garvey, Black Arts and the Harlem Renaissance* (Dover MA: Majority Press, 1987).

[32] Howe, *Afrocentrism*, 36.

[33] Howe (*Afrocentrism*, 48–49) characterizes Houston's book as heavily ideological and not very attentive to actual historical facts and realities.

[34] Drusilla Dunjee Houston, *Wonderful Ethiopians of the Ancient Cushite Empire* (1926; Baltimore MD: Black Classic Press, 1985), vol. 1: 1.

my point that a strong diasporic awareness – in cultural, to a lesser degree
political terms – informed the arts and aesthetic of the Harlem Renaissance.
In the following passage, Houston formulates her own Ethiopian prophecy
in which the severed ties between Ethiopia and Afro-America are reunited,
and pan-African unity, the imagined black community of Ethiopia, is re-
stored and celebrated:

> The Ethiopian is a great race, probably the oldest. It is a race that does not die
> out under adversity. [...] We need our eyes opened, this type that we in ig-
> norance despise, built the eternal pyramids of Egypt and laid the foundation of
> the civilization of the historic ages. Because the slave trade broke the threads
> of remembrance, they walk among us with bowed heads, themselves ignorant
> of the facts that this story unfolds. Lift up your heads, discouraged and down-
> trodden Ethiopians. Listen to this marvelous story told of your ancestors, who
> wrought mightily for mankind and built the foundations of civilization true
> and square in the days of old.[35]

Houston also merges her Victorian-derived, Du Bois-inspired focus on high
culture – the true, the good, the beautiful – with a claim to the political
fitness of Africans for self-government and world leadership. Crucially, she
casts her appeal in an Ethiopian framework: "If we knew just what contribution each race has made to art, science and religion, we would know what
would be its fitness to take part in world government and control."[36]

More than a decade before Drusilla Houston, an African voice was heard
in the black diaspora, J.E. Casely–Hayford's *Ethiopia Unbound* (1911). Like
Houston, who might have read his work, Caseley–Hayford, a Gold Coast
lawyer and politician, transforms the Ethiopianist myth into a prophecy of
Africans' divinely ordained role of world leadership. *Ethiopia Unbound*
was dedicated "to the sons of Ethiopia the world wide over." Black Americans, who have obviously inspired African intellectuals like Caseley–Hayford, are in one passage tellingly referred to as "the teeming millions of
Ethiopia's sons in America."[37] What is intriguing about this argument is
that Caseley–Hayford still argues along the lines of religiously inspired

---

[35] Houston, *Wonderful Ethiopians*, 10–11.

[36] Houston, *Wonderful Ethiopians*, 12. Houston's ultimate appeal, however, does
not derive from a separatist impulse. Her ultimate goal is the universal elevation of
mankind, an opinion which links Houston to the Negritude movement and the
humanist ideal envisioned by Léopold Sédar Senghor.

[37] J.E. Caseley–Hayford, *Ethiopia Unbound: Studies in Race Emancipation* (1911;
London: Frank Cass, 1969): 167.

nineteenth-century African-American exceptionalism, turning to the "sons of Ethiopia" in America to help to uplift Africa and aid in its modernization.

An important intellectual figure for the Harlem community arts scene who also popularized interest in ancient African history was Charles C. Seifert, a West Indian by birth and founder of the Ethiopian School of Research. Seifert's academic institution was later converted to a research library and studio (1939) where artists could study and paint from ancient African art.[38] His 1938 study reflects a notion of black contributionism that was at the center of the aesthetic debate during the Harlem Renaissance. Seifert's argument twisted the vindicationist rhetoric based on the black origins of ancient civilization in such a way that it reflected back on the essential role of black culture and its enrichment of American life:

> Any attempt, then, to estimate Western Culture, or 'Our Culture' without taking into consideration the Negro's or Ethiopian's contribution to that culture would not only be false, but a travesty on Culture itself.[39]

Seifert, further, addresses the fundamental cultural contradiction that peoples of African descent in Western society were relegated to a culturally inferior position – colonized, segregated and lynched – yet in the artistic life they became the very source of modernity, eagerly consumed and celebrated:

> This causes us to remember the statement 'Negroes are not leaders in our culture' – etc.; 'not much' even though all Europe and America have gone African Negro art crazy in many ways besides adorning themselves in the sculpture and painting of the Negro.[40]

The Harlem Renaissance and the Visual Arts

The visual artists that are usefully associated with the Harlem Renaissance hardly followed one canon, genre or style. However, the role of Africa as an inspirational yet also vindicationist source loomed large. As the alter ego of primitivism, Ethiopianism was related to Locke's ideal of "representative-

---

[38] Romare Bearden & Harry Henderson. *A History of African-American Artists from 1792 to the Present* (New York: Pantheon, 1993): 250.

[39] Charles C. Seifert, *The Negro's or Ethiopian's Contribution to Art* (New York: Ethiopian Historical Publishing Co., 1938): 28.

[40] Seifert, *The Negro's or Ethiopian's Contribution to Art*, 14.

ness."[41] The Ethiopianist tradition that these artists drew upon not only emanated from a cultural project of black vindicationist nationalism of which excellence in the arts became the medium as well as the message, but, as we can clearly see in Aaron Douglas' "Aspects of Negro Life" and Lois Mailou Jones's "The Ascent of Ethiopia," it effected a privileging of narrative and performance.[42] The deliberate choice of visual theatricality[43] characterizes these artists' narrative strategy as diasporic, but also indicates their deep rootedness in black American tradition and popular culture.[44] I would like to suggest that popular forms of black drama at the time might have influenced Douglas in his choice of what he represented and how he represented it to tell his story, to re-construct[45] and offer positive identification for African Americans, who were, according to Locke, in the process of overcoming the burden of white stereotypization. Michel Feith deconstructs the notion of heritage as established by Harlem Renaissance intellectuals and artists by asking "what claims to authenticity can a definition of identity have when it is based on an invention of origins?"[46] Precisely owing to the Renaissance project of linking culture, race and civilization, ancestral Africa was usually symbolized by Ethiopia, which encompassed by association Egyptian as well as West African culture. Feith thus appro-

---

[41] The cultural-historical framework I am applying to the visual arts is based on Wilson Moses *Afrotopia*, where he differentiates between two varieties of afrocentric cultural discourse – primitivism and vindicationism.

[42] On the privileging of the performative in African-American visual art, see Richard J. Powell, "Art History and Black Memory: Toward a 'Blues Aesthetic'" (1994), in *The Jazz Cadence of American Culture*, ed. Robert O'Meally (New York: Columbia UP, 1999): 182–95,

[43] Michel Feith refers to this strategy as diasporic, thus explaining Douglas' choice of the historic panorama or Jones' choice of fusion of past and present. Feith, "The Syncopated African: Constructions of Origins in the Harlem Renaissance (Literature, Music, Visual Arts)," in *"Temples for Tomorrow": Looking Back at the Harlem Renaissance*, ed. Geneviève Fabre & Michel Feith (Bloomington: Indiana UP, 2001): 51–73.

[44] I am indebted to Alessandra Lorini's essay on W.E.B. Du Bois' pageant "The Star of Ethiopia" – vastly popular at the time and featuring prominently in the *Crisis*; Lorini, "'The Spell of Africa is Upon Me': W.E.B. Du Bois's Notion of Art as Propaganda," in Fabre & Feith, ed. *"Temples for Tomorrow"*, 159–77.

[45] See Henry Louis Gates, Jr.,"The Trope of the New Negro and the Reconstruction of the Image of the Black," *Representations* 24 (1988): 129–55.

[46] Feith, "The Syncopated African," 52. I would like to add that this critique of identity was a by-product of 'Ethiopianism', as a myth set against someone else's myth, and it also questioned the project of white supremacy.

priately speaks of pan-African images in the arts of the Harlem Renaissance
which were meant to express the fusion of traditions.[47] Meta Warrick Fuller's "Ethiopia Awakening"[48] anticipates the cultural credo of the Harlem
Renaissance in a twofold sense. Fuller's allegorization of Africa and its
diaspora emerged from the same nascent New Negro cultural moment as Du
Bois' pageant "The Star of Ethiopia." That Fuller might have been inspired
not only by New England scholars of Ethiopianism such as Du Bois and
Hopkins, but also by the surge of pan-African sensibility symbolically triggered by Menelik II's defense of the Italian Army at Adwa and its impact
on African-American cultural identification seems likely. As Theresa Leininger–Miller mentions, Fuller created a plaster relief (1913) and a statuette
(1914) entitled "Menelik II of Abyssinia" (370). Like her contemporary
Tanner, Fuller emerged from the Philadelphia art scene, where she studied
at the Pennsylvania Museum School of Industrial Art, completing her
degree in 1899. She left Philadelphia to study in Paris, where she met Du
Bois and visited the American Negro exhibition at the Exposition Univer-
selle in 1900, where Du Bois assisted Thomas J. Calloway, its collector,
with installing the exhibition and himself was responsible for its highly
acclaimed "Georgia Negro section."[49] The catalogue of the first of the annual art exhibitions to be held at the 135th Street Branch during the Harlem
Renaissance – under the auspices of a curatorial committee that consisted of
such key cultural spokespersons as Du Bois, James Weldon Johnson and
Schomburg himself – lists a sculpture entitled "The Sphinx."[50] "The
Sphinx" would fit well into the Ethiopianist tradition, since pan-African
scholars such as Edward Blyden claimed that the Sphinx at Gizeh's features
were "decidedly of the African or Negro type."[51]

---

[47] "The Syncopated African," 54.

[48] See Figure 2, end of essay. The provenance of "Ethiopia Awakening" is a
matter of controversy – the sculpture is usually dated 1914. For an in-depth discussion of Fuller's work, see Judith Wilson, "Will the 'New Internationalism' be the
Same Old Story? Some Art Historical Considerations," in *Global Visions: Towards
a New Internationalism in the Visual Arts*, ed. Jean Fisher (London: The Institute of
International Visual Arts, 1994).

[49] Michel Fabre, *From Harlem to Paris: Black American Writers in France,
1840–1980* (Urbana & Chicago; U of Illinois P, 1993): 46–47, Judith Wilson, "Will
the 'New Internationalism' be the Same Old Story?" 75.

[50] Deborah A. Deacon, "The Art & Artifacts Collection of the Schomburg Center
for Research in Black Culture," *Bulletin of Research in the Humanities* ("The
Schomburg Center Issue," Summer 1981): 147.

[51] Quoted in W.E.B. Du Bois, *The Negro* (New York: Henry Holt, 1915): 19.

Du Bois' pageant "The Star of Ethiopia" indicates that Ethiopianism represented an elitist myth with popular appeal. Through his editorship of *The Crisis*, which featured an equally popular art form, the illustration, he was able to successfully funnel his message to the broad majority of African Americans. Looking at the content and symbols of the episodes in the first performed version – "The People of People and Their Gifts to Men" – which was presented at the National Emancipation Exposition in New York in October 1913[52] and then published in *The Crisis*, one can hardly imagine that those black visual artists drawing upon Ethiopianist symbolism were not inspired by this doubly 'monumental' piece of cultural work. The cultural agenda, contributionism and vindicationism, of Du Bois' pageant, structured according to the "gifts" of the black race to the world, could not have been more obvious. This familiar subject is already introduced in the first scene, set in ancient Africa, where a veiled woman appears during a storm bringing the Promethean "gifts of fire and iron."[53] Scene number two is centered on the "gift of civilization" given by the ancient Nilotic cultures, embodied by Ra, the Queen of Sheba, and Candace of Meroë.

Twelve years later, and some months after "The Star of Ethiopia" was performed at the Los Angeles Hollywood Bowl in 1925 (15 and 18 June), Du Bois published an essay calling for the creation of a racial school of art and artistic group-expression. Blending monumentalist metaphors with a rhetoric of illumination suggesting enlightenment, Du Bois articulates the

---

[52] As Du Bois himself phrased it, his dramatized history of the black race, driven by a similar impulse that inspired his historiography *The Negro*, was "first attempted in the New York celebration of Emancipation in 1913"; quoted in Freda L. Scott, "The Star of Ethiopia: A Contribution Toward the Development of Black Drama and Theater in the Harlem Renaissance," in *The Harlem Renaissance: Revaluations,* ed. Amritjit Singh, William S. Shiver & Stanley Brodwin (New York: Garland, 1989): 258. Richard Powell mentions a commissioned work Fuller was to create for a New York city exposition on occasion of the Centennial, of which Du Bois was a member of the Board of Governors, a group of figures entitled "Emancipation"; Powell, "Art History and Black Memory: Toward a 'Blues Aesthetic'" (1994), in *The Jazz Cadence of American Culture*, ed. Robert O'Meally (New York: Columbia UP, 1999): 194. Significantly, Du Bois early draft of "The Star" – dating back to 1911 – was first conceived not as a pageant, but "a masque" entitled "The Jewel of Ethiopia" suggesting an allegorical form, as Freda Scott shows in her discussion of the pageant's origins; like Fuller's piece, obviously, Du Bois dramatic performance underwent a series of highly suggestive permutations regarding its title, in which historical presentation began to gain precedence over allegorical presentation (Scott, "The Star of Ethiopia," 259).

[53] Freda L. Scott, "The Star of Ethiopia," 259.

need to make the African-American experience and heritage visible in order
to free the (black) world from the shackles of white racist discourse:

> two things may happen: on the one hand, the walls of race, class, and econo-
> mic hate and prejudice may grow more strait and dark so as to shut out the
> light from these prophets and maker of the Word [capitalized here and thus
> endowed with symbolic meaning]; and on the other hand, this same stone may
> crumble away before reason and decency and the spreading of real civilization
> so that the very blaze of coming light may illuminate the former darkness and
> make the intricate path over which this group has come all the more thrilling
> for its shadows, turns and twists.[54]

Alessandra Lorini considers Du Bois' "Star of Ethiopia" a celebration of
African-American cultural and artistic achievement as well as a theatrical
version of the prophetic and redeeming role Du Bois attaches to the arts: the
"Du Bois pageant went beyond the historical reconstruction of African-
American past and delivered a visionary message to the whole human
race."[55]

The African-American painter Laura Wheeler Waring (1887–1948) was
based in Philadelphia, where she was trained in the academic style of the
time. Her contemporary Albert Alexander Smith was also an illustrator for
The Crisis and *Opportunity* and very close to Arthur Schomburg, who commissioned Smith to execute a series of etched portraits of "famous Negroes."[56] Wheeler Waring was a frequent exhibitor with the Harmon Foundation (1928, 1930, 1931) and contributed to the Harmon portrait series of
"outstanding Americans of Negro origin" among others, with a portrait of
W.E.B. Du Bois.[57] Smith, who received an equally conservative art educa-

---

[54] Du Bois, "The Social Origins of American Negro Art," *Modern Quarterly*
(October–December 1925), repr. in *W.E.B. Du Bois: A Reader*, ed. Meyer Weinberg
(New York: Harper & Row, 1970): 250. Valentin Y. Mudimbe speaks of "epistemo-
logical violence"; Mudimbe, "Discourse of Power and Knowledge of Otherness," in
Mudimbe, *The Invention of Africa: Gnosis, Philosophy and the Order of Knowledge*
(Bloomington: Indiana UP, 1988): 1–23.

[55] Lorini, "'The Spell of Africa is Upon Me'," 175.

[56] James A. Porter, *Modern Negro Art* (1943; Washington DC: Howard UP, 1992):
147.

[57] Bearden & Henderson. *A History of African-American Artists from 1792 to the
Present*, 495.

tion at the notorious National Academy of Design,[58] was soon to become a life-long African-American expatriate in Paris, where he moved permanently in 1920. I believe that it is significant that Fuller, Waring and Smith all received a classical education. Thus, they embodied the New Negro ideal of cultural refinement which partly explains their interest in Ethiopianist themes. In "Negro Art Past and Present," Locke speaks of Fuller's career as a "great vindicating example in the American Negro's conquest of fine arts" (28).[59] Black publications such as *The Crisis*, *Opportunity*, and *The Messenger* featured pen and ink drawings by black artists such as Wheeler Waring and Smith, who also supported themselves through the graphic profession; as illustrators, these artists were the visualizers of the respective magazine's opinion, another means by which art was placed in the service of cultural propaganda as "race illustration."[60]

Around the same time that we find Laura Wheeler Waring's illustrations of Ethiopianist themes of racial uplift, Smith's etchings of similar subject matter also appeared on the cover of *The Crisis*, among them "Visions of Ethiopia" (1923) and "The Builders of the Temple" (1924). A list titled "Heads of Famous Negroes" (presumably commissioned by Schomburg), which Smith compiled in the years 1937 and 1938, indicates among other black heroic figures, the following, who were not only seminal sources of black pride and identification to the inkling movement of Negritude, but also of African Americans in the Depression era who identified with the

---

[58] He was the first African American to study there; see Theresa Leininger–Miller, *New Negro Artists in Paris: African American Painters and Sculptors in the City of Light, 1922–1934* (New Brunswick NJ: Rutgers UP, 2001).

[59] Locke, *Negro Art Past and Present*, 28. James A. Porter offers important insights into the opportunities open to black artists coming of age in the early twentieth century: "The strongest single influence on the Negro artist in the first decade of this century remained the academic tradition perpetuated by the schools; and the schools were not likely to stimulate many artists to treat Negro subjects either for their own sake of for the sake of original art"; *Modern Negro Art*, 76. As Porter notes, it was exhibitions at State Fairs – at least those which offered the Negro a place in the celebration of American History, no matter how segregated – which constituted one of the few possibilities for black artists to exhibit their art. Porter concedes that "at least they provided the occasions for the showing of Negro-made wares and afforded some relief from the usual public indifference to Negro cultural progress" (76). Porter also – the only slight reference to the provenance of Fuller's "Ethiopia Awakening" – argues that it was created for the New York State Centennial. This would, then, imply an immediate correlation between "Ethiopia Awakening" and the first showing of "The Star of Ethiopia."

[60] Porter, *Modern Negro Art*, 147.

Abyssinian crisis: Toussaint L'Ouverture, Menelik I and Menelik II, Henri Christophe, Haiti, and Makonnen. The fact that Smith had actual pictures of the Ethiopian rulers in his personal possession indicates that he must have had an active interest in the Ethiopians' plight and the country's history, which was certainly also inspired by Schomburg's commissions.[61] In June 1928, a most peculiar representation of Ethiopianism, after an etching by Smith, appeared on the cover page of *Opportunity* magazine. Typically, all the major classical arts are included in this allegory of the arts – painting, music, architecture, and writing – suggesting the symbolic function of African-American artists' connection with the ancient Empire as a source of inspiration upon which to build new (temples) of art.

Waring's cover drawings for *The Crisis* date from the same time as Smith's early ones, yet are executed in a different style: art deco. In "Egypt and Spring" (*The Crisis*, April 1923), a black female allegory of Egypt is visually connected with a display of ornamentation. In this piece, Waring seems deliberately to adapt fin-de-siècle "Egyptomania" and raise it to symbolic significance in the context of the Harlem Renaissance. In June 1924, Waring created "Africa in America" for the cover of (once again) *The Crisis*, pursuing a similar aesthetic connection between the decorativeness of black beauty and historical allusion to the ancient Nilotic civilizations on the one hand, and African-American history (the Middle Passage) on the other. As in Hughes' "The Negro Speaks of Rivers," Nile and Atlantic Ocean merge into one mnemonic route connecting the African American to his (mythic) origins. The woman to the left, an allegory of Africa, looks more like an Egyptian or Ethiopian queen than a person of West African origin – which, in view of the slave ship and the Middle Passage represented on the right, would, in a historical sense, be more appropriate. Here myth and cultural memory merge to fashion a powerful vessel for instilling pride and racial uplift.

As syncretic works of art, Aaron Douglas' images combine Ethiopian, Egyptian, West African and modern Western styles such as Art Deco, primitivism and cubism. He successfully incorporates several 'inherited' legacies into his work – modernist primitivism on the one hand, and the ancestral legacy of Ethiopianism on the other – and blends them into a pan-African collage of diasporically inflected cultural and stylistic fragments.[62]

---

[61] In a list compiled in Aug 1937, Smith lists, among others: Tahiti ("EMPRESS OF ABYSSINIA and wife of Menelik II. From a photo in my possession") and Makonnen ("RAZ of ABYSSINIA: Copied from photo in my collection") (Schomburg Collection).

[62] See Michel Feith, "The Syncopated African," passim.

Thematically as well as stylistically, they testify to the modernizing impulse of the African diaspora and to the Ethiopianist tenet of the black origins of Western civilization. Alain Locke praises such African-American artists as Douglas working in a modernist pan-African vein, inspired as they are by "African" as well as "Africanist" art – tribal art, primitivist modernist art and black folk traditions such as the spirituals. His observation therefore lead him to the seemingly paradoxical conclusion that "it is, thus, an African influence at second remove upon our younger Negro modernistic painters and sculptors; in being modernistic, they are indirectly being African."[63] In his art, then, Douglas not only endeavours to tell how African-American identity is historically constituted – ontologically and phenomenologically – but also expresses it in his very style. His Egyptianism thus represents a cultural as well as an aesthetic strategy. In the "Untitled" cover image for *Opportunity* magazine (June 1926), for instance, a black male thinker – his body reaching forward, his gaze looking back – embodies a chronology of cultural influences. The past he faces is represented by a blazing sun suggesting black cultural enlightenment, the glory of the ancient high cultures of the Nile. Yet it also prophetically encapsulates the credo of the New Negro generation and its awakening, by visually alluding to the first line of the traditional Negro spiritual "Rise Shine for Thy Light has Come."[64] The same theme also constituted the epigraph of the *New Negro* Anthology – "dedicated to the younger generation."

In "Song of the Towers," intermediality and pan-African impulse are blended to express a visual history of the arts and their role in the Harlem Renaissance. Here black ethics and aesthetics merge – after all, it is song that is the most enduring medium of black creative expression, container of cultural and historical memory. As Douglas himself once characterized the iconography of "The Song of the Towers,"

> the song is the most powerful instrument for representing all of the other arts as well as a perfect vehicle for conveying all of our various moods and conditions of life. I use three different types in this picture; Songs of Deliverance, Songs of Joy, and the Dance and Songs of Depression or the blues. Among the songs of deliverance we find such well known spirituals as "Run, Mourner,

---

[63] Locke, *Negro Art Past and Present*, 70.

[64] This is a theme Douglas also explored in a gouache drawing entitled "Rise Shine Thy Light Will Come" which was acquired by Locke for the Howard University collection; Richard J. Powell & Jock Reynolds, *To Conserve a Legacy: American Art from Historically Black Colleges and Universities* (Andover MA: Addison Gallery of American Art & New York: Studio Museum of Harlem, 1999): 113).

Run," "Steal Away," "Let My People Go," "Did My Lord Deliver Daniel,"
etc. The second group would include rag time, jazz, and all other popular
tunes. The third group would be made up of sorrow songs and the blues.[65]

In yet another exemplary work by Douglas, the "Fisk University Library
Murals," references to the ancient Greeks and their achievements are projected over/against towering skyscrapers. Allusions to contemporary American urban culture, they comment upon the ancient as well as modern origins of the Harlem Renaissance. Douglas' use of Ethiopianist rhetoric in the
"Fisk University Library Murals" is remarkably close to that of Lois Mailou
Jones' painting "The Ascent of Ethiopia" The star of freedom, for instance,
which appears in the panel entitled "Poetry," can be also found in Jones'
work. Pyramids, concentric circles and towering skyscrapers, suggesting a
similar teleology and historical consciousness, are zoomed together in
Jones' image. The comic and the tragic masks which we see in Douglas'
"Drama" panel also reappear in "The Ascent of Ethiopia."[66]

I have demonstrated that the aesthetic debate on black origins and originality which emerged during the Harlem Renaissance was characterized by
two primary strategies of black representation – the primitivist modernist
one, and the traditionalist, 'Victorian' or "Nile style." Although these strategies frequently clashed in the aesthetic debate over what constituted "representative" black subject matter in the arts, they successfully merged in
Aaron Douglas' truly pan-African work. Yet primitivism and Ethiopianism
were also essentially manifestations of the same cultural impulse: both conflated African-American and African identity. As black-centered mythologies they served a similar purpose – "to offer through art an emancipating
vision," as Locke once phrased it in the *New Negro*.

---

[65] Douglas' address here was occasioned by the replica of the Countee Cullen
Library panel which he re-created for the Governor's residence at Madison, Wisconsin, in 1968. Schomburg Center for Research in Black Culture, New York Public
Library, New York. David Lewering Lewis Collection, Schomburg Collection, 52–
53.

[66] See Figure 1, end of essay. Whether Jones has actually seen and was inspired by
Douglas murals is not documented, it seems evident, however, that both artists were
employing codes of recognition appealing to the Ethiopianist prophecy.

WORKS CITED

Baker, Houston A., Jr. *Modernism and the Harlem Renaissance* (Chicago & London: U of Chicago P, 1987).

Bearden, Romare, & Harry Henderson. *A History of African-American Artists from 1792 to the Present* (New York: Pantheon, 1993).

Burkett, Randall K. *Garveyism as a Religious Movement: the Institutionalization of a Black Civil Religion* (Metuchen NJ: Scarecrow, 1978).

Caseley–Hayford, J.E. *Ethiopia Unbound: Studies in Race Emancipation* (1911; London: Frank Cass, 1969).

Clifford, James. "Diasporas," *Cultural Anthropology* (1994): 302–38.

Deacon, Deborah A. "The Art & Artifacts Collection of the Schomburg Center for Research in Black Culture," *Bulletin of Research in the Humanities* ("The Schomburg Center Issue," Summer 1981): 145–63.

Delafosse, Maurice. "Sur des traces probables de civilisation égyptienne et d'hommes de race blanche," *Anthropologie* 11 (1900): 431–51, 543–68, 677–90.

Drake, St. Clair. *Black Folk Here and There: An Essay in History and Anthropology*, vols. 1–2 (Los Angeles: Center for Afro-American Studies, University of California, 1991).

——. *The Redemption of Africa and Black Religion* (Chicago: Third World Press, 1970).

Du Bois, W.E.B. *The Negro* (New York: Henry Holt, 1915).

——. "The Negro in Literature and Art," *Annals* (September 1913), repr. in *W.E.B. Du Bois: A Reader*, ed. Meyer Weinberg (New York: Harper & Row, 1970): 231–37.

——. "The Social Origins of American Negro Art," *Modern Quarterly* (October–December 1925), repr. in *W.E.B. Du Bois: A Reader*, ed. Meyer Weinberg (New York: Harper & Row, 1970): 247–51.

Eschen, Penny von. *Race Against Empire: Black Americans and Anticolonialism 1937–1957* (Ithaca NY & London: Cornell UP, 1997).

Fabre, Geneviève, & Michel Feith. "'Temples for Tomorrow': Introductory Essay," in Fabre & Feith, ed. *"Temples for Tomorrow"*, 1–31.

——, & Michel Feith. ed. *"Temples for Tomorrow": Looking Back at the Harlem Renaissance* (Bloomington: Indiana UP, 2001).

Fabre, Michel. *From Harlem to Paris: Black American Writers in France, 1840–1980* (Urbana & Chicago: U of Illinois P, 1993).

Feith, Michel. "The Syncopated African: Constructions of Origins in the Harlem Renaissance (Literature, Music, Visual Arts)," in Fabre & Feith, ed. *"Temples for Tomorrow"*, 51–73.

Gates, Henry Louis, Jr. "The Trope of the New Negro and the Reconstruction of the Image of the Black," *Representations* 24 (Fall 1988): 129–55.

Gilroy, Paul. *The Black Atlantic: Modernity and Double-Consciousness* (London: Verso & Cambridge MA: Harvard UP, 1993).

Gruesser, John Culler. *Black on Black: Twentieth-Century African American Writing About Africa* (Lexington: UP of Kentucky, 2000).

Gubar, Susan. *Racechanges: White Skin, Black Face in American Culture* (New York & Oxford: Oxford UP, 1997).

Harris, James. *African-American Reactions to the War in Ethiopia 1936–1941* (Baton Rouge & London: Louisiana State UP, 1994).

Hopkins, Pauline E. *A Primer of Facts Pertaining to the Early Greatness of the African Race and the Possibility of Restoration by its Descendants* (Cambridge MA: Hopkins, 1905).

——. "Venus and Apollo Modelled from Ethiopians," *Colored American Magazine* 6 (May–June 1903): 465.

Houston, Drusilla Dunjee. *Wonderful Ethiopians of the Ancient Cushite Empire* (1926; Baltimore: Black Classic Press, 1985).

Howe, Stephen. *Afrocentrism: Mythical Pasts and Imagined Homes* (London & New York: Verso, 1998).

Humbert, Jean Marcel. *L'Egyptomanie dans l'art occidental* (Paris: ACR, 1989).

Jenkins, David. *Black Zion: The Return of Afro-Americans and West Indians to Africa* (London & New York: Wildwood House, 1975).

Kirschke, Amy H. *Aaron Douglas: Art, Race and the Harlem Renaissance* (Jackson: UP of Mississippi, 1995).

Leininger–Miller, Theresa. *New Negro Artists in Paris: African American Painters and Sculptors in the City of Light, 1922–1934* (New Brunswick NJ: Rutgers UP, 2001).

Locke, Alain. *Negro Art Past and Present* (Washington DC: Associates in Negro Folk Education, 1936).

——. "The New Negro," in *The New Negro*, ed. Locke (1925; New York: Touchstone, 1992): 3–19.

Lorini, Alessandra. "'The Spell of Africa is Upon Me': W.E.B. Du Bois's Notion of Art as Propaganda," in Fabre & Feith, ed. *"Temples for Tomorrow"*, 159–77.

McKay, Claude. *Home to Harlem* (New York: Harper & Brothers, 1928)

Martin, Tony. *Literary Garveyism: Garvey, Black Arts and the Harlem Renaissance* (Dover MA: Majority Press, 1987).

Martin, Wendy. "'Remembering the Jungle': Josephine Baker and Modernist Parody," in *Prehistories of the Future: The Primitivist Project and the Culture of Modernism*, ed. Elazar Barkan & Ronald Bush (Stanford CA: Stanford UP, 1995): 310–26.

Michaels, Walter Benn. *Our America: Nativism, Modernism, and Pluralism* (Durham NC & London: Duke UP, 1995).

Moorland–Spingarn Research Center, Howard University. Papers of Alain Locke. Washington DC.

Moses, Wilson J. *Afrotopia: The Roots of African-American Popular History* (Cambridge: Cambridge UP, 1998).

Mudimbe, Valentine Y. "Discourse of Power and Knowledge of Otherness," in Mudimbe, *The Invention of Africa: Gnosis, Philosophy and the Order of Knowledge* (Bloomington: Indiana UP, 1988): 1–23.

Porter, James. *Modern Negro Art* (1943; Washington DC: Howard UP, 1992).

Powell, Richard J. "Art History and Black Memory: Toward a 'Blues Aesthetic'" (1994), in *The Jazz Cadence of American Culture*, ed. Robert O'Meally (New York: Columbia UP, 1999): 182–95.

——, & Jock Reynolds. *To Conserve a Legacy: American Art from Historically Black Colleges and Universities* (Andover MA: Addison Gallery of American Art & New York: Studio Museum of Harlem, 1999).

Rowell, Charles H. "An Interview with Lois Mailou Jones," *Callaloo* 12.2 (1989): 357–78.

Schomburg Center for Research in Black Culture, New York Public Library, New York. David Lewering Lewis Collection, Schomburg Collection.

Schomburg, Arthur A. "The Negro Digs up his Past," in *The New Negro*, ed. Alain Locke (1925; New York: Touchstone, 1992): 231–38.

Scott, Freda L. "The Star of Ethiopia: A Contribution Toward the Development of Black Drama and Theater in the Harlem Renaissance," in *The Harlem Renaissance: Revaluations*, ed. Amritjit Singh, William S. Shiver & Stanley Brodwin (New York: Garland, 1989): 257–69.

Scott, William R. *The Sons of Sheba's Race: African-Americans and the Italo-Ethiopian War 1935–1941* (Blacks in the Diaspora; Bloomington & Indianapolis: Indiana UP, 1993).

Seifert, Charles C. *The Negro's or Ethiopian's Contribution to Art* (New York: Ethiopian Historical Publishing Co., 1938).

Stuckey, Sterling, comp. *The Ideological Origins of Black Nationalism* (Boston MA: Beacon, 1972).

Wiegman, Robyn. *American Anatomies: Theorizing Race and Gender* (Durham NC: Duke UP, 1995).

Wilson, Judith. "Will the 'New Internationalism' be the Same Old Story? Some Art Historical Considerations," in *Global Visions: Towards a New Internationalism in the Visual Arts*, ed. Jean Fisher (London: The Institute of International Visual Arts, 1994): 68–81.

❖

FIGURE 1. "The Ascent of Ethiopia" (1932) by Lois Mailou Jones,
Milwaukee Art Museum.

FIGURE 2."Ethiopia Awakening" (ca. 1914) by Meta Warrick Fuller,
Schomburg Center for Research in Black Culture, New York Public Library,
New York.

Carnaval of Los Congos of Portobelo, Panama
Feathered Men and Queens

JUDITH BETTELHEIM

A FTER HAVING PUBLISHED extensively on Cuban *carnaval* and other Caribbean festivals, I decided to profit from a unique opportunity and attend Carnaval 2000 in Portobelo, Panama to see Los Congos de Portobelo celebrate.[1] I was excited about the opportunity to document a rural celebration, and one where there was less government involvement than in Cuba. After having accomplished some research on Congo-based traditions in the Americas, I was also anxious to extend my research to a new area.[2] I easily admit that I commenced this trip with certain clear expectations, or should I say preconceptions, resulting from both scholarly research and fieldwork in Cuba with practitioners of the Congo-based religion Palo Monte. I not only wanted to begin to understand what constituted a *carnaval* celebration in Portobelo, but I was interested in fleshing out what might be considered signs of 'Congo-ness', as I understand it, in Portobelo, and compare that evidence with other former slave and free Afro-communities in the Americas.

---

[1] In 1999–2000 I was a visiting professor at Emory University and I would like to thank the Art History department there for helping to fund my research trip to Panama.

[2] See Bettelheim, "Costume Types and Festival Elements in Caribbean Celebrations;" *ACIJ Research Review* 4 (Kingston: African Caribbean Institute of Jamaica, 1999): 1–46, and "Palo Monte Religion, Initiation and Art in Cuba," *African Arts* (forthcoming).

In the Americas during the nineteenth and twentieth centuries, there were scattered reports and articles concerning folk traditions and ritual dramas performed by groups who both identify themselves with Congos and/or are so called. Often these groups are led by a King and/or Queen and emulate in one way or another royalty and a courtly hierarchy. For example, an 1873 report on the Día de Reyes celebrations in Santiago de Cuba included this comment: "These are not ordinary masqueraders, be it known, but grave subjects of his sombre majesty King Congo, the oldest and blackest of all the blacks: lawfully appointed sovereign of the coloured community."[3] During my years of research in Santiago de Cuba I also documented many of the *cabildos* which are still led by Queens and Kings.[4] In March 2000, I was fortunate to be able to meet another one of these groups, the Congos of Portobelo, Panama, and to attend a three day-long *congada* (or festival) in celebration of *carnaval*. Historically, for the most part, these Congo *congadas* derive from sixteenth- and seventeenth-century practices which in turn may refer back to events and ideas from Central Africa. Although Afro-Americans from various ethnicities elected, and may still elect, Kings and Queens, here I am specifically interested in those groups which identify themselves as Congo, or perhaps demonstrate strong cultural signs which may be understood as Congo.[5] Relevant to the discussion below is the increasing possibility that a form of Christianity, particular to areas of West

---

[3] Walter Goodman, *The Pearl of the Antilles, or An Artist in Cuba* (London: Henry S. King, 1873): 137. I agree with Elizabeth Kiddy when she remarks that "Africans from many different ethnicities named kings as their leaders" and that there exists the possibility that in the Americas observers called any royally-dressed Afro a "Congo King" without really knowing his ethnic heritage; Kiddy, "Who is the King of Congo? A New Look at African and African-Brazilian Kings in Brazil" (unpublished paper, 1999). Yet, in this case, having documented the importance of Congo-derived culture in eastern Cuba, I tend to accept this particular designation at face value. See Bettelheim, "Ethnicity, Gender and Power in Carnaval in Santiago de Cuba," in *Negotiating Performance in Latin/o America*, ed. Diana Taylor & Juan Villegas (Durham NC & London: Duke UP, 1994): 176–212.

[4] See, for example, Bettelheim, ed. *Cuban Festivals: An Illustrated Anthology* (New York & London: Garland, 1993), or the revised edition, *Cuban Festivals: A Century of Afro-Cuban Culture* (Kingston, Jamaica & London: Ian Randle, 2001).

[5] I do not intend to rehearse the numerous articles and books documenting the strong Congo historical and cultural heritage in the Americas. For the relevant history of the Kongo empire of central Africa and European powers, specifically Portuguese and Spanish, see the Works Cited below for many excellent sources.

Central Africa, arrived in the Americas along with the slave trade, a particular Christianity that the Central Africans themselves practiced.[6]

As I rethink many of the contemporary debates surrounding questions of modernity, the subaltern community, the role of race in dialogues about nationalism and the 'sub-national' status of many black communities, I wonder how these discussions may be applied to, or have influenced, my understanding of these *carnaval* celebrations. Some scholars cite Benedict Anderson's suggestion that the communities we study are "imagined," in that "the members of even the smallest nation will never know most of their followers [...] yet in the minds of each lives the image of their communion."[7] This, I believe, does not do justice to the power of Los Congos and their annual *carnaval*, for it seems that the hundreds of people roaming around the town during the four-day celebration knew Los Congos and supported their performance, either as participants or spectators. Afro-Panamanians, especially the Congos, have yet to enter into a national dialogue within Panama concerning nationhood and modernity. I agree with scholars like Jean Muteba Rahier, who, in describing the celebration of Semana Santa among the Afro-Esmeraldes population of Ecuador, decides that race consciousness defines the limits of the discourse of modernity in contemporary Latin countries.[8] Race consciousness exists outside of the constructs of modernity, for one of modernity's most salient claims is the universality of its constructs. And when race enters a national dialogue it reverberates

---

[6] In a recent piece, the historian John Thornton writes of the long-range success that Kongo King Afonso had "in developing a syncretic and acceptable Christianity which became a fundamental part of Kongo's self identity from his day through to the colonial period" (published by H-Net List for African Expressive Culture, 14 March 2000). For more precise information, see John K. Thornton, *Africa and Africans in the Making of the Atlantic World, 1400–1680* (1992; Cambridge & New York: Cambridge UP, 1998), Thornton, "The Regalia of the Kingdom of Kongo: 1491–1895," in *Kings of Africa: Art and Authority in Central Africa*, ed. Erna Beumers & Hans–Joachim (Utrecht: Foundation of Kings of Africa, 1992): 57–63, and Linda M. Heywood, "The Angolan–Afro-Brazilian Cultural Connections," *Slavery & Abolition* 22 (1999): 9–23. For information on Kongo-related art and ritual, see Wyatt MacGaffey, *Religion and Society in Central Africa: The Bakongo of Lower Zaire* (Chicago: U of Chicago P, 1986), and Robert Farris Thompson, *Face of the Gods: Art and Altars of Africa and the African Americas* (New York: The Museum for African Arts, 1993).

[7] Benedict Anderson, *Imagined Communities: Reflections on the Origin and Spread of Nationalism* (London: Verso, rev. ed. 1991): 4–6.

[8] Rahier, lecture at the conference "'Race' & Anti-Black Racism in Latin America" at the Wolfsonian, Miami Beach, 15 March 2000.

against any notion of modernity in a 'non-racial' nation-state. It is as Samuel Kinser makes clear in his discussion of Carnival in Mobile and New Orleans: "Carnival deals with the barriers in daily life not by tearing them down or turning them topsy-turvy but by stepping over them and back again in an exemplary although impractical enlargement of the everyday."[9] And he reminds the reader that in the south of the USA the rituals of Carnival "all make reference [...] to race relations" – in other words, "marginality is etched in black and white."[10] Rather than seeing it as an inversion in the Bahktinian sense, let us look at Portobelo Carnaval as a celebration, a reminder, of a vital part of Panama's history, a history that is repeated yearly as Los Congos de Portobelo assume the responsibility of ruling and purifying the town for the oncoming year. The public transcript that *carnaval* enacts may derive from the Christian Bible, but the hidden transcript is one that reminds the town of Congo history on the Atlantic coast of Panama, and, by extension, in the Americas.[11] Historically, in Panama it is not only a matter of race relations, but of the particular status of the powerful and threatening free *cimarrón* (maroon) communities, initially composed of escaped slaves, that populated the entire Atlantic coast. Portobelo is one of these communities. It is important to keep this in mind when reading the descriptions below.

Carnaval in Portobelo, Panama

It is the first day of Lent, Ash Wednesday, 8 March 2000. The street in front of Portobelo's main park, in the center of town, is lined with spectators, sometimes three deep. All around there are families and small crowds of youth, mingling, talking, laughing and running. On the hillside facing the old customs house and running onto and then away from the main road parallel to the park, I counted at least twenty Devils. These were *jovenes*, young men and boys dressed in elaborate Devil costumes, and they were chasing other young men their own age, who were not in costume; it was like an "I Dare" contest. A boy without a costume would step in front of a

---

[9] Samuel Kinser, *Carnival, American Style: Mardi Gras at New Orleans and Mobile* (Chicago: U of Chicago P, 1990): xvii.

[10] Kinser, *Carnival, American Style*, xx.

[11] See James C. Scott, *Domination and the Arts of Resistance: Hidden Transcripts* (New Haven CT: Yale UP, 1990).

Devil, and, as the Devil attempted to whip the boy's legs, the youth without the costume would try to jump above the rope whip. Often the youth would be wearing jeans with some kind of padding underneath, but often, too, there was no padding to be seen (cf Figure 1, below). As the whip cracked and oftentimes hit, I could see the youth wince in momentary pain. I noticed one lone teenage girl who continually challenged one Devil and then another. She wore black jeans and her legs were thoroughly padded. Sometimes a Devil would charge into a small crowd of spectators (cf Figure 2), and all the women and children would dash away while screaming and giggling, only to reassemble to continue watching the action on the hillside.

There are certain community rules which dictate behavior on this the final day of *carnaval* celebrations. Ideally, the whip must never strike above the knees, and ideally there should be no knots in the rope whip. If any spectator chose not be whipped, all that was needed was to squat as a Devil approached. (I was given explicit instructions to do this when I first ventured out to the central square at about 2 pm.) Sometimes a young lad, of about seven or eight, would take off his Devil mask as he approached a family member and take a rest alongside his mother or aunt, who had a supply of drink or food ready. Then he would put the mask back on, grab his whip, and rejoin the battle. Sometimes, too, I noticed an 'older' Devil, maybe in his early twenties, find a victim and chase him for a few blocks, or charge into a crowd looking for a particular young woman, who would hide behind her friends. Twice I saw a Devil confronting an elder in the community, and both times the whip stopped in mid-air as the older man stared defiantly at the Devil. At times the action did get rough, and I marveled that a fight had not broken out. By 7 pm, though, as the light faded and I was back at the house, I was told that a serious fight had erupted and the police had been called in.

I must admit that I did not stay out on the hillside for four hours. I got bored watching the boys playing, so I wandered back to the house a few times, leaving to check out the scene again and again. At first I found myself mumbling "Boys Will Be Boys." But toward the end of the afternoon I realized something else was happening.

All along, a chorus of Congo female singers and a few drummers had been playing and singing in a corner on the hillside, away from the action (cf Figure 3). Early in the afternoon I had wandered over to greet them and to see if I could catch some lyrics, or see if anyone was dancing. Every once in a while, a Devil would break through the singers, then return to play with the other Devils. Sometimes an older Devil, about thirty, would stop on the hillside, or near the chorus, and perform. He would snort and grunt, and, with his masked head looking down at the ground, would then stomp. Then he too ran off to confront another non-costumed 'onlooker'. At around 5 pm, the Queen[12] came out to dance alone and walked over to the center of the hill, surveying the games going on around her. It was semi-choreographed pandemonium. An older Devil, one I recognized from the previous day's events, came onto the hillside to stand near her, and suddenly a group of men, roped together at the waist, ran by the Queen. These men were in their thirties or forties; each had on a white slip over his street clothes and wore a tightly wrapped white head-tie – the Angels had arrived. The first in line carried a simple wooden cross. (See Figure 4.) The Angels began to rope in certain Devils and deliver them to the area where the chorus was singing. It was then I realized that play was occurring on two levels.

The Angels were only roping in certain of the Devils, the older ones. The youth were still performing their own version of the play. The Queen did not look happy. I had been told that in years past fewer young people took part in the final afternoon's play, and more Devils kept to the script. The afternoon 'should have' ended when the Angels finally roped in the Diablo Major and the Queen subdued him with her dancing while holding the wooden cross up in front of him. This year, the Queen, the chorus, the drummers, and some of the Devils left the hillside, but the rowdy youth remained. Some Devils played the game; others didn't.[13]

---

[12] References to black Kings and Queens are numerous throughout the Americas, although most research on their history and performance has been done in Brazil. Although both a King and a Queen celebrated *carnaval* in Portobelo, the Queen was decidedly more important and exerted considerably more power. According to Elizabeth Kiddy, "records of the practice of crowning African kings, in fact, first emerged in Brazil in the seventeenth century in runaway slave communities and brotherhoods"; Kiddy, "Who is the King of Congo?" (10). The first recorded ritual performance that included a King was "during the visit of the ambassador of the King of Kongo to Dutch Recife in 1642" (12). By the 1700s, local Brazilian governments recognized the connection between brotherhoods electing Kings and Queens and rebellion, and in 1728 in Bahia the authorities enacted a proclamation declaring such elections illegal. The evidence from other slave communities in the Americas agrees with this statement, but the evidence of documented Kings and Queens exerting political power from Panama may push the date even further back. And in Panama during the 1800s and 1900s the Queen wielded much more power than the King. This is evident both from Ronald Smith's research in the mid-1970s – "The Society of Los Congos of Panama: An Ethnomusicological Study of the Music and Dance Theater of an Afro-Panamanian Group" (unpubl. doctoral dissertation, Indiana University, Bloomington, 1976) – and my own observations in Portobelo.

[13] During the few days I spent in Portobelo I heard conversations about the number of youth who were participating as Devils, and how violent these games had

To put the above action in perspective, I'll go back to the first evening of *carnaval* celebrations, the evening of Monday, 6 March. I had come to Portobelo with Arturo Lindsay to see the Congos of Portobelo celebrate the *congada*, a festive gathering of the Congos. Lindsay has been coming to Portobelo yearly since 1993. A Panamanian by birth, he wanted to work with Los Congos as a source for his own art works, and he continues to work with various Congos on a long-term art project. Portobelo is one of the small towns scattered along the Caribbean coast to the west and east of Colón, many of which (including Portobelo itself) used to be isolated villages harbouring *cimarrones* (escaped slave communities). The coastal road from Sabanita, west of Colón, was paved only in the 1970s. Today Portobelo's residents number around two thousand.

At 11 pm on Monday, when Lindsay and I walked to the town square, I first saw the *palacio*, a temporary rectangular wood structure approximately 15′x20′, with a thatched roof and rafters strung with strips of colored cloth. Inside, a chorus of women sang behind four drummers. They wore an assortment of street clothes, but most had on the long, full, flared skirt, the *pollera montuno* [rustic overskirt], that has become an emblem of Panama itself; many wore small bowler-style hats.[14] All danced in bare feet. First the drummers struck up; a few of the more elderly women would begin a song, and then the others would start to clap and join in. As each older woman came out to the center of the *palacio* to dance, a younger male entered from the crowd of onlookers to dance with her. She had bare feet; he wore street clothes and shoes. These older women were definitely in control. The dance resembled a form of mild flirtation; I am not sure if the 'goal' was to steal a kiss, but as the couple danced around one another, the young man would often lean forward and try to kiss the woman. She would maneuver herself away, or hold the end of her long skirt over her face.[15] If any of the young men acted too aggressively, the older women would grab him and throw him out of the *palacio*. Often the young dancers would offer money to the singers. So these were the famous Congo women, the ones

---

become. There is genuine concern that rival social factions may use this opportunity to act out other problems.

[14] This particular style is actually "the Panama hat"; what is known as a Panama hat in the USA is actually made in Ecuador.

[15] This reminds me of the Cuban rumba, where the woman is also in control. The male partner may attempt a side-kick, known as the *vacuna*, or vaccination, but the female partner can reject these advances by covering her genital area with one end of her long skirt, which she can maneuver at will.

ultimately in control of the *juegos* [games] or theater (action) of the *carnaval* celebrations.

I would like to comment on the dance itself, for this was one of the first
'hints' I saw that resonated with a Central African Congo aesthetic. The
couples move their lower bodies in a sway-shuffle. The arms are held low,
also swaying or swinging in a parallel side-to-side movement. There is
virtually no upper-body movement, no syncopated shoulders. The two dancers move around one another in a circular pattern. The footwork especially
reminds me of a Jamaican dance, Kumina, where the hips and shuffling feet
move in a strikingly similar pattern. Kumina is known to be of Congo heritage, and its Congo-based vocabulary and belief system have been well-
documented.[16] The famous Kingston-based Kumina Queen Imogene Kennedy, known as "Queenie," passed away in spring 1998. But I did not see
the Portobelo Queen herself or the male Congos de Portobelo until midnight
of Tuesday, Mardi Gras.

All day long on Mardi Gras, there was singing and dancing inside the
palacio. A visiting troupe of Congos from Colón arrived by bus to dance
inside the *palacio* and romp with other Portobelo youth on the town square.
I noted certain 'characters', as many of the troupe members wore costumes.
But this seemed like a *divertissement* devised by a cultural commission or
town officials. The visitors wore name tags, many were in their early
twenties, and all left together on their bus.

It was not until about 11 pm on Mardi Gras that the main *juego* began. I
had pestered Lindsay during the day: "Are you sure I am going to see some
Congos in feather head-dresses?" (For me, one of the main identifying
'signs' of Congos in the Americas is the feathered head-dress.).[17] Lindsay
knew these men; many were part of the Taller Portobelo, an art cooperative
he works with. This workshop had been organized by Lindsay, along with

---

[16] See Kenneth M. Bilby & Kia Bunseki Fu-Kiau. *Kumina: A Kongo-Based
Tradition in the New World* (Cahiers du CEDAF 8.4, 1983), Cheryl Ryman,
"Kumina: Stability and Change," *ACIJ Review* 1 (Kingston: The African Caribbean
Institute of Jamaica, 1984): 81–90, and Monica Schuler, *"Alas, Alas Kongo": A
Social History of Indentured Immigration into Jamaica, 1841–1865* (Baltimore MD:
Johns Hopkins UP, 1980).

[17] See Bettelheim, "Costume Types and Festival Elements in Caribbean Celebrations;" *ACIJ Research Review* 4 (Kingston: African Caribbean Institute of Jamaica,
1999): 1–46.

Sandra Eleta and Yaneca Esquina, a leading figure in the Congo community, some ten years earlier.[18]

We walked past the *palacio*, where the singing and dancing continued, and up a dark hillside, where the Congos were gathering. And yes, they wore an assortment of tattered clothes and feathered head-dresses, and had darkened their faces with charcoal (see Figure 5).[19] Specifically, their costumes consisted of solid-color pants, and sometimes mismatched shoes and socks. Their white long-sleeved shirts had patches of multicolored cloth sewn on, along with some fringing. Multicolored multiple strands of beads were worn around the neck, and one or two wore shoulder bags made from cloth or plastic. The King wore a home-made crown covered with shiny paper or shiny fabric. Many of the Congos had an eclectic assortment of objects hanging from a waist rope: gourds, plastic dolls, stuffed animals, and perhaps a lone shoe.[20] One member often carries the Congo flag, always black-and-white, although in Portobelo during the celebrations it flies above the *palacio*. We greeted them; I was introduced, and after a conversation and some photography Lindsay and I went down and entered the

---

[18] Arturo Lindsay, born in Panama, is a professor at Spelman College in Atlanta, and Sandra Eleta is a Panamanian photographer who resides in both Panama City and Portobelo.

[19] There are many festival traditions throughout the Caribbean where male Afro-performers blacken their skin as a sign of their ancestors, or of those individuals who lived close to or during the period of slavery. I have seen these performers in Cuba, and have read documentation of their performances in the Dominican Republic, Martinique and Trinidad. For a fascinating discussion of the Trinidad tradition, see Ana Maria Alonso, "Men in 'Rags' and the Devil on the Throne: A Study of Protest and Inversion in the Carnival of Post-Emancipation Trinidad," in *Carnival in Perspective*, ed. Thomas M. Fiehrer & Michael W. Lodwick (Plantation Society in the Americas; New Orleans: U of New Orleans, 1990): 73–120.

[20] When I asked the significance of all these objects, I was told (by Lindsay and one Congo) that in "former times" the Congos wore chains and locks and even some iron objects around their waists. This reminded people of slavery and escaped slaves, who were constantly on the run and had to carry essentials with them. Once a group of Congos was coming to Portobelo from a close-by island and their boat overturned. Because of the weight of their chains and objects, many drowned. Since then, Congos have worn store-bought lightweight objects. By the way, the visiting troupe from Colón had more elaborate costumes, attesting to their greater "wealth" and patronage. For example, the Pajarito character wore a goured green and yellow knee length courtier-style overdress, with yellow 'wings' attached to the long sleeves. His head-dress consisted of matching green and yellow commercial feathers.

palacio, waiting for the *juego* to begin. This was the section of the celebrations when the Diablo Major is first subdued, but not conquered.

The *palacio* became crowded as more female chorus members arrived, and more men entered to dance. The crowd outside also got larger; there was jockeying to get a better view, as the older Congas made sure no 'spectators' actually entered the *palacio*. I noticed that the crowned Congo Queen had also arrived and was dancing with a few of the men. The singing became louder, and all of a sudden five costumed Congos bounded into the *palacio*, madly swirling about, while the Queen danced solemnly to the side, carrying a small wooden cross (see Figure 6). Then the costumed Diablo Major arrived; he made ferocious attempts to grab the Queen; the Congos pushed and shoved each other, trying to protect her. Then another female Conga joined the fray, holding up a small wooden cross against the Devil. There was real jostling, as Congos or the Devil fell to the ground or ran after the Queen in the small amount of open interior space remaining. Some Congos were actually hit by the Devil. Other Congos reached into straw shoulder bags and took out pieces of wrapped hard candy, which they threw at the crowd and on the ground. So, in the midst of all the action, small boys ran between the fighting actors to retrieve candy. At one point, the drumming and singing got very intense when both Congos and the Devil tried to grab the Queen. Yet, in the end, thanks to the concerted effort of some Congos and the Queen holding up her cross, the players managed to chase the Devil away into the darkness. For the moment, the Congos were again in control, at least until the next *juego* at 5 am, in the square in front of the town church.

Ideally, the Queen would again confront the Diablo Major and subdue him before the Lenten Mass begins at about 6 am (cf Figure 7). But it was not going to happen this morning. A few of the Congos began to gather; members of the chorus arrived, as did a few drummers. They set up next to the church door and began to sing, but the remaining Congos were not there, and neither was the Diablo Major. The Congo named Pajarito (little bird) went up and down adjacent streets, blowing his whistle in an attempt to summon the others. (The Congo named Pajarito functions as a trickster/ messenger). The church bell sounded and townspeople arrived for Lenten Mass. The Congos did not enter the church, but took a break until after mass.

During the mass, Lindsay and I followed a few of the Congos, who were then joined by the Devil. We went up a dark street as Pajarito blew his whistle, and a group of neighborhood boys joined the Congos, who were obviously looking for their brothers. At a certain house, Pajarito went to the front door to knock, as the Devil jumped up onto the front porch, where he discovered a young boy asleep. As the Devil cracked his whip, the young boy jumped up, did a back flip off the porch, and ran down the street, chased by the laughing youth. Then Pajarito and the Devil went up another street to round up more Congos. Finally, the *juego* at the church began as the mass ended, at about 7 in the morning.

Many of the people leaving the church stopped to watch the *juego* as the Congos began to gather and dance. The Queen danced while holding the cross and the Devil and Congos wrestled with each other. There was rough tumbling, but this time on the concrete square in front of the church. Soon Pajarito arrived, blowing his whistle. It was time for the final confrontation, the ultimate taming of the Devil, for this year at least. As the Queen and the Diablo Major danced close to one another, she handed the cross to her assistant. The Queen grabbed the Devil from behind and literally wrestled him to the ground (see Figure 8). She then 'rode' him (sat on top of him) while he struggled to get away. When they rose, she grabbed him again and dragged him over to the drummers. With one strong shove, she fell onto the drummers, never letting go of the Devil. As they crashed into the drums, the singing reached a crescendo. The Congo Queen had subdued the Devil in front of the church, before the official Catholic authority. This *juego* was complete. The Congos, not the church, had driven the Devil away. (But remember, this 'should have' happened just before the mass began.) What remains is the ultimate chase, when the Angels rope in the Diablo Major and his assistants until the next year, as described earlier.

I am reminded of Rara celebrations in Haiti, many aspects of which also resonate with a Central African aesthetic. Rara begins on Lent and continues during Catholicism's most holy week. Its adherents take to the streets, taking them over from official Catholic culture. I see a real parallel in the Congos' *carnaval*. The Congos are in charge of the yearly purification of Portobelo. Through a series of confrontations they cleanse the town of evil; they dance and enact a series of *juegos* to assure the townsfolk that the Congos are in charge and that they will return each year.

During the more relaxed atmosphere of late afternoon on Ash Wednesday, a few interesting events are notable. While I was taking a break at Taller Portobelo, two young boys who were playing Devils also came in to rest and get a drink. They are members of the extended family of Congos associated with the *taller* (or workshop). They left their masks outside and covered their mouth with one hand as they backed in and out the house. One of them was sure to play a Diablo Major eventually. Also, in the early evening the Diablo Major came to pay his respects to the neighborhood. He was followed by a small chorus of women and by children; there were no drummers. As they stopped at each house, they were given some food, drink, and cash. I was able to listen carefully to the singing and picked out one familiar word, *"puya,"* and the refrain *"esa es la puya que no me gusta compay"* (It's the insult that I don't like, brother). A *puya*, I had learned years ago in Cuba, is a verbal assault that can be answered verbally. Relevant to my present concerns is the fact that the word and action of the *puya* recall Central African aesthetics. According to Wyatt MacGaffey, "[puya] refers to a genre of ritualized verbal insults and indirect speech among the Bakongo."[21]

As the Devil came into the Taller Portobelo to greet the owner, another man was sitting around. The Devil and this man jumped up to face each other; after a ritual salute, the Devil left. The visitor without the costume used to play a Devil, and he demonstrated respect in this greeting.

Before and After Thoughts

The Atlantic coast of Panama is not densely populated. There are at least 120 inches of rainfall yearly, and the ground is not very suitable for agriculture. In the 1970s only five percent of Panama's population lived along this coast. The small towns dotting the area mostly contain descendants of slaves and free *cimarrones*, and the isolation of the area has been both physical and economic. Each town has its own Congo tradition. There are even *barrio* areas in Colón that have Congo traditions. Interestingly, one famous such quarter is called Malambo, a distinctly Congo name. In the 1970s, Ronald Smith did fieldwork in Colón, but the smaller communities and their rural traditions have not been documented.[22] More recently, members of a theater group in Panama City, and independent folklorists, have begun to visit the coastal villages. And on 20 March 2001, a cultural committee in Portobelo, with the assistance of Sandra Eleta, organized a 'convention' of Congos from all the coastal towns, in order to establish a Congo cultural union. March 20 is the date of the founding of the town of Portobelo, which was named by Columbus on his fourth and final trip to the Americas. As an important Atlantic port, Portobelo played a major part in

---

[21] MacGaffey, *Religion and Society in Central Africa*, 159. I thank David H. Brown for checking this reference for me.

[22] One of the most important in-depth studies of the Congos of Panama, was accomplished by Ronald Richard Smith, as a doctoral dissertation in folklore and ethnomusicology at Indiana University in 1974–75.

the commerce between Panama City and Spain. The Camino Real, established by the Spanish to provide a land road where slaves were the backbone of commerce, ran from Panama City, on the Pacific, to Portobelo, on the Caribbean Sea. By the mid-1700s, the number of free blacks in Panama numbered around 10,000, while the slave population numbered only c.2,700.[23] The Atlantic coast was (in)famous for its *cimarrón* communities, primarily founded during wars with the Spanish between 1549 and 1582. By the early 1700s,

> free Negroes functioned as scribes and notaries, and they also formed military units which were used for the suppression of pirates, hostile Indians, and even *cimarron* bands, which constantly attacked the Camino Real and the ranches near Panama [City] and Portobelo.[24]

Records from the 1500s cite the names of rebellious *cimarrón* leaders, referred to always as Kings, such as Felipillo or Bayano. The war with Bayano and his followers lasted from c.1553 to 1558, when he was finally captured. But there are reports of *cimarrón* guerrilla warfare well into the late 1500s.

The town of Portobelo was established by 1579, and it grew as a center of economic activity and a center for the importation of slaves to work in the mines of the interior. By the 1600s, there were many independent *cimarrón* settlements around Portobelo, providing a refuge for escaped slaves, ruled by named kings and queens, and apparently existing in relative peace with the nearby mixed-race communities. During the height of economic activity in Portobelo, the *aduana*, or customs house, served as a warehouse for items from Europe, and as an *entrepôt* for the gold and silver mined in Peru. The area also became a major slave port, and subsequently the surrounding dense rainforest became a refuge for runaways. Smith established a list of communities with strong self-identifying Congo traditions in the mid-1970s, and compared this list with the centers of *cimarrón* activity and independent *palenques*, the name given to the communities established by runaway slaves. There is a remarkable correlation between the two. On the Caribbean coast these include Colón, Portobelo, Garrote, Palenque, and Nombre de Dios.

It is noteworthy that the Caribbean coast of Panama is just above the Caribbean coast of Colombia, and the important Afro-Colombian city of Cartagena and the equally important Afro-Barranquilla coastal region. There has

---

[23] Smith, "The Society of Los Congos of Panama," 34.
[24] "The Society of Los Congos of Panama," 35.

been extensive documentation of the rich Congo culture of Atlantic Colombia, where Afro-*cabildos* paraded with kings and queens, followed by an entourage of Congo drummers.[25] There is even a tradition of parading as "fieldworkers," when the Afro-Colombians would darken their skin with "charcoal syrup," much like the Congos of Portobelo today.[26] By the 1770s the Afro-Colombians had developed strong festival traditions on major Catholic holidays, such as *carnaval*. The importance of the Afro-Colombian Congo-based traditions is relevant because it creates a continuity of such culture along a long stretch of the Caribbean coast. These twenty-first-century Congo communities ultimately derive from the coastal *cimarrón* communities. Today the Congos still assert a presence and an authority in ritual matters that resonate with their strong history.

WORKS CITED

Alonso, Ana Maria. "Men in 'Rags' and the Devil on the Throne: A Study of Protest and Inversion in the Carnival of Post-Emancipation Trinidad," in *Carnival in Perspective*, ed. Thomas M. Fiehrer & Michael W. Lodwick (Plantation Society in the Americas; New Orleans: U of New Orleans, 1990): 73–120.

Anderson, Benedict. *Imagined Communities: Reflections on the Origin and Spread of Nationalism* (London: Verso, rev. ed. 1991).

Bettelheim, Judith. "Costume Types and Festival Elements in Caribbean Celebrations," *ACIJ Research Review* 4 (Kingston: African Caribbean Institute of Jamaica, 1999): 1–46.

——. "Ethnicity, Gender and Power in Carnaval in Santiago de Cuba," in *Negotiating Performance in Latin/o America*, ed. Diana Taylor & Juan Villegas (Durham NC & London: Duke UP, 1994): 176–212.

——. "Palo Monte Mayombe and Its Influence on Cuban Contemporary Art," *African Arts* 34.2 (2001): 36–49, 95–96.

——, ed. *Cuban Festivals: A Century of Afro-Cuban Culture* (Kingston, Jamaica & London: Ian Randle, 2001).

——, ed. *Cuban Festivals: An Illustrated Anthology* (New York & London: Garland, 1993).

Bilby, Kenneth M., & Kia Bunseki Fu-Kiau. *Kumina: A Kongo-Based Tradition in the New World* (Cahiers du CEDAF 8.4, 1983).

Carámbula, Rubén. *El Candombe* (Buenos Aires: Ediciones del Sol, 1995).

Friedemann, Nina de. *Carnaval en Barranquilla* (Bogotá: La Rosa, 1985).

---

[25] See Nina de Friedemann, *Carnaval en Barranquilla* (Bogotá: La Rosa, 1985), and Nina de Friedemann & Richard Cross, *Ma Ngombe: Guerreros y Granaderos en Palenque* (Bogotá: Carlos Valencia Editores, 1979).

[26] See note 19 above.

——, & Richard Cross. *Ma Ngombe: Guerreros y Granaderos en Palenque* (Bogotá: Carlos Valencia Editores, 1979).

Goodman, Walter. *The Pearl of the Antilles, or An Artist in Cuba* (London: Henry S. King, 1873).

Heywood, Linda M. "The Angolan–Afro-Brazilian Cultural Connections," *Slavery & Abolition* 22 (1999): 9–23.

Kiddy, Elizabeth. "Who is the King of Congo? A New Look at African and African-Brazilian Kings in Brazil" (unpublished paper, 1999).

Kinser, Samuel. *Carnival, American Style: Mardi Gras at New Orleans and Mobile* (Chicago: U of Chicago P, 1990).

Kubik, Gerhard. "Transplantation of African Musical Cultures into the New World," in *Slavery in the Americas*, ed. Wolfgang Binder (Würzburg: Königshausen & Neuman, 1993): 421–52.

MacGaffey, Wyatt. *Religion and Society in Central Africa: The Bakongo of Lower Zaire* (Chicago: U of Chicago P, 1986).

——, & Michael Harris. *Astonishment & Power* (Washington DC: Smithsonian Institution P, 1993).

Ryman, Cheryl. "Kumina: Stability and Change," *ACIJ Review* 1 (Kingston: The African Caribbean Institute of Jamaica, 1984): 81–90.

Schuler, Monica. *"Alas, Alas Kongo": A Social History of Indentured Immigration into Jamaica, 1841–1865* (Baltimore MD: Johns Hopkins UP, 1980).

Scott, James C. *Domination and the Arts of Resistance: Hidden Transcripts* (New Haven CT: Yale UP, 1990).

Smith, Ronald R. "Arroz Colorado: Los Congos of Panama," in *Music and Black Ethnicity: The Caribbean and South America*, ed. Gerard H. Béhague (New Brunswick NJ: Transaction Publishers, 1994): 239–66.

——. "The Society of Los Congos of Panama: An Ethnomusicological Study of the Music and Dance Theater of an Afro-Panamanian Group" (unpublished doctoral dissertation, Bloomington: Indiana University, 1976).

Thompson, Robert Farris. *Face of the Gods: Art and Altars of Africa and the African Americas* (New York: The Museum for African Arts, 1993).

Thornton, John K. *Africa and Africans in the Making of the Atlantic World, 1400–1680* (1992; Cambridge & New York: Cambridge UP, 1998).

——. "The Regalia of the Kingdom of Kongo: 1491–1895," in *Kings of Africa: Art and Authority in Central Africa*, ed. Erna Beumers & Hans–Joachim (Utrecht: Foundation of Kings of Africa, 1992): 57–63.

❖

FIGURE 1. Youth taunting Devil with whip

FIGURE **2**. Devil accosting spectators

FIGURE 3. Congo female singers and drummer

FIGURE 4. Group of Angels

FIGURE 5. Congo youth in typical garb and decoration

FIGURE 6. Congo Queen with her wooden cross

FIGURE 7. Woman confronts the Devil with his whip

FIGURE 8. Congo Queen wrestling Devil to the ground

❖   POSTSCRIPT

The Middle Passage
A Visual Narrative

TOM FEELINGS

I T WAS A COOL FALL NIGHT in 1969. I came out of the NYC subway headed for a midtown New York University and its brand-new art gallery. The invitation said, "for the showcase of new Black and other minority group talents." The opening show was featuring a prominent young black artist whose recent works were accepted by one of America's leading museums. I hadn't heard of the artist before, but this wasn't unusual. I had been living in Africa for two years, and in that time it seemed as if a new Black Renaissance in Art – reminiscent of the Harlem 1930s – had taken place.

What really whet my appetite, besides the fact that the artist was young and came out of my old neighborhood of Bedford–Stuyvesant, Brooklyn, was that the paintings on exhibit portrayed the Middle Passage. What could hold more challenging an undertaking both visually and spiritually for a black artist than the horrific crossing of the Atlantic ocean by Africans, stolen from their homes by the European slave traders, our ancestors forcibly packed into slave ships and chained together like animals through-out the long voyage from Africa to the Americas? Millions dying from the awful conditions on board. These scenes flashed through my mind as I walked quickly up the stairs into the gallery.

The first painting I saw was done on light-blue plexiglass plastic – a modern-day product. The choice of material didn't bother me, however, for any material can be redefined and given new tasks and powers. But the figures of the captured Africans were all done in flat gray paint in silhou-ette, with thin black lines suggesting veins and muscles, showing through the skin on the surface like a diagram in an anatomy textbook. I moved slowly from painting to painting trying to understand what the artist was saying to me. Was he saying that this experience was a cold inhuman one, and had he chosen materials and colors to reflect this? Then I came to a painting of a backview cross-section of a slave ship divided into two halves. Enslaved Africans were seated, bent over and chained to each other on one side; and, on the other, like a mirror image, were white men, painted in flat white paint and chained in exactly the same way. At once I could understand the intellectual point the artist was making: that slavery had psychologically enslaved both sides, both groups. But emotionally it left me cold. The painting was cold, sterile. How clean the experience of the Middle Passage looked, how ghostly gray and abstract the black people appeared!

I had expected to be forced emotionally back through time to the horrible Middle Passage, to feel myself packed, below filthy decks, stifled in foul air, feces, urine, and vomit. But for me these paintings seemed more like intellectual exercises in technique, style, and form. The words of the Harlem Renaissance painter Aaron Douglas flashed through my mind: "Technique in itself is not enough. It is more important for the artist to develop the power to convey emotion. [...] The artist's technique, no matter how brilliant it is, should never obscure his vision."

And yet white and black people were standing before these paintings, leisurely drinking champagne; some actually making comments about the "universal quality" of this show. It just depressed me. For me, paintings of the Middle Passage should make you run screaming from its inhumanity, or draw you closer to the human beings who suffered this particular agony. They must make you feel something extreme. But was I being too critical? Expecting the artist to share my way of thinking because we were both black and came out of the same neighborhood? I did respect the artist for taking on such a monumentally difficult subject. But as I rode back home to Brooklyn, I was aware of being terribly disappointed. Powerful artwork by any artist, but especially a black artist, always fired me up, encouraged me to do better work, showed me the possibilities of even going beyond myself. What could have made those paintings a deeper emotional and more meaningful experience for his most important audience, his black viewers? And how much is one willing to give up towards that end?

Since I returned to America and started illustrating books for black children, I had been reluctant to deal with the most painful side of the black experience. I wanted to concentrate on the joy in our lives, especially for the children who were daily bombarded with negative images of Africa and its people. I wanted to share those positive experiences that I had living in Ghana, and felt it was important to concentrate on life-affirming themes. But a year earlier I had illustrated Julius Lester's *To Be a Slave*, a story right from the mouths of the people who lived through slavery. Working on those images with a short deadline took me many times right to the edge. I felt I had done a good job. I still felt, however, I had much more to say. Remembering the pain it caused me, though, I didn't exactly yearn for that experience again. I kept asking myself, was it possible for anyone to tell this complete story of the Middle Passage in a way that would illuminate and re-define blackness and de-center whiteness at the same time? Hadn't my life, right up to that point, taught me the need for balance, to reflect this sometimes in the same artwork, both pain and joy, that bittersweet duality? Didn't my African experience show me that those two major elements of our lives never just sit side by side, that they interact and build on each other? This is expressed so clearly in our music, especially the blues. The sorrow and pain have always been tempered by the strength of black people and our joy tempered by the pain.

Lynn Ward, a book illustrator, points out in his autobiography that pictorial narrative art has a long history that includes visual sequences in many media – from wall decorations in ancient Egyptian tombs to contemporary comic strips. When some text was also involved, this type of media was called "illustration." But when communication is happening entirely in visual terms and can be fully understood without any words or text, it may no longer be seen as illustration, but perhaps moves into the realm of illumination.

The first books that children 'read', even when they can't actually read, are picture books. Even when they have some limited reading ability, they still take in the images. They listen to an adult reading and start to repeat their words. But they read those images first. Thus picture books for the very young are primarily known for introducing them to the wonders and joys of life, including the world of fantasy. In general they are supposed to be life-affirming and optimistic. But narrative art, in the functional form of a picture book, can both stimulate the imagination in a creative way and stretch the mind and spirit with the hard truths of the past.

The illustrated book can show both the young and the old that history is more than facts, and illustration more than decoration. Narrative art can fill that gap between the seductive desire just to be entertained and the un-conscious hunger for knowledge; it can transform painful historical truths into a powerful visual narrative; it can take a humiliating experience and make a creative one out of it. In many ways, the lack of knowledge and of memory is responsible for much of the conflict, confusion, denial and pain now felt today, especially on the touchy subject of America's original sin, slavery and the horrific Middle Passage.

The Brooklyn artist whose work I was seeing was about twenty. What was I doing at twenty? How much did I understand then? My mind started racing back over the years: What were all the experiences I had in those thirty-seven years that had brought me to my present conclusions about life and art? What had I seen, done, felt, learned, that helped me be surer of what I had to struggle for as a black person? Yet still I asked myself: am I a graphic artist, a storyteller, an illustrator? Were these questions still there because I was not sure that, in my art, I could show that right balance of beauty and ugliness? Was I avoiding the emotional risk of failure? Above all, was it that I feared stepping back into the most agonizing experience for any black person to confront? Was I feeling deep down that not only could it totally overwhelm my life and drive me crazy, but that it might even kill me? Yet I knew I had to do it.

As a storyteller in visual form who tries to reflect and interpret black life as I see and feel it, and as an African born in America, I can bring to my work a quality which is rooted in the culture of Africa and expanded by the experience of being black in America. Storytelling is an ancient African tradition where the values and history of a people are passed on to the young verbally. To me, illustrated children's books are a natural extension of this African oral tradition. I consider myself to be a functional artist. I use my skills of drawing and painting to tell a story, and the story, our story, is the most important element.

In the *Middle Passage*, I've tried to innovate within a restrictive form, to open up a physically small frame of reference – the form of a children's picture book past its actual size. I am trying to arrest, captivate, and expand the viewer's senses with dynamic compositions, combining realism, abstract design and social content, passionately expressed. I wanted the whole picture to feel large, panoramic, huge, so that you could see that this affected millions of Africans as it did, in order to focus on the personality of that group. But I also wanted it to feel close, intimate, on a personal level, so that you could not distance yourself from it, although it happened centuries ago.

I believe my living in Africa gave me a sense of my own importance as an artist, with respect to the power of the image, to reach into the psyche of the people and provide an instrument for healing. No matter how debasing the situations depicted in this journey, I tried to show a sense of dignity about the bodies of my ancestors, many times using photos of dancers as reference material (not as an evasion of the pain, but as a reflection of Africa's celebratory dance consciousness, our rites of rhythm). Still, I could not pass over, under, or go around the trip; I had to go through it in order to take you (the reader) with me.

Elizabeth Bowen, a writer, has said that two things are terrible in childhood: helplessness (being in other people's power) and perceived apprehensiveness – the apprehension that something is being concealed from us because it is too bad to be told and the feeling of being lied to about the past.

Books can be wonderful tools for enlightenment because through them we are capable of reaching and intensifying children's perceptions of reality and can stimulate their imaginations in a creative way. With this form we can stretch their minds and strengthen their spirit by telling them the truth of the past, therefore preparing them to face reality, reject the shallow and the slick. This book of mine, the *Middle Passage*, or a book like it, should have been available for every white child right after the first slave ship docked into the so-called New World harbor, centuries ago. Of course that wasn't possible for many obvious reasons, but if most Americans today had seen this kind of book as a child, they would clearly understand that there is a sin at the core of this country's culture. Only by giving into that sorrowful, painful truth can we start to grieve for all our ancestors, grieve for those who made it across those treacherous waters, grieve for those who didn't, and grieve for those who enslaved them. Because even while celebrating the survival strength of my African ancestors, I realize that only by grieving first can the Europeans release that pain that holds them and their children's future hostage to the lie – to a history, a reality, that has been distorted, hidden, ignored, and denied.

I will continue reaching back into the past, involving myself in the process of retrieving and re-creating our values and images even while I live in the midst of our difficult society. I still celebrate the joys of innocence, but I choose to try in my art to do justice to the complex and the convoluted experience. I am still optimistic. I still believe in the ability of human beings – especially of children – to change the wrongs to right.

Our writers and artists must continue to reach back into our past, involving themselves in the process of retrieving and re-creating, even amidst confusion and pain. I feel that maybe we are going through a series of stages, moving towards a greater level of understanding of our larger selves. And all these current agonizing experiences are labor pains, forcing us to see and seek concrete connections with the larger African community. Collectivity is our strength, and whether you call it pan-Africanism (as in my youth) or afrocentricity today, it is still striving towards an African world-view, seeing the world first through our own eyes. The Middle Passage is the one thing, consciously or unconsciously, that Africans all over this world share through race memory. If this painful experience, this part of our history, can constantly be told in such a way that those chains of the past, those shackles that physically bound us together against our wills, could in the re-telling be spiritual links that willingly bind us together now and into the future, then slavery's Middle Passage can, ironically, become a positive connecting line to all of us, whether living inside or outside of the continent of Africa.

I now realize how important Toni Morrison's words have become to me:

> There is so much to remember and to describe for purposes of exercising and purposes of exorcising and purposes of celebrating sites of passage. Things must be made – some fixing ceremony, some memorial, some altar – somewhere where these things can be released, thought, and felt. But the consequences of slavery, only artists can deal with – and it's our job.

For me, that "altar" was the Middle Passage.

❖ APPENDIX

The Power and Place of Black Diasporan Autobiography

An Annotated Bibliography of Autobiographies

PHYLLIS B. BISCHOF

T HE OCCASION OF THE PARIS CONFERENCE on "African
 Diasporas" caused me to reflect on our lack of a bibliography of
 contemporary life-writings by black diasporan authors. The power
and place of autobiographies in black literature are self-evident, and the
need for a bibliography of such works is compelling. Diasporan autobiographies not only illuminate individual lives but also bring to life the
experience of entire peoples and of historical periods. This Appendix discusses several key examples of autobiographies of the black diaspora, both
individual and collective, and it also addresses the difficulty of identifying
and separating out primary from secondary sources in biographical writing.
The essay is followed by an annotated bibliography of selected autobiographies from many countries and regions presented geographically: African
Americans Abroad, Africans in the USA, the Caribbean, China, France,
Germany, Latin America, the Soviet Union, the United Kingdom, and
finally International Travel. Authors of these autobiographies are musicians,
students, statesmen, journalists, prisoners, educators, asylum seekers, noted
authors, and working-class women.

Slave narratives and political autobiographies and the changes they have
helped bring about illustrate the centrality of autobiographical writing in
black life and literature. Slave narratives, among early black autobiographies, clearly fueled the antislavery movement. They provided first-hand
information about the effect of slavery on the lives of individuals who suffered its cruel injustice, and thereby hastened its end. The ubiquitousness of

racism has often served as an impetus for political autobiography. The effect of racism is to mark the black experience so profoundly by the political that virtually no aspect of life remains beyond its scope; indeed, in periods of rank injustice the political touches on essentially all aspects of life. Political autobiography is one avenue, one weapon, to bring about change.

As slave narratives dominated mid-nineteenth-century writing by blacks, political autobiography was central to black American literature during a later period of liberation, the 1960s and 1970s. C.W.E. Bigsby points out how potent autobiographies – *The Autobiography of Malcolm X* (1965), Eldridge Cleaver's *Soul on Ice* (1968), Claude Brown's *Manchild in the Promised Land* (1965), and *Angela Davis: An Autobiography* (1974) – written by activists committed to changing not only their own community, but indeed all of American society documented injustices and gave voice to the black power and civil rights movements.[1]

Several works of collective autobiography lie at the heart of the contemporary diasporan experience. Two seminal works published in what might seem unlikely venues, Germany and Jamaica, illustrate the far reach of the black diaspora. Berlin, Germany, was the site of the 1986 publication of *Farbe bekennen: Afro-deutsche Frauen auf den Spuren ihrer Geschichte*, later published in English in 1992 as *Showing Our Colors: Afro-German Women Speak Out*. This work essentially liberated the thousands of mixed-race men and women born in Germany after World War II when black American soldiers met German women, producing at least 3,093 highly visible mixed-race children. *Farbe Bekennen* and other books which followed have helped to form positive identities for members of a minority who were frequently subjected to harsh discrimination. Their autobiographies helped these people to call themselves by a new name, Afro-Germans, as opposed to the old names, *Neger, Farbige, Mischlinge, Mulatten, Bimbos*, etc. by which they had been called. This remarkable book helped Afro-Germans to learn their history and to find and to establish solidarity with each other. Audre Lorde declared in her foreword:

> We are the hyphenated people of the Diaspora whose self-defined identities are no longer shameful secrets in the countries of our origin, but rather declarations of strength and solidarity. We are an increasingly united front from which the world has not yet heard.[2]

---

[1] C.W.E. Bigsby, "The Public Self: The Black Autobiography," *LiLi: Zeitschrift fur Literaturwissenschaft und Linguistik*, Jhrg 9, Nr. 35 (1979): 28.

[2] Audre Lorde, Foreword to *Showing Our Colors: Afro-German Women Speak Out*, tr. Anne V. Adams, ed. Katharina Oguntoye, May Opitz & Dagmar Schultz (Amherst: U of Massachusetts P, 1992): viii.

Lorde helped the editors to create the term "Afro-German," borrowing from the term Afro-American.[3]

In 1986, the same year *Farbe Bekennen* appeared, Die Initiative Schwarze Deutsche, the Initiative of Black Germans [ISD], the first national organization of black Germans, was established by Afro- and Asian Germans. By 1992, chapters of this association met annually in over ten German cities.[4] In addition, the ISD issued two quarterly publications, *Afro Look* and *Afrekete*.

> The primary purpose of ISD is to strengthen the self-esteem of its individual members and to assert the rights of Blacks in German society, but it also aims to develop contacts with Black movements in other countries.[5]

These Afro-German writings are emblematic of twentieth-century diasporan autobiographies, in that they flourish and empower. They have helped to establish a community of individuals who, though visible singly, had been for the most part denied an understanding of a common past until this writing made entirely clear its existence, its claims, and the beauty of its strength in the face of adversity.

The timing of the publication of *Farbe Bekennen* was surely related to the Civil Rights Movement of 1960s America and to the French student revolts of 1968. Dagmar Schultz, a white German woman who spent time in the USA during the 1960s and early 1970s and one of the three editors, was a moving force in the publication of *Farbe Bekennen*.[6] Although the book addresses the lives of persons born in Germany and not those born abroad, certainly the community and awareness that the book engendered have caused foreign students and others, including asylum seekers, to enter into dialogue with Afro-Germans.

The bibliography which follows this essay includes a number of autobiographies by black Germans, including Hans J. Massaquoi's *Neger, Neger, Schornsteinfeger!* This highly popular full-length memoir appeared in Germany in 1999, and in the USA as *Destined to Witness: Growing up Black in Nazi Germany*. In December 1999 the title was among the top ten bestsellers in Germany; I myself saw it prominently featured by bookstores in Bremen in May and in July of 2000. The German title conveys far more of the young Massaquoi's suffering during his first twelve years in Hamburg than

---

[3] Lorde, Foreword to *Showing Our Colors*, xxii.
[4] Foreword to *Showing Our Colors*, xvi.
[5] Foreword to *Showing Our Colors*, xv.
[6] Foreword to *Showing Our Colors*, xxiii.

does the relatively bland English-language title. The book chronicles the life
of a child born to a Liberian diplomat's son and a German nurse, and is
among the first accounts of a mixed-race child's youth in Germany during
the Nazi era. His parents never married; his father returned to Africa, while
his mother remained his best friend and staunchest defense against the
dangers and evils of the times of his youth. Later Massaquoi traveled to
Liberia to become acquainted with his father, and ultimately moved to the
USA, where he became a Managing Editor of *Ebony* magazine. This book
is a pageturner which provides remarkable documentation of one man's
triumph over one of history's most racist eras.

Coincidentally, another work of collective biography, in this case telling
the stories of fifteen Jamaican women, also appeared in 1986. The Women's
Press in London published *Lionheart Gal: Life Stories of Jamaican Women*,
a work in mixed Patwah (Jamaican creole) and English. In a program sponsored by Michael Manley's government in 1977 to alleviate unemployment,
the editor, Honor Ford–Smith, brought together a group of working-class
women, who formed Sistren, a theatre collective. From these women have
come plays, *Sistren* (a periodical), and these stories, which grew out of a
project to document the work of the collective. Because Sistren's work is
perceived by some to be radical, the collective has faced societal opposition
as well as censorship by local media, and thus the editor protected the
anonymity of the fifteen authors. These stories were first done as interviews, then reviewed and edited by the group. Themes include male–female
relationships, "migration pulling like a magnet, female unemployment or
under-employment, the failure of the educational system, rapid urban indus-
trialisation, inadequate housing, violence [...], the failure of present political
structures."[7] This book, among the most heavily circulated titles in the University of California Library, shows the use of autobiography in working
toward solutions to the problems these life stories address. *Lionheart Gal* is
like *Farbe Bekennen,* in that it has created an important niche in twentieth-
century Jamaican women's history, and it gives voice to previously hidden
stories, empowering narrators and readers alike.

Margaret Wilkerson, Professor of Theatre Arts at the University of California at Berkeley, emphasizes the importance of a more intensive study of
the lives of people of color:

> We will not, I now believe, have a comprehensive understanding of the
> history of the USA, of the history of peoples of color, or of artistic

---

[7] Sistren [Collective], with Honor Ford–Smith. *Lionheart Gal: Life Stories of
Jamaican Women* (London: Women's Press, 1986): xvi.

institutions such as theatre, until we have more biographical work done on people of color, especially women of color. The story of individual lives is a critical component precedent to any serious exploration of differences and affirmation of connections.[8]

Gerhard Grohs would concur:

for all studies which are interested in the change of attitudes within social groups under the influence of cultural change and especially in the succession of different generations, autobiographies should be used not only as supplementary sources but as independent sources of interpretation.[9]

Rebecca Stuhr–Rommereim writes of a doubling of autobiographies published by Americans of color in the years 1985–1995.[10] This trend also occurs in the production of autobiography around the world. Two major English-language journals are devoted to autobiographical and biographical studies. *Biography: An Interdisciplinary Quarterly*, published since 1978, was joined in 1986 by *a/b: auto-biography studies*, sponsored by the Autobiography Society. Both carry articles devoted to the theoretical, cultural, and historical study of all forms of life-writing, and also publish special issues on such topics as cross-cultural or intercultural life-writing. The summer 1999 issue of *a/b* reviewed *the First International Conference on Auto/ Biography: Approaching the Auto/Biographical Turn, held in Beijing, China. 21–24 June 1999*. The convening of the Beijing conference is another marker of increased international attention to the genre.

James Olney has written extensively on autobiography, offering thoughtful analyses of the genre. In *Tell Me Africa*, he defines the African autobiography – "(how an individual or a group live, as recorded from within), [...] the most direct narrative enactment and immediate manifestation of the ways, the motives, and the beliefs of a culture foreign to the reader."[11]

---

[8] Margaret B. Wilkerson, "Excavating Our History: The Importance of Biographies of Women of Color," *Black American Literature Forum* 24.1 (Spring 1990): 73.

[9] Gerhard Grohs, "Changing Social Functions of African Autobiographies with Special Reference to Political Autobiographies," in *Autobiographical Genres in Africa: Papers presented at the 6th International Janheinz Jahn Symposium: (Mainz–Bayreuth 1992)*, ed. Janos Reisz & Ulla Schild (Mainzer Afrika-Studien 10; Berlin: Dietrich Reimer, 1996): 202.

[10] Rebecca Stuhr–Rommereim, *Autobiographies by Americans of Color 1980-1994: An Annotated Bibliography* (Troy NY: Whitston, 1997): 1.

[11] James Olney, *Tell Me Africa: An Approach to African Literature* (Princeton NJ: Princeton UP, 1973): 6.

> Autobiography offers, I think, a uniquely clear and persuasive testimony about African life that comes from the very heart of African experience, from the central consciousness that participates in and registers the experience.[12]

Olney stresses that autobiography offers an ideal opportunity for those outside a particular culture to learn about it. An African autobiographer

> looks with African eyes and records and analyses with an African mind; this gives the account an interior integrity that one can never hope for or expect in the alien, if sometimes sympathetic, view of a non-African Being himself the center and seismograph of the experience he records.[13]

Olney discusses at considerable length the features that distinguish African life, hence African life-writing, from other world-views, most particularly the Western. He makes clear the African concept of the unity of all life, the unbroken circular connections between the unborn, the living, and the dead. This view results in a grounded sense of self and of the world, a certainty of perception which Olney describes as

> less a belief than a certainty: human life, here and now, lived in the present moment and on a known, very precise piece of land, is the summary and the necessary conclusion of family and ancestral experience, the climax of all history, the focus of all spiritual being, both human and extra-human. This certainty determines the shape of autobiography and the mode of fiction from Africa as surely as it decides the nature of African politics, education, economics, and religion.[14]

Olney's reflections summarize insights which may help in understanding the meaning of the life stories discussed in this essay. Next we shall turn to another category of first-hand diasporan accounts, travel writing.

Travel writing is an important type of autobiographical writing; the number of such volumes published and interest in reading them have burgeoned in recent years. For far too long, the masses of Africans and their fellows abroad found neither travel nor emigration, nor living abroad, easy options. Today, however, improved economic status for some combines with such imperatives as war in the Horn of Africa, Liberia or Sierra Leone, genocide in Rwanda, desertification and climate change in other locales to

---

[12] Olney, *Tell Me Africa*, 7–8.

[13] *Tell Me Africa*, 10.

[14] Olney, *Tell Me Africa*, 56.

encourage or even mandate African peoples to move elsewhere. These conditions have created massive transfers of populations, and it is my belief that no power on earth will hold back the peoples whose destinies call for transborder migration. If W.E.B. Du Bois, (or "Web Du Bois," as a student charmingly named him when he asked a question about him at the Berkeley Library's Reference Desk) were alive today, I suspect he might say that the problem of the twenty-first century will be large-scale transborder movements of Southern Hemisphere peoples. These movements have been and will continue to be documented in autobiographical writings. In fact, I suggest that travel and/or longer-term changes in one's country of residence enhance the need and desire to record one's life experiences. Perhaps the increasing mobility of populations we see at present is in part responsible for a significant increase in the production of life-writing.

A frontpage *New York Times* article by Norimitsu Onishi describes the fiercely intense pressures to migrate experienced by today's West Africans. Yusuf Marwan, a twenty-seven-year-old Ghanaian migrant, describes in the following words his plight while traveling to Libya over a dangerous Saharan route: "We are like running water [...] We know our source, but we don't know where we are running to."[15] The story of Africans on the move, creating new lives in new lands, will continue to be revealed in poignant statements like Mr Marwan's and in autobiographical writings such as Ezekiel Mphahlele's *Afrika My Music*, in which he comments: "You got to know that the immigrant's journey is a long, long road, a heavy road."[16]

The editors of a fine collection of travel writing, *A Stranger in the Village: Two Centuries of African-American Travel Writing,*, comment: "Much of the black experience in the New World is characterized by migration, mobility, and travel."[17] From this work one can glean incomparably revealing observations made by writers such as Langston Hughes on his Russian trip in the 1930s. Hughes became friendly with Russian train workers, learning to his surprise that two-man crews on long trips were provided with a compartment in each coach with berths in which to rest, change clothes, etc., while "Negro porters on American trains have no such conveniences. [...] In the USA. a single man takes care of a car, working

---

[15] Norimitsu Onishi, "Out of Africa or Bust, With a Desert to Cross," *New York Times* (4 January 2001): A12.

[16] Ezekiel Mphahlele, *Afrika My Music: An Autobiography, 1957–1983* (Johannesburg: Ravan, 1984): 21.

[17] Farah J. Griffin & Cheryl J. Fish, ed. *A Stranger in the Village: Two Centuries of African-American Travel Writing* (Boston MA: Beacon, 1998): xiii.

throughout a long trip, and perhaps managing to catch a little sleep on the bench in the men's toilet."[18]

A very similar work, published in the same year, is *Always Elsewhere: Travels of the Black Atlantic*, edited by Alasdair Pettinger. It includes some of the same content – for example, Gwendolyn Brooks' pungent essay "African Fragment," on her trip to Kenya, although the coverage of *Always Elsewhere* is far wider, including material by Africans and West Indians as well as African-American travellers. Another difference is that *Always Elsewhere* reaches back to a number of writers of the eighteenth century, including material as early as 1768.

In this bibliographic project, I plan to collect and improve access to twentieth-century autobiographies by black authors living in Western Europe, the Caribbean, and elsewhere. Two exclusions will be autobiographies with their chief focus on life either in Africa or in the USA. The latter are already reasonably well covered, while persons living solely in Africa do not reflect diasporic movement out from the center. Thus, omitted will be books like Bloke Modisane's *Blame Me On History*, which focusses on his life in South Africa's Sophiatown at the time of its destruction by the apartheid regime and brings the author's life up to the point of his illegal departure for Bechuanaland. Included will be works such as Philippe Wamba's *Kinship*, the life story of a son whose father is Congolese and mother African-American, and who grew up in the USA. I do not include the life stories of African Americans who published autobiographies covering their lives abroad before 1984 which are included in Brignano's work cited below. I do, however, provide references to earlier titles not identified by Brignano, eg, *Bricktop*, a 1983 title, and also to autobiographies of black Americans who lived or traveled abroad subsequent to 1984, eg, the well-known jazz musician Bill Coleman's *Trumpet Story* (1991), which discusses his life in France and elsewhere. James Haskins, Bricktop's collaborator, conveys something of the power and place of autobiography in black life when he writes that in the small Alabama town where he grew up

> Negroes who had made it were a common topic of discussion [...] it was a peculiar fact of existence for the average American black to be on intimate terms with the stories of those few of us who had managed to burrow out from under. The grownups talked about Josephine Baker, Ralph Bunche [...] and Bricktop as familiarly as they talked about Cousin Eliza and Aunt Cindy.[19]

---

[18] Langston Hughes, "Soviet Russia and the Negro" (1923), from *The Crisis*, in Griffin & Fish, ed. *A Stranger in the Village*, 219.

[19] James Haskins, *Bricktop* (New York: Atheneum, 1983): xii.

A model for my project is Russell Brignano's *Black Americans in Auto-biography*. This bibliography facilitates access to 710 primary sources which – without this guide – would be far more difficult to identify. Why so? The difficulty in their identification stems from the cataloguing practice of American libraries, which has been to classify under the subject-heading "Biography" both autobiographies and biographies, even though the two genres are quite different literary forms. I discovered in working on this essay that sorting out which entries under the heading "Biography" are autobiographies, hence primary sources, and which are secondary can be far more time-consuming than one would wish.

I will, like Brignano, consider as autobiographical books not only those formally designated as autobiographies, but also "diaries, travelogues, col-lections of letters, collections of essays, and narrations of events in relatively brief periods of time, all of which address some phases of the authors' lives."[20] In addition to these, I shall also include interviews, an example of which is Françoise Pfaff's *Conversations with Maryse Condé* (1996). Reading this fascinating collection of informal interviews conducted over a number of years allows one to understand many aspects of Condé's uniquely diasporan life. Born on the island of Guadeloupe, she has lived and worked in the Caribbean, in many West African countries during the important years of their early independence, in London, where she worked for the BBC, in Paris, and in many cities of the USA. In these interviews, she shares insights and information concerning her research and writing, her personal life, and her teaching.

A particularly useful aspect of the Brignano bibliography is a section called "Index of activities, experiences, occupations, and professions." Worth noting with respect to this index is the wide range of occupations covered and its inclusion of headings for certain behaviors and varied ex-periences, both positive and negative. He includes prison experiences, for example, a category all too familiar among diasporan populations. In the years covered, 1789–1982, Brignano identified ninety-four works describing foreign travel experiences and only seventeen for US travel. Like Brignano, I will not include autobiographical novels. Although these fictions offer a rich vein of material for scholarly exploration, they are beyond the scope of this bibliography. Not well covered bibliographically, the novels need separate attention.

---

[20] Russell Brignano, *Black Americans in Autobiography: An Annotated Biblio-graphy of Autobiographies and Autobiographical Books Written since the Civil War* (Durham NC: Duke UP, 1984): Preface.

Creation of the proposed bibliography, accompanied by a similarly detailed index, will significantly enhance scholarly access to diasporan autobiographies. Unlike Brignano, I do not plan to include holdings information.
Since 1984 the ready availability of online union catalogs like WorldCat or
the Research Libraries Information Network [RLIN] catalogs, which provide instant information internationally on library holdings, renders obsolete
the need to do so.

Tyler Stovall, in his compelling study *Paris Noir*, has masterfully interwoven autobiographical testimony into his historical text. This book mar-
velously captures the black experience in this city, beginning with World
War I, when some 200,000 black American servicemen made their way to
Europe. Stovall brings his account of expatriate blacks in Paris up through
the 1990s, when he estimates their number to be about a thousand. The
experience of France not only changed forever the lives of 200,000 servicemen; it also broadened the perspective of their fellow black Americans as
returning soldiers shared stories of their time in a freer society. Stovall's
bibliography led me to a number of the works included in this diasporan
bibliography.

When Toni Morrison spoke at Berkeley in 1987 regarding her work as an
editor at Random House, she spoke of the necessity she finds "to enter the
text," a beautifully expressive phrase for what I suspect most writers would
like to see happen when editors touch their text. In the course of historical
and cultural research, students and scholars often want to enter the lives of
persons in the places and periods they study. This bibliography of autobiographies of the black diaspora will help others to enter the lives of far-
flung diasporan peoples. It is my hope that it will help to illuminate issues
of race relations, of migration, and of diasporan studies generally.

A working *Bibliography of Autobiographies* follows, the first stage of a
project which I expect to complete over time. In fact, I told my son that I
had found the project on which I would happily work for the rest of my life.
His response was that he hoped it would not be published posthumously! In
any case, what follows is the first stage of a bibliography in which I plan to
annotate those entries not yet read and to add a great many more entries.

African Americans Abroad

Bricktop (1894–), with James Haskins. *Bricktop* (New York: Atheneum, 1983). xviii, 300 pp.

In Bricktop's Chicago girlhood, her mother raised her strictly. She could barely wait to be old enough to become a vaudeville and saloon singer, in both of which activities she excelled. In 1911 she worked for Jack Johnson in his elegant, integrated saloon, before moving on to Harlem in the early 1920s. In 1924 at age twenty-nine she took Paris by storm, becoming the darling of café society including Cole Porter, Elsa Maxwell and F. Scott Fitzgerald. She was at the center when "the whole city was like a great big celebration" (94). In 1939 she fled France as the Germans threatened Paris, returning to New York, where she was unable to live successfully. In Mexico City she opened a club, remaining in that city until 1949. She later opened a club in Rome, living in Italy until the mid-1960s. While attaining celebrity herself, she remained refreshingly her own person. She shares her adventurous spirit in her choice of words in dedicating this book "to the world in general," and in her prefatory quotation "To heck with yesterday! What are we gonna do tomorrow?" (vii).

Coleman, Bill. *Trumpet Story* (Paris: Éditions Cana, 1981). Tr. as *Trumpet Story* (Boston MA: Northeastern UP, 1990). 259 pp.

Immensely detailed memories of a fifty-year career as a jazz musician. Coleman grew up in Ohio, where he taught himself to play trumpet. Before moving to New York in 1927, he played with many bands in cities around the USA. In 1933 he joined a band in Paris, and was later invited to play in India and Egypt. He returned to the USA in 1940, where he remained during World War II, after which he toured the Philippines and Japan for the USO. In 1948 he returned to Europe, where he remained. In 1953 he married Lily, a Swiss woman, the love of his life.

Griffin, Farah J., & Cheryl J. Fish, ed. *A Stranger in the Village: Two Centuries of African-American Travel Writing* (Boston MA: Beacon, 1998). xvii, 366 pp.

Forty-seven entries for the nineteenth and twentieth centuries, excerpted from larger works. Organized by theme – Adventurers; Missionaries and Activists of the Nineteenth Century; Truth Seekers, Statesmen, Scholars and

Journalists (from 1930 to the Civil Rights Era); Visitors, Tourists, and "Others" – and by Geography: Africa, France, Russia. Many, though not all, of the writers are well-known, eg, James Baldwin, June Jordan, Katherine Dunham, Edward Wilmot Blyden, Mary Seacole.

Pettinger, Alasdair, ed. *Always Elsewhere: Travels of the Black Atlantic* (London & New York: Cassell, 1998). xix, 300 pp.

Fifty accounts from 1768 onward by traveling Africans, West Indians, and African Americans, almost all taken from larger works, in a thematic arrangement. The black Atlantic is construed broadly, for pieces on Australia, Indian, and Japan are found in these pages. Includes a biographical sketch for each author at the beginning of each selection; wide-ranging suggestions for further reading (283–87); a bibliography ([289]–95); and an index.

Africans in the USA

Achebe, Chinua. *Home and Exile* (Oxford & New York: Oxford UP, 2000). x, 115 pp.

[Nigeria.] With masterful concision, Achebe shares insights and memories in three essays which came out of lectures at Harvard in 1998: "My Home Under Imperial Fire," "The Empire Fights Back," and "Today, the Balance of Stories." When he was five, his father, having retired from work as a Christian missionary, returned to Ogidi, his ancestral Igbo town. He recalls riding then for the first time in a motor vehicle. Originally enrolled in medicine, after "an academic year of great sadness I switched to the Faculty of Arts" (21). He criticizes the arrogance of V.S. Naipaul in his writings on Africa, describing his novel *A Bend in the River* as being "downright outrageous." He also discusses Joyce Cary's *Mister Johnson*, assigned to Nigerian students in the 1950s, which they uniformly rejected as an inauthentic portrayal of Africa. Achebe uses Igbo proverbs to illuminate his own life and that of his people, who are devoted to democratic institutions and to the belief that each person and community is unique.

Barry, Kesso. *Kesso, princesse peuhle* (Paris: Seghers, 1988). 232 pp.

[Guinea.] Kesso, a Peul or Fula, was born into the royal family of the kingdom of Fouta–Djalon, Guinée, Kesso. As part of an adolescent rebellion, she demanded to attend school, thereby contravening custom. At the age of twelve she satisfied custom when she underwent a terrifying excision, after which she left for Dakar. At fifteen, rather than enter an arranged marriage, she chose her own husband, later to divorce him and become a steno-grapher. Her second marriage was for love, to a French industrialist who took her to Paris. There she became a renowned model, and had two child-ren who knew nothing of their mother's earlier years; it is for them that she wrote this book.

Clark–Bekederemo, J.P. (John Pepper Clark). *America, Their America* (London: André Deutsch, 1964, 221 pp.; London: Heinemann Educational in association with André Deutsch, 1968, 224 pp.; New York: Africana, 1969, 224 pp.).

[Nigeria.] Clark, a journalist and author of poetry and plays, reports acerbi-cally on a fellowship year at Princeton. He takes strong exception to Ameri-can values, including the prevalent racism and capitalism, and even the sometimes superficial adoption of African clothing and lifestyles by American blacks. As he says in his introduction, "if the picture of America that you want to see is a rosy one, you had better stop reading this book now" (12).

Gatheru, R. Mugo. *Child of Two Worlds: A Kikuyu's Story*, intro. St. Clair Drake (New York: Praeger, 1964). xiv, 216 pp.

[Kenya.] Gatheru, a Kenyan of Kikuyu descent, is among the small number of first-generation college-educated Africans. He documents the indignities and injustices suffered by Kenyans forced to wear clothing unlike that worn by Asians and Europeans, and paid only a fraction of the wages they earned though doing the same work. His protests concerning the conditions of life of Africans earned him the attention of the authorities, and finally he was forced to resign from his position as a lab assistant. He became a journalist and, in 1946, associate editor of the *African Voice*. After British colonialists refused him a passport to the USA, he made his way there via India. He met Professor St. Clair Drake, who counseled him, helping to obtain a full scholarship at Lincoln University in Fall 1951. He successfully completed his degree, married an American woman, and went on to London to study criminal law. His studies kept him away from Kenya for fourteen years.

Kassindja, Fauziya. *Do They Hear You When You Cry?* With Layli Miller Bashir (London & New York: Delacorte, 1998). 518 pp.

[Togo.] Upon the death of her father Fauziya, a young Muslim woman of sixteen, was about to be married to a 45-year-old man with two wives already and forced to undergo excision. With the help of her sister Ayisha she fled to Germany, landing in Düsseldorf in October 1994. There Rudina, a German woman kindly took her into her home for two months, and a friendly Nigerian told her of potential asylum in the USA. When she flew to the USA, where she had a distant cousin, the Immigration and Naturalization Service imprisoned her harshly for sixteen months. After a long struggle she won political asylum, thereafter becoming a junior college student in Virginia.

Kayira, Legson. *I Will Try* (Garden City NY: Doubleday, 1965). 251 pp.

[Malawi.] Kayira was born in then Nyasaland to a family so poor his father could afford to pay poll taxes only once; thereafter, in an act of kindness, the village tax collector declared his father dead. Legson began school about 1946 and became a highly competent student who was financially assisted to attend secondary school. In 1958, wanting to attend school in the USA, he began walking to America, a trip which took him through Tanganyika and Uganda, and on 25 September 1960 he reached Khartoum. There an embassy official helped him to fulfil his dream. He received a full scholarship to Skagit Valley College in Washington State, and an American family invited him to live with them.

Mbele, Cosbie. *Lady Africa in America* (Lea Glen FL: Vivlia Publishers & Booksellers, 1996). 119 pp.

[South Africa.] Cosbie's mother, a teacher, and her father, a filing clerk, become evangelists and left their children with family members while going off to do missionary work. Born into poverty in South Africa, the author struggled to gain an education and also to become a teacher. In 1981 she left an unfaithful husband and twin sons to travel to New York, where she attended Queensborough Community College and acted and sang in a variety of musical productions. Ultimately she built a life in both countries and became a US citizen.

Mphahlele, Ezekiel [now Es'kia]. *Afrika My Music: An Autobiography, 1957–1983* (Johannesburg: Ravan, 1984). 260 pp.

[South Africa.] This is Mphahlele's second autobiographical work; because of the scope of this bibliography his first, *Down Second Avenue*, shall not be annotated herein, since its focus is exclusively on the author's South African childhood and youth. In 1957 Mphahlele and his family left South Africa for Nigeria, where he taught for four years. There he met major West African intellectuals, artists, writers, and politicians and joined the editorial board of *Black Orpheus* in 1958. In 1961 he went on to Paris, moving out from this base to lecture in eleven European and African countries. In 1963 he transferred to Kenya, and in 1966 to Denver, where he taught and earned a doctorate in English literature. His novel *The Wanderers* served in lieu of a dissertation. He also taught in Zambia and at the University of Pennsylvania before returning to South Africa in 1977 with his wife; their children opted to remain in the USA.

Nkosi, Lewis. *Home and Exile* (London: Longmans, 1965). 136 pp. Expanded ed. as *Home and Exile and Other Selections* (London & New York: Longman, 1983). xi, 164 pp.

[South Africa.] Born in Durban, Nkosi worked as a journalist at *Drum* magazine during the 1950s. In 1960, when he left South Africa to travel to the USA to take up a one-year fellowship at Harvard University, he was forced to leave on a one-way exit visa. The book covers his South African life in chapters 1–5, and his life in the USA and Paris in chapters 6–11. Offers impressions of New York, Paris, and Los Angeles. The later chapters of the 1983 edition are made up of literary essays added to material in the first edition.

Ojike, Mazi Mbonu. *I Have Two Countries* (New York: John Day, 1947). viii, 208 pp.

[Nigeria.] Ojike, an Igbo, won a scholarship to a normal college in Nigeria. Thereafter, in 1939 he enrolled at Lincoln University in Philadelphia, a traditionally black college. In May 1946 he attended the United Nations Conference on International Organization in San Francisco, where he met with W.E.B. Du Bois and many Afro-American and African delegates and others from still-colonized parts of the world. He also reports on a three-week trip through the American South. This book was written prior to the author's return to Nigeria after seven years as student, lecturer, and traveler.

Siwundhla, Alice Princess (Msumba). *Alice Princess: An Autobiography* (Mountain View CA: Pacific Press Publishing Association, 1973). 192 pp.

[South Africa.] Alice Princess, named after the sister of the King of England, was born into a loving family in Johannesburg, where Alice's father was a hospital orderly. When her mother died, her father returned to his village in Nyasaland with his children. After he contracted tuberculosis and died, the children attended a Seventh Day Adventist mission school. There Mr and Mrs Lowell A. Edwards, missionary teachers, befriended Alice and ultimately brought her, her husband and child to America. The Siwundhlas entered a program of study after an appearance on *This is Your Life,* the television program hosted by Ralph Edwards. This book was "introduced and given its prevailing tone of simpering idiocy by Ralph Edwards."[21]

Wamba, Philippe E. *Kinship: A Family's Journey in Africa and America* (New York: E.P. Dutton, 1999). xiv, 383 pp.

[Congo.] Wamba's Congolese father arrived in the USA as a student in 1964 and married an African-American woman. Wamba grew up in the USA and is a graduate of Harvard University. Includes a perceptive discussion of relationships between Africans and African Americans.

Zamenga Batukezanga. *Lettres d'Amérique* (Kinshasa, Zaire: Zabat, [1982?]). 175 pp.

[Zaire.] In 1981 the American Cultural Center in Kinshasa invited the author, a Zairian writer and director of a school for the physically handicapped, to be the guest of the US government on a thirty-day visit to the USA. These letters to his son recount his trip. His goal was to learn about African culture amongst black Americans and to observe the interaction between European and African cultures in the USA. Places visited included Washington DC, Atlanta, Memphis, Philadelphia, and Los Angeles. Highlights included a visit with his countryman Professor Valentine Mudimbe and to the house of Alex Haley, author of *Roots*.

Canada

Clarke, Austin. *Growing Up Stupid Under the Union Jack* (Havana: Casa de las Américas, 1980). 188 pp. Also as *Growing Up Stupid Under the Union Jack: A Memoir* (Toronto: McClelland & Stewart, 1980). 192 pp.

[Barbados.] Born in humble circumstances to a loving Barbadian mother, the distinguished author evokes island life. This lyrical memoir focusses on school days, beginning in 1944, when he entered secondary school and on island life during World War II. Clarke emigrated to Canada in 1955, where his writing in a variety of genres has frequently addressed the black immigrant exprience.

---

[21] James Olney, *Tell Me Africa*, 36.

Talbot, Carol. *Growing Up Black in Canada* (Toronto: Williams–Wallace, 1984). 96 pp.

The author grew up in Windsor, Ontario, in a family greatly valuing education. Her family dates back five or more generations; her mother's hometown was Amherstburg, settled by blacks as early as 1812, and "the most southerly Canadian terminous of the Underground Railway" (20). Grandfather Talbot was an ordained Baptist minister. After completing university, the author was hired as a teacher at Waterdown District High, a school near Hamilton. Includes poems.

Caribbean

Condé, Maryse. *Entretiens avec Maryse Condé: suivis d'une bibliographie complète*. With Françoise Pfaff; postface de Regis Antoine (Paris: Editions Karthala, 1993). 203 pp. Tr. as *Conversations with Maryse Condé*, ed. Françoise Pfaff (Lincoln: U of Nebraska P, 1996). xvi, 178 pp.

[Guadeloupe.] The author of novels, plays, essays, short stories, and children's books, Condé discusses her life and work with Françoise Pfaff in a series of interviews in France and the Americas conducted over several years. These frank and wide-ranging interviews reflect Condé's international perspective; born in Guadeloupe, she has since lived in France, Africa, the UK, and the USA. In 1959 she married Mamadou Condé, a Guinean actor, and traveled to West Africa, where she was to reside and work in Côte d'Ivoire, Guinea, Ghana, and Senegal until 1970. She had four children with Mamadou, and entered a second marriage to the Englishman Richard Philcox, which has endured. In 1975 she gained a doctorate in Caribbean literature from the Sorbonne, and has taught at many institutions in the USA and elsewhere. The translation includes an additional chapter based on a 1994 interview on newer works not covered in the 1993 French-language edition, and the bibliography has been revised and updated.

——. *Le cœur à rire et à pleurer: Contes vrais de mon enfance* (Paris: Robert Laffont, 1999). 135 pp. Tr. by Richard Philcox as *Tales from the Heart: True Stories from my Childhood* (New York: Soho, 2001). 147 pp.

Born to parents of advanced years, closer by far to her mother, yet keeping her mother at a distance, Condé grew up a spoiled but fiercely independent child. She was the eighth child and fourth daughter of acutely class-conscious parents who prevented their children from speaking creole and playing with mulattoes. Her mother was one of the first black school teachers in Guadeloupe, and her father a banker; her favorite brother Sandrino told her: "Papa and Maman are a pair of alienated individuals" (20). Her parents lived for their annual trip to France, which was sadly missed for seven years during World War II. As a child she loathed the girl scouts and camping, but loved making up stories. At sixteen she left Guadeloupe to study in France.

——. "Pan-Africanism, Feminism and Culture," in *Imagining Home: Class, Culture, and Nationalism in the African Diaspora*, ed. Sidney J. Lemelle & Robin D.G. Kelley (London & New York: Verso, 1994): 55–65.

Condé discusses culture and pan-Africanism in the context of her experiences as an activist and writer. She describes fighting for Guadeloupe's independence and changes in culture in terms of women's roles and the place of education, reading and writing on the island during the span of her own lifetime. Condé's life abroad for over thirty years in Europe, Africa, and America affords her comparisons between earlier and present generations on her island. In 1988, to help create inter-Caribbean understanding, she wrote *Haïti chérie*, intended to help foster understanding between Guadeloupean and Haitian children.

Danticat, Edwidge. *After the Dance: A Walk Through Carnival in Jacmel, Haiti* (New York: Crown, 2002).

[Haiti/USA.] Danticat, who now lives in New York, returned in 2001 to her Haitian homeland; here she visits the Carnival celebration in the city of Jacmel, and traces the stories behind the masked figures in the parades to illuminate the history of a place.

Lorde, Audre. *A Burst of Light: Essays* (Ithaca NY: Firebrand Books, 1988). 134 pp.

[USA.] The first essay, "Sadomasochism: Not About Condemnation: An Interview with Audre Lorde by Susan Leigh Star," covers June and July 1980. Other essays and brief diary entries from the year she turned fifty, 1984, run through August 1987. Two weeks prior to her birthday in 1984 she was diagnosed with liver cancer, metastasized from the breast cancer she had suffered six years earlier. She continued with plans to travel to Berlin and taught there, and worked with Dagmar Schultz, a moving force behind *Farbe Bekennen: afro-deutsche Frauen auf den Spuren ihrer Geschichte*, and other Afro-German women.

——. *The Cancer Journals* (Argyle NY: Spinsters, 1980, 77 pp.; London: Sheba, 1985, xii, 69 pp.; San Francisco: Aunt Lute Books, special ed. 1997, 99 pp.; San Franciso: Spinsters, 2nd ed. 1980, 77 pp.).

Selected journal entries, of varying length, "which begin 6 months after my modified radical mastectomy for breast cancer [...] exemplify the process of integrating this crisis into my life" (8).

——. *Sister Outsider: Essays and Speeches* (Trumansburg NY: Crossing Press, 1984). 190 pp.

Fifteen pieces include "Manchild: A Black Lesbian Feminist's Response," an examination of her relationship with her fourteen-and-a-half-year-old son Jonathan. Also the distillation of three hours of interviews with Adrienne Rich in which Lorde discusses her early life as the daughter of Grenadian immigrants, her essays and poetry, her teaching, why she became a librarian, and much else. Other essays discuss issues of race, feminism, and sexuality. The book opens with "Notes from a Trip to Russia," and concludes with "Grenada Revisited," a recounting of travel to the Caribbean island in 1983.

Manley, Edna. *Edna Manley: The Diaries*, ed. Rachel Manley (Kingston, Jamaica: Heinemann Caribbean, 1989). xi, 308 pp.

[Jamaica.] Daughter of an English Methodist missionary and his Jamaican wife, the author was born in Cornwall, England and later married her first cousin, Norman Manley, who was to be Jamaica's first Premier. A talented sculptress and political activist who earned the love and respect of the Jamaican people, she was also the mother of Michael Manley, the Jamaican Prime Minister. Diary entries, which address both personal and public concerns, begin in February 1939 and end in December 1986. The editor is her granddaughter.

Ollivier, Émile. *Mille eaux: récit* (Paris: Gallimard, 1999). 172 pp.

[Haiti.] Although he did not know his father, his mother figures prominently in this recollection of the author's Haitian childhood and youth. Ollivier lived in Quebec from 1965 until his death in 2002, and taught sociology at the University of Montreal. He received the Grand Prix littéraire de la Ville de Montréal for *Passages,* published in 1994.

Sistren; with Honor Ford–Smith. *Lionheart Gal: Life Stories of Jamaican Women* (Toronto: Sister Vision, 1987). xxxi, 298 pp.

[Jamaica.] Fifteen interviews of members of the theatre collective were issued anonymously to protect their identities. These oral histories in a mixture of Patwah (Jamaican creole) and English were edited collectively by members of the Sistren, an organization founded in 1977. These working-class women devote themselves to the production of plays growing out of their experience. The collective has published several plays, as well as *Sistren,* its journal. One story is in the form of diary entries, from July 1968 to November 1984. Stories begin with childhood innocence and move toward a sense of political understanding and collective action; the period covered overall is roughly from 1945 through the mid-1980s.

China

Hevi, Emmanuel John. *An African Student in China* (New York: Praeger, 1963). 220 pp.

[Ghana.] Hevi, a Ghanaian student who went to Beijing in November 1960 on a Chinese government scholarship, directs his words to fellow Africans as a warning against the dangers of Chinese communism, calling the book "my argument against communism in Africa" (9). Having left his wife in Ghana, he intended to study medicine. Hevi is highly critical of Chinese housing, hygiene, the paucity of food, propaganda, communes, and most particularly the ubiquitous regimentation and racism. Ninety percent of African students demanded repatriation in the year he was there (141). Two appendices are "Zanzibari Students' Standpoint" and "Resolution of the Camerounian Students"; they are documents which outline the grievances of these foreign students.

France

Faye, N.G.M. *Le debrouillard* (Paris: Gallimard, 1964). 223 pp.

[Senegal.] After running away from his Senegalese home to escape his father's harsh demands, Faye worked for six years earning money any way he could, by working as a porter and photographer, and by selling cocoa.

Then he entered a boxing club, where he learned to excel in this sport; he became boxing champion of Senegal and West Africa, and thereafter enjoyed a professional boxing career in France. François Reichenbach invited him to star in the movie *Un cœur gros comme ça.* This won the Delluc Prize for the best French film of 1962 as well as first prize at Lucarno's international film festival.

Guilao, Gamé. *France, terre d'accueil, terre de rejet: l'impossible intégration* (Paris: L'Harmattan, 1994). 271 pp.

[Guinea.] The life story of a Guinean who arrived to study in France in 1956 and because of Guinean politics stayed on. This book received the Prix du salon français 1994 décerné par l'Association des Écrivains Régionalistes du Maine-et-Loire.

Heath, Gordon. *Deep Are the Roots: Memoirs of a Black Expatriate*, intro. Doris Abramson; afterword by Ekwueme Mike Thelwell (Amherst: U of Massachusetts P, 1992). 200 pp.

[USA.] A black American actor whose father immigrated from Barbados lived his adult life chiefly in Paris and, more briefly, in the UK. His acclaimed performances were in the USA, in France, and in England. In 1947 he and his longtime companion Lee Payant became owners of L'Abbaye, a popular nightclub, where they sang and played guitar. As director of the Studio Theatre of Paris in the 1960s, Heath produced English-language drama.

Sarrazin, Albertine. *Biftons de prison*, intro. Brigitte Duc (Paris: J.–J. Pauvert, 1977). 170 pp.

Julien Sarrazin gave Albertine a ride as she escaped from prison. They were both subsequently arrested, and while in prison they were married. Albertine was twenty-one years old when she wrote *bifton 1*, and went on to write 26 *biftons,* or clandestine letters, to Julien, while both were imprisoned at Amiens. The *biftons* speak of her passionate love, and convey something of her excitement of enjoying the forbidden as she spoke privately to her husband, thereby contravening prison regulations. These letters begin in 1958 and run through September 1960. Brigitte Duc speaks of their ability to erase prison walls (Introduction, 8).

——. *Journal de prison* (1959), préface de Josane Duranteau (Paris: Sarrazin, 1972). 239 pp.

Sarrazin, born a foundling in Algiers, was adopted by a French colonialist couple of advanced years who took her to Southern France. There, as her parents failed to understand her, she became alienated and in adolescent rebellion ran away from home. She engaged in prostitution and theft, and was arrested and imprisoned several times. A gifted writer who had kept a journal from early childhood days, she lived to see her novels published. After medical malfeasance led to her early death at the age of thirty, her husband Julien founded a publishing house and issued posthumously her previously unpublished writings (preface, 9–55). Her first diary entry is dated 23 December 1958 and the last 3 November 1959. Sarrazin reflects on love, longing, and death as she writes of her boredom and her simultaneous rage to live.

Soukouna, Hawa. *Hawa*, [raconté par] Catherine Vigor (Paris: Flammarion, 1991). 232 pp.

[Mali.] Hawa Soukouna, a Soninke woman born in a small Malian village, has lived in Paris from the age of sixteen, She recounts traditional life in her village, her marriage, and her arrival in Paris to a world totally other than she had known. Living in a third-floor apartment was cause for panic for her, as was delivering her first child while quite alone in a hospital where she understood not a word said to her. Gradually she learned French, and since petty commerce was the work of women in her home country she took up selling Tupperware and Avon products at parties. She corresponded with her friends and family in Mali via videotape cassettes. As a Muslim, her husband planned to take a co-spouse, although the intended marriage did not actually occur. She says she finds her life is not bad, and that in fact she is better off living in France than she would be had she remained in her village. Nonetheless, one thing bothers her: "c'est que je ne suis pas chez moi en France" (230). [It is that I do not feel at home in France].."Où est-ce que je serai chez moi?" [And where shall I feel at home?] "Au paradis seulement..." [Solely in paradise...] With these words Hawa expresses the pangs of her exile.

Germany

Ajao, Aderogba. *On the Tiger's Back* (Cleveland: World, 1962). 149 pp.; ill.

[Nigeria.] Born 1930 in Oyo, into a wealthy Yoruba family headed by a chief, Ajao was raised in Lagos. Like many other African students of his generation, he was sent in 1948 to study abroad. After living as an anti-colonialist, leftist student in Scotland and England, he returned to Nigeria to enter the import business. On a business trip to Europe he was in effect kidnapped and taken to East Germany, where he spent seven years of unwilling indoctrination into communism, as well as in further study. He describes these years in East Germany as being partly attraction, partly enterprise, and partly conspiracy. Relations with German women were a continual problem for him and his fellow students. He reports that he married a German girl, but does not discuss this marriage, saying only that "it is part of my private life, and in the outcome, a tragic part" (130). Disillusioned with communism, he eventually escaped via Berlin and returned to Lagos.

Oguntoye, Katharina, May Opitz & Dagmar Schultz, ed. *Farbe bekennen: Afro-deutsche Frauen auf den Spuren ihrer Geschichte*. Mit einem Beitrag von Audre Lorde (Berlin: Orlanda Frauenverlag, 1986, 243 pp.; Frankfurt am Main: Fischer, rev. ed. 1992 & 1997, 251 pp.; ill.). Tr. by Anne V. Adams as *Showing Our Colors: Afro-German Women Speak Out*, foreword by Audre Lorde (Amherst: U of Massachusetts P, 1992). xxv, 239 pp.

Two elders, sisters Doris Reiprich and Erika Ngambi ul Kuo (aged 67 and 70) and thirteen young woman born after World War II write of their lives; some include poetry. Chronologically arranged, beginning in the precolonial period, each chapter begins with a historical overview by May Opitz placing the period in context *vis-à-vis* the position of blacks in Germany. The overview is followed by one or more autobiographical sketches with photographs of the authors, who include the children of black Americans and of Africans with German women. The 1992 English translation includes a preface by the three editors which assesses the impact of the first edition in 1986 on German life and culture. According to Audre Lorde, this is "The first book to be published in Germany dealing with Afro-Germans as a national entity" (ix). The book resulted in the creation of the Initative of Black Germans, an organization formed in 1986, which by 1990 had affiliate groups in over ten cities. Its periodical, *Afro Look*, was published by the IBG in Berlin, and a second periodical, *Afekete*, was published by the Afro-German Women's Group.

Hügel–Marshall, Ika. *Daheim unterwegs: Ein deutsches Leben* (Berlin: Orlanda Frauenverlag, 1998). 154 pp.

One of 3,093 children of mixed race born in Germany following World War II, the author – daughter of a white German mother and a black American father who returned to America prior to her birth – writes determinedly that "I will know who I am." Her mother married a German man with whom she had a second child, a sister to Ika. Ika's life in a small South German town,

at first tranquil, was increasingly hindered by racism. After a long search
she located her father and, in 1993, happily visited him in the USA. She
returned to Germany, and in time came to be content in her dark skin as she
accepted herself fully.

Kenna, Constance, ed. *Homecoming: The GDR Kids of Namibia* (Windhoek: New Namibia Books, 1999). 226 pp.

[Namibia.] In the 1980s, many Namibian children were sent to East Germany, where they remained until their repatriation in 1990. In their own
words, they tell their stories in songs, poems, and essays, each preceded by
biographical information. The first chapter provides background on how the
children came to be exiled to the German Democratic Republic and on
organizations involved in the program.

Massaquoi, Hans J. *Neger, Neger, Schornsteinfeger! Meine Kindheit in
Deutschland* (Berne, Munich & Vienna: Fretz & Wasmuth, 1999). 413 pp.
Tr. as *Destined to Witness: Growing up Black in Nazi Germany* (New York:
William Morrow, 1999). 443 pp.

The grandson of a Liberian diplomat whose mother was a German nurse recounts his mixed-race childhood in Germany during the Nazi era. His
parents never married; his father returned to Africa, while his mother
remained his best friend and staunchest defense against the dangers and
evils of the times of his youth. Later, Massaquoi traveled to Liberia to meet
his father, and ultimately moved to the USA.

Nwajiuba, Chinedum Uzoma. *The Unknown Foreigner = Der unbekante*
[sic] *Ausländer* (Owerri, Nigeria: Readon Publishers, 1997). 123 pp.

[Nigeria.] An Igbo's somewhat random reflections on nearly five years
spent in Germany. In 1991 he arrived in Freiburg to spend six months at the
Goethe Institute, and stayed on for additional study. The author comments
on his experiences of racism and discrimination while expressing appreciation for some aspects of German life and culture.

Latin America

Da Silva, Benedita. *Benedita da Silva: An Afro-Brazilian Woman's Story of
Politics and Love*. As told to Medea Benjamin and Maisa Mendonça. Fore-

word by Rev. Jesse Jackson, Sr. (Oakland CA: Institute for Food and Development Policy, 1997). 215 pp.

[Brazil.] Rio di Janeiro's first black city councilwoman, subsequently Senator, overcame a life of abject poverty to become a highly successful political activist.

Soviet Union

Amar, Andrew Richard. *A Student in Moscow* (London: Ampersand, 1961). 64 pp.

[Uganda.] Amar, a Luo from the Lango District of Northern Uganda, studied at Makerere University before going on to study in London in 1957. He received a coveted scholarship to study medicine at Moscow University in 1959. He remained there for just one year of a six-year program before leaving to continue his education elsewhere in Europe. In Moscow he shared a small single room with two Russians, one of them a member of the state security police, and another African; he claims that all foreign students were similarly housed, with their activities and movement closely monitored. Guineans were the most numerous among African students in Moscow and in Tashkent.

Anti-Taylor, William. *Moscow Diary* (London: Robert Hale, 1967). 192 pp.

[Ghana.] Among some 4,000 African students brought to Russia, Anti-Taylor was one of the first from Ghana to study on a prestigious scholarship. Hailing from a small Ghanaian village, he arrived at Friendship University, shortly to be renamed Lumumba University. Becoming thoroughly disillusioned with Communism, he joined five hundred African students to march through Red Square to protest the murder of Asare Addo, a fellow Ghanaian student who had dared to fall in love with a Russian girl. The irony of the march lay in the fact that the students, who had been thoroughly schooled in producing 'spontaneous' demonstrations on cue, followed those instructions, in this instance, to register their own outrage at the racism they constantly experienced. Documents indoctrination, constant surveillance, and regimentation. He remained in Russia for three years only, 1960–1962.

United Kingdom

Emecheta, Buchi. *Head Above Water* (London: Ogwugwo Afo, 1986). 243 pp.

[Nigeria.] Emecheta, married and a mother by the age of seventeen, accompanied her student husband to London in 1962. There she had four more children and learned that her husband expected her to support not only the children but himself as well while he continued to live the life of a layabout student. Not surprisingly, she left him. Perhaps more surprisingly, she supported her children, returned to school, and earned sociology degrees, including ultimately the Ph.D, while earning renown as the writer of books she called "documentary novels." In the course of these exertions, she became so exhausted that for some five years she would simply "fall in the street." Her novels, such as *Second-Class Citizen*, frequently have autobiographical elements. *In the Ditch,* her first novel, was perhaps the first book on the English working class written by a foreigner living in the UK.

Gilroy, Beryl. *Black Teacher* (London: Cassell, 1976). ix, 196 pp.

[Guyana.] The author, a Guyanese teacher, lived with her husband in London, and was headmistress of a North London infants' school with students from twenty nationalities registered in 1969, a number that rose to forty-four. The first and last chapters frame an account of how the author overcame distrust to move from working as a filing clerk and a maid to teaching and finally to becoming a headmistress. There are vivid accounts of the elementary school classroom and of the challenges of racism and poverty; the book is full of vignettes of winning children's cooperation to establish a climate conducive to learning in difficult settings.

Gladwell, Joyce. *Brown Face, Big Master* (London: Inter-Varsity Press, 1969). 126 pp.

[Jamaica.] A Jamaican who traveled to London University in 1953 to study psychology; religiously observant, Gladwell termed God "Big Master." She describes her childhood as a twin and Jamaican school days, when her mother and father, who was head teacher, both taught at her school. In London she experienced discrimination when her proposed marriage to an Welshman was opposed by his family; also discusses early marital adjustments in what became a happy and fulfilling mixed marriage.

Sikakane, Joyce. *A Window on Soweto* (London: International Defence and Aid Fund, 1977). 80 pp.

[South Africa.] A journalist for the *Rand Daily Mail* and the *World* who was imprisoned and banned under the Terrorism Act documents daily life in Soweto under apartheid, interwoven with her particular life story and ordeals. Covers the economy, schooling, medical services, pass laws, crime, nutrition, and her trials, imprisonment, and banning. In 1973 she left South Africa and settled in Britain. There she married a Scottish physician and established a family.

Udoji, J.O. (Jerome O.). *Under Three Masters: Memoirs of an African Administrator* (Ibadan: Spectrum Books, 1995). xii, 169 pp.

[Nigeria.] In 1944 on his ship to England were twenty-nine students, including Obafeme Awolowo, H.S.A. Adedeji, and other Nigerians who would become well known upon their return. Udoji, urbane and well-educated, attended Cambridge until 1948; during this period he brought his wife to the UK for eighteen months. On return to Nigeria he became an administrative official in the colonial service, continuing in administration after independence. Subsequently he joined the Ford Foundation in East Africa, 1962–1971. Based in East Africa, he traveled widely throughout the continent to set up seminars on such themes as "Regional Cooperation in Africa: Prospects and Problems," a 1969 seminar he organized in Liberia. Later he returned to government service in his home country.

International Travel

Ajala, Olabisi. *An African Abroad*, intro. T.J. Mboya (London: Jarrolds, 1963). 255 pp.

[Nigeria.] The author's foreword briefly reports on how he made his way from Nigeria to acquire an undergraduate degree in the USA, accomplished on his own with part-time and summer employment. Ajala exhibits constant ingenuity in intrepid travels, mostly via motor scooter, to some eighty-six countries, including India, Russia, Iran, Israel, Egypt, and Australia. He met with such figures as Nehru, Khrushchev, the Shah of Iran, Golda Meir, and Nasser – and wryly comments that "Without the sometimes reluctant cooperation of most of these 'controversial figures' the writing of this book would not have been possible" (15).

Hutchinson, Alfred. *Road to Ghana* (New York: John Day, 1960). 190 pp.

[South Africa.] Hutchinson taught at the only school in South Africa staffed by Indians, Coloureds, Africans and Europeans (18). He fell in love with Hazel, a European teacher at the school, thereby complicating his life considerably. He recollects a party at Joe Slovo's and Ruth First's house to celebrate release from prison after the withdrawal of treason charges. He recounts how he fled the country clandestinely, joining a trainload of miners returning to Nyasaland. He reached Tanzania, where Julius Nyerere helped him on his way, and at length he arrived in Ghana after a rough journey. The book eloquently captures the immense difficulty and dangers experienced by Africans traveling in pre-independence Africa.

Nkrumah, Kwame. *The Autobiography of Kwame Nkrumah* (London & New York: Nelson, 1957). xv, 310 pp. Also published as *Ghana: The Autobiography of Kwame Nkrumah* (London: Panaf, 1973) x, 246 pp.

[Ghana.] Two chapters cover Nkrumah's ten years in the USA, where he earned a Bachelor of Theology degree at Lincoln, Philadelphia, in 1942 and a M.Sc. in Education from the University of Pennsylvania the same year, followed by an M.A. in Philosophy in 1943. Nkrumah worked uncommonly hard to pay his expenses, some of the time in all-night work outdoors, which led to his contracting pneumonia. He also taught at Lincoln, where in 1945 the *Lincolnian* voted him "the most outstanding professor of the year" (27). In the summers he worked in New York wherever he could, including a job at a soap factory; until 1939 he joined ship as a dishwasher and waiter, graduating to bellhop. Also discussed is his stay in England.

Additional Autobiographies (not yet examined)

The following titles (see overleaf) have been identified as almost certainly being autobiographies of the black diaspora; however, for a variety of reasons these have not yet been examined.

| Africans and Afro-Latin Americans in the USA

Azikiwe, Nnamdi [Nigeria]. *My Odyssey: An Autobiography* (London: C. Hurst, 1970). xii, 452 pp. Includes material on his student life in the USA.

Dadié, Bernard Binlin [Côte d'Ivoire]. *Un Patron de New York* (Paris: Présence Africaine, 1964). 308 pp. Tr. by Jo Patterson as *One Way: Bernard Dadié Observes America*, foreword by Claude Bouygues (Urbana: U of Illinois P, 1994). xi, 165 pp. This book received the Grand Prix Littéraire d'Afrique Noire in 1965.

Chipenda, Eva de Carvalho [Angola]. *The Visitor: An African Woman's Story of Travel and Discovery* (Geneva: WCC Publications, 1996). viii, 87 pp.

Lopes, Belmira Nunes [Cape Verde]. *A Portuguese Colonial in America, Belmira Nunes Lopes: The Autobiography of a Cape Verdean American.* By Maria Luisa Nunes (Pittsburgh PA: Latin American Literary Review Press, 1982). 215 pp.

Zapata Olivella, Manuel [Colombia]. *He visto la noche* (Bogotá: Editorial Los Andes, 1953; Biblioteca del pueblo; San Rafael, Impr. Nacional de Cuba, 1962; Medellín: Editorial Bedout, 1969). 127 pp.

— See also:

Drachler, Jacob, comp. *Black Homeland/Black Diaspora: Cross-Currents of the African Relationship.* Prefatory essay by Boniface I. Obichere (Port Washington NY: Kennikat, 1975). 270 pp.

| Africans and Afro-Caribbeans Abroad

Kpomassie, Tête–Michel [Togo]. *L'Africain du Groenland*, preface by Jean Malaurie; tr. by James Kirkup as *An African in Greenland* (San Diego CA: Harcourt Brace Jovanovich, 1983). xix, 298 pp.

Nzenza–Shand, Sekai [Zimbabwe]. *Songs to an African Sunset: A Zimbabwean Story* (Melbourne & Oakland CA: Lonely Planet, 1997). 239 pp.

— France

Cousturier, Lucie [French Guinea]. *Mes inconnus chez eux* (Paris: F. Reider, 1925). 2 vols.

Diallo, Bakary [Senegal]. *Force-bonté*, ed. Jean Richard Bloch (Paris: F. Rieder, 1926). 208 pp.

Dibango, Manu [Cameroon]. *Trois kilos de café: Autobiographie*. En collaboration avec Danielle Rouard (Paris: Lieu commun, 1989). 221 pp. Tr. by Beth G. Raps as *Three Kilos of Coffee: An Autobiography*, in collaboration with Danielle Rouard; foreword by Danielle Rouard (Chicago: U of Chicago P, 1994). xi, 146 pp.

Diop, Ababacar [Senegal]. *Dans la peau d'un sans-papiers* (Paris: Seuil, 1997). 199 pp.

Elizé, Raphaël [Haiti]. *Des Antilles au Maine: itinéraire entre politique et art de vivre* (Sablé-sur-Sarthe: Passé Simple, 1994). 214 pp. Elizé, a veterinarian who published a study of animal tuberculosis in 1927, was the first black mayor in metropolitan France.

Guéry, Fortuna Augustin [Niger]. *Témoignages* (Port-au-Prince: Henri Deschamps, 1950). 108 pp.

Hama, Boubou [Niger]. *Kotia-Nima, recontre avec l'Europe* (Paris: Publication de la République du Niger/Présence Africaine, 1968), 3 vols. Vol. 3 has the subtitle *Dialogue avec l'Occident*.

Julian, Hubert Fauntleroy [Ethiopia/Algeria]. *Black Eagle: Colonel Hubert Julian,* as told to John Bulloch (London: Jarrolds, 1964; subscription edition, London: Adventurers Club, 1965). 200 pp.

Whily–Tell, A.E. [French Antilles] *Je suis un civilisé* (Paris: Société d'impressions de Lancry, 1953). 253 pp.

Yamgnané, Kofi [Togo]. *Droits, devoirs et crocodile*. With Robert Laffont (Aider la vie; Paris: Robert Laffont, 1992). 235 pp. See also Hervé Quemener, *Kofi de Saint-Coulitz: Histoire d'une integration*, préface de Pierre–Jakez Hélias (Paris: Payot, 1991). 241 pp. Socialist mayor and French Deputy.

— Germany

Oji, Chima [Nigeria]. *Unter die Deutschen gefallen: Erfahrungen eines Afrikaners* (Wuppertal: Hammer, 1992). 288 pp.

Sankoh, Osman Alimamyu [Sierra Leone]. *Hybrid Eyes: An African in Europe* (Germany: self-published, 1999). 196 pp.

— United Kingdom

Cole, Robert Wellesley [Sierra Leone]. *An Innocent in Britain, or, The Missing Link: Documented Autobiography* (London: Campbell Matthews, 1988). xvii, 416 pp.

Marke, Ernest [Jamaica]. *Ol' Man Trouble* (London: Weidenfeld & Nicolson, 1975). 159 pp. Political activist in the Midlands and London.

— United Kingdom: see also:

Dennis, Ferdinand. *Behind the Frontline: Journey into Afro-Britain* (London: Victor Gollancz, 1988). xv, 216 pp.

——, & Naseem Khan, ed. *Voices of the Crossing: The Impact of Britain on Writers from Asia, the Caribbean and Africa* (London: Serpent's Tail, 2000). vii, 179 pp.

Africa

Casely–Hayford, Adelaide, & Gladys Casely–Hayford [Sierra Leone]. *Mother and Daughter: Memoirs and Poems*, ed. Lucilda Hunter (Freetown: Sierra Leone UP, 1983). 111 pp.

Laye, Camara [Guinea]. *L'enfant noir: roman* (Paris, Plon, 1953). 256 pp. Ed. Joyce A. Hutchinson (Cambridge: Cambridge UP, 1966). vi, 189 pp. Tr. as *The Dark Child*, intro. Philippe Thoby–Marcellin, tr. James Kirkup, Ernest Jones & Elaine Gottlieb (New York: Noonday, 1954). 188 pp.

Makeba, Miriam [South Africa]. *Makeba: My Story*. With James Hall (New York: New American Library, 1988). 249 pp.

Caribbean

Chamoiseau, Patrick [Martinique]. *Antan d'enfance.* Tr. Carol Volk as *Childhood* (London: Granta, 1999). viii, 117 pp.

Ega, Françoise [Martinique]. *Le temps des madras: Récit de la Martinique* (Paris: Éditions Maritimes et d'Outre-Mer, 1966). 207 pp.

Johnson, Amryl [Trinidad]. *Sequins for a Ragged Hem* (London: Virago, 1988). 272 pp.

Phillips, Caryl [St Kitts]. *The European Tribe* (New York: Farrar, Straus & Giroux, 1987 and London: Faber & Faber, 1987, xiii, 129 pp.; Boston MA: Faber & Faber, 1992, xv, 129 pp., with updated foreword; New York: Vintage, 2000, ix, 133 pp.).

Salkey, Andrew [Guyana]. *Georgetown Journal: A Caribbean Writer's Journey from London via Port of Spain to Georgetown, Guyana, 1970* (London & Port of Spain: New Beacon, 1972). 416 pp.

Shore, Louise [Jamaica]. *Pure Running: A Life Story* (London: Hackney Reading Centre at Centerprise, 1982). 64 pp.

African Americans Abroad

Dunbar, Ernest, ed. & intro. *The Black Expatriates: A Study of American Negroes in Exile* (New York: E.P. Dutton, 1968). 251 pp. Includes interiews with American blacks living in five European countries.

Harris, Eddy L. *Native Stranger: A Black American's Journey into the Heart of Africa* (New York: Simon & Schuster, 1992). 315 pp.

Harrington, Oliver W[endell]. *Why I Left America, and Other Essays*, ed. & intro. M. Thomas Inge (Jackson: UP of Mississippi, 1993). xxix, 113 pp.

McElroy, Colleen J. *A Long Way from St. Louie: Travel Memoirs* (Minneapolis: Coffee House Press, 1997). viii, 241 pp.

Murphy, George. *A Journey to the Soviet Union* (Moscow: Novosti Press Agency Publishing House, 1974). 71 pp.

Richburg, Keith B. *Out of America: A Black Man Confronts Africa* (New York: Basic Books, 1997). xiv, 257 pp.

WORKS CITED

a/b: Auto/biography Studies (New York: Auto/Biography Studies, 1985–).

Bigsby, C.W.E. "The Public Self: The Black Autobiography," *LiLi: Zeitschrift für Literaturwissenschaft und Linguistik*, Jhrg. 9, Nr. 35 (1979): 27–42.

Biography: An Interdisciplinary Quarterly (1978–; Honolulu: UP of Hawaii for the Biographical Research Center).

Brignano, Russell. *Black Americans in Autobiography: An Annotated Bibliography of Autobiographies and Autobiographical Books Written Since the Civil War* (Durham NC: Duke UP, 1984).

Brown, Claude. *Manchild in the Promised Land* (New York: Macmillan, 1965).

Cleaver, Eldridge. *Soul on Ice*, intro. Maxwell Geismar (New York: McGraw–Hill, 1967).

Davis, Angela Yvonne. *Angela Davis: An Autobiography* (New York: Random House, 1974).

Encyclopedia of Life Writing, ed. Margaretta Jolly, 2 vols. (London & Chicago: Fitzroy Dearborn, 2001). Includes essays on varied aspects of autobiographical writing, including Caribbean and African.

Griffin, Farah J., & Cheryl J. Fish, ed. *A Stranger in the Village: Two Centuries of African-American Travel Writing* (Boston MA: Beacon, 1998).

Grohs, Gerhard. "Changing Social Functions of African Autobiographies with Special Reference to Political Autobiographies," in *Janheinz Jahn Symposium* (6th: 1992: Mainz and Bayreuth, Germany). *Genres autobiographiques en Afrique:*

actes du 6e Symposium international Janheinz Jahn = Autobiographical genres in Africa: Papers Presented at the 6th International Janheinz Jahn Symosium: (Mainz–Bayreuth 1992), ed. Janos Reisz & Ulla Schild (Mainzer Afrika-Studien 10; Berlin: Dietrich Reimer Verlag, 1996): 191–203.

Gruesser, John C. "Afro-American Travel Literature and Africanist Discourse," *Black American Literature Forum* 24.1 (Spring 1990): 3–20.

Hughes, Langston, "Soviet Russia and the Negro" (1923), from *The Crisis*, in Griffin & Fish, ed. *A Stranger in the Village*, 215–20.

Malcolm X. *The Autobiography of Malcolm X*, with the assistance of Alex Haley, intro. M.S. Handler, epilogue by Alex Haley (New York: Grove, 1965).

Massaquoi, Hans J. *Neger, Neger, Schornsteinfeger! Meine Kindheit in Deutschland* (Berne, Munich & Vienna: Fretz & Wasmuth, 1999). Tr. as *Destined to Witness: Growing up Black in Nazi Germany* (New York: William Morrow, 1999).

Oguntoye, Katharina, May Opitz & Dagmar Schultz, ed. *Showing Our Colors: Afro-German Women Speak Out*, foreword by Audre Lorde; tr. Anne V. Adams (Amherst: U of Massachusetts P, 1992).

Olney, James, ed. *Tell Me Africa: An Approach to African Literature* (Princeton NJ: Princeton UP, 1973).

Onishi, Norimitsu. "Out of Africa or Bust, With a Desert to Cross," *New York Times* (4 January 2001): A1, A12.

Pettinger, Alasdair, ed. *Always Elsewhere: Travels of the Black Atlantic* (London & New York: Cassell, 1998).

Sistren [Collective], with Honor Ford–Smith. *Lionheart Gal: Life Stories of Jamaican Women* (London: Women's Press, 1986).

Stovall, Tyler. *Paris Noir: African Americans in the City of Light* (Boston MA: Houghton Mifflin, 1996).

Stuhr–Rommereim, Rebecca. *Autobiographies by Americans of Color 1980-1994: An Annotated Bibliography* (Troy NY: Whitston, 1997).

Weixlmann, Joe. "African American Autobiography in the Twentieth Century: A Bibliographical Essay," *Black American Literature Forum* 24.2 ("20th-Century Autobiography" issue; Summer 1990): 375–415.

Wilkerson, Margaret B. "Excavating Our History: The Importance of Biographies of Women of Color," *Black American Literature Forum* 24.1 (Spring 1990): 72–84.

❖

Notes on Contributors

KLAUS BENESCH is Professor of English and Chair of American Studies at the University of Bayreuth (Germany). Among his publications are *The Sea and the American Imagination* (ed. 2003), *Romantic Cyborgs: Authorship and Technology in the American Renaissance* (2002), *Technology and American Culture* (ed. 1996), and *The Threat of History: Narrative Discourse and Historical Consciousness in Contemporary Afro-American Fiction* (1990).

JUDITH BETTELHEIM is a professor of Art History at San Francisco State University. Recent publications include *Cuban Festivals: A Century of Afro-Cuban Culture* (2001) and essays on Mayombe and its influence on contemporary Cuban art (2001) and on costume types and festival elements in Caribbean celebrations (1999).

PHYLLIS B. BISCHOF is Librarian for African and African American Collections at the University of California, Berkeley. Themes of her writings are Africana bibliography, cooperative activities among Africana librarians nationally and internationally, and publishing in Africa. In 1999 she received Berkeley's Distinguished Librarian Award. She is former editor (1986–2003) of the *African Book Publishing Record* (Oxford, England).

KATHIE BIRAT teaches American literature at the University of Metz. She has published articles on the African-American writers Jean Toomer, Toni Morrison, Alice Walker, and John Edgar Wideman. She recently contributed to a special issue of *Callaloo* devoted to Wideman. She has also published on writers from the Caribbean, in particular Caryl Phillips, Fred D'Aguiar, Earl Lovelace and Wilson Harris.

SUJAYA DHANVANTARI is a PhD candidate at the University of Alberta. Her dissertation focuses on twentieth-century Caribbean literary and political writing, especially the work of Frantz Fanon and theories of nationalism and diaspora.

BRENT HAYES EDWARDS teaches in the Department of English at Rutgers University. He is the author of *The Practice of Diaspora: Literature, Translation, and the Rise of Black Internationalism* (2003).

GENEVIÈVE FABRE is professor emerita at the University Paris 7 where she has been directing the Center of African American and Diasporas Studies. Co-author of books on *F.S. Fitzgerald* and *En marge: Les minorités aux États Unis* (1970), she is the author of *James Agee* (1977), *Le théâtre noir américain* (1982), translated as *Drumbeats; Masks and Metaphor: Contemporary Afro-American Theatre* (1983). She has edited various collections of essays on Hispanic literature and barrio culture in the USA, on ethnicity and identity, two volumes on feasts and celebrations among ethnic communities, on history and memory in African American culture, and a book on Toni Morrison. More recently she has co-edited *Jean Toomer* (2000), *"Temples for Tomorrow": Looking Back at the Harlem Renaissance* (2001), *Celebrating Ethnicity and the Nation* (2001), and *Écritures et représentations des diasporas* (2002).

TOM FEELINGS (*19 May 1933 – †25 August 2003) was an award-winning graphic artist, and a professor of Art at the University of South Carolina, in Columbia, from 1988 to 1996. His work *Soul Looks Back in Wonder* and the *Middle Passage* (1995), a visual narrative of the Atlantic slave trade, has been often exhibited, notably at the Schomburg. The artist lived in Ghana and Guyana and lectured at many European universities. He worked with poets such as Margaret Walker and Maya Angelou (with the latter he collaborated on *Now Sheba Sings the Song*, 1987). He illustrated some twenty books, including *Something on My Mind* and *Daydreams* (both winners of the Coretta Scott King Award of the American Library Association), and *Moja Means One* and *Jambo Means Hello* (both winners of the Caldecott Honor Book award), A new book by the writer and critic Kwame Dawes, *I See Your Face* (forthcoming 2004), incorporates drawings bequeathed by Feelings.

MICHEL FEITH is an associate professor of American Literature at the University of Nantes, France. His experience of living in Australia, Japan and the USA has sensitized him to issues of multiculturalism. His publications include articles on Maxine Hong Kingston, John Edgar Wideman, and the Harlem Renaissance, and he is the co-editor, with Geneviève Fabre, of *Jean Toomer and the Harlem Renaissance* (2001) and *"Temples for Tomorrow": Looking Back at the Harlem Renaissance* (2001).

SYLVIA R. FREY is Professor of History and Director of the Deep South Regional Humanities Center at Tulane University. Among her recent publications are *Water from the Rock: Black Resistance in a Revolutionary Age* and, with Betty Wood, *Come Shouting to Zion: African American Protestantism in the American South and the British Caribbean to 1830*.

ARLETTE FRUND teaches American literature in the Department of English of the University of Tours. She is secretary of the Cercle d'Études Afro-Américaines. She is about to edit a special issue of *BMA: The Sonia Sanchez Literary Review*, and to co-edit a special issue of *The Annals of the Anglophone World* on the African American historiography.

WINSTON JAMES teaches history at Columbia University. Among his recent publications are *Holding Aloft the Banner of Ethiopia: Caribbean Radicalism in Early Twentieth-Century America* (1998) and *A Fierce Hatred of Injustice: Claude McKay's Jamaica and His Poetry of Rebellion* (2001). He is currently completing a book-length study of McKay's political development.

AMY KIRSCHKE is an assistant professor of Art History and African American Studies at the University of North Carolina, Wilmington, and chair of the Cultural Diversity Committee for the College Art Association. She is the author of *Aaron Douglas: Art, Race and the Harlem Renaissance* (1995) and "Joy and Sorrow: Art, Memory and Identity," in *W.E.B. Du Bois's CRISIS Magazine* (forthcoming).

SETH MOGLEN is an assistant professor in the English Department at Lehigh University. He is currently completing a book entitled *An Other Modernism: John Dos Passos and the Politics of Literary Form*. He is also at work on a second book, *Black Enlightenment: A Study in African-American Literature and Politics, 1845–1945*.

DAVID PALUMBO–LIU is Professor of Comparative Literature and Director of the Program in Modern Thought and Literature at Stanford University. His most recent book is *Asian/American: Historical Crossings of a Racial Frontier* (1999). He has most recently published essays on

"Civilization, National Identity, and Difference Before and After September 11th" and "The Morality of Form."

CARLA L. PETERSON is a professor in the department of English at the University of Maryland, and affiliate faculty of the Women's Studies and American Studies departments as well as the Afro-American Studies Program. She is the author of *Doers of the Word: African-American Women Speakers and Writers in the North (1830–1880)*. She has also published numerous essays on nineteenth-century African American literature and culture. Her current project is a social and cultural history of African Americans in nineteenth-century New York City as seen through the lens of family history.

IRIS SCHMEISSER is a doctoral student at the Amerika-Institut of Munich University. She is currently completing a dissertation in the field of African-American/postcolonial studies entitled "Transatlantic Crossings and Confluences: Cultural Panafricanism and the Visual Arts."